THE CHANGING
FACE OF WORLD
MISSIONS

A. Scott Moreau, *series editor*

Also in the series:

Introducing World Missions: A Biblical, Historical, and Practical Survey
  A. Scott Moreau, Gary R. Corwin, and Gary B. McGee

THE CHANGING FACE OF WORLD MISSIONS

*Engaging Contemporary
Issues and Trends*

MICHAEL POCOCK
GAILYN VAN RHEENEN
DOUGLAS McCONNELL

Baker Academic
Grand Rapids, Michigan

© 2005 by Michael Pocock, Gailyn Van Rheenen, and Douglas McConnell

Published by Baker Academic
a division of Baker Publishing Group
P.O. Box 6287, Grand Rapids, MI 49516-6287
www.bakeracademic.com

Printed in the United States of America

Library of Congress Cataloging-in-Publication Data
Pocock, Michael, 1942–
    The changing face of world missions : engaging contemporary issues and trends / Michael Pocock, Gailyn Van Rheenen, and Douglas McConnell.
        p.   cm. — (Encountering mission)
    Includes bibliographical references and indexes.
    ISBN 10: 0-8010-2661-X (pbk.)
    ISBN 978-0-8010-2661-4 (pbk.)
    1. Missions—Theory. 2. Globalization—Religious aspects—Christianity. I. Van Rheenen, Gailyn, 1946– II. McConnell, Douglas, 1951– III. Title. IV. Series.
    BV2063.P63 2005
    266′.009′0511—dc22   2005007228

Contents

Preface

The *Changing Face of World Missions* appears at a moment when sufficient time has passed to determine whether developments in the late twentieth century have continued as trends in the context and conduct of missions in the twenty-first. This volume is the second of an eight-volume series titled Encountering Mission. As noted in *Introducing World Missions* (2004), J. Herbert Kane's textbooks—such as *Understanding Christian Missions* (1976), *Life and Work on the Mission Field* (1980), *The Christian World Mission: Today and Tomorrow* (1981), and *Wanted: World Christians* (1986)—were widely used in schools to introduce a generation of students to missions. Those works, however, are now dated, and Baker decided the time had come to develop a new series of books to replace them.

The Changing Face of World Missions is intended for upper-level undergraduate and graduate students preparing for a career in intercultural service and for laypeople and church leaders wanting to understand the changing world that forms the context in which missions are now conducted. Missionaries on home assignment will find this volume helpful in providing an understanding of the developments beyond their specific fields of service.

We the authors join in expressing our appreciation to our wives and families, who encouraged and bore with us in the production of this book. We also extend our thanks to Brian Bolger of Baker Academic for his patience, grace, and encouragement; to the series editor, Scott Moreau, for giving us the opportunity to produce what we hope is a significant help to the mission community; and finally to those entering cross-cultural service for Christ, for whom the Great Commission is as compelling today as it was when Christ gave it.

We also offer thanks for specific technical and research assistance provided by Angel Crow (administrative assistant, Dallas Theological Seminary), Mark Heavener (research assistant, Dallas Theological Seminary), and Kevin and Jenny McGill (manuscript alignment and coordination). Larry and Carol Jeffus and Dave and Wendy Chavanne provided vacation homes that served as quiet havens for planning and writing the text.

Finally, without the help and encouragement of the academic communities in which we work and the prayers of many friends, the work of finishing this volume would have been impossible. For them we give thanks to God.

Introduction

CROSSING THE MILLENNIAL DIVIDE

Toward the end of the twentieth century, evangelical missiologists put on their reflective hats and attempted to summarize and evaluate the past and to anticipate what lay ahead in the new millennium. Keenly aware of the number of years since Christ gave his Great Commission and conscious of the possibility that he could come again at any moment, they pondered how best to respond to the global developments around them.

The sovereign hand of God had been apparent throughout the chaotic movements of the twentieth century, including the rise and decline of two major ideologies (Marxism and national socialism), two world wars and countless regional conflicts, the closing and opening of huge areas (e.g., the former Soviet Union and Eastern Europe), and the appearance of life-changing technologies (e.g., the airplane and the Internet) as well as life-saving medicines (e.g., antibiotics and vaccines). The twentieth century was one of tremendous numerical growth and geographical spread for Christianity. Against a backdrop of incredible resistance to the program and the people of God and the near collapse of Christianity in some of its Western strongholds, God continued to fulfill his promise to Abraham to bless all peoples (Gen. 12:3). But still the task of world evangelization remained unfinished by the year 2000, despite much prayer and bold initiatives. What were missiologists thinking as they approached the end of the last century and the beginning of the new? Where are they now that we are several years into the new millennium?

PLANNING FOR COMPLETION OF THE GREAT COMMISSION

Their desire to finish the task stimulated soul-searching and research to discover how the barriers to evangelism could be overcome. The first Lausanne Conference on World Evangelization was called by Billy Graham in 1974. Church and mission leaders from around the world attended the conference. They were challenged by men such as Donald McGavran and Ralph Winter to adopt a church-planting focus on *people groups* rather than on geographic or national entities and to think afresh about *closure,* actually finishing the task committed to them by Christ (Douglas 1975). The Lausanne Committee for World Evangelization (LCWE) created a Strategy Working Group to focus on unreached peoples rather than on countries. The group prepared profiles of the major segments of unreached humanity, while World Vision's Missions Advanced Research and Communication Center (MARC) created a list of individual unreached people groups, published descriptions of them, and advocated strategic planning to engage them (Dayton and Fraser 1990). But all the targeting and strategizing would not help if Christian workers lacked the spiritual power to overcome the barriers of revitalized world religions—Islam, Hinduism, and Buddhism—and the spiritual opposition of Satan epitomized in Paul's declaration: "The god of this age has blinded the minds of unbelievers, so that they cannot see the light of the gospel of the glory of Christ, who is the image of God" (2 Cor. 4:4).

The Fuller School of Intercultural Studies championed an emphasis on prioritizing church planting and church growth among the responsive peoples of the world (McGavran 1979). Later, some of its faculty developed an emphasis on power encounter (the demonstration of God's power to heal and to overcome demonic opposition) to overcome barriers among the more resistant peoples (Kraft 1989, 1992; Wimber 1986; Wagner 1996). The spiritual warfare orientation to missions became a trend during the latter part of the twentieth century and focused efforts on stimulating prayer and offsetting satanic opposition through identifying and "binding" demons thought to control resistant people groups.

Ralph and Roberta Winter founded the U.S. Center for World Missions in 1978 to coordinate research on unreached peoples and to mobilize Christians to minister to them. At Edinburgh in 1980, focus on closure became clearer, and by 1986, Thomas Wang was calling for "A Church for Every People by the Year 2000" (1989). Later the theme was enlarged to include "and the Gospel for Every Person" (Bush 2003, 19). Patrick Johnstone continued the periodic update of *Operation World*, a guide to prayer for all the nations of the world (Johnstone and Mandryk 2001). The database behind much of this effort was made available through David Barrett's *World Christian Encyclopedia* (1982). Clearly, twentieth-century missions were energized by an organized, focused, well-managed, and even scientific approach to ministry, all hallmarks of modernity.

Quantification, prioritization, and demographics were first applied to missions by William Carey in 1792. His *Enquiry into the Obligations of Christians to Use Means for the Conversion of the Heathens* shows why he is generally regarded as the father of modern missions. His approach epitomized an Enlightenment, or modern, orientation with charts taken from the journals of Captain James Cook, confidence that all obstacles could be overcome, and a willingness to use emerging business corporations as models for mission societies (Baker 2003). His thoroughly Bible-centered approach, coupled with the application of science, good management, and careful strategy, marked missions for the next two hundred years. The results were amazing, as later chapters will develop. Toward the close of the twentieth century, however, new voices were raised in cautious evaluation and even criticism of what was called "managerial missiology" (Escobar 2000a, 112), and modernity was questioned for its overconfident assumptions about humanity's ability to clear all obstacles in the way.

GROWING CONCERN ABOUT THE LIMITS OF WESTERN MISSION MINISTRY

Lesslie Newbigin (1993, 1–6) explained that, as the modern period progressed, Christianity and Western Enlightenment principles tended to coalesce in the missionary endeavors launched from Europe and North America. This resulted in a kind of syncretism in which key elements of the supernatural became deemphasized. As a result, modern missionaries knew little or nothing about how to deal with events such as demon possession. Kenyan John Mbiti, in a humorous and yet realistic way, tells the story of an African who was sent to Europe for academic theological training but was completely unprepared to resolve the first problem he encountered on his return—the need to exorcise his aunt (1976, 6–8). Uneasiness with the previously unquestioned value of modernity is one of the marks of postmodernism. Such uneasiness was found in both the West and the majority world cultures long before its current, more evident manifestation.

> *The experience of European churches suggests that the synthesis between Christianity and the Enlightenment, which was inherent in much of the missionary thrust of the last century, is not sustainable forever.*
>
> Lesslie Newbigin (1993, 4)

A tension exists between the growing disillusionment with modernity and the increasing use of modern technology. Clearly, technology has facilitated missions in the areas of communication, distance learning, translation, and generally increased mobility. It has also introduced nontransferable rather than appropriate technology, created tension between those who have access to certain capabilities and those who do not, and exposed Christian workers to workplace temptations they never had before the Internet. Appropriate technologies are those that can be used in a given context because they rely on locally available and affordable materials rather than on the ongoing resources or presence of outsiders. Of what use is it to teach indigenous pastors using Power-Point and data projectors if such an act produces in those pastors the sense that they cannot teach or preach without that technology, which is unobtainable for them and unusable without electricity? Storytelling and chalk art may be more appropriate technology in undeveloped contexts. As modernity yields to postmodernity, those working in the field of missions need discernment so that they do not simply exchange one set of problems for another.

LOOKING AHEAD TO THE TRENDS AFFECTING MISSION IN THE NEW MILLENNIUM

As missiologists turned their attention to the new millennium, they considered the trends and the issues most likely to affect missionary ministry. For example, David Hesselgrave wrote *Today's Choices for Tomorrow's Mission: An Evangelical Perspective on Trends and Issues in Missions* (1988). He admitted that predictions and prophesies were perilous, and he urged his readers to do what they could to make the right choices, since it is from today's choices that tomorrow's trends emerge. He also emphasized the need to keep decision making and predictions in line with the Word of God:

> In the final analysis, human predictions do not enjoy the status of prophesy. In the first place, our reading of what is actually happening may be faulty. Second, that which is unlikely may well occur. History is full of surprises. Third, the options we choose today will mightily affect what will happen tomorrow. There will be an intimate connection between today's choices and tomorrow's mission.
>
> Despite the difficulties connected with biblical interpretation, for the Christian nothing—absolutely nothing—is as important as the prophetic Word of God when it comes to understanding whence we have come, where we are now, where we are going, and the best way of getting to our destination. To neglect that Word is to neglect our only sure guide. Human predictions that are out of "sync" with Bible prophesy are automatically disqualified. (1988, 21)

One of the most difficult processes involved in writing this book was choosing the trends to discuss. We paid careful attention to what others decided were the trends that would mark missions in the new millennium. Hesselgrave, for example, distinguished ten (1988). Stan

Guthrie, former managing editor of *Evangelical Missions Quarterly,* listed twenty-one (2000). A guiding principle in choosing the trends for this volume arose from agreement over the distinction between a *trend* and an *issue.* The word *trend* refers to a relatively enduring and growing phenomenon. As Hesselgrave notes, trends are "broad outlines . . . broad enough and deep enough to possess explanatory and predictive potential" (1988, 18–19). An *issue,* on the other hand, is more temporally limited and the focus of debate or discussion among those who reflect on global outreach. *Trends* are what is characteristically happening, and they intensify over a period of time. *Issues* are points often raised by those trends that become the focus of debate. For example, global migration is a major component of the globalization *trend,* but whether churches established in communities that are culturally diverse by reason of migration should be homogeneous or heterogeneous in makeup is an *issue.* Both are important and related, but they are not the same.

The informed reader may ask why we omitted suffering and persecution as trends worthy of their own chapters. It is true that as many as 150,000 Christians die annually for their faith (Stearns 1999, 4), including missionaries such as Australian Graham Staines and his children in India, Martin Burnham in the Philippines, the Petts of Africa Inland Mission in Uganda, and several workers of the International Mission Board of the Southern Baptist Convention in Yemen, Lebanon, and Iraq. To those unacquainted with the broad sweep of church history, these tragedies of the new millennium may signal a trend toward greater persecution of missionaries and believers in general. In reality, however, persecution and struggles have always been a part of the Christian experience. Christian missions began the twentieth century with the Boxer Rebellion in China (1900) in which hundreds of missionaries and thousands of Chinese Christians lost their lives. The new millennium also began with significant loss of life. Suffering, like persecution, is not as much a recent trend as it is a continuing mark of Christian life and witness. Jesus predicted for those who follow him, "In this world you will have trouble. But take heart! I have overcome the world" (John 16:33; see also John 15:20–21). For that reason, we chose not to treat suffering as a trend, although it is an all-too-present reality for the church.

RECKONING WITH THE REALITY OF A GLOBALIZED HUMANITY AND A WORLDWIDE CHURCH

In a globalized world in which missions are conducted from all nations to all nations, it is fitting that the voices of majority world Christians are heard in regard to the conduct of missions. Global consultations include Christian leaders from around the world. The collected works of these conferences bring the reflections of majority world Christians to the attention of Western readers. Readers will find many citations of majority world leaders in this volume, although the authors of this volume are themselves from the West.

The conviction of the authors is that North American evangelical schools and their graduates can remain relevant only to the extent that they read, listen, and interact with believers from around the world about the conduct of the missionary enterprise. This means that students and educational leaders should be reading material developed by Christians from other cultures. Beyond reading, they should avail themselves of the wisdom of the international students among them, many of whom bring much wisdom and experience in ministry. They too are on a pilgrimage toward increased usefulness in God's service. They share the same passion to reach culturally different peoples with the gospel and to build up the body of Christ worldwide. Because this is a shared concern, Christians should learn together with respect and mutual love for one another.

THE ORGANIZATION OF THIS TEXT

This book has three sections: The global context describes major trends in the world in which we minister; the missional context deals with trends internal to the body of Christ and the mission community; the strategic context focuses on trends of a strategic or procedural nature. In each chapter, the author *identifies* a trend by describing, quantifying, or illustrating its development. He then *evaluates* the trend in terms of its importance to and impact on missions, generally showing the negative and the positive aspects of the trend. Next, the author *reflects* on the trend, examining it in light of relevant scriptural and theological considerations, frequently showing how other thinkers have dealt with the trend. Finally, the author *engages* the trend, recommending workable, emerging models and best practices.

Discussion of many of the trends requires the use of special vocabulary. The following sidebar briefly defines terms used in more than one chapter of the book. Terms that are exclusive to a particular chapter are defined in a sidebar in that chapter.

The text includes case studies that readers can use to focus reflection on a particular issue raised by each trend. Many chapters contain a sidebar listing Internet and other resources, enabling readers to explore the issues in depth. Each of the authors brings a wealth of personal and academic experience in dealing with the trends under discussion. All

SIDEBAR I.1
IMPORTANT TERMS USED IN THIS BOOK

(Adapted from Moreau, Corwin, and McGee 2004, 12–13; used with permission)

10/40 Window: An imaginary rectangular "window" between the 10th and 40th latitudes, bordered by Africa, the Middle East, and Asia. This window contains the bulk of the unreached peoples in the world and the bulk of non-Christian religions.

4/14 Window: Developed as a spin-off of the term 10/40 Window, this refers to the ages in which children are most likely to commit their lives to Christ as well as the ages in which they are most vulnerable.

contextualization: The core idea is that of taking the gospel to a new context and finding appropriate ways to communicate it so that it is understandable to the people in that context. Contextualization refers to more than just theology; it also includes developing church life and ministry that are biblically faithful and culturally appropriate.

creative-access country: Formerly referred to as a *closed country,* a creative-access country is a nation-state in which traditional missionary work is illegal or banned. Missionaries who want to work in such countries must be creative in the means they utilize for entry and residence.

globalization: The trend toward an increasing interdependence of economies and businesses on a global scale, especially in trade, the movement of money, manufacturing (e.g., outsourcing the manufacture of consumer goods), and service provision (e.g., computer technicians living in India answering questions from people in the United States).

hidden peoples: People groups (see below) that currently have no access to the gospel. They are "hidden" not in the sense that they are invisible but in the sense that there is no way, given current conditions, that they could hear the gospel in their own language in a way that makes sense to them.

holistic mission: Mission that takes into account the whole of human needs: spiritual, social, and personal. Holistic mission includes both evangelism and church planting as well as development and social transformation.

incarnational mission: Just as Christ was incarnated as a person, so missionaries, it can be said, need to incarnate themselves into a new context. They cannot enter as newborns, but they can learn the language and the culture of their new context in such a way that they can behave like those who were born in the culture.

indigenous church: A church that fits well into a local culture. Traditionally, this is defined in terms of three "selfs": self-governing (not dependent on outside agencies to make decisions), self-financing (not needing outside funding to carry on its work), and self-propagating (able to evangelize effectively within its own culture). More recently, self-theologizing—the ability of a church to develop its own theological understandings from Scripture—has been added to the criteria.

15

indigenous missionary: A missionary from what was once considered a receiving nation. This term tends to be broadly used of both indigenous evangelists (who do not cross cultural boundaries) and indigenous missionaries (who may cross significant boundaries even though they stay within their country of residence).

majority world: That part of the world's population living outside Europe and North America. Terms such as *non-Western, third world, two-thirds world, developing nations,* and *undeveloped nations* have been used to designate such areas and peoples. No single term has been accepted by all, and all such terms have a negative political, economic, or social connotation. By using the term *majority world,* we simply recognize that the peoples living outside Europe and North America constitute the largest demographic block in the world. *See also* Southern Christianity.

marginalized: Individuals and groups who live on the margins of a society, "not fully able to participate in its socioeconomic, political, or religious life, due to cultural, political, religious, or socioeconomic differences" (Klaus 2000, 597).

missional: Being oriented toward mission in thinking, acting, and living. Missional churches are churches that have mission as their heartbeat.

nongovernment organization (NGO): Often a charitable or social service organization that provides government-like support but is not government directed or controlled (e.g., the Red Cross, Tear Fund, Habitat for Humanity, World Vision).

nonresidential missionary: A missionary who, for whatever reason, is unable to live permanently in the country that is the main focus of his or her ministry. This tends to be the case more often with creative-access countries.

peoples, people groups: A people is usually defined by ethnic or linguistic terms. It is estimated that there are twelve thousand distinct languages and dialects and as many as twenty-four thousand people groups in the world today.

pluralism: The idea that there is more than one correct approach to truth or reality. In their most extreme form, pluralists advocate the blending of all sets of competing ideas, each having only a portion of the whole and each true in its own way. In religious terms, those who promote pluralism claim that no religion has an exclusive hold on religious truth; all are legitimate in their own spheres of influence.

praxis: From the Greek word used in the New Testament book of Acts meaning "to work" or "to execute." The focus in mission literature tends to be on acts that work toward God's goals for humanity. Depending on the author, these may include such things as salvation, redemption, justice, and liberation.

short-term missions: Trips with a mission focus that range from one week to one or two years. They may be organized by churches, agencies, or even individuals for a variety of reasons (from English language camps to church-building projects to evangelistic campaigns).

Southern Christianity: The forms and types of Christian faith found in the majority world.

spiritual warfare: Reflects the reality that Satan does not want unbelievers to come to Christ or believers to live fruitful, holy lives. The warfare Christians face involves Satan and his hosts constantly trying to maneuver them toward spiritual lethargy or depression while they seek to live the abundant life Jesus promised.

syncretism: The replacement of core or important truths of the gospel with non-Christian elements (Moreau 2001d).

tentmaking: Coined from Paul's stay at Corinth when he made tents so as not to be a burden on the Corinthian church. Tentmaking is the practice of using paid employment to gain and maintain entry in a cross-cultural setting. Tentmakers work as professionals and engage in ministry activities in addition to their wage-earning work.

have several years of experience in mission field ministry, administration, research, and teaching. The chapters were written as follows:

    chapters 1, 4, 5, 7: Michael Pocock
    chapters 2, 9: Douglas McConnell
    chapters 3, 6, 10: Gailyn Van Rheenen
    chapter 8: Mike Barnett
    chapter 11: Douglas McConnell and J. Ted Esler
    chapter 12: A. Scott Moreau

We hope this book will positively affect the progress of the missionary task, not simply in numerical expansion but also in qualitative depth. If we move beyond *acquaintance* with the trends to *engaging* the people affected by them, we will have made some progress. Such engagement involves a renewed focus on God's glory and a renewed love for one another. Jonathan Bonk's synopsis deserves thoughtful reflection: "The real test of progress is how we love God and our neighbor. Everything else is fluff, and potentially dangerous fluff, at that. It gets in the eyes, so that we no longer see clearly as God sees" (2003, 16).

It is our hope that readers will see the trends of this book through the eyes of God. May our hearts be sensitive to the things that must break God's heart but also alive to the marvelous things he is doing in our day.

PART 1

The Global Context

Globalization

New York's in New Delhi, Manila's in Los Angeles

MICHAEL POCOCK

Whether you look at the label on your shirt (from Guatemala), your shoes (from China), your watch (from Taiwan), or the newest English-language issue of the World Evangelical Alliance's (WEA) *Connections* (printed in India), it is clear that you are wearing, using, and thinking on a global scale. But as we do with computers, we can use this entire system with only minimal understanding of its makeup. Life is fast paced, highly scheduled. Most of us do not have time to learn how to program computers; we only need things to work for us.

That is the level at which many of us think about globalization. We may have heard the term. We may be generally aware that products we use are made all over the world and that we seem to hear very quickly about events a continent away. Ethnically diverse people address us on television news programs. Some of us are aware that a Japanese cello player, YoYoMa, is one of the most famous musicians in the world, even though his expertise is on a Western musical instrument. Some will remember that Ravi Shankar introduced Indian musical themes to the Beatles and taught them to play the sitar. If you are a Generation X or

Millennial reader, you are more likely to know that singer Nora Jones, raised in Texas, is Shankar's daughter.

Global interaction has intensified. The dynamics behind globalization, its meaning, and its implication for missions need to be understood by everyone involved in living for Christ and making him known in our global context. We need to ask some serious questions. What is globalization? Is globalization new? Does globalization matter? Is it good or bad? Must there be winners and losers in globalization? Does globalization have a life of its own? Where is God in this entire process? For missionaries and other cross-cultural workers, the application question is crucial: In what ways does globalization make cross-cultural service different?

IDENTIFYING THE TREND: WHAT IS GLOBALIZATION?

Thomas Friedman, who gave the world a great, fast-paced reader on globalization in *The Lexus and the Olive Tree* (1999), says in a later work:

> Globalization involves the integration of free markets, nation-states and information technologies to a degree never before witnessed, in a way that is enabling individuals, corporations and countries to reach around the world further, faster and cheaper than ever. . . . Globalization means the spread of free-market capitalism to virtually every country in the world. (Friedman 2000, 7)

John Powell maintains that *globalism*, used in a sense very close to *globalization*, "refers to the process in which goods and services, including capital, move more freely within and among nations. As globalism advances, national boundaries become more and more porous, and to some extent, less and less relevant" (Powell and Udayakumar 2000).

Powell and Friedman both focus on economics or the market to define globalization. Many writers give the impression that globalization is essentially a movement from the West to extend its influence worldwide through the free-market economy. But globalization is not a one-way street, nor does it relate solely to economics. Malcolm Waters, an Australian, captures the idea that globalization lifts restraints on interaction at every level. He calls it "a social process in which the constraints of geography on economic, political, social and cultural arrangements recede, in which people become increasingly aware that they are receding and in which people act accordingly" (2001, 5).

Globalization began with the emergence of empires marked by expansion and the control of large territories by single cultures or civilizations.

The Roman and Greek empires spread far beyond their points of origin, taking their ideas, innovations, and systems of governance with them. Islamic faith and culture spread widely around the Mediterranean world after AD 732, and the Mongol Empire spread from Mongolia into China and across Asia to Vienna by 1241 (Moffett 1998, 407). In South America, the Incas established an empire covering what today are several nation-states, and the Spanish, English, and French became dynamic catalysts for the spread of commerce, culture, and religion over extended areas of the world from 1500 onward.

Historically, empires expanded outward from the center. Over the course of history, centers have included Athens, Rome, Beijing, Cuzco, Seville, and London. There was some interaction when people at the center of an empire received input from those on the periphery. Many spices and condiments, for example, were unknown in Europe until the dark chapter in church history known as the Crusades brought Europeans into contact with the Middle East. Gunpowder and paper-making technologies reached Europe from China in the fourteenth century. Tomatoes, tobacco, and potatoes became common staples in Europe following the colonization of the Americas after 1500. There was, however, markedly less cultural, philosophical, or religious movement from the peripheries to the centers of civilization until the modern era.

> *Taken as a whole, globalization is a trend of accelerating, compressed interaction between peoples, cultures, governments and transnational companies. It is a heightened multi-directional flow of ideas, material goods, symbols and power facilitated by the Internet and other communication, technologies, and travel.*
>
> Michael Pocock (see Waters 2001, 20; Robertson 2000, 53)

In 1969, human beings first stood on the moon. As the American and Russian space programs progressed, we saw for the first time photographs of the entire planet. Seeing earth in this way reinforced the idea that we are all on a single globe. The possibility of a change in perspective occurred. Indicative of this was the coining of new terms in the 1960s such as *global village* (McLuhan 1964). The general use of the word *global* began in the 1960s, although it is much older in origin. The term was still relatively rare in literature in the early 1990s but is much more common in the new millennium. For example, in 1993, the Library of Congress listed 34 volumes with *globalization* in the title; by 2000, the number had risen to 284 (Waters 2001, 2).

The reality is that globalization has developed over centuries as people have engaged in trade, conquest, and religious expansion. Globalization has progressed in fits and starts. The rapid expansion of peoples and ideas, followed by stagnation or reaction, has been going on throughout human history. The more modern version of globalization has been linked to the appearance of capitalism and especially to the recent mobility of capital. The world has reached near total and instantaneous interconnectivity since the emergence of the Internet in the 1990s. "All arguments accept that there has been a sudden acceleration of globalization in recent years" (Tiplady 2003b, 4).

More than a fad, this is a fundamental transformation to a new reality likened by Robert Schreiter to the emergence of feudalism, the creation of modern nation-states, or the ending of the colonial era (1990, 29). Globalization is both dynamic and developing as an enduring reality in which nation-states and geographical distance are less relevant than ever. As such, it merits serious consideration for the implications it has for Christianity and world missions.

EVALUATING THE TREND: HOW SIGNIFICANT IS GLOBALIZATION?

There is scarcely a Christian organization, alliance, or individual writer in the new millennium who discounts the reality of globalization. This applies to Catholics such as Robert Schreiter (1990), Protestants such as Max Stackhouse (2000), evangelicals such as Bob Goudzwaard (2001), and organizations such as the World Evangelical Alliance (WEA), which in June 2003 held an international consultation titled "The Impact of Globalization on World Mission."

> *Globalization matters because it fundamentally changes the contexts in which we minister, the way people and cultures perceive each other, how people think, and the means available to reach them. We cannot dismiss the effects of globalization on ourselves as communicators of the gospel message.*
>
> Michael Pocock

The discussion that follows looks at four interrelated aspects of globalization and evaluates their impact on ministry today: world migration, air travel, the Internet, and the free-market economic system.

World Migration

Widespread and rapid migrations have the potential to make geographical and nation-state issues seem almost irrelevant. During the last twenty years of the twentieth century, the vision of missions to unreached people was focused on the 10/40 Window. Such a vision expressed the idea that mission efforts needed to be focused on the peoples living between 10 degrees and 40 degrees north of the equator and from the west coast of Africa to the eastern limits of Asia.

This was a helpful concept, but it did not take into account the fact that millions of people from the 10/40 Window have migrated outside it. Six million Muslims live in the United States, but only 30 percent of them are American born. Over 1 million Muslims live in the United Kingdom, and an additional 3.4 million live in Germany. Within the 10/40 Window, people of various religions and nationalities work outside their own nation. Patrick Johnstone notes that the expatriate population of the United Arab Emirates is 82 percent. Many of these people are from 10/40 Window nations (Johnstone and Mandryk 2001, 650). Similar figures are also true of Saudi Arabia (Johnstone and Mandryk 2001, 647) and Kuwait (Johnstone and Mandryk 2001, 270). The expatriate populations in these countries illustrate that even when people do not live among their people groups in their traditional homes, it is often possible to live among them somewhere else. Those who migrate for work also travel back and forth to their home areas. The boundaries imposed by geographic distances simply do not mean what they once did (George 2003b, 18–22).

Migration brings non-Christians into areas more strongly Christian and more open to evangelism and religious change. A Hindu Indian in England or a Muslim Turk in Germany may not face ostracism from the community, loss of employment, and family violence if he or she converts to Christianity. Migration also brings vibrant Christians from Africa or the Caribbean to post-Christian areas of Europe. Church planters in Europe can often find Christian immigrants there who understand what the church planter is trying to do and are willing to become part of the nucleus of newly forming churches.

Air Travel

An important dynamic of globalization is rapid air travel. Nowhere in the world is more than thirty hours from where you presently sit. If you have a bank account, a computer, a television, and a job, you are in the top 30 percent of the world's population and are considered "connected" in the process of globalization. For those who are connected, travel is relatively affordable, and opportunities exist to influence and be influenced by other cultures around the globe. Those who are connected can learn about countries more prosperous or stable than their own and have the means of getting there. Often they choose to leave their home countries to live elsewhere. On the other side are the disconnected, those left behind who are increasingly poorer and less prepared for employment.

25

Fast and affordable travel has revolutionized the mission scene, bringing millions of people we would otherwise never meet into close proximity. It has also made nonresidential and short-term missions possible. More North American church people than ever before have seen other cultures, learned directly from nationals overseas or on their U.S. campuses and jobs, and become more aware of global contexts simply because air travel has made the world smaller.

The Internet

Instantaneous information exchange facilitated by the Internet is a prominent feature of globalization. This exploded in the 1990s. Anyone from Azerbaijan to Zimbabwe can set up a Hotmail account and join the Internet at a village cybercafe—even those who cannot afford a computer. In fact, as with public transportation systems, cybercafes are far more numerous in majority world areas, where there is less computer ownership than in North America.

The Internet greatly facilitates any investigative or learning process. The possibilities are almost limitless. In the field of Christian missions, interested people can educate themselves about a people or a nation-state. Just as easily, those who are being studied can in turn investigate those researching them. People can sit at a laptop and learn about Bhutan and the Bhutanese. Anyone who is connected can learn what Christian researchers are saying about a given people group in *Operation World* (Johnstone and Mandryk 2001; see http://www.gmi.org/ow), *The World Christian Encyclopedia* (Barrett, Kurian, and Johnson 2001; see http://www.worldchristiandatabase.org/wcd), or on websites such as the Joshua Project (http://www.joshuaproject.org), Global Mapping International (http://www.gmi.org), and MisLinks (http://www.mislinks.org).

Mission organizations must both reckon with and capitalize on the near total interconnectivity of a globalized world. The question is, Should agencies list the people groups they wish to reach on their websites so that interested people can pray for them? Should they say where their personnel are working or express their plans for the future? They can, but do they really want the entire world to know? It would be difficult for mission planners and practitioners to survive without the Internet and electronic interconnectivity, but they are also limited by it. Opposition has been mounted against Christian workers based on what anti-Christian extremists have learned about the plans of agencies from the agencies' websites.

Yet the Internet has also made it possible for interested non-Christians to investigate Christianity or the Bible, asking questions and receiving answers, all without exposing themselves to risk if they live in sensitive circumstances. Evangelism, discipleship, and leadership training are more available at a distance than ever before. The Internet reduces barriers of distance, occupation, and funding.

The Free-Market Economic System

Multinational or transnational corporations (TNCs) have burgeoned as the major economic phenomenon of globalization. Forty thousand corporations operate across national boundaries (Anderson and Cavanagh 2000, 1). At $7.1 trillion, the combined sales of the top 200 TNCs is larger than the combined gross domestic product of 181 nations ($6.9 trillion; Anderson and Cavanagh 2000, 2). Although free-market capitalism has definitely brought jobs to millions around the world and may be the best hope for the poor and marginalized, the free market desperately needs a conscience and a moral commitment to help the 70 to 80 percent who are disconnected and getting progressively poorer and destabilized (Anderson and Cavanagh 2000, 3).

As global business expands, it industrializes areas that previously were traditionalist, often agrarian, cultures. Malcolm Waters has shown that industrialization has a tendency to homogenize culture (2001, 31) because the very essence of industrial productivity is standardization. Chinese people making shirts in factories in Macao must make them to Western tastes, styles, and specification. The production line looks like a similar factory in South Carolina or the assembly plants just inside the Mexican border. Yet while working hours and working styles are standardized, the new workplace values mix with local cultural distinctives, generating distinctly different patterns of living and values.

> *I believe you dare not be a globalizer without being a safety-netter and social democrat, because if you don't equip the have-nots, know-nots and turtles to survive in the new system, they will eventually produce a backlash that will choke off your country from the world. . . . It means articulating a politics, geo-economics and geo-politics of sustainable globalization.*
>
> Thomas Friedman (2000, 12–13)

Transnational corporations tend to homogenize their cooperating partners in the name of efficiency and profit. Transnational mission agencies and the churches they establish in other cultures face the same set of issues. It is difficult to tell if one is really in another country when a church looks like, acts like, and sings like the churches in the West. Presentations of Rick Warren's *Purpose Driven Church* or Bill Hybels's Willowcreek Church model are known and duplicated around the world. Benny Hinn is as well known—if not

27

SIDEBAR 1.1
KATHIE LEE GIFFORD GOES GLOBAL

In 1995, Kathie Lee Gifford, a well-known talk-show host and Christian (Gifford 2004; Solomon 2004), offered a woman's line of apparel intended to be both fashionable and affordable. The line was marketed in the United States by Wal-Mart.

Gifford's line of clothes was produced in Honduras. Investigators checking on working conditions at the plant discovered girls 13 to 15 years of age working fourteen- to fifteen-hour workdays. Gifford was mortified. She did not know about the conditions at the plant that made her line of clothing "affordable" in the United States.

The Giffords attempted to compensate workers for their labor and have since condemned unfair and child labor practices worldwide. They donated profits from the clothing line to a variety of charities and called for monitoring of garment workers and factories worldwide.

As unfortunate as the conditions were at the Honduras garment factory, the fact is that many families who previously had no income obtained a way out of poverty through their employment there. There were practically no assembly plants in Honduras before 1985, but within 10 years, 160 plants sprang up, employing 75,000 people (Anderson and Cavanagh 2000). After the publicity connected with the Gifford case, many plants were closed in Honduras. The work moved elsewhere, resulting in a loss of employment for many Hondurans. In 2003, Wal-Mart canceled its agreement with Kathie Lee Gifford.

REFLECTION AND DISCUSSION

1. Were the measures taken by Kathie Lee Gifford appropriate for a Christian entrepreneur?
2. What appropriate actions could missionaries in Honduras have taken in the situation described above?
3. What limitations and risks are involved in such actions?

---

better known—in Latin America and South Africa as in the United States. Biblical Instruction and Leadership Development (BILD) is a biblical training program for pastors taught around the world and available in many languages. Many ministry approaches originating in North America may seem biblical and sound, but they are certainly contextualized to their original setting. Should missionaries maintain their home-grown ministry methods in different cultural settings? Is what they do any different from what TNCs do as they globalize industry and business?

The globalizing free-market system has benefits and risks. Many from the majority world have prospered as the West has outsourced its manufacturing and technology service industry. However, the mobility of capital and the lack of consideration for the long-term well-being of workers can create hostility among societies that fall victim to exploitation.

Mission agencies and missionaries must minister at both extremes—to the beneficiaries *and* to the marginalized losers of globalization. If we are Westerners working in economically struggling societies, we may be perceived with anger, not solely for our religious faith but also because we represent a socio-cultural-economic juggernaut and a dominating free-market system that drowns or crushes other peoples and cultures. Thomas Friedman, in his inimitable style, uses the famous painting *American Gothic* to describe how disconnected, marginalized people perceive Americans and the globalization process. The painting pictures a simple farmer standing protectively by his daughter in front of their farmhouse. The new *American Gothic* would be two twenty-something "software engineers who come into your country wearing beads and sandals, with rings in their noses. . . . They kick down your front door, overturn everything in the house, stick a Big Mac in your mouth, fill your kids with ideas you never had or can't understand, slam a cable box on your TV, lock in the channel to MTV, plug an Internet connection into your computer and tell you, 'download or die'" (Friedman 2000, 9).

This is the perception that fuels the anger of extremists such as Al-Qaeda in marginalized societies. It is the new context of missions. If we do not understand the phenomenon of globalization, we will miss golden opportunities for service, and we will fail to understand the antagonism that swirls around us. "Unless we understand some of these undercurrents of our time, our ministries will fail to have lasting legacies" (George 2003b, 21).

REFLECTING ON THE TREND: GLOBALIZATION IN LIGHT OF SCRIPTURE AND THEOLOGY

Biblically Positive Elements of Globalization

Globalization can be seen as the phenomenon that fulfills the creation mandate of God in Genesis 1:26–28. Before there was ever a covenant people of Israel or the body of Christ, people were to move out from the creative center into the entire earth, establishing a benevolent steward-ship over all created things. Idolatry, pride, and failure to spread out were judged by God at Babel (Gen. 11:1–9).

God has a purpose in globalization, and while we may not have clarity on that purpose, he will not permit it to be thwarted. History bears witness to humanity's movement toward the ends of the earth. Like a flood that flows to the farthest extent possible and then moves back in choppy waves, people have migrated, flowing around the planet, mingling and swirling until the entire earth finds itself fully populated

29

with people in considerable but not complete control of the environment around them.

Paul, guided by the Holy Spirit, explained the Babel event to pagan philosophers gathered on the Areopagus (Acts 17:16–34). He declared:

- that God made everyone from one person; hence, the human race is a unity of similar essence (vv. 25–26).
- that God's original purpose was for the earth to be globally populated (v. 26).
- that all people live where they do because God has put them there (v. 26).
- that God's creation and providential care demand recognition of him as the one God to be worshiped in the person of his Son, whom he sent (vv. 27–31).
- that the placement of peoples and God's presence among them are intended to help them reach out and find God, who is not far from any of them (v. 27).

Paul maintains that God is a global God who created humanity and prompts our movements around the globe. God lives providentially with his creation. Regenerate and unregenerate people are never far from him (v. 28). God always transcends creation but at the same time is immanent or present with it.

How does this relate to globalization? The movement and presence of people around the globe are not simply products of market forces. Globalization is not simply the product of a human desire for betterment, a working out of aggression, or a flight from danger. Rather, God himself orchestrates the globalizing phenomenon of human migration. The fundamental fact of population migration, the presence of people of many cultures living together the world over, is not a theological "problem." It is a phenomenon we are called to embrace and even to engage.

Every area of life touched by people will have both wonderful and woeful aspects. Since the whole of creation participates in the fall, it exhibits the negative qualities named as the thorns and difficulties in Genesis 3:17–24. But the environment also responds to care and cultivation, which is part of the fundamental creation mandate issued before the fall to humankind. From the very beginning, humans had a responsibility to care for the environment (Gen. 2:15). Lordship over the earth (Gen. 1:28) does not imply a destructive battle with the elements or greedy and indiscriminate use of them. Rather, it means that we should exercise a constructive stewardship over what God has entrusted to us.

SIDEBAR 1.2
MISSIONS AND GLOBALIZATION

Ruth Valerio, working for Cred in the United Kingdom by helping churches understand globalization and related issues, writes the following. As you read it, consider the implications for missions:

Mike Perreau (personal communication) talks about moving from "job faking" (using a job as a disguise to enter a country) to "job taking" (i.e., "tentmaking") to "job making." Two of the greatest needs that people have in order to be able to survive in today's world are business skills and the finances to support those skills. Hence, micro-business and enterprise are a key factor in development. Mission agencies should be, and are, looking at how they can equip their personnel with enterprise-making skills. English comes into play again here. Many missionary activities are focused on the developing nations, where three needs predominate: health, education, and economics. Since English is a key factor in all three areas, teaching English can help a country access these areas. (2003, 24)

REFLECTION AND DISCUSSION

1. What opportunities are there to share the gospel and to show Christian values at work in businesses created overseas?
2. In what ways might teaching English help the process of development?
3. How might direct gospel sharing be compromised in mission work focused on combating economic and social ills in a community?

Biblically Negative Elements of Globalization

The globalizing of the globe also bears negative marks left by the hands of people who are "fearfully and wonderfully" (Ps. 139:14) made in the image of God (Gen. 1:26). Since the fall, that image has been incredibly marred. Isaiah says that the wicked are "like the tossing sea, which cannot rest, whose waves cast up mire and mud" (57:20).

There is something wonderful about even an unregenerate person. Having been made in God's image—including elements of God's wisdom and creativity—people have produced marvels such as the tower of Babel. Even so, these wonders have often been attempts by individuals and societies to assert themselves and to avoid obeying and giving honor to the God who created them. This was the story of Babel.

The Babel incident (Gen. 11) shows that the mechanical ingenuity of people is boundless. God recognizes this fact (11:6). But we can use our ingenuity to attempt to subvert his sovereign purposes. The people of Babel were anti-globalists. They built a city and a tower so that they would not be scattered (11:4). But God destroyed their project and caused

31

linguistic diversification, which forced people to move out (11:9) and to obey the globalizing mandate of Genesis 1:28. The judgment of Babel is presented as the event through which cultural diversity began. The seventy-two nations mentioned in Genesis 10 are actually the product of the Babel incident recorded in Genesis 11, though described prior to that incident (Ross 1988, 243).

The Glorious Potential of Globalization

Mission agency consultant Richard Tiplady notes a tendency among people to take one side or the other in evaluating globalization. Some see it as nothing less than the evil of this present age, others as the greatest aid to world evangelism ever witnessed. We should be cautious because globalization is complex. Tiplady says:

> As human beings, made in the image of God, we are capable of cultural innovations that are good. As fallen people, all our actions and thoughts are corrupted throughout by sin. But, the image of God remains. We may be entirely in need of redemption, but we are not entirely evil. (2003a, 15)

People have a tendency to subvert even their divinely given ingenuity. At Babel, people built an impressive and no doubt beautiful tower, but they used it to exalt themselves and to resist the creation mandate. In the same way, an incredibly wonderful innovation such as the Internet can be used positively to educate, socialize, plan, or connect or negatively to disseminate pornography, recipes for weapons of mass destruction, hate-based philosophies, and so on.

As globalization brings diverse peoples together, God has a method to move people past the mono-cultural prejudices held almost universally. God's people—the church—live among the rest of the nations as God's "priestly nation" (1 Pet. 2:9–12). God keeps track of the nations; he knows their names and dwelling places. He uses his own people as a ministerial or priestly nation to minister to all the other nations. The church is thus a type of "supranation"—its people are from all nation-states, languages, and tribal groups, but their united task is to glorify God among the nations (Ps. 96) and to "live such good lives among the pagans that . . . they may see your good deeds and glorify God on the day he visits us" (1 Pet. 2:12).

But how are the people of God from various cultures united in light of their natural inclination to resist unity? Jesus Christ destroyed the hostility that renders reconciliation impossible. Paul explains that Christ "is our peace, who has made the two one and has destroyed the barrier, the dividing wall of hostility" (Eph. 2:14). The key to getting along in a globalized world with diverse peoples is the Spirit of Christ, who bears witness to the work of Christ.

Amazingly, the first thing we learn about the Holy Spirit when he makes his appearance in Acts 2 is that in the Spirit the linguistic differences of people, which originated at Babel, are overcome. The Spirit is an international or global Spirit. The key dynamic for people getting along in a globalized world is the Lord Jesus Christ and his indwelling Spirit. This is why all believers should preach the uniqueness of Christ as God's provision for sin and the cure for divisiveness (Acts 4:12; Eph. 2:14). We should teach and embody the work of the Spirit around the globe wherever God places us. However, we do this in the context of many competing claims. The challenge is to remain Bible centered in our orientation without obscuring the issues or being unloving toward those who disagree. As Harold Netland puts it, "Within this context [of increasing pluralism] . . . the church should seize the opportunity and lead the way, demonstrating how to be both deeply committed to one's own beliefs and also appropriately tolerant and accepting of diversity" (2001, 347).

Competing Dynamics within Globalization

The hand of God is discernible in globalization. However, we must also consider the hand of other unseen entities, including human self-interest as well as the demonic. Secular writers have referred to globalization as if it had a mind of its own, as if free-market dynamics are irresistible and opposition futile (Friedman 1999, 8). Some writers are as deterministic regarding free-market capitalism as Karl Marx was about economic determinism and the proletarian revolution. Francis Fukuyama, for example, says, "The laws of economic efficiency and growth have replaced the divine plan" (cited by Sine 1999, 67).

The real possibility is that the unseen yet evident dynamic behind much of globalization is collective human self-interest. Michael Pocock has labeled "the world"—the cosmos of which the New Testament speaks so frequently—"the group-think of unregenerate humanity" (1997, 19–23), by which he means the conventional wisdom of the culture around us. In other words, without resorting to theories of satanic empowerment of world forces (discussed in chap. 9), we have to reckon with people themselves and their unregenerate sinfulness.

James and John speak of both individual and collective sinfulness as the dynamics behind the acquisitiveness that marks unregenerate people and Christians whose focus is on the world rather than on Christ. The cravings for more that mark so much of the free-market capitalism that drives the hidden side of globalization are "the cravings of sinful man, the lust of his eyes and the boasting of what he has and does. . . . [These come] not from the Father but from the world" (1 John 2:16).

The unbridled, self-aggrandizing aspect of globalization not only proceeds from depravity but also leads to it. Life has improved for the minority in the world who benefit from globalization. The wealth of some individuals and companies has increased immensely, but this has not produced spiritual interest, nor has it spread widely to the rest of the world's population. In the West, religious faith has dwindled with prosperity. In addition, growing prosperity among the globally connected can be linked to the increasing impoverishment of 70 percent of the world's population, including the disconnected in North America.

The depravity of the top dogs and the desperation of the underdogs require prophetic voices willing to demand a curb on rampant capitalism. Such voices already exist in people such as Mustard Seed Associates founder Tom Sine (1999) and popular lecturer Tony Campolo (2004). Solid teaching on stewardship and self-limitation for believers who too easily buy into the spirit of the world are also needed. A plan for reformation and transformation has been advanced by economist Bob Goudzwaard that merits serious study. He outlines five steps that have possibilities for moderating the negative impact of globalization and maximizing its positive aspects (2001). The closing section of this chapter discusses them further.

> *God did not put us into this time in order to curse the wind, but to sail the ship. We will not stop the gathering storm of globalization. We will, with God's help, harness the forces of globalization so that those very forces take us in the direction God wants, not the direction they are trying to blow us (see Gen. 50:20).*
>
> Stan Nussbaum (2003, 31)

The opposite of consumerism is contentment with sufficiency. Contentment is close to what the Bible calls shalom. The shalom of which the Bible speaks includes peace with God, peace with others, and general well-being. It includes prosperity, not in the sense of wealth but in the sense of sufficiency and an achievement of legitimate ends. The shalom of Scripture is not as the world gives but as Jesus gives (John 14:27). There is no true shalom apart from God in Christ. This is what makes proclamation of the gospel to the lost and teaching on biblical stewardship global imperatives.

Beyond the human tendencies of sin and rebellion, another dynamic fuels the negative side of globalization. Most simply stated, it is the ruler of this world. As John noted, "The whole world is under the control of the evil one" (1 John 5:19). This rulership does not preclude the sovereign lordship of Yahweh, God of the universe, but it represents the temporal controlling power of Satan over unredeemed humanity and all its structures. Satan, though already judged (John 16:11), has not been confined, and therefore he still acts within the permissive will of God.

Ethics professor Max Stackhouse is intrigued and troubled by the reality of apparent causative agents acting within the process of globalization, for "no one knows for certain what percentage of life can be explained by mechanical and organic factors" (Stackhouse, Browning, and Paris 2000, 34). He is skeptical of any traditional understanding of demons or angelic beings manipulating events or influencing trends, and yet he understands that something beyond the material is a partially understood dynamic behind globalization. He is not interested in the paranormal, but he believes that "moral and spiritual energies" are "more than myth and are critical to personal and social life" (2000, 34). Stackhouse finds these causative agents in Scripture, primarily as Paul refers to them—the authorities, powers, and principalities (2000, 31–52). He relates them all to the biblical concept of the world and believes that they represent constellations of spiritual and moral energies invested in complex configurations ruling life today.

To Stackhouse, "people carve out 'spheres' of social activity, clusters of institutions that house, guide, constrain, and permit, even encourage these powers to operate" (2000, 39). He builds his analysis on the observation that every field of endeavor develops a system by which it is ruled and that sets out a defined relationship to those outside the field. Religion is a principality and a sphere of concern that points to an "ultimate creative power that encompasses and that is present in every sphere" (2000, 43). Religion then develops subsets such as Christianity or Islam. Within these exist authority structures or linkages such as denominations or brotherhoods, and each of these has a life of its own. In the case of economies, the World Trade Organization (WTO) is such an authority, and the European Economic Community and the North American Free Trade Act serve as subset authorities that maintain and extend WTO authority.

Stackhouse helps us to see that something more than free-market capitalism drives globalization and that these powers are embedded in human institutions, even if they are energized by darker powers. If Stackhouse's contention is true, then humans can take responsibility for accepting or rejecting the temptation to serve their personal aims by acquiescing to the expectations of associations, corporations, or trade pacts by which society is controlled.

Clinton Arnold offers a more strictly biblical and theological treatment of the powers, authorities, and rulers (1992). Putting Stackhouse's argument in biblical terms, if Satan was judged and the authorities and powers were defeated at Calvary (Col. 2:15), then one who has been rescued from that dark domain and brought into the kingdom of the Son (Col. 1:12–13) is no longer paralyzed by these forces. This is a major facet of the good news. As John says, "The reason the Son of God appeared was to destroy the devil's work" (1 John 3:8).

Put in this way, globalization has a spiritual warfare component at its heart. The WEA acknowledged this in its Iguassu 1999 declaration:

> We welcome the renewed attention given in recent decades to the biblical theme of spiritual conflict. We rejoice that power and authority are not ours but God's. At the same time, we must ensure that interest in spiritual warfare doesn't become a substitute for dealing with the root issues of sin, salvation, conversion, and the battle for truth. We commit ourselves to increase our biblical understanding and practice of spiritual conflict while guarding against syncretistic and unbiblical elements. (Araujo 2000, 20)

There are three spiritual realities within and behind the phenomenon of globalization. First is God, who created us with cultural distinctiveness and who oversees the globe-encircling spread of humanity. Second, this humanity, infinitely valuable yet tragically flawed by sin, is moved not only by God but also by its own sinfulness and its national and community associations. It is also moved by the third spiritual reality, namely, satanic power working against the glory of God and his creation. The combination of sinful human endeavor and satanic intervention results in systems that exalt the powerful and stamp on the powerless.

This negative aspect of globalization can be remedied only as individuals accept the transforming work of God in Christ. We need to work, as Daniel and Joseph did, within the institutions of this world for the shalom of both the unredeemed and the redeemed. We must create modules of the new community, Christ's church, in which he reigns and his loved ones act in care for one another, their fellow human beings, and the creation in which God has placed them while they await the final establishment of harmonious balance between them and the world around them (Rom. 8:19–25).

ENGAGING THE TREND: WHAT SHOULD MINISTRY LOOK LIKE IN A GLOBALIZED WORLD?

As the new millennium dawned, evangelical mission agencies and associations worldwide worked to evaluate the progress of missions in the twentieth century and to explore the possibilities of ministry in the new millennium. The WEA, the Interdenominational Foreign Mission Association (IFMA), the Evangelical Fellowship of Mission Agenices (EFMA), the Evangelical Missiological Society (EMS), the Association of Evangelical Relief and Development Organizations (AERDO), and others met individually and together to consider the future, as did evangelical denominations and Roman Catholic orders. Most of these consultations at the very least touched on globalization.

The deliberations and findings of all the groups merit study, but this section focuses primarily on the WEA as a representative global fellowship of missiologists and practitioners. The WEA held two significant consultations, the Iguassu Missiological Consultation in 1999 and the consultation titled "The Impact of Globalization on World Mission" in 2003. The Iguassu dialogue produced the volume *Global Missiology for the Twenty-first Century* (Taylor 2000b). *One World or Many? The Impact of Globalisation on Mission* (Tiplady 2003b) was produced prior to the second meeting as reading for the meeting itself.

Responding to Free-Market Capitalist Expansion

The typical view of many secular observers is that globalization is essentially free-market capitalist expansion. Alex Araujo, a Brazilian bicultural evangelical, concurs. He also acknowledges rapid worldwide informational interchange facilitated by technology as a key aspect of globalization. However, his evaluation of globalization as a whole is largely negative, in part because he sees what it has done to those left in the cracks or crushed under the wheels of globalization.

In evaluating globalization, Araujo asks the question, "Are there safe ways to take advantage of elements of globalization without at the same time being exposed to its harm?" (2000, 58). He notes that "the key principle for Christians looking at globalization, then, is to refuse to be lured, intimidated or pressured by it," and he concludes, "We don't need to learn how to adjust. . . . [The church] is called to speak to people caught up in globalization's tidal wave, just as it did with all the previous tidal waves in human history" (2000, 60).

Araujo's proposed antidote to globalization is the church as God's intentional, transnational community. Christians must not permit ecclesiology or missiology to be shaped by the terminology of the commercial world but must restore every facet of the biblical foundation. What are appropriate responses to the negative aspects of globalized commercialism? Four things may be noted.

First, we must look at humanity as *homo spiritualis* rather than *homo economicus*—the status to which economic globalism reduces humankind.

Second, we should refuse to quantify or assess ministry progress in numerical terminology. Araujo feels that Scripture minimizes numbers and that an emphasis on them is a distinctly Western approach to assessment that fits the globalizing tendency. While he does not directly address New Testament numerical citations (e.g., the four thousand fed; the three thousand who believed at Pentecost; the growth of the church to five thousand in Acts 4), he does follow the lead of many majority world Christians who charge that Western missiologists rely excessively on numerical goal setting and quantification.

Third, we must come to terms with the overwhelming perception of globalization as an American phenomenon. In this Araujo agrees with Thomas Friedman, whose alarming picture of *American Gothic* was noted earlier. American culture, films, and music and American evangelistic, educational, and worship materials have circulated around the world in English and other languages. Much of this has been done with the best of intentions, but like globalization in general, these things are essentially American in outlook and ethos. This results in feelings of cultural suffocation on the part of those who are on the receiving end.

There have been many attempts to contextualize Western-flavored Christian communication, and this must continue. The best contribution of Westerners to the majority world church is the provision of tools to produce indigenous worship and educational materials. Examples of this approach are found in the July 2002 issue of *Evangelical Missions Quarterly*, which focuses on missions and the arts. Articles deal with such topics as the use of indigenous art to communicate the Christian message (Jordan and Tucker 2002, 302–9) and indigenous worship (Pierson 2002, 314–22). In addition, it contains a guide to websites to help continue the conversation (Moreau and O'Rear 2002, 364–71; see http://www.mislinks.org/practical/arts.htm). Mission agencies such as Wycliffe Bible Translators and Pioneers and seminaries such as Southwestern Baptist Theological Seminary (Fort Worth) have seriously interacted with the need for culturally appropriate worship through their consultations on ethnomusicology. In the end, the solution lies in full participation by Christians of all cultures in the provision of new educational and worship aids for churches.

Fourth, we must recognize the anguish of the marginalized in the wake of globalization. "People from all countries can experience globalization, not all can participate in shaping it or reaping its benefits" (Araujo 2000, 66). The majority of believers in majority world countries where great church growth is occurring come from the underside of globalization. Those who have resources have a disproportionate influence on decision making and must deliberately invite participation from those often at globalization's mercy, especially those who have nonfinancial contributions to make. WEA does this, as does Orbis Books, whose mission is to make the contributions of majority world Christians known to Western Christians.

SIDEBAR 1.3
GLOBALIZATION: WINNERS AND LOSERS

WINNERS	LOSERS
1. Corporations in search of cheaper, quality labor.	1. Those without skills needed to work for foreign corporations.
2. People living under restrictive, exploitive governments whose plight is shown to worldwide audiences.	2. Restrictive governments that cannot hide their brutality in a globalized world.
3. Consumers who enjoy less expensive products made abroad.	3. Majority world families uprooted by centralized factory systems making products for export.
4. Corporations seeking raw materials that have been depleted in their own nations.	4. Hardwood forests in Asia and Latin America.
5. People with disposable income seeking new travel and adventure venues.	5. Indigenous peoples affected by licentious behavior of Western tourists.
6. Western Christians seeking exposure to and ministry among unreached peoples.	6. Unreached peoples who need long-term rather than short-term missionary presence.

REFLECTION AND DISCUSSION

1. As you look over the list of winners and losers, consider specific countries, companies, ministries, or churches that have been positively or negatively impacted by globalization.
2. What is the Christian responsibility toward the losers in globalization?

3. What is the Christian responsibility toward the winners in globalization? For further resources, see http://www.globalization.about.com (secular site) and http://www.tiplady.org.uk.globalizationbook.org (Christian site).

Responding to Human Migration

In *Cultural Change and Your Church* (Pocock and Henriques 2002), Pocock deals extensively with the issue of human migration as globalization. This phenomenon continues as people move in response to push and pull effects. The collapse of colonialism in the 1950s and 1960s left millions of indigenous people in colonized countries, speaking the language and understanding the cultures of their colonizers but lacking jobs and living in insecure areas. Many of these migrated to the colonizers' home countries—Francophone Africans and Asians to France,

Anglophone Africans and Asians to the United Kingdom, Dutch-speaking Indonesians and Caribbean peoples to the Netherlands, and Filipinos to the United States.

Mission strategists have been aware of people groups migrating for employment for quite some time. To some extent, mission organizations have risen to the call, sending workers to minister exclusively to Muslims and Hindus in the United Kingdom, France, and other parts of Europe. American Chinese churches have sent workers to Latin America and Europe to reach migrating Chinese. Groups such as Church Associates have targeted English-speaking internationals who are semipermanent businesspeople in the major cities of Europe. Many of these migrating peoples see themselves as homogeneous units even though they are nationally or ethnically heterogeneous. They prefer to gather as internationals more than as culturally restricted ethnics. This is both a product and an opportunity of globalization. Mission agencies that have focused on a certain ethnicity, nationality, or religion must see the full validity and significance of migrant internationals as a target group.

> *The God who scattered the nations at the tower of Babel is in these days bringing the nations back together through the millions of immigrants who are filling our cities. It is only the power of the gospel lived out in the community of believers that can make such diversity into a new humanity.*
>
> John Leonard (2004, 70)

Responding to Accelerated Intercommunication

Al Gore did not invent the Internet, but it certainly came of age in the years of the Clinton presidency (1993–2000). It plays a crucial role in the accelerated development of communication technologies made widely accessible through cheaper hardware and better software. People have been putting together systems of communication since before the first postage stamp, the Penny Black, was issued in England in 1840. Erla Zwingle notes:

> Humans have been weaving commercial and cultural connections since before the first camel caravan ventured afield. In the nineteenth century the postal service, newspapers, transcontinental railroads, and great steam powered ships wrought fundamental changes. Telegraph, telephone, radio, and television tied tight and more intricate knots between individuals and the wider world. Now computers, the Internet, cellular phones, cable TVs, and cheaper jet transportation have accelerated and complicated the connections. . . . The difference now is the speed and scope of these changes.

It took television 13 years to acquire 50 million users; the Internet took only five. (2000, 154)

Missionaries have utilized every one of the means of information exchange and travel Zwingle names, from Livingstone's rescue by an Arab caravan in Africa (which led to his horror over slavery and made him a leading light in the abolitionist movement) to the use of SAT-7 Christian radio and television programming, which has overcome national barriers to Christian ministry in North Africa and the Middle East. Two significant questions concern whether there is a better way to use available technology than we have seen so far and whether we are called to offset the negative side of globalization technology.

For all the efficiency of rapid communication and the enhancement of border-obliterating technology, personal relationships and simple acts of kindness may, in the end, constitute the best strategies—and they may have the most appeal in a postmodern era. Jonathan Bonk of the Overseas Ministries Study Center (OMSC) tells the story of Prem Predahn, the apostle of Nepal. Predahn may be more responsible than any other person in seeing a handful of Christians in Nepal in the 1950s become one hundred thousand today (Bonk 2000).

Predahn was a Nepali Air Force officer stationed for a period in North India, where he heard the famous Indian Christian Bakht Singh speak at his military base. Predahn was converted, went back to Nepal, and continued as a witness, even during frequent imprisonments. But what about Bakht Singh, the person who led Predahn to Christ? Singh was used of God in tremendous ways in India, starting a church-planting movement that eventually brought more than five hundred churches into existence. How did Bakht Singh come to Christ? As an international student in Winnipeg, Manitoba, Singh had nowhere to go during Christmas break. While working out at the local YMCA, he met an old man. Struck by the peaceful face of the man, Singh commented on it. The elderly man, a Christian, asked Singh to spend Christmas with him and his wife. Singh did and became a believer. What, then, was the secret of the conversion of two great men of God and Christian movements in two Asian countries? It was the simple obedience of one Canadian follower of Christ to two simple words of admonition by Paul: "Practice hospitality" (Rom. 12:13; Bonk 2000, 149–61).

As the story illustrates, we dare not let the existence of increasingly sophisticated communication technologies blind us to the continuing efficacy of simple presence and personal proclamation. At the same time, however, we must use available media and communication advances.

For example, distance learning has improved with the use of the Internet and satellite technology. The Technical University of Monter-

---

SIDEBAR 1.4
GLOBALIZATION AND SHORT-TERM MISSIONS

One reality that has come with globalization is the dramatic increase of short-term mission projects. Mission agencies alone reported almost 350,000 short-termers (from two weeks to one year) in 2001 (Moreau 2004, 13). This did not include the uncounted short-term projects coming from local churches and schools, and if the projects of less than two weeks had been added in, the total may well have been as high as 1 million!

All of this raises complicated questions about short-term missions.

REFLECTION AND DISCUSSION

1. What are the potential benefits of short-term mission trips?
2. What is necessary to make short-term trips successful?
3. What factors may make a short-term trip less than ideal?

---

rey, Mexico (UTM) is an outstanding Latin American educational entity that runs a virtual university in addition to its residential program. Over eighty thousand students are enrolled in UTM's distance learning

---

CASE STUDY: DEALING WITH THE DOWNSIDE OF GLOBALIZATION

Two years ago, Abdul Abraham was thrilled when he found an opportunity to use one of the two official languages of India in a technical support position for an American company. He had taken a course in American-style English to interact more easily with the Americans referred to him daily from half a world away. Although he did not earn as much as the Americans who had previously done his job, he did make more than he ever had before. His improved pay enabled him to move his family to a better apartment. As Christians, he and his wife were able to support an effective indigenous Indian ministry as well. Everything seemed to be going well.

Unfortunately, it did not last long. Abdul vividly remembers the shock that came with the termination notice he received. At first, he was confused. He knew he had consistently good job ratings from his superior, and he had never been late or absent from work. Then he noticed that everyone around him was far more subdued than normal. As they began to talk, they realized that everyone had received the notice. They dug deeper and discovered that the Indian technical support division had been closed down because workers in yet another Asian country were willing to do the same work for lower pay and less benefits. The American company, sensing greater

program. This kind of educational venture is becoming commonplace for evangelical seminaries in many parts of the world. Even students without personal computers in poorer economies can learn through distance education through a local cybercafe—as long as they can afford the connection rate of less than a dollar per hour.

At issue in the use of Internet education is the relative lack of interaction among learners and between learners and the professor. Interaction of a sort is certainly possible through chat rooms on the Internet, but the Association of Theological Schools in North America has voiced concern that real value in ministerial preparation is lost when peer interaction is compromised (Pond 2004).

How might missionaries, hoping to utilize the benefits of Internet training for believers and emerging leaders, retain the value of face-to-face interaction among students? One possible answer is to require all students pursuing an educational program at a distance to meet with a minimum of three other students in the same geographical area. Schools can assist students by matching them with others in learning cohorts. Face-to-face interaction facilitates reflection, accountability, and spiritual disciplines. It also reflects the biblical orientation that people learn in

---

profits, had simply shut the Indian division to save money.

What could Abdul do? His mind raced through the issues he faced. Should he start looking for less expensive housing immediately? Should he hang on and hope that another transnational company would hire him? What could he tell the Indian believers in the ministry his American job helped him to support? He could already imagine the shock on their faces when he told them he could no longer support them. Even harder to face was the fact that he would have to tell his wife and children. How would they cope?

As he churned on the inside, shock give way to deep disappointment, and disappointment to anger. His questions took a new direction. How could an American company do this to Indian workers? Wasn't America supposed to be a Christian nation? Weren't the owners of this business Christians themselves? How could they simply dump dozens of people—people with families—so quickly in pursuit of greater profit? Wasn't America full of Christians? Couldn't they tell these companies how badly it hurts when they pursue free-market policies? Weren't there any rules against creating jobs in other countries, raising people's hopes, and then dashing them to the ground? Maybe the Indian Labor Board would have something to say to the American company!

Then he remembered a new friend he had recently made. Mark was an American missionary working in Abdul's city. Maybe Mark could answer some of his questions. Abdul left work that day and went straight to Mark's apartment. He poured out his heart and his hurts. He and Mark prayed over the situation and together decided that the best course of action would be to …

communities (e.g., the twelve disciples, Paul's missionary band, a local church, or even two or three gathered in Christ's name).

Part of the curse of globalization is the pressure to produce ever more cheaply better technology, generally at the expense of personalization and the reduction of people to *homo economicus*. Those engaged in cross-cultural service for Christ and the agencies and companies they represent must find ways to avoid depersonalizing the very people they serve when faced with the consistent need to economize. Christians cannot afford to promote the dehumanizing tendency of globalization.

There are other important considerations for missions in the context of globalization, many of which are treated in later chapters. Globalizing information technologies do not simply provide advantages for ministry. They also bring risks, such as the avalanche of online pornography, the frustration of proliferating email, and the endangerment of Christian workers in sensitive areas by communicating on the Internet details that alert the enemies of the gospel.

None of the risks associated with globalization means we should reject the trend wholesale nor that, taken as a whole, globalization is evil. God himself has an agenda in globalization. Globalization is not the antichrist. However, both Christ and Satan work and are served through globalization. Believers must critically engage and use the possibilities that come with globalization, guided by the criteria Paul gave the church at Philippi:

> Finally, brothers, whatever is true, whatever is noble, whatever is right, whatever is pure, whatever is lovely, whatever is admirable—if anything is excellent or praiseworthy—think about such things. Whatever you have learned or received or heard from me, or seen in me—put it into practice. And the God of peace will be with you.
>
> Philippians 4:8–9

2

Changing Demographics

The Impact of Migration, HIV/AIDS, and Children at Risk

Douglas McConnell

As a plane descends into the haze of any large city, the passengers are faced with the staggering reality of unchecked population growth. Visible from the air are a range of houses, office buildings, factories, roads, and the inevitable urban blight that quickens the pulse and reminds the traveler that the globe is filling with people. It is no wonder this impression is so sobering; during the twentieth century, the human population grew from 1.4 billion to 6.2 billion. Increasing the degree of impact has been the regional disparity of the growth. Economically less developed regions account for 4.6 billion people, and it is projected that 98 percent of the global population growth will occur in these regions in the next thirty years (Population Issues 1999). However we consider it, demographics, or the study of populations, has emerged as a significant source of information for missions.

As challenging as the sight of a large city is from the air, it is even more startling when you get into a car and begin to drive through the streets. If you are unsure of your destination, it is easy to wander around trying to find important landmarks all the while wishing you were in the safety of familiar surroundings. The field of demographics contains similar problems. In both cases, knowing where you are going is essential to

your journey. Choosing a destination requires some important considerations. First, why do demographic trends matter to us as followers of
Christ? Of the many responses that will be given in this chapter, none
is more compelling than the fact that the people represented by these
trends are on the heart of God. Therefore, we dare not ignore them by
isolating ourselves from the world, even when it appears unstable and
changing. One of the first verses many of us learned was the wonderful statement of the plan of salvation: "For God so loved the world that
he gave his one and only Son, that whoever believes in him shall not
perish but have eternal life" (John 3:16). This precious truth, for those
who believe in the Lord Jesus Christ, is like a treasured jewel. It is also
an inescapable motivation for obedience to the mission of God to the
world. This was captured by the theme of the Lausanne II Congress
on World Evangelization: "Our manifesto at Manila is that the whole
church is called to take the whole gospel to the whole world" (Lausanne
Committee for World Evangelization 1989).

IDENTIFYING THE TRENDS: MIGRATION, THE HIV/AIDS PANDEMIC, AND THE PLIGHT OF CHILDREN AT RISK

The analogy of traveling to a world-class city is a helpful way to remember that there is much more to explore than can be dealt with in
one chapter. As with a trip to the city, we are forced to choose certain
roads that will lead to a particular destination. Of the many significant
demographic trends, this chapter deals with only three: (1) migration,
(2) the HIV/AIDS pandemic, and (3) the plight of children at risk. Each
of these trends is raising vital and complex issues that must be addressed by those working in missions. Due to the limitations of space,
we will not address other vital trends such as the status of women, the
aging of the world's population, and other current global, cultural, and
economic issues. The three trends discussed here provide a starting
point for assessing the role of churches and agencies in responding to
demographic changes.

Migration

As noted in chapter 1, the growth of international migration as a
population trend has captured the attention of demographers and
missiologists alike. According to the "International Migration Report
2002" issued by the United Nations Population Division, over 175 million migrants live in countries other than those of their birth. In fact,
international migration has doubled since 1975. The total number of
migrants is larger than the total population of all but four countries
(DeLung and Jones 2003). In the more developed regions of the world,

nearly one in ten persons is a migrant. Thus, in 2002, migrants accounted for 18 percent of the total number of births and two-thirds of the total population growth in the more developed regions (United Nations Population Division 2002).

International migration has positively affected countries with declining fertility rates by helping them maintain appropriate ratios between aging and working populations. In real terms, the birthrate of a nation must be 2.1 children per woman of childbearing age to maintain its population. In parts of Europe and Japan, this rate has dropped below the replacement needs, threatening the critical population balance. To fully achieve the goal of population ratios, even greater numbers of migrants are needed in the coming fifteen years. In Europe, 20.3 million migrants are needed, and 14.3 million are needed in the United States (Bonilla 2001). Increasing the rate of international migration is readily achievable because of the rapid growth of populations in many areas of Asia, Latin America, and Africa.

Another outcome of the migration toward more developed countries is the flow of capital from migrants back to the developing world. In 2000, at least nine countries received over 10 percent of their gross domestic product in money sent home from abroad (United Nations Population Division 2002). The impact globally accounts for an estimated annual remittance of $62 billion (DeLung and Jones 2003). It is unlikely that this trend will slow down given the fact that developed nations account for only 15 percent of the world's population yet over 60 percent of the world's gross domestic product.

The complexities of such massive migration challenge our ability to evaluate the impact. To illustrate this fact, we can again look at the money sent home from abroad by populations migrating to the developing world. While it is true that capital flows into less developed countries, the money is used primarily by individuals or groups for current consumption needs such as health care or education (DeLung and Jones 2003). In many cases, those who benefit from the educational opportunities in turn become migrants to the developed world

> *Eddie Perez was not a typical gang leader. He was scrawny, read books and went to school. A Puerto Rican boy growing up in Hartford's mostly black North End, he founded the Ghetto Brothers in the early 1970s. And though he was younger than the rest of his crew, they followed him. In those days, he was known on the street as "The Professor." These days, he is Mayor Perez.... Raised by a single mother on welfare, Perez is now the most powerful mayor in Hartford [Connecticut] history.*
>
> CNN.com (2004a)

47

SIDEBAR 2.1
THE WORLD'S POOR

(Myers 2003, 30, 41, 45)

- In the last thirty years, the developing world has improved as much as the industrial world did during the entire nineteenth century.

- The number of people living on less than $1 a day has decreased by 400 million since 1970 but was unchanged in the 1990s.

- Yet still today one in five—1.2 billion people—do not have access to the basic social services of health care, education, safe drinking water, and adequate nutrition.

- Women make up 70 percent of the world's poor and two-thirds of the world's illiterates.

- Of the 925 million absolute poor in the world, 211 million (or 23 percent) are Christians.

- In the last twenty years, income inequality has risen in 66 percent of the countries of the world, particularly in Latin America, parts of Africa, China, and the West.

REFLECTION AND DISCUSSION

1. How do you account for the improvement in the developing world?

2. What are the factors contributing to the growing disparity?

3. What changes are needed to address the needs of the 211 million Christians trapped in poverty? Should they differ from responses to the non-Christian poor?

---

seeking better pay and greater access to resources. This phenomenon is a contributing factor to "brain drain," with its crippling effects on the developing world. Rather than assisting in overall development, remittances tend to create financial and social dependencies, further complicating unequal global economic growth.

Economic migrants, those who migrate in search of employment, constitute the vast majority of the increase in global migration. Of the 175 million people living outside the country of their birth, 91 percent are economic migrants (United Nations Population Division 2002). It is estimated that this trend will continue unabated in the coming decades. The largest diaspora is of the Chinese, with an estimated 55 million living outside mainland China, followed by the 22 million Indians living outside India (Myers 2003, 36). In many countries, migrants comprise a major population block. For example, 8.4 million Chinese migrants live in Indonesia, and another 6.4 million live in Thailand. The same phenomenon may be observed among Indian migrant populations in Fiji, Kenya, and Canada. The economic nature of migration is illustrated by the flow of migrants from Mexico to the United States, accounting for 8 percent of global migration (Myers 2003, 37).

Migrating populations bring many resources to their new countries, not the least of which are their religious beliefs. The impact of this trend should not be underestimated. Historically, the spread of religions through migration may be seen in the expansion of Christianity in the first five centuries AD, then again in what Kenneth Latourette called the "Great Century" from 1815 to 1915 (1939). The same may be observed in Islam, with its continuous spread from 750 to 1750 known as the Islamic Age. In his research on migration and missions, J. J. Hanciles postulates, "Recent migration movements, as a critical dimension of contemporary global transformations, have the potential to significantly affect the geographic and demographic contours of the world's major religions and provide a vital outlet for proselytism and missionary expansion" (2003, 146).

The causes of migration, although predominantly economic, include a variety of pathologies experienced by developing countries. For example, in 2000, there were 16 million refugees, over half of whom (9 million) were in Asia. Another 4 million were in Africa (United Nations Population Division 2002). According to Jane De-Lung and Becca Jones, "In 2002, over 40 million—16 million refugees and an estimated 25 million internally displaced persons—fled their homes because of persecution, war, and human rights abuses" (2003, 4).

> *One striking example [of the spread of religious beliefs through migration] is the El Shaddai movement in the Philippines . . . a [Catholic] lay charismatic group designed to combat Protestant penetration. . . . The Movement probably has 7 million members across the Philippines, making them a potent political force, and it also has the nucleus for a truly global presence. The large army of expatriate Filipino workers worldwide permits El Shaddai to operate congregations or chapters in over twenty-five countries.*
>
> Philip Jenkins (2002, 67)

Historically, one of the more serious threats posed by migrating populations is the spread of disease.

The HIV/AIDS Pandemic

From the first documented cases in the United States in June 1981, the AIDS disease caused by the HIV virus has emerged as a global pandemic. The rapid spread of HIV/AIDS makes it the deadliest epidemic of our time. The disease has killed 22 million people, with another 42 million infected. This number continues to rise as 16,000 individuals

Botswana currently has the highest HIV prevalence rate in the world: more than one in every three adults is HIV positive. Life expectancy had reached 65 years in 1990–1995, but it dropped to 56 years by 1995–2000 and is currently around 40 years because of deaths related to AIDS. The population will likely begin to decline within a few years. Although the full economic impact of HIV/AIDS is still to come, population projections for Botswana show a severe deficit in working-age people by 2025.

United Nations Population
Division (2003)

are infected daily. As with the other demographic trends, there is a disparity of distribution worldwide. Estimates show that sub-Saharan Africa, the hardest hit, has 28.1 million cases. The disease is also spreading rapidly through the massive populations of Asia, where it is estimated that 6 million people are infected in India and 1 million in China. These mind-numbing statistics bear witness to the claim that HIV/AIDS is the greatest humanitarian crisis in the twenty-first century.

The HIV/AIDS pandemic negatively affects families and households far beyond the millions of tragic deaths. Over 13 million children have lost one or more parents, accounting for one-third of all orphans in the world. Countries where the disease is widespread are experiencing a dramatic drop in life expectancy, further destabilizing families. Financial strain caused by the loss of income from infected members and the cost of treatment also creates a spiraling decline in family stability. Some of the more significant results are an increase in malnutrition, higher rates of school dropouts, and adoption of orphans into families already bearing heavy financial and social burdens. In the worst hit areas, there have been rapid increases in the number of single-parent-headed households, grandparent-headed households, and, sadly, orphan-headed households.

Juliet, a 21-year-old Zambian, lost both her parents to AIDS and is now looking after 11 of her younger brothers and sisters. The plight of Juliet and her siblings is not unique. By the year 2010, one out of four children in Zambia will be orphaned. As the growing number of children who lose their parents to AIDS overwhelms fragile social safety nets, many believe that strengthening community-based efforts is the only hope for building effective, sustainable support systems for children who are now orphans, for those who will become orphans, and for other children affected by AIDS.

USAID (2003)

The economic impact of HIV/AIDS is as widespread as the disease itself, particularly in the developing world. Among young adults in the prime employment years, there is a high incidence of contracting HIV and dying from AIDS. In agricultural areas, this trend has forced a reduction in land under cultivation—because of the loss of available labor—with correspondingly lower yields. In industrial and manufacturing firms, the disproportionate number of cases among younger workers has created increases in sickness-related absenteeism and placed greater demands on health care and death benefits. Another negative trend is the reduced demand for goods and services related to loss of personal income and lower levels of consumption. To illustrate, "In South Africa, economic growth will be reduced by 0.3–0.4% annually by AIDS, resulting in a gross domestic product that will be 17% lower than it would have been without AIDS" (Rosen 2001, 4–5).

> *Today some 3 million children are living with HIV/AIDS. And the disease has killed the mother, father or both parents of 13.4 million children still under the age of 15. The vast majority of these children—11 million—live in Sub-Saharan Africa. Their ranks will soon be swelled by millions of additional children who are living with sick and dying parents. By 2010, the total number of children orphaned by HIV/AIDS is expected to nearly double, to 25 million.*
>
> UNICEF (2002)

The United Nations continues to monitor the impact of the HIV/AIDS pandemic. The Declaration of Commitment adopted at the twenty-sixth special session of the U.N. General Assembly noted that "the global HIV/AIDS epidemic, through its devastating scale and impact, constitutes a global emergency and one of the most formidable challenges to human life and dignity" (United Nations Population Division 2003, xv). The effects of this pandemic are readily identifiable on the growing population of at-risk children.

The Plight of Children at Risk

In the last decade of the twentieth century, exponential population growth created an unprecedented number of children who were affected by natural disasters, wars, and poverty. In an effort to identify this vulnerable section of the population, the phrase *children at risk* emerged as a widely accepted classification. In broad categories, the risks faced by children include:

- disabling or bonded child labor
- war and other forms of violence

- sexual abuse and exploitation
- disease, drug abuse, or disability
- neglect or loss of family or primary caregiver
- extreme poverty
- oppressive institutions (Viva Network 2004a)

A major reason for the emergence of this new category was a spike in fertility rates worldwide during the 1960s and 1970s. The global impact of this change was heightened by a significant decline in mortality rates, particularly among infants, leading to an exponential growth of the global population. Specifically, there was a drop in infant mortality in the developing world from 141 deaths per 1,000 births in 1960 to 63 deaths per 1,000 births in 2000 (Himes and Olmo 2002). Overall, the population grew from 3 billion in 1960 to 6.1 billion in 2001.

Demographically, it is helpful to differentiate between two primary age groups: children (ages 0–14) and youth (ages 15–24). According to Judith Himes and Angelique Olmo, "Almost a third of the population is below age 15 in both Asia and Latin America, 30 and 32 percent respectively. Africa, with 43 percent of the population or 338 million young people under the age of 15, continues to be the youngest region" (2002, 1). Children are not only the largest population block but also the most vulnerable and dependent. One of the more sobering statistics is that 1.5 billion of the world's children face life-threatening risks (Viva Network 2004a).

> *A lot of the crime is carried out by so-called "rascals." Typically, these are gangs of young single men, who come to the cities, and, finding no jobs, turn to crime. A worrying trend is that these gangs are increasingly using weapons. . . . The population of PNG is about 4 million, and barely a quarter of this number has received formal education.*
>
> Post Courier (1998, 4)

The next older population block is the source of more urgently felt challenges. Estimates of the global youth population are less precise, varying from 18 percent, or 1.1 billion, to 30 percent, or 1.83 billion. The regional impact is again significant, with 80 percent living in the developing world, where access to education and employment is significantly reduced. Populations of young adults are a major social resource, either for building a strong future or for creating a destructive force within society.

In the coming decade, it is estimated that the labor force will grow by 1 billion people, largely coming from the current bulge in youth. In contrast, "Worldwide over 70 million young people are unemployed"

(Himes and Olmo 2002, 3). The majority of these young people are ill prepared to enter the workforce because of the disparities in education and job opportunities. Despite gains in universal primary education, the developing world suffers from significant attrition within the education system. Himes and Olmo report that only 75 percent of students in the developing world reach the fifth grade, with even higher dropout rates occurring among secondary school–aged youth (2002, 3).

Youth are also the most vulnerable in regard to political and military ideologues. While young people ages 18 to 24 constitute the greatest number of soldiers globally, the more sinister phenomenon is that of child soldiers. UNICEF states, "It has been estimated that over 300,000 children under the age of 18 are currently being used in more than 30 conflicts worldwide" (2003, 1). Factors contributing to child participation in armed conflict range from poverty to forcible recruitment and abduction. The production and ready availability of light weapons, such as the AK-47, facilitate the deadly engagement of children in warfare. According to the Viva Network, "The advantages of using children in warfare are chillingly simple: they are easy to manipulate, do not demand anything in return and are expendable" (2004b). The negative consequences of the physical, psychological, and sexual abuse suffered by children in armed conflicts are beyond calculation.

> *One U.S. shelter has rescued 10,000 child prostitutes. Sociologist Lois Lee has spent 24 years working with children from 11 to 17 years old who have been trafficked by pimps. One young resident, at her Children of the Night shelter in southern California, was forced to work as a prostitute in Oregon, Washington, Idaho, and Nevada before escaping her captor. "The sexual exploitation of American children cuts across every economic, ethnic, and social line," Lee says. "This is not just a Third World problem."*
>
> Andrew Cockburn (2003, 23)

The sexual exploitation of children has reached epidemic proportions globally. It is estimated that 10 million children are in the sex industry, with an additional million entering each year. Two extreme economic factors drive the sex trade among children: profitability and poverty. Fed by international tourism and the Internet, profits from the exploitation of children make it a lucrative alternative for depraved entrepreneurs. In many cases, the economic crises faced in the developing world foster a weak response by governments to stem the growth of the sex industry. On the supply side, poverty creates an intolerable situation in which children become a marketable commodity with little to offer but their bodies. Studies indicate that even parents succumb to the promise of a better life from increased income resulting from the sale of children into prostitution (Viva Network 2003).

The list of risks facing children worldwide grows in staggering proportion to the population. Although the responses among churches, agencies, and nongovernment agencies are expanding rapidly, the plight of children remains one of the most vexing of all the demographic trends at the beginning of the twenty-first century.

EVALUATING THE TRENDS: SERIOUS IMPLICATIONS OF EXPONENTIAL CHANGE

The impact of these demographic trends is truly overwhelming. The efforts of agencies and churches to deal with the realities of demographic shifts have, sadly, lagged behind the exponential rate of change. Yet at the outset of the twenty-first century, hopeful signs exist of a growing concern among Christians, including a renewed understanding of the place of holistic mission. Resources are increasingly available that provide substantive analysis of the trends and implications for strategic engagement (see sidebar 2.2).

SIDEBAR 2.2
DIGGING DEEPER

The following websites are useful for further study in the area of children at risk, demographics, the HIV/AIDS pandemic, and missional responses to global population issues.

AIDS Research and Information: http://www.aegis.com; http://www.aids.org; http://www.critpath.org/aric; http://www.unaids.org

Compassion International: http://www.compassion.com

Lausanne Committee on World Evangelization: http://www.gospelcom.net/lcwe

MAP International: http://www.map.org

Medical Ambassadors International: http://www.medicalambassadors.org

Population Resource Center: http://www.prcdc.org

Support for Analysis and Research in Africa Project, Academy for Educational Development: http://sara.aed.org

TEAR Fund: http://www.tearfund.org

U.N. Population Fund: http://www.unfpa.org

UNICEF: http://www.unicef.org

U.S. Census Bureau: http://www.census.gov

Viva Network: http://www.viva.org

World Relief: http://www.worldrelief.org

World Vision International: http://wvi.org

Evaluating Migration

During the last decade of the twentieth century, a number of critical works appeared that analyzed the global changes. Fundamental to the analysis was the recognition of dynamic changes in the political, social, economic, and religious landscape. From the critical analysis of a bifurcation in the political world called *Jihad vs. McWorld* (Barber 1995) to the broader assessment of civilizations in conflict (Huntington 1996), these works provided help to those trying to understand the upheaval, particularly from the perspective of globalization. One of the most glaring oversights, however, was the role of religion in these monumental changes. In the works by Benjamin Barber and Samuel Huntington, the primary acknowledgment of religion concerned the growth and the accompanying impact of Islam. The authors saw Christianity as a Western religion with a diminishing influence on the world scene. Yet as Philip Jenkins so perceptively stated, "The gravest challenge to 'McWorld' might not come from Jihad, but rather from what we might call the forces of Crusade, from the Christian Third World" (2002, 6).

In a more positive analysis of globalization, Thomas Friedman assessed its nature as that of bringing technology, information, and economies together into a powerful global force (1999). In common with the other works, Friedman also observed a powerful reactionary force to globalization.

It is interesting that the major works on globalization have noted that a form of dialectic is shaping the globe in inescapable ways. As previously noted, one of the by-products of globalization has been the increasing disparity in the distribution of income. The old adage "the rich get richer and the poor get poorer" has never been more valid. It is difficult to assess this phenomenon in terms of cause and effect, yet the dialectic suggested by various scholars is applicable here: Economic migration is one of the most powerful outcomes of globalization.

The movement of migrant populations around the world, coupled with the rapid spread of cultural knowledge through media, the Internet, and various technologies, is felt in profound ways the world over. The once common homogenous populations now face issues of multiculturalism little known in previous generations. On the positive side, migrants bring a range of traditions such as ethnic foods, which find their way into the marketplace through new restaurants and ethnic grocery stores. These cultural changes are readily adaptable and act as a greeting card to the peoples of the host country. Other positive contributions were noted earlier, such as a balance in age ratios and people to fill out gaps in the local workforce. Studies in the United States demonstrate that if the interaction between migrant groups and the dominant cultural groups

55

is positive, differences are reduced and tolerance results, leading to assimilation (Fischer 1982).

The opposite is also true. If the interaction is negative, differences are accentuated and hostility increases, feeding the stereotypes so prevalent in all intercultural encounters. Most urban environments are littered with examples of this social phenomenon. Some years ago, for example, while traveling on the commuter train from downtown Sydney to the western suburbs, Doug McConnell noticed profanity in the form of graffiti targeting the growing Asian population. The effect of such racist slander can have devastating consequences. In the weeks following the tragic events of September 11, 2001, a sheikh, mistakenly viewed as a Muslim, was killed in a southwestern U.S. city. Another example occurred in a prosperous city in California where local children beat Muslim children walking home from school. Such anti-migrant sentiments can be identified in all cultures. With the increase in international migration, the accompanying problems will inevitably escalate.

The presence of diverse cultural groups introduces changes far beyond those of dress and cuisine. Groups carry with them their religious beliefs as well as their unique lifestyles, with all the cultural demands. The challenge of living in close proximity with adherents of other religions is a reality for all countries receiving migrants. It is only natural that in a democratic society tolerance of religious diversity is the norm. This is far easier to articulate in words than to accept in practice. In a class on urban anthropology that McConnell taught at Fuller, the students were encouraged to attend services of various religions. After sitting through prayer services in mosques and temples, the students were faced with the difficulty of determining how to witness to these followers of different faiths while still affirming their religious freedom.

Two common responses to religious pluralism exist among Christians: outreach and ambivalence. The first conceives of people of other faiths as unreached people groups to target with outreach. This approach has been strongly held in mission agencies and evangelical churches. As long as there is a geographic separation between those motivated for missionary service and the unreached people group, the thorny issues of strategic outreach are left to those answering the call to go. Ambivalence—being uncertain about what is right—is a second common response. The number of people who are ambivalent is growing, particularly among those who are deeply affected by globalization. The tendency toward universalism is often the logical conclusion in a secular society in which everyone has the right to be and, by default, the right to be right. In contrast, many Christians adopt a low-profile approach to pluralism that allows for a comfortable coexistence based more on passivity than on proactive engagement. Such ambivalence requires a degree of denial of both the lostness of humanity and the unity of the family of God globally. From the perspective of the unity of believers, one of the inescapable tasks in the face of international migration must be advocacy for religious freedom on behalf of brothers and sisters in the faith who are living in countries antagonistic toward Christ.

The right to gather and worship is one that, while taken for granted in many countries, is a precious experience that unfortunately can result in persecution. This is felt acutely by those who have converted to Christianity, particularly from Islam, in North Africa and in many areas of the Middle East. Recently, a well-known Christian worker who grew up as a Muslim spoke of the pain of Muslims who become believers in Christ. These new believers feel the pain of rejection from their home communities and even families while also being characterized as the enemy, particularly by some outspoken Christians in the West.

While the intercultural nomenclature of the New Testament refers primarily to two groups, Jews and Gentiles, Gentiles were far from a homogeneous unit. One of the primary concerns in the early church was the need not only to know that in Christ we are one new people but also to live accordingly (Eph. 2:11–22). The kind of newness proclaimed is the reality of being members of the household or family of God. All Christians must be proactive in accepting one another both in word and in deed to overcome racism (McConnell 1997a). Our primary allegiance is to Christ Jesus our Lord, while the most visible expression of that allegiance is our love for one another (John 13:34–35). In the twenty-first century, that love must be extended beyond national and ethnic borders to believers globally.

From the potent news images of people fleeing war zones to the stories of brave pilgrims searching for religious freedom, immigration is a reality of all time. The expulsion from the Garden of Eden marked the beginning of the biblical record of people in migration. Often the motivation was obedience to God in fulfilling a calling to deeper commitment. The great example of faithful obedience is Abraham, who "when called to go to a place he would later receive as his inheritance, obeyed and went, even though he did not know where he was going" (Heb. 11:8). Less spiritually motivated moves are also recorded, such as Joseph's migration to Egypt (Gen. 50:19–20), yet with no less dramatic effect. Other times, people moved because of fear of persecution, as happened in Jerusalem following the stoning of Stephen (Acts 8:1). Even the picture of heaven is one of "a great multitude that no one could count, from every nation, tribe, people and language" (Rev. 7:9).

The missiological evaluation of migration as a trend was greatly assisted by the works of David Barrett (1982), Andrew Walls (1996, 2002a, 2002b), Philip Jenkins (2002), and J. J. Hanciles (2003). Building on the thesis that Christianity has progressed through historical phases in the transmission of the faith, these authors believe we are living through the transition from Western to Southern (or majority world) Christianity. The locus has already shifted, yet within the next five decades, a dramatic shift will more than likely take place in which only one in five Christians will be a non-Hispanic white (Jenkins 2002, 3). There are far-reaching implications of this demographic shift that exceed simply a numeric assessment. Most startling is the extent to which Christianity will continue to shape the social, political, and religious contours of the world.

This view stands in opposition to predictions that Christianity is declining and has to make major adjustments to survive. In more liberal Western settings, the call to change radically the presentation of the faith in an effort to prevent extinction was a common theme in the late twentieth century. Among the most outspoken were Episcopalians led by the bishop of Newark in the United States whose 1998 book titled *Why Christianity Must Change or Die* highlights the understanding. Others were equally critical of the antiquated views and lack of credibility of the Christian faith that threatened its demise (Peacocke 1993; Spong 1998; Staples 2000). The fruit of such views may be seen in the attempts to adjust the historical positions of the church to include changing social norms.

The battle over same-sex relationships among clergy in the Anglican Church is a landmark confrontation between the Western social agenda and Southern conservatism, notably led by the strong voices of the bishops of Africa (see sidebar 2.3). Although it is still too early to predict the outcome, the potential split of the Anglicans demonstrates not only the numerical strength of the Southern church but also the strength of its theological position. Theological conservatism is one of the primary characteristics of the newer churches spreading rapidly in the Southern Hemisphere. Anglican leaders of the churches in Africa and Asia have a voice that is now heard by the centers of missions of the previous generations.

The growth of the Southern church, which will account for 70 percent of all Christians by 2025, is taking place almost exclusively among Roman Catholics, evangelicals, and Pentecostals. Even among traditional evangelicals and Roman Catholics, Pentecostal forms of worship and interpretations of the role of the Holy Spirit, gifts, and revelation are widespread. From a few scattered groups in 1900 to an estimated 1 billion in 2050, Pentecostal believers comprise one of the most remarkable social movements in history. To put this in perspective, by 2050 it is estimated that there will be "roughly as many Pentecostals as Hindus, and twice as many as there are Buddhists" (Jenkins 2002, 8).

SIDEBAR 2.3
A STRONG SOUTHERN VOICE: THE ANGLICAN EXPERIENCE

(Anglican News Service 2003)

The Primates of the Anglican Communion and the Moderators of the United Churches, meeting together at Lambeth Palace on the 15th and 16th October, 2003 . . . seek to discern, in an atmosphere of common prayer and worship, the will and guidance of the Holy Spirit for the common life of the thirty-eight provinces which constitute our Communion.

At a time of tension, we have struggled at great cost with the issues before us. . . . Our firm desire [is] to remain part of a Communion, where what we hold in common is much greater than that which divides us in proclaiming Good News to the world. . . . At this time we feel the profound pain and uncertainty shared by others about our Christian discipleship in the light of controversial decisions by the Diocese of New Westminster to authorise a Public Rite of Blessing for those in committed same sex relationships, and by the 74th General Convention of the Episcopal Church (USA) to confirm the election of a priest in a committed same

sex relationship to the office and work of a Bishop.

These actions threaten the unity of our own Communion as well as our relationships with other parts of Christ's Church, our mission and witness, and our relations with other faiths, in a world already confused in areas of sexuality, morality and theology, and polarised Christian opinion. . . . We recognise that we have reached a crucial and critical point in the life of the Anglican Communion and we have had to conclude that the future of the Communion itself will be put in jeopardy.

REFLECTION AND DISCUSSION

1. What factors caused the African bishops to call for such a strong stand against the 74th General Convention of the Episcopal Church (USA)?
2. To what extent does a growing awareness of global Christianity influence theological discussion? To what extent should it shape the discussion?

These dynamic changes set the stage not only for a shift in the locus of influence but also for "new themes and priorities undreamt of by ourselves or by earlier Christian ages" (Walls 1996, 24). As the Christian faith spreads through migration and witness, new sets of issues confront believers in new places. In some cases, they will try to use the forms and structures of faith from their own social backgrounds. In other cases, they will respond by trying to create new ways of living their faith. It is in the newer, experimental ways of living the faith that the most radical transformations in the practice and views of Christians will be seen. These transformations are "the result of the great principle of translatability which lies at the heart of Christian faith and is demonstrated both in the Incarnation and in the Scriptures" (Walls 1996, 25).

The full impact on the missionary movement of the shift from Western to Southern Christianity remains to be determined, yet its significance as a major trend in the twenty-first century is unquestionable. The role of migrants in the transmission of the faith is a strategic consideration in the preparation of men and women for world missions. A missionary's ability to discern the work of God is a foundational skill for intercultural service.

Evaluating the Response to the HIV/AIDS Pandemic

The HIV/AIDS pandemic, called "the greatest human emergency in history," merits inclusion as one of the most pressing issues facing all Christians (Myers 2003, 68). Because of the rapid spread of the disease, available information tends to be statistical. Impact studies are needed to fill out the analysis of raw data (see sidebar 2.2). Some attempts have been made to integrate the scientific study, epidemiological and demographic, with a more sociological analysis (Baylies 2002; Mann, Taratola, and Netter 1992; Smart 2000; Williamson 2000). A helpful study of the search for a cure for AIDS is the book *Beyond Love* by French journalist Dominique LaPierre (1990). Yet the rapid spread of the pandemic means that assessments and reports are difficult to validate.

Misunderstandings of HIV/AIDS have abounded since the earliest recorded cases. In Christian circles, many churches and leaders spoke out against AIDS as a direct judgment by God on the evils of society. In other cases, AIDS was largely ignored. The earliest positive responses to the crisis by Christians came primarily from mission agencies and nonprofit organizations. For example, MAP International launched HIV/AIDS church and youth education and prevention programs in 1984 in Africa. The

> *Now those who had been scattered by the persecution in connection with Stephen traveled as far as Phoenicia, Cyprus and Antioch, telling the message only to Jews. Some of them, however, men from Cyprus and Cyrene, went to Antioch and began to speak to Greeks also, telling them the good news about the Lord Jesus. The Lord's hand was with them, and a great number of people believed and turned to the Lord. News of this reached the ears of the church at Jerusalem, and they sent Barnabas to Antioch. When he arrived and saw the evidence of the grace of God, he was glad and encouraged them all to remain true to the Lord with all their hearts.*
>
> Acts 11:19–23

accompanying workshops have reached more than 56,000 people in sub-Saharan Africa alone (MAP International 2004). MAP International works across denominational and organizational lines, providing a Christian perspective in response to both prevention of HIV/AIDS and care of the disease's victims. In the words of Debbie Dortzbach, the first director of MAP's Kenya project, "Churches . . . are right where the people are in the community. There's a good structure for a multiplier effect when church leaders talk to their congregations" (MAP International 2004). Building on its experience in Africa, MAP International has developed programs that are reaching people in the Americas and beyond.

Another global response is World Vision's HIV/AIDS Hope Initiative, which focuses on prevention, care, and advocacy. Recognizing the challenge AIDS poses to human development and its impact on children, World Vision has taken a leadership role in mobilizing the global Christian response to HIV/AIDS. Dean Hirsch, president of World Vision International, stated, "World Vision can play a key role in addressing the AIDS epidemic. Our faithfulness in Christ calls us to both comfort the sick and demand justice for the oppressed. AIDS is a health and social issue. But it is also an ethical and human rights issue" (World Vision 2002). World Vision is committed to a global response by helping to connect churches, agencies, and other Christian groups with government and nongovernment organizations.

One of the most encouraging examples of collaborative efforts to respond to the HIV/AIDS pandemic has been the work of faith-based organizations in Africa. A 2002–3 study jointly sponsored by the World Conference of Religions for Peace (WCRP) and UNICEF documented the efforts of religious groups to meet the needs of orphans and vulnerable children in eight sub-Saharan African countries (Foster 2003). The range of findings indicates that faith-based organizations, primarily at the level of congregations, are a major new force in the response to the crisis. Of the 686 organizations studied, over half started between 1999 and 2003. The faith-based efforts included institutional responses (18 percent) and community-based responses (82 percent), with local congregational initiatives accounting for 59 percent of the total. The proliferation of initiatives was strongest among Pentecostal groups, accounting for 64 percent of the total. Uganda had the highest number of faith-based organizations (194) and was the only country in which estimates indicate that the total number of orphans will decrease by the year 2010 (Foster 2003, 10, 20, 24).

The HIV/AIDS pandemic is also drawing concern from high-profile leaders, including many Christians. For example, a recent move to Johannesburg, South Africa, by well-known author Bruce Wilkinson attracted the attention of a feature story in *Christianity Today* (Morgan

2003). Among the activities sponsored by the initiatives of Wilkinson and others are increased financial commitment to orphans, micro-agricultural projects such as the Never-Ending Gardens, and increases in advocacy and support for local initiatives. While the profile of leaders such as Rick Warren of Saddleback Community Church and Wilkinson helps to accelerate awareness and brings needed resources, the greatest human resource is still the local congregation, whose members have relationships within the community.

An important finding emerged from the study of faith-based responses in Africa. Because of the small, idiosyncratic nature of congregational initiatives, they have been largely overlooked by external agencies seeking to create partnerships (Foster 2003, 14). Yet despite the rather recent establishment of many congregational responses and their small-scale nature, these initiatives are expanding, resulting in a significant cumulative impact. These faith-based organizations have "improved the situation of thousands of vulnerable children, their families, and communities" (Foster 2003, 15). However, Geoff Foster concludes that these initiatives are potentially limited in their long-term effect because of the lack of financial support available in poor communities. At the same time, despite potential limitations, the reality of the growing impact of congregational initiatives reinforces a belief long a hallmark of evangelicals: The local church has a central role in God's mission.

The Manila Manifesto, issued at the conclusion of the Lausanne II Congress, affirmed the role of each local congregation to "turn itself outward to its local community in evangelistic witness and compassionate service" (Lausanne Committee for World Evangelization 1989). This statement of affirmation by leaders of churches and agencies underscores the responsibility of congregations to respond to the HIV/AIDS pandemic in the manner observed in Africa. These good works of compassionate service demonstrate anew what happens when people love their neighbors as themselves (Matt. 22:39). Love for Christ is demonstrated publicly by acts of kindness and love toward the weak and the marginalized, who cannot care for themselves, and toward one another as disciples (Matt. 24:44–45; John 13:34–35; James 1:27). Given this mandate, local churches around the globe are among the greatest single resource for responding to this human emergency.

Evaluating the Response to the Plight of Children at Risk

A characteristic of Christian missions through the ages has been its response to children. The teaching of Jesus raised the level of importance of children in the eyes of his disciples (Matt. 10:42; 18:3; 19:14). The early churches, made up of entire households, included the children.

Following this tradition, missionary movements soon saw the care and education of children as foundational to their mission (Brewster 2003, 179–80; McDonald 2003, 151–53). Schools, orphanages, vocational training programs, and clinics were established, often where no other social institutions existed. This continued throughout the twentieth century, particularly in the developing world, where mission institutions were sanctioned by colonial governments and permitted by the governments of newly emerging independent nations.

The dramatic changes in the population in the late twentieth century, with an increase in the number of children at risk, brought new challenges to agencies and churches. A solid indicator of the Christian response to children is in the field of education. David Barrett and Todd Johnson estimated that in 2000 there were 170,000 Christian primary schools, 50,000 Christian secondary schools, and 1,500 Christian colleges and universities worldwide (2001, 40). In many areas where the church has long been established, social conditions have threatened the stability of public education, thereby fostering even greater numbers of Christian schools and the homeschooling movement, particularly in the United States. Because the developing world lacks the financial resources necessary to provide alternative models, the proliferation of Christian schools has not been as dramatic there. This disparity of response is disconcerting given the increasing attrition rates in the developing world. In 2002, 25 percent of children had dropped out by grade 5.

On a global scale, the disparities in access to education are greatest among female children. In 1980, 29 percent of females compared to 43 percent of males were enrolled in secondary school in the developing world. In contrast, 87 percent of females and 85 percent of males were enrolled in secondary schools in the more developed world (Gould 2001, 3). By 2000, the number of females in high school in the developing world jumped to 47 percent, while the number of males rose to 56 percent. On the surface this improvement is encouraging, but the escalating number of school dropouts in the developing world diminishes it. According to Melissa Gould, "Women's access to education is key to improving their health, employment, and education and that of their family" (2001, 5). A lack of access to education is only one of the problems faced by girls. The situation is exacerbated by other inequalities such as less access to health care and the challenges of early marriage and early childbearing.

In the last two decades of the twentieth century, there was a renewed emphasis on finishing the task of world evangelization. Barrett and Johnson estimated that in 2000, of the 845 global plans, 260 were making progress (2001, 29). Unfortunately, few of these strategies were specifically targeting the needs of children and even fewer the development of educational responses. It is estimated that 14 percent of the $270 billion of the annual expenditure of organized global Christianity goes specifically toward education. Ninety-seven percent of the total annual expenditure is on Christians (Barrett and Johnson 2001, 661). The irony of such a significant oversight is that "nearly 85% of people who make a decision for Christ do so between the ages of four and fourteen" (Brewster 2003, 176).

In contrast to these apparent oversights in strategic planning, there have been many positive developments in responding to children at risk, beginning with the efforts of Bob Pierce to support the orphans of the Korean War in 1953, thereby launching World Vision. Other groups such as Compassion International and Christian Children's Fund joined in an unprecedented effort to respond to the needs of children globally. Agencies and churches were also mobilized to assist children through groups such as Scripture Union, Young Life, Awana, and Boys and Girls Brigades. As the twentieth century closed, it appeared that the needs of what D. Brewster calls the 4/14 Window were going to be addressed by a renewal in the global mission community (2003).

During the 1990s, a different response emerged through a group of young people committed to caring for children at risk (McDonald and Garrow 2000). Led by Patrick McDonald, a visionary young Dane, the Viva Network was launched in Oxford, England, in 1994. Patrick and Emily McDonald and a couple of bright collegians began a prayer movement for children at risk coming out of their experiences in Bolivia and Mexico. Through these humble beginnings, God touched the lives of many young people during the following years. By 2003, Viva Network had grown into a global movement of committed Christians, bringing together 66 network initiatives in 43 countries and linking 16,000 workers.

At the beginning of the twenty-first century, missiological research on the plight of children at risk remains in the early stages. It has been greatly assisted by the emergence of the Viva Network and conferences such as the Cutting Edge Conference, which brings together leaders and practitioners from organizations, churches, and agencies worldwide. Based on preliminary estimates, it appears that more than 25,000 projects are touching the lives of 2 million children full-time, with partial care extending to millions of others through the ministries of approximately 100,000 full-time Christian workers (McDonald 2003, 153). A significant response to the need for a more informed approach began in 1998 as a series of workshops that gathered international educators, missiologists, and practitioners to design a curriculum for training people to work with children at risk. These gatherings were instrumental in launching two important collaborative efforts. The first was a comprehensive work on ministry to children at risk edited by Glenn Miles and Josephine-Joy Wright (2003) and published under the title *Celebrating Children*. The second is a growing network of evangelical colleges and seminaries worldwide that offer courses in the study of children at risk.

In evaluating the responses to children at risk, it is tempting to ask the question, What would Jesus do? symbolized by WWJD, an acronym that adorned bracelets, bumpers, and book covers in the past decade. The difficulty is that we cannot provide an answer without changing the acronym to WDJD, What did Jesus do? In the case of children, Jesus called the disciples together and asked a little child to sit with them. Addressing the disciples, Jesus said, "And whoever welcomes a little child like this in my name welcomes me" (Matt. 18:5). What a powerful statement to a group who had spent months with Jesus on the roads of Palestine. Jesus exhorted the disciples to take seriously the children among them, even identifying himself with them. The significance of this action provides a strong motivation to engage in missions to children at risk at a point in history when there are more to welcome than ever before.

REFLECTING ON THE TRENDS: A DELIBERATE RESPONSE

Having introduced and evaluated the changing demographics, this chapter now turns to the critical need for theological reflection to make sense of these overwhelming trends. The extent of the reflection is limited to a few theological and biblical themes, despite the magnitude of the issues. The following sections reflect on three themes that apply to the trends already discussed: the nature of welcoming others, the dignity of humanity, and evangelism and the mission of the church.

The Nature of Welcoming Others

As one reads through the Epistle to the Romans, one is struck by a succinct statement at the end of the section dealing with the practice of the righteousness of God lived by faith in Christ. "Accept one another, then, just as Christ accepted you, in order to bring praise to God" (Rom. 15:7). The Greek word used may be translated "accept" (NIV) or "welcome" (NRSV). The idea is to take something or someone to oneself, illustrated by inviting someone into your home. The root of the word is used in a theological sense when Jesus takes our infirmities (Matt. 8:17; cf. Isa. 53:4) and as believers receive the Holy Spirit (John 7:39; Acts 10:47) (Bromiley 1985, 496). It would be difficult to overstate the strength of this command. As John Murray warned, "If we place restraints upon our acceptance of believers, we are violating the example of that redemptive action upon which all fellowship in the church rests" (1965, 203–4).

In the context of the Romans passage, believers are to accept not only those who are weaker (Rom. 14:1) but also Jews and Gentiles (Rom. 15:8–9). The principle is that the new humanity shared by all believers in Christ (Eph. 2:15) crosses the barriers of separation inherent in our views of ethnicity. "Consequently, you are no longer foreigners and aliens, but fellow citizens with God's people and members of God's household" (Eph. 2:19). The practice of welcoming one another as believers, a tangible expression of obedience to the new commandment, is a hallmark of our witness to the world, according to Jesus (John 13:35). From the beginning, churches were called to be places of welcome for all who truly believe in Christ. The fact that throughout the New Testament the issue of ethnic divisions is a recurring theme indicates the difficulty of keeping this example of Christ's redemptive act. As John Stott noted in his comments on Ephesians, "This does not mean that the whole human race is now united and reconciled. We know from observation and experience that it is not" (1979, 102). As difficult as it may be, we are not left with an alternate or easier expression of our unity. Accepting one another must be openly practiced in the family of God.

When we take these practices into the world of the twenty-first century, we find immediate relevance. The force of international migration spreads Christians across the face of the globe in unprecedented numbers. Swelling the ranks of believers in many cities, these migrants are an important part of God's mission. The continuing challenge is to embrace the injunction to welcome one another as part of the life of the local church. The manner of acceptance may vary from incorporation into the life of an individual church to providing assistance for new congregations through sharing facilities, extending financial assistance, or extending moral support. Whatever the form of acceptance in the face of international migration, the call to Christians remains the same.

Two significant types of acceptance found in most world-class cities are international congregations and local church plants in partnership with established churches in other countries. In Beijing, Christians from all over the world gather for worship in a major convention center. One unique element is the simultaneous translation of the message given in English into Cantonese, Korean, and French, for the West Africans present. In Tashkent, a service is supported by the Young Nak Presbyterian Church in Los Angeles. The service is led by a Korean-speaking pastor and a Russian Uzbek student, who translates the sermon from English into Russian for a congregation of ethnically Korean Uzbeks.

Another aspect of welcoming others is hospitality. While not solely a Christian virtue, it is a practice established among the people of God in the Old and New Testaments. The Old Testament expectation of hospitality included providing a safe haven to travelers (Gen. 19:1–9; Judg. 19:20–28) and the provision of food and personal care (Gen. 18:4, 7–8; 24:14; Deut. 23:4). Failing to practice hospitality was taken seriously (1 Sam. 25:1–39), while generous hospitality was a practical sign of commitment approved by the Lord (Isa. 58:6–7). Hospitality was even to be extended to strangers, who could be messengers from God (Gen. 18:1–8; Judg. 13:9–16; 2 Kings 4:8–10; cf. Heb. 13:2). The New Testament also demands hospitality of believers: "Share with God's people who are in need. Practice hospitality" (Rom. 12:13). Again, the requirement extends beyond the household of faith, even to those who curse or persecute believers (cf. Matt. 5:38–47; Rom. 12:14–21). "Jesus even taught that a hospitable attitude on the part of others towards him and his followers was a sure indication of their acceptance of the gospel—and vice versa—with eternal consequences (Matt. 10:11–15; 25:31–46)" (Field 1995, 460).

Hospitality is a powerful witness to those who are displaced and marginalized. The universal experience of alienation among migrants creates opportunities for the church and individual believers to demonstrate the love of the Savior in terms of kindness that translate across cultural and social barriers. When Christians extend hospitality, it highlights their understanding that they are servants of the living God, whose love of all persons is seen in the sacrifice of Jesus Christ. The demonstration of kindness and hospitality can be an important bridge to relationships of trust that invite others to inquire regarding the motivation. This is particularly important for those who come as refugees or as economic migrants from situations of great poverty. The practice of Christian hospitality is encapsulated in Jesus' words, "But when you give a banquet, invite the poor, the crippled, the lame, the blind, and you will be blessed. Although they cannot repay you, you will be repaid at the resurrection of the righteous" (Luke 14:13–14).

> *Hospitality should be understood as a way of life rather than as a task or strategy. It is easy to slip into viewing hospitality as a strategy for reaching migrants and refugees, or for that matter, for reaching postmodern youth or homeless people. But such an approach misunderstands the basic orientation of hospitality. Hospitality is not a means to an end; it is a way of life infused by the gospel.*
>
> C. D. Pohl (2003, 11)

The call to extend hospitality to those who are unable to reciprocate applies directly to those with HIV/AIDS and to children at risk. Care given in the name of Christ is not an optional activity for those who are so inclined. It is the expectation clearly modeled and taught by the

Lord. The persuasive nature of welcoming hospitality is seen in the life of one of the most visible Christian missionaries of the last century, Mother Teresa. A Macedonian missionary to Calcutta, this Nobel Peace Prize winner spent her life serving the poorest of the poor. She was also given audience in the halls of religious and political power, not because of what she could do but because of what she did. The Missionaries of Charity, the society she founded in 1950, follows her example, resulting in a global impact. Other examples, such as congregational responses to orphans and vulnerable children in Africa, further testify to the powerful gospel witness of hospitality to those who cannot repay.

The Dignity of Humanity

Given that hospitality is a tangible expression of God's love, the question of motivation remains. Why should we as believers invest our resources in those who are outside the family of God? Are they not part of the world set in rebellion? As one friend asked, "Why should Christians get involved in the HIV/AIDS pandemic or with children at risk, even if it does tug at the heart strings?" Although we have already explored the nature of Christ's call to show hospitality, the worth of those to whom we go is an important consideration. "For God so loved *the world*" is a powerful statement about the heart of God for his creation. It is also the place where we must begin to answer the question.

In the creation story, we begin to find the answer in the uniqueness of humanity. Genesis 1:27 states, "So God created humankind in his image, in the image of God he created them, male and female he created them" (NRSV). Human beings are created in the image of God, bearing a likeness in which there is dignity apart from any action of human origin. No longer in the state of goodness present in creation, all humanity equally exists under the disastrous consequences of sin as a result of the fall (Gen. 3; Rom. 3:23). Yet despite the fall, the image of God remains (Gen. 9:6; James 3:9). "The infinite value of each person rests on the divine image" (Grogan 1995, 476). As part of the created design of humanity, every new child, male or female, is the offspring of parents who bear the image of God and are therefore worthy of respect.

The coming of Jesus Christ added a glorious new dimension to the dignity of humanity. Through the incarnation, God himself became human in order to reconcile us to himself. Our collective uniqueness as humans, therefore, is grounded in the image of God, the event of the incarnation of God to reconcile the world, and the promise of his coming kingdom, which will bring to consummation all human history (Moltmann 1984, 20). Because we as human beings are made in the image of God, we are also responsible to the Creator for our actions and relationships, individually and collectively. As Christians, we affirm that all human beings receive life from God and must give account to God. The dignity we share as humans is, therefore, both in our being and in our common responsibility.

Looking into the face of a child who is suffering has a way of penetrating the soul. The sheer number of those who suffer compounds the pain. Traveling through the back roads of Uganda in 1996, Doug McConnell was struck by the magnitude of the problem and the weakness of the response. You can imagine the delight in his heart when he discovered in 2003 that the churches in the country known as the Pearl of Africa were actually making a difference in regard to the mind-numbing statistics of the HIV/AIDS pandemic. Having met Ugandan leaders from FOCUS, the national InterVarsity group, and the Scripture Union ministries, he was encouraged by the knowledge that people can actually make a difference. It is wise to remember our calling as servants of God. We do not bring God's love to the problems of the world. Rather, his amazing love draws us to serve in those places where hope fades and humans suffer. The mission is God's.

As we examine the demographic challenges through the lens of human dignity, we are reminded that every person who suffers from the horror of HIV/AIDS has the indelible mark of the Creator printed on the DNA of his or her being. When Jesus answered the question concerning which is the greatest commandment by adding, "And the second is like it: 'Love your neighbor as yourself'" (Matt. 22:39), he gave a command that must be obeyed by the exercise of our will, not by the tug of an emotional appeal. As in the case of the good Samaritan, the lack of an ethnic or social relationship does not exempt a neighborly response. Every human being is the object of God's love, the bearer of God's image, and responsible to God.

The sobering reality of this view is that a child orphaned by the loss of her parents to AIDS shares the inalienable human dignity with a child soldier forced to become a murderer by armed rebels. Equally true is that both children, the orphan and the soldier, as well as every human being, may be reconciled to God only through the Savior. We proclaim the truth that "there is no other name under heaven given among mortals by which we must be saved" (Acts 4:12 NRSV).

Evangelism and the Mission of the Church

In a plan that surpasses contemporary strategies, Christ instituted a structure that is the ideal unit of response to the issues of the world. This divine design seeks to establish congregations of believers in every people group who share the same purpose and a common source of power with gifts and abilities to achieve the will of the one who holds them together. What a wonderful plan to touch the world at the point where it most needs hope, in the hearts and homes of every individual. Yet that great plan has a mystery of major proportion. It requires the congregations to respond in obedience to Christ's call to go into the world. Lest we forget, the changing demographics of our globe are not a news item in the courts of heaven. God's heart for the masses, seen in the tears of Jesus weeping over Jerusalem, desires that each and every one is touched with the same gracious love experienced by those who know Christ as Savior. The church spread throughout the world as communities of redeemed people forms the structure of Christ's plan (Eph. 2:19–22).

Mission history reveals that God comes to each person right where he or she is on the basis of the work of Christ alone, thereby making the church a place to feel at home (Walls 1996, 7). As we look at the response of Jerusalem (Acts 2:42–47) to the "ends of the earth," the observation holds true. God in Christ is reconciling the world to himself by reaching people wherever they are found. The local church, then, is the community of God's people called to be both a witness to the lost and a welcoming family to those who respond. This biblical mandate is the foundation for the missional engagement of believing congregations in local and global outreach. Until the return of Christ, the church is called to set apart those who will go in obedience to the Great Commission.

In the face of global migration, the HIV/AIDS pandemic, and the plight of children at risk, there is a demand for an urgent missional response. Those who serve Christ must serve the spiritual and physical needs of the people to whom he calls them. A hospitable welcome includes a clear communication of the hope of eternal life found in the Son of Man, who came to seek and to save the lost (Luke 19:10). To the multitudes that have been damaged by the injustices of life, believers communicate with the graciousness of the Lord in words and deeds. The call to missions in the twenty-first century is a call to be rooted in the Word of God and the church of Christ and to be obedient to the fullness of the gospel.

ENGAGING THE TRENDS: A GLOBAL RESPONSE TO DEMOGRAPHIC CHANGES

Missiological reflection involves answering the question, What are the implications? Missiology is by nature an intentional engagement with the issues emerging from careful contextual, historical, and theological study. Therefore, these demographic trends must be approached with a renewed sense of calling to follow Christ through the changing dynamics of his world. In the words of Jesus, "As the Father has sent me, I am sending you" (John 20:21).

This section reflects on the necessity of engaging the three trends already discussed. The previous section asked the pertinent biblical question, What did Jesus do? It is now time to personalize the question and ask, What would Jesus have us do?

Engaging Migration

The role of migration in shaping the landscape of the world continually offers new opportunities for work and witness. As J. J. Hanciles reminds us, "Christianity is a migratory religion and has been from the outset" (2003, 152). Recognizing this fact is a critical aspect of engagement. Welcoming brothers and sisters in Christ who are new migrants is a call for all churches and individual Christians for all time. This includes the practical issues of both sharing resources and extending church facilities to those who seek a place to worship. It is incumbent upon those who are at home to extend security to others in the body of Christ. Being a missional church involves developing creative strategies for partnership with and outreach to newly formed migrant congregations.

Accepting migrants into our churches does not stop with the household of faith. We are to offer hospitality to those who are different from us. Extending grace to those who are displaced is an expression of Christ's love. However, it is not without a set of complexities that require wisdom. We are welcoming people, but we are also uniquely committed to a particular belief in Jesus as "the way and the truth and the life" (John 14:6). Engagement with those of other faiths requires both the demonstration of God's love and the witness of the Savior. It requires great discernment to advocate for the rights of others based on the dignity of humanity while continuing to reach out to them as people in need of redemption.

There are many practical means of engaging migrants. Among the most visible is identification with those who are persecuted either in the land of their origin or in the land to which they have migrated. Churches must learn to advocate for the displaced in the public arena. Muslim children should not fear walking home from school in traditionally Christian lands any more than the opposite should be tolerated in a Muslim country. Any form of ethnic discrimination or racism is intolerable and demands the proactive involvement of believers. Other opportunities for advocacy both locally and globally involve employment, housing, health care, and education.

An area mentioned earlier is the advocacy for religious freedom in contexts where believers are persecuted. A leading group in this area is

Christian Solidarity Worldwide, an international, interdenominational Christian human rights organization that focuses particularly on serving the persecuted church. Regular news on the persecuted church may be obtained through the Religious Liberty Prayer Bulletin, a ministry of the World Evangelical Alliance. Another significant organization is the International Justice Mission, a U.S.-based organization involved in global advocacy (Haugen 1999). In an increasingly fractured world, persecution will continue and must be challenged by those who have a voice. As is the case in all areas of missional response, prayer is a vital element of the ministry.

> *The settlement of both Christian and non-Christian immigrants in Europe has enormous consequences for the Christian congregations and churches. Today, all congregations and churches in Europe need wholeheartedly to welcome all non-European (mainly majority world) Christians as fellow Christians. At the same time, they need to talk intensively with them about both the community of all believers (ecclesiology) and the missionary responsibility to communicate the gospel with the adherents of non-Christian religions and ideologies (missiology).*
>
> J. A. B. Jongeneel (2003, 31)

International migration has escalated the missional outreach of the church in many parts of the world, noticeably in Europe. Congregations dwindling in numbers are being revived by the presence of Christian migrants who bring a spiritual vitality and a keen sense of missions and evangelism. Partnership with this new infusion of spiritual life is a strategic consideration for the future. Agencies, churches, and denominations are faced with the reality of the majority world missionary movement in ways that have only begun to surface. New approaches to collaboration in training, funding, and networking are required to engage fully this exciting trend.

Engaging the HIV/AIDS Pandemic

Any human emergency calls the church into immediate action. The exponential growth of the HIV/AIDS pandemic requires a humble assessment of the capacity of the church to engage it on a global scale. The church needs a sustained commitment to holistic responses that emphasize evangelism as an integral part of the physical care given through ministries of local congregations. The findings of the Africa Research Project on orphans and vulnerable children demonstrate the value of these micro-level projects. Despite difficulties in sustaining funding, local projects sponsored by congregations have the strength of culturally sensitive care that is part of an expression of faith in Christ.

Historically, churches and agencies have leaned toward institutional responses that were both resource and personnel intensive. The difficulty with these responses has often been most acute in the second generation and beyond. Issues of vision, purpose, and sustainability have raised serious questions as to the long-term viability of institutions. The scale of the HIV/AIDS pandemic, however, requires a serious review of strategic missional responses through hospitals, clinics, schools, and other institutions. Health care, employment, financial assistance, and educational opportunities for AIDS orphans and families of victims are a few of the more difficult issues that must be addressed. While Christians have a vital part to play, engaging in established programs of governmental and nongovernmental organizations may be more effective than attempting a renewal of the practice of establishing Christian institutions.

In keeping with the local emphasis, Christians in the developed world must find appropriate means of engaging in financial partnership with local congregational efforts in the less developed world to help children and families of victims. These alliances between churches, agencies, and individual believers continue to be an important part of the stewardship of the resources God has given to the body of Christ. Part of the responsibility of missional responses is to discern the issues involved in stewardship and to honor God both in expectations and in practice.

An important aspect of the HIV/AIDS pandemic is the moral issue. The spread of the disease is radically influenced by premarital and extramarital sex. Attempts to reduce the spread of the disease must go beyond advocacy for safe sex. Abstinence and marital fidelity are vital elements of the message of hope. God's intent that the joys of physical intimacy should take place within the bonds of marriage continues to be the greatest plan to counter the potentially abusive and life-threatening elements of multiple sexual partners. Churches, agencies, and other Christian groups must include a clear message of abstinence and fidelity as a central feature of their holistic engagement. New initiatives should explore the use of media, educational and teaching opportunities, and broad-scale advocacy for moral purity.

At the early stages of engagement, churches and agencies should support the efforts of World Vision, MAP International, World Relief, Compassion International, TEAR Fund, and other nonprofit organizations that have launched global efforts to provide support and resources to fight the HIV/AIDS pandemic. Such organizations give significant attention to the spiritual and physical needs of victims and their families. They also partner with local congregational initiatives, which are important in maintaining a long-term influence.

In an effort to stem the tide of the disease and provide professional care, churches, agencies, and volunteer associations should mobilize their members to join a network of sustainable care. Thankfully, there is no shortage of short-term responses among groups of Christian health care professionals. However, the impact of such efforts needs to be evaluated by those who are familiar with the cultural and sociopolitical contexts. Mission agencies and nonprofit organizations should identify knowledgeable, locally based people to assist such efforts. Greater involvement in collaborative efforts should be a stated goal of both individual and congregational efforts to mobilize Christians for appropriate holistic missional responses.

There have been encouraging movements among Christian health care professionals. In 1996, Southeast Christian Church in Louisville, Kentucky, launched the annual Global Health Missions Conference. In 2004, Fuller Theological Seminary in Pasadena, California, began the annual Healthcare Missions Conference. A Christian nonprofit organization that has worked to integrate health care and evangelism is Medical Ambassadors International, with their Community Health Evangelism programs. Other initiatives such as Project MedSend are aimed at reducing the debt of medical students through grants in an effort to mobilize health care workers. In a growing missions movement, committed Christian health care professionals in Australia and New Zealand are being mobilized to work with missionaries around the world through the efforts of Pioneers of Australia. These are but a few of the growing responses to the HIV/AIDS pandemic and other global health crises.

Committed Christians who are called to work as volunteers or as professionals should consider the potential impact of various types of educational opportunities. Programs with a focus on intercultural studies exist in many evangelical seminaries and Christian colleges. The disciplined perspectives of these programs are invaluable to a contextually appropriate engagement with the challenging situations in which Christian workers or missionaries serve. Degrees or certificates in intercultural studies with a strong integration of biblical and theological study provide vocational support. Perhaps the most significant contribution is the ability of individuals to integrate their faith and practice as they seek solutions to the complexities they face.

Engaging the Plight of Children at Risk

The plight of children at risk challenges the hearts and minds of every committed Christian. Successful programs such as the child-care sponsorship programs of World Vision and Compassion are commendable examples of both the concern of Christians and the wisdom of solid, practical responses. Many of the responses to migration and the

HIV/AIDS pandemic are also applicable to the needs of children at risk. From the practice of hospitality to holistic congregational responses, the engagement opportunities are the same. In the engagement process, it is helpful to remember that all Christians are adopted into the family of God through the atoning work of Christ on the cross and are called to serve others as part of their commitment to Christ.

Over the past half century, there has been a renewed vision for church planting among peoples unreached by the gospel of Jesus Christ, seen in both the emergence of new agencies such as Frontiers, Pioneers, and Antioch Mission of Brazil and the renewed commitment of older mission societies such as Africa Inland Mission (AIM), Overseas Missionary Fellowship (OMF), Serving in Mission (SIM; formerly Sudan Interior Mission), and other mission organizations founded during the nineteenth and early twentieth centuries. The ongoing commitment to a mighty multiplication of churches, as Donald McGavran put it, remains a vital component of agencies and churches (1979). Yet given the commitment to the unreached people groups and the necessity of church planting, there has been a significant oversight in the nature of outreach to children. Following the traditions of established churches, the approach to children has followed the Christian education and youth ministries models of segregating children into age-based groups for a combination of discipleship and interest-based activities. Children tend to be catered to by ministry specialists or missions and parachurch groups apart from the intergenerational strengths of the local churches. Responses to children outside the nurture of families or churches have a distinct disadvantage in the process of reintegrating children into society because of an absence of social networks for support.

The most common surrogate family structures open to children at risk are gangs. These "families" provide security, acceptance, financial support, and identity for children who lack the basic support necessary for human existence. It does not take much imagination to recognize the inadequacies of the traditional youth group, Sunday school, or after-school program. To address the issues that make gangs such an attractive alternative for at-risk children, Christian responses must include the establishment of functional families that incorporate children not only for their future potential but also because of their dignity. The actions and teaching of Jesus toward children provide the best model. Jesus said, "Let the little children come to me, and do not hinder them, for the kingdom of heaven belongs to such as these" (Matt. 19:14).

From the perspective of a missional engagement with children at risk, there is no replacement for the establishment of churches among every group of children who suffers the atrocities of a fallen world. Congregations of redeemed people who live as the people of God and incorporate

CASE STUDY:
WHAT ABOUT KIKU?

As he approached the small dwelling where yet another family was struggling with "Slim," the name given to AIDS, the cries of pain blended with the smells of poverty in an all-too-familiar scene. "Welcome, Pastor," Kiku said. "Please pray for my mother. She is much worse today." The other children moved aside as the pastor knelt beside the cot from which their mother had not moved in days. Looking into the face of the woman in her early thirties, David knew the end was near. His prayer stopped short of asking for healing even though it was a plea for her eternal health. The thought that raced through his mind was, What about Kiku?

As he walked through the dusty passageways in Four Mile settlement, Pastor David reflected on the struggles of his growing congregation. It was a long way from the tranquil seminary campus in the United States where he had completed his studies in missiology three years earlier. On returning to his homeland of Kenya, he had served tirelessly in planting a church that would be a center where people could experience the love of God in Christ. In all the settlements surrounding Nairobi, families devastated by "Slim" continued to pour in with little to gain but proximity to the hospital. The growing congregation led by Pastor David had a burden for the hurting masses and had built a modest building on the edge of Four Mile. In the months since its completion, the church had rapidly gained the reputation for being a place of refuge in this harsh landscape.

A new challenge for the church was how to sustain the growing demands for practical ministry in Four Mile. Initially, David drew upon his contacts with the Fellowship of Christian University Students (FOCUS) from his university days. Now among the ranks of business and professional leaders, these committed Christian friends had supported David through the days at seminary in the United States and had given generously to the establishment of Four Mile Church. A number of them were members of the congregation, but the majority of church growth had come from families of those suffering from HIV/AIDS. The reality facing the church now was a surplus of human need and a shortage of material resources.

Kiku's family was typical of those coming to Four Mile Church. Her father had been a laborer who traveled forty miles by bus from their village into Nakuru each week for work. During the weeknights in the Kenyan regional center, he found comfort among the prostitutes. On the weekends he returned home carrying not only the meager wages from his work but also an unseen killer spreading through the population of Africa. Kiku remembered when her father began to show signs of the dreaded disease.

children into God's family are the divine response to the human condition. Every Christian who desires to enter into ministries to children at risk must be committed to the local church as a community of God's

His weight loss was followed by other symptoms as his life disappeared before the eyes of her mother and seven younger siblings. Others in the village experienced similar problems, resulting in a depletion of men. When Kiku's mother began to lose weight, she knew it was time to move to the city in hope of getting help at the Nairobi Hospital.

Pastor David met Kiku as he visited various people in the densely populated squatter settlement. She was a bright young person with wisdom and responsibilities far beyond her fifteen years. At their first meeting, he invited Kiku and her siblings to the youth group at Four Mile Church. Kiku found that she could leave her mother only for a few hours, but she was delighted to have time with others her own age. Because Kiku was an increasingly typical case, the church elders established a fund to help with food, clothing, and other practical needs. This practical sign of God's love communicated to Kiku in a way she could not dismiss. After several months of attending the church, Kiku responded to an invitation by Pastor David to receive the greatest gift of all, new life in Christ.

After the service that evening, David sat down to write an email to his seminary friends. Since returning, he had tried to stay in touch with several of his classmates, and they shared in the joy of partnering with this new work. Words did not come easily to mind that night. David knew that before too long Kiku would join the ranks of a new category in the census data, an orphan-headed household. Remembering the shortage of funds available to keep up with the practical needs of the poor, David wondered what he could say to these friends so far away. He knew they could help by supplying needed funds. They had proven their commitment in this way many times before. So had the leaders of Four Mile Church. But the growing pressures from too many needy people that far exceeded their capacity to help weighed heavily on his heart.

"Dear Friends, the Lord has blessed us with so many opportunities to exercise our faith here in Four Mile settlement. You are witnesses to his provision. Every time I hear from you and receive your generous gifts, I thank God for each of you." David paused to collect his thoughts. "Tonight I had the great privilege of leading Kiku to Christ. She is a fifteen-year-old who will soon take over the responsibility of caring for her seven brothers and sisters. I am overjoyed by the grace God is showing our new little sister in Christ. Yet to be honest, I am equally troubled to know what we can do to ease her burden. She is so young to bear so much." David's eyes filled with tears as he typed the words. He knew too well the road ahead for this family of children. "In all honesty, I wonder if we can keep going. I am tired but convinced that God is calling us to this ministry. Please help me to know how to walk this path. It is far harder than we ever imagined. As you pray, please help me to answer my question, What about Kiku? I await your thoughts. Your brother, David."

people, his earthly family. Given that central belief, churches are the greatest resource to influence the world of children at risk.

On a broader scale, Christian involvement with efforts that address all the needs of children at risk are essential. Advocacy concerning the global atrocities of the sex and slave trade, child soldiers, orphans, child labor, children of war, street children, and a host of other abuses should become a priority for Christians worldwide. The Viva Network, mentioned earlier, has one of the most extensive networks of committed Christian responses. Involvement can introduce individuals and local churches to the amazing body of believers who are affecting children at risk on a global scale. The world day of prayer for children at risk is a strong beginning for an obedient response to the call of Christ to love the children of the world.

Responding to the changing demographic trends of migration, the HIV/AIDS pandemic, and children at risk is a daunting task. If humility is not our attitude at the outset, it certainly will be after engaging these trends. A personal experience of faith in action may be helpful, but it is far from sufficient to prepare us. It would be easy to walk away from these trends with a sense of abject fatalism, if it were not for Jesus.

Jesus knew our weaknesses and the failings of our spiritual resolve before we knew them ourselves. In the face of such overwhelming need, we serve one who knows our every weakness and the full extent of the need. It is Christ alone who will come again at the conclusion of human history. Until that day, we who are called according to his purposes must look to him for the strength and the wisdom to serve. There is good news of hope found in the message carried by those who serve the living God.

3

Religionquake

From World Religions to Multiple Spiritualities

GAILYN VAN RHEENEN

Who could have imagined the religious changes taking place in this generation? Linda, for example, is a member of the First Christian Church. She also practices Reiki therapy (the Japanese art of therapeutic touch). Gailyn Van Rheenen met Linda on the day she went public concerning her involvement in New Spiritualities. Her speech, given at an occult fair, was titled "Can You Be a Christian and a Psychic? Yes." As a prayer partner and Van Rheenen arrived for the presentation, she turned from her conversation and said, "I perceive that one of you is a preacher." Recovering from their surprise, they listened as she led participants through a personality profile enabling them to ascertain whether they had the spiritual propensities to be clairvoyants, clairaudients, intuitives, and prophetics. She then equated these psychic abilities with the gifts of the Holy Spirit in 1 Corinthians 12.

Van Rheenen later learned that Linda's Reiki training began with an "attunement," when she was "opened to the flow of Reiki energy." During her attunement, Linda received what she called "the gift of vision." Thus, each time she performs Reiki therapy she sees images of light. Although they are not distinct, these images have a vague human form. Linda calls these figures her "light workers." Linda, while believing in

God and salvation in Jesus Christ on a cosmic level, uses therapeutic touch and meditation to heal, relax, and rejuvenate both herself and her patients on a functional level.

IDENTIFYING THE TREND: MULTIPLE SPIRITUALITIES

Linda typifies one type of religious transformation in our generation, that is, people looking to the East for spiritual direction and frequently absorbing these beliefs and customs into the fabric of Christianity. As Ray Yungen notes, "Christianity has opened the door to a blending of the gospel of Jesus Christ with mystical pantheistic thoughts" (2002, 15).

The major world religions have gravitated to places where governments and customs allow freedom of expression. As these religions compete in the religious marketplace, they adapt themselves to become more attractive to local populations, creating a consumer mentality and multiplying the religious options available. Such contexts produce a pluralistic ethos, which "celebrates diversity of religious experience" as "something good and healthy" and "is deeply suspicious of attempts to privilege one tradition or teaching as normative for all." Christianity, consequently, is considered just one of many religious options, one way of truth, one belief system that should be accepted with all others (Netland 2001, 14).

In the Western world, religion has been increasingly separated from public life: "Functions once performed by the church—marriage, education, health care, conflict resolution, funerals—are assumed by nonreligious institutions, which in turn dominate and define the public sector" (Netland 2001, 15). This pluralistic religious environment, however, has seen a general decline in secularism, with two possible exceptions: Europe and the educated elite, who profess humanistic options in educational institutions throughout the world (Berger 1999, 1–18). While some societies have become tolerant of religious options, Hinduism, Buddhism, and Islam have become increasingly militant and evangelistic, both in their countries of origin and in the West. Perhaps the most interesting phenomenon, however, is the mushrooming of new religious movements (NRMs).

At the height of the Enlightenment, philosophers and religionists predicted two differing scenarios about the future of religion (Netland 2001, 124–25). For three centuries, as secular understandings eroded religious beliefs, social scientists and a wide assortment of other intellectuals forecast the decline of religion. According to this secularization theory, human self-confidence and rational ability would free people from religious superstition so that there would no longer be a need for religion. Religion would progress from animism to polytheism to monotheism until humans became mature enough to live without religion. Modernization, guided by education and science, would eventually dislodge religious influences. In 1969, renowned sociologist Peter Berger told the *New York Times* that by "the twenty-first century, religious believers are likely to be found only in small sects, huddled together to resist a worldwide secular culture" (Lester 2002, 39). Missiologists predicting the disappearance of animism were also influenced by this thinking. For example, in 1964, Phil Elkins claimed, "Within the present century the progress of the world will bring all primitive or animistic people into some advanced religion" (1964, 10), and in 1973, Alan Tippett gave animism "ten years, at the very utmost twenty" to disappear (1973, 9). The secularization perspective held that advances in rational understandings would inevitably diminish the influence of "religious irrationality."

> *During the nineteenth and twentieth centuries, theologians in the Western world sought to prove Christianity, to enshrine it as the queen of the sciences, or at least to give a rational foundation for believing God and the Christian way of life. In the new climate of the twenty-first century the most significant theological issue is the relationship between Christianity and the other world religions.*
>
> Gailyn Van Rheenen

The expectations of the Western mission community, however, were quite different. They optimistically anticipated the collapse of non-Christian religions as Christianity advanced throughout the world. In 1900, the general secretary of the Norwegian Missionary Society, Lars Dahle, looked at statistics of the growth of Christianity since 1800 and projected such growth into the future. His conclusion was that the world would become Christian by 1990. A few years later, Johannes Warneck's book *Die Lebenskrafte des Evangeliums*, translated optimistically as *The Living Christ and Dying Heathenism* (1909), described the superiority of Christianity over other world religions (Bosch 1991, 6). The general belief was that the other world religions would collapse before the onslaught of the superior ideologies of Christianity. Both predictions, however, have proven to be false.

To the amazement of Enlightenment philosophers, religion did not fade away during the twentieth century but began to explode—in both intensity and variety. New religions are springing up everywhere. Old ones are, according to Toby Lester, "mutating with Darwinian restlessness" (Lester 2002, 37). Nicholas Kristof writes that his grandfather was a devout and active Presbyterian elder, who nonetheless "believed firmly in evolution and regarded the Virgin Birth as a pious legend." These "mainline Christians," however, "are vanishing away, replaced by evangelicals."

In the postmodern era, the United States is becoming increasingly religious, more so than any industrialized country except possibly South Korea (Kristof 2003a). Peter Berger confesses that the unexpected has happened: The world has become "massively religious." It "is *anything* but the secularized world that had been predicted (whether joyfully or despondently) by so many analysts of modernity" (1999, 9).

Berger sees two exceptions to the now current desecularization thesis: First, secularism continues unabated in Western Europe. Nevertheless, even in this secular context, many younger people are borrowing religious beliefs and customs from Eastern and animistic sources to form various types of religions. Second, an international elite has been culturally shaped by Western education to serve as "carriers" of Enlightenment beliefs and practices throughout the world (1999, 9–11). Many of these carriers of secularism teach in the areas of religion, the humanities, and the social sciences.

In a recent article, Van Rheenen described another cultural wave, perhaps more powerful than either traditional animism or revitalizing theism, that is sweeping Africa. This spreading force is almost imperceptible but is present in statements such as, "We need education so that our children will have jobs," "How can the church go forward if preachers are not trained?" and "We need to develop our country, and technology will enable us to do so." Underneath many Christian movements is the desire for progress. These perspectives are not animistic or theistic but secular (Van Rheenen 2004b).

On the other hand, Christianity has not flourished as the optimists expected. Cannon Max Warren, general secretary of the Church Missionary Society, commented, "We have marched around alien Jerichos the requisite number of times. We have sounded the trumpets. And the walls have not collapsed" (Netland 2001, 125; cf. Smith 1976, 7). In many cases, Christian missions have motivated Hinduism, Islam, and Buddhism to revitalize and militarize. For example, D. D. Pani writes that instead of moving India toward Christ:

> the missionary movement has helped to re-ignite, reform, and revitalize Hinduism. . . . During the twentieth century, various elements of the nineteenth century Hindu renaissance movement evolved into militant forms of Hinduism. And these fanatical brands of Hinduism have merged into the most powerful political force in the country today. (2001, 23)

Today, Hindus, Buddhists, and Muslims are as active in converting those of a Christian heritage as Christians are in evangelizing them. Mosques and temples of the world's religions dot the landscape of most large North American and European cities.

EVALUATING THE TREND: RELIGIOUS RESURGENCE

What factors gave rise to this great religious resurgence? How has Christianity, in particular, been able to withstand the onslaught of secularism and to revitalize in spite of the fact that secular influences have been strongest in areas of Christian strength?

Reasons for Resurgent Religion

Spirituality is intrinsic to human nature. Because they are created in the image of God, humans have an embedded conscience reflecting the imprint of God (Gen. 1:26–27; Rom 1:20; 2:12–16). Paul writes that the Gentiles, even though they do not have a written law, possess an inward law, one "written on their hearts," a conscience that guides them in making moral decisions (Rom. 2:15). Religion, although molded and shaped by culture, is more than a cultural phenomenon. The search for God and the need for relationship with him—the inner essence of religion, its spiritual core—are embedded within the human psyche.

Consequently, the world has almost always been religious, except for brief periods of secularism promoted by ancient Hellenism, Confucianism, and, more recently, modernity (Berger 1999, 11–13). During modernity, secularism, especially at the hands of the educated elite, suppressed religion through ridicule and pressure, thus undermining the "certainties by which people lived through most of history" (Berger 1999, 11). Because human spirituality is innate, this suppression could not continue indefinitely. In communistic lands, the belief that "religion is the opiate of the people" survived only as long as the sociopolitical controls that maintained it. In the West, secularism exerted a more covert pressure through the educated elite. The social sciences—psychology, sociology, anthropology—were all birthed during modernity and until recently promoted constructs of thinking that upheld secularism: Humans created God and Satan to personalize good and evil in society; dreams express the desires of our inmost egos; religion is merely a myth used to control others. These statements illustrate attempts to explain a human-focused world with no need for God. Thus, Berger now maintains that "it would take something close to a mutation of the species to extinguish this impulse for good. . . . Human existence bereft of transcendence is an impoverished and finally untenable condition" (Berger 1999, 13).

Religion is triumphing over secularism because humans realize that they need a strength beyond themselves to solve their problems. Jeremiah rightly said, "A man's life is not his own; it is not for man to direct his steps" (10:23) and, "Cursed is the one who trusts in man, who depends on flesh for his strength and whose heart turns away from the LORD"

83

(17:5). Sometimes, however, humans turn to gods instead of God (Deut. 32:15–18) or, according to some contemporary ideologies, they vainly look within, thinking they have the stuff of God, not realizing that they are merely creatures of God.

Catalysts of Religious Resurgence

Some religious movements are growing faster than others and thereby have become catalysts of religious resurgence. The most dynamic religious surges worldwide are among Muslims; evangelicals, especially Pentecostals; and participants of new religious movements. The growth of these movements is reconfiguring the religious climate of the world.

THE GROWTH OF ISLAM

The worldwide growth of Islam is currently well known because of contemporary political concerns. It continues unabated and is frequently underrated. According to David Barrett and Todd Johnson, Islam is growing at 2.11 percent per year and Christianity at a rate of only 1.27 percent, compared with the world population growth of 1.22 percent (2001, 384). Patrick Johnstone and Jason Mandryk's figures are slightly higher: Islam is growing at a rate of 2.17 percent and Christianity at a rate of 1.43 percent (2001, 2). Islam grew rapidly during the twentieth century—from 12.3 percent of the world's population in 1900 to 21.1 in 2000 (Johnstone and Mandryk 2001, 14).

In recent years, Islam's influence has spread from its traditional domain, which stretches from North Africa to southeast Asia. Radical religious commitment and the use of oil wealth to build mosques and finance missionaries have propelled Muslim growth from sub-Saharan Africa to the burgeoning cities of Europe and North America. While much growth has resulted from high birthrates and migration, growth through conversion has been significant in West Africa, Indonesia, and the United States (Johnstone and Mandryk 2001, 14). Paradoxically, Islam generally meets greater resistance from Christianity in Africa than in Europe and North America, where a pluralistic ethos celebrates diversity as good and healthy without realizing Islam's intrinsic militarism and exclusiveness. Whether in Europe and North America or its traditional domain of influence, Islam seeks to restore not only Islamic beliefs but also "distinctively Islamic lifestyles, which in many ways directly contradict modern ideas" (Berger 1999, 7).

Islam at various points has waned in influence and world power, but it has only marginally experienced geographical declines or reverses. Andrew Walls compares the geographical spread of Islam to that of Christianity:

Islam can point to a steady geographical progression from its birthplace and from its earliest years. And over all these years it has hitherto not had many territorial losses to record. Whereas the Jerusalem of the apostles has fallen, the Mecca of the prophet remains inviolate. When it comes to sustaining congregations of the faithful, Christianity does not appear to possess the same resilience as Islam. It decays and withers in its very heartlands, in the areas where it appears to have had the profoundest cultural effects. Crossing cultural boundaries, it then takes root anew on the margins of those areas, and beyond. Islamic expansion is progressive; Christian expansion is serial. (Walls 2003, 13)

The rapid growth of Islam continues to be one of the greatest challenges to Christianity.

Since the bombing of the World Trade Center on September 11, 2001, thousands of missionaries have made the commitment to serve God among the Muslims. This mission, however, is fraught with difficulty. How do Christians make disciples in areas of religious exclusivity, where conversion to another religion is against the law and converts are disinherited and imprisoned? Should Christians always meet in secret as a distinct body of Christ, or can they also become Muslim follow- ers of Isa (Christ), studying the Ingili within their own mosques? By what means must the Christ of the Gospels be communicated? Is the idea of the triumphal Christ who defeated the principalities and pow- ers frequently more effective than that of substitutionary atonement? What are some creative-access platforms for missionaries in Muslim countries? How can strategy coordinators who live adjacent to areas closed to traditional missionaries effectively develop tools and training for national leaders to carry the gospel to their own people? How can entrepreneurial Christian businesspeople create environments of disciple making within Muslim countries? These questions have launched new, creative patterns of missions among Muslims.

The Growth of Evangelicalism

Evangelicalism is likewise growing throughout the world. Johnstone and Mandryk report that evangelicalism grew from 2.8 percent of the world's population (84.5 million) in 1960 to 6.9 percent (420 million) in 2000. While most of the postwar evangelical growth took place in traditional evangelical churches, the current evangelical surge is taking place primarily in indigenous evangelical movements (2001, 5).

The most significant growth in recent years has taken place in Latin America, where evangelicals have grown from 50,000 in 1900 to 64 million in 1997. Pentecostal and charismatic churches make up three- quarters of this number (Taylor 2000a). A recent Latin American Catholic bishops' conference estimated that every day 8,000 Latin Americans turn from Catholicism to evangelicalism (Moreno 1999, 50). Protestantism (composed mostly of evangelicals) has grown from 1 percent of the population in 1930 to 4 percent in 1960 to 12 to 15 percent in 1999 (Sigmund 1999, 2).

These statistics on Latin America, however, do not tell the full story. Within the historically Catholic cultures of Latin America, evangelicals are creating a new understanding of reality, a "new cultural ethos" (Moreno 1999, 62). Historically, Catholicism accommodated prevailing cultural norms so that popular theology reinforced traditional culture, frequently absorbing popular folk religious beliefs. Evangelicalism, by contrast, emphasizes a radical break with the traditional, frequently calling it demonic. Catholic priests are ordained representatives of the traditional church, authorized to administer sacraments to the common person; evangelical leaders are charismatic, self-ordained, and frequently iconoclastic. Catholic symbols are tangible and visual (e.g., statues, rosary); evangelical ones are verbal and abstract (e.g., blood, cross, reconciliation). Catholic worship forms are generally traditional and liturgical, following prescribed forms; evangelical forms are contemporary, celebrative, emotional, and participatory (Van Rheenen 2001b). Evangelicals have also broken down traditional social and racial boundaries so that rich and poor, educated and uneducated, whites and blacks, mestizo and Indian celebrate their Christian faith in unity, frequently holding hands and hugging one another. Thus, evangelical belief systems, conversion, and lifestyles are transforming how Latin Americans think and relate to one another.

> *Christianity had never been more itself, more consistent with Jesus and more evidently en route to its own future, than in the launching of the world mission.*
>
> Ben Meyer (1986, 206)

Evangelicals are also growing significantly in the United States. According to a study by Glenmary Research Center, evangelical churches continued to grow during the 1990s, while mainline Protestant denominations struggled "to stem an exodus from their pews." The study, titled *Religious Congregations and Membership: 2000* (Jones et al. 2000), shows that those identified by most scholars as moderate or liberal are on the decline. Catholic publisher and statistician Kenneth Sanchagrin says, "The churches that are demanding in some way—that expect you to come two or three times a week, or not wear lipstick, or dress in a certain way—but at the same time offer you great rewards—community, a salvation that is exclusive of other faiths—those are the churches that are growing" (Cho 2002, A3).

86

SIDEBAR 3.1
HOW SHOULD CHRISTIANS APPROACH ADHERENTS
OF THE WORLD'S RELIGIONS?

As you read the following three options for approaching adherents of the world's religions, consider the strengths and weaknesses of each.

Reconciliation is based on the idea that truth is found equally in all world religions. Reconcilers employ interreligious dialogue to arrive at common understandings of at least some truth.

Confrontation is based on the idea that non-Christian religions are demonic, estranged from God, contortions of ultimate reality as formed by God. Confrontational ministry is thus defined as a type of spiritual warfare. Confrontational methods may range from gentle admonishment and exhortation to prophetic denouncement.

Incarnation is based on the idea that God enables divinity to embody humanity. Christians, like Jesus, are God's incarnations, God's temples, tabernacling in human flesh (John 1:14; Phil. 2:3–8) Christians, spiritually transformed into the image of God, carry out God's ministry in God's way. Incarnationalists relate to seekers from other world religions personally and empathetically (as Jesus taught Nicodemus). Sometimes, however, they declare God's social concerns by shaking up the status quo and "cleaning out the temple." The end result of incarnation in a non-Christian world is always some form of crucifixion.

Almost every religious group in the United States is growing with the exception of those firmly rooted in modernity. For example, the membership of mainline Protestant denominations dropped from 29 to 22 million adherents between 1960 and 2000 (a 21 percent drop), probably due to loss of message and accommodation to secular culture. Overall church membership in the United States grew at a rate of 33 percent during this same period (Hamilton and McKinney 2003, 37). Yet these same groups are now undergoing renewal from below. The laity is objecting to the secularism of older clergy and seeking to return to traditional orthodoxy (Hamilton and McKinney 2003, 34–40). In 1972, the General Conference of the United Methodist Church declared that their doctrine was "not to be construed literally" and advocated "theological pluralism" as characteristic of Methodism. In 1988, the tide began to turn when the General Conference "voted into the *Book of Discipline* a declaration avowing the 'primacy of Scripture' for theology, and removed the term *pluralism*" (Hamilton and McKinney 2003, 37). According to Michael Hamilton and Jennifer McKinney, renewal movements in the mainline denominations spring from "widespread theological discontent among ordinary Christians"—from the laity rather than the clergy (2003, 40).

Much of evangelical growth is occurring in new independent churches, which have little or no organizational relationship with Western churches. David Barrett estimates that these new independent churches claim roughly 394 million members, or about 20 percent of Christians (Lester 2002, 44). In North America, new "emerging churches," which are evangelical in theology, are rapidly growing because they creatively contextualize the gospel for postmoderns. The truth is being re-clothed in new cultural garments, releasing Western Christianity from the bounds of rationalistic Enlightenment paradigms (Webber 2002). The growth of evangelicalism throughout the world is truly one of the greatest religious realignments in the world.

This growth illustrates that Christianity must be distinctive in order to grow in non-Christian contexts. When Christianity accommodates to contemporary culture rather than contextually communicating the essentials of the Christian faith, the church ceases to be light in the midst of darkness. The end result is decline and demise.

THE GROWTH OF NEW RELIGIOUS MOVEMENTS

The growth of new religious movements (NRMs) rivals the evangelical advance. As the world has continued to internationalize and individualize, the mixing of cultural forms and meanings to create new religious movements has amplified. The availability of religious options in global cultures and the freedom to innovate allow individuals to pick and choose their own forms and beliefs and to systematize them in new ways.

For example, Van Rheenen met Julie on an airplane. Her books about power points and flows of energy enthralled him. She told him about the altar in her house. Numerous crystals line the circumference. Within the circle three pyramids form a triangle. Statues of Buddha, Krishna, and Jesus, representing Buddhism, Hinduism, and Christianity, stand between the pyramids. In the background is a large cross. A Bible, a Koran, and Sutras lie among the images. Julie's religion integrates beliefs and forms from different world religions. She believes that the life energy radiating from these elements gives her peace and power.

If numerous people were to accept Julie's mixing of ideas and forms and were to develop narratives and rituals to affirm them as plausible, a new religious movement would be born. Otherwise, Julie's religion is merely a distinctive do-it-yourself spirituality. The influences of Satan, who contorts human creativity to improvise new forms, and a pluralistic environment in which people are able to combine various religious beliefs come together in the formation of NRMs. Ravi Zacharias says, "Religion is making a revival, but often as a hybrid of Western marketing techniques and eastern mythology—a devastating combination of seduction through media and mysticism" (2000, 4). As Harold Taylor points out:

> One of the new realities of our times is that the so-called "Christian" West has now become a mission field. In many Western countries there are increasing numbers of people who have either moved from a "church" faith, to no faith, or are seeking for meaning and purpose in "alternative" spiritual paths. As the decline in church involvement continues, there has been a dramatic increase in spiritual and religious experimentation as people develop their own spirituality, sometimes by a return to pre-Christian Pagan religion, or by an "amalgam" spirituality which draws on many different sources to provide a personalized "Do-it-Yourself" religion. This contemporary search, often described as "New Age," or "Self Spirituality," is one expression of many "new religious movements," and is one of the major frontiers of mission confronting the church in the "Christian" West. (2004, 1)

David Barrett says that the major thing he has learned from his continual research into world religions is the "enormous religious change going on across the world all the time. It's massive, it's complex, and it's continual. We have identified nine thousand and nine hundred distinct and separate religions in the world, *increasing by two or three new religions every day*" (Lester 2002, 38, author's emphasis). This era, according to Toby Lester, could be called the "rush hour of the gods." "The implication is clear," he says. "What is now dismissed as a fundamentalist sect, a fanatical cult, or a mushy New Age fad could become the next big thing" (2002, 37).

Missionaries must not be frightened by the presence of people of new religious movements. They must instead realize that such people are receptive to Christian witness when Christians empathetically relate to them as spiritual friends. Christian evangelists must learn to listen to those holding new religious beliefs, engage them spiritually as equals, invite them into vibrant Christian community that provides an embodied apology for Christian truth, demonstrate authentic spirituality, and learn to tell and retell the stories of divine work in their lives that also reflect God's ongoing narrative as revealed in Scripture. New religionists are much more open to Christianity than the traditional secularists of the modern era.

New Religious Movements: Contextualized Global Cultures

New religious movements are newly contextualized global cultures that borrow heavily from various religious heritages but are not specifically aligned with any. As global cultures they "selectively combine aspects of many traditions to create new cultures" (Hexham and Poewe-Hexham 2004, 91). They are not "revitalization movements" within existing religious traditions, such as Pentecostalism within Christianity or Ahmadis within Islam. Nor are they "the results of missionaries planting an existing tradition in a new cultural environment." They are, rather, self-contained emerging religions (Hexham and Poewe-Hexham 2004, 91).

New religious movements result from the intertwining of at least four factors: globalization, syncretism, consumerism, and individualization. Through globalization, ideas from various parts of the world are brought together in new religious configurations and become rooted in specific cultural traditions. "Essentially the ideas that help create new religions travel as fragments of traditions, not distinct traditions, that continue to fragment and unite with other fragments in order to bear new fruit in the form of distinct folk religions" (Hexham and Poewe-Hexham 2004, 92). As these NRMs travel the world, they take on the color of local cultural contexts. "As such, global cultures have both a global, or meta-cultural, and a local, or situated distinct cultural dimension" (Hexham and Poewe-Hexham 2004, 92). People in pluralistic contexts choose from the many options available to them. They may either creatively fashion their own religion, as in the case of Julie, or adhere to a NRM that fits their personality, philosophy, and persuasion. They become participants of NRMs, according to Rodney Stark, because of relationships formed within the community of the religion and active participation in its activities and rituals (Lester 2002, 42). These new movements meet needs, provide friendship, and offer a plausible structure for life.

In the urban centers around the world, these movements are frequently called New Spiritualities and tend to be of two types. Some, like Wicca, are highly animistic, drawing beliefs and practices from ancient, premodern heritages to form contemporary rituals. Others are highly pantheistic, attempting through meditation to find the oneness of the universe that permeates all reality. The focus is on monism ("All is one"), self-actualization ("We are indeed gods"), and meditation ("We can access the potential, the godness or universal energy, that is within us"). Although these two streams are distinct, they are interrelated. For example, adherents of both channel spiritual beings and use objects for power.

A significant change has occurred in the nature of new religious movements in Africa. During the twentieth century, the most successful African Christian NRMs synthesized Christianity and African traditional religion. Founders played the role of powerful prophets able to provide spiritual power to overcome sickness and to achieve success in life. Worship forms were "self-consciously and deliberatively African." A new wave of African NRMs, however, "downplays traditional African

SIDEBAR 3.2
SYNCRETISM AS A WAY OF LIFE

(Adapted from Sadowitz 2004)

One of the most prevalent aspects of the Japanese worldview is the predisposition to syncretize new ideas with existing ones. It is well documented that religions that enter Japan retain very few of their original aspects once they have merged with the Japanese worldview. In this worldview, *heiwa* (peace) is one of the highest virtues to which humans can attain. Buddhist writings exalt *heiwa* as the supreme goal. The Japanese are seen as having mastered the art of controlling their emotions even in the most difficult of circumstances. Syncretism helps protect this ideal of peace by preventing religious thoughts from conflicting. In Japan, it is not either-or but both-and.

In this syncretistic society, it is not surprising that the fervency of one's faith is more important than the content of that faith. The heart takes precedent over the head (Ayabe 1992, 24). Syncretism seeks to unify and to do away with differences by ignoring them or allowing them to coexist without any real attempt to address the discrepancies. In this kind of worldview, people become the ultimate authority as they decide to bury truth for the sake of unity.

Japanese Christians face the constant challenge of taking the basic teachings of Christianity, which resist syncretism (such as "I am the way, the truth, and the life" and "There is no other name under heaven given among men whereby we might be saved"), and internalizing them as convictions. The pressure to syncretize the Word with Japanese customs and ancient beliefs is staggering, and churches that mix Christianity with Japanese religions abound. Even pastors have problems standing by the fundamentals of the faith.

Because syncretistic secular humanity is the final authority, many Japanese create gods to fit their own needs, gods that can be beckoned or dispelled by rituals. Belief in the one true creator God who tells humankind what it needs is challenged because the Christian God is one of a number of choices. They think the God of heaven can be controlled by mere word and ritual. When they are in need, they petition the gods. In good times, however, they do not bother the gods lest they become annoyed.

REFLECTION AND DISCUSSION

1. Define *syncretism*. Give an example from your own culture.
2. Describe the beliefs and practices giving rise to syncretism in Japanese culture.
3. What guidelines would help Japanese Christians overcome syncretism?

features and instead promotes modern lifestyles and global evangelism" (Lester 2002, 45). Thus, African independent churches frequently pride themselves on their global connections, which, they believe, give them legitimacy.

Christians in dialogue with adherents of a new religious movement must listen closely to determine the mix of global and local aspects in the religion. Based on these understandings, they must find ways to convey the narratives of Scripture so that they sound new and alive, pertinent to life, intensely counter-cultural, and unique. Christians must learn to tell the story of the gospel in new and distinctive ways.

REFLECTING ON THE TREND: A THEOLOGY OF RELIGION

Globalization, which allows people to choose their own religious orientations, is strongly challenged by fundamentalist religious groups, creating a clash of civilizations. These clashes have only begun and will amplify in the future.

Samuel Huntington writes about the changing nature of international conflict. After the Peace of Westphalia, conflict was essentially between *rulers* attempting to expand their economic and political power, especially the territory they ruled. In the process, they created nation-states. From the French Revolution until World War I, conflict occurred between these *nations*. After the First World War, conflict occurred between *ideologies*, "first among communism, fascism-Nazism and liberal democracy, and then between communism and liberal democracy" (1993, 25). With the disintegration of the Soviet Union and the fragmentation of Yugoslavia, the clash has become one of *civilizations*. Civilizations are broad cultural entities held together by similar history, customs, languages, traditions, and especially religion. According to Huntington:

> The people of different civilizations have different views on the relations between God and man, the individual and the group, the citizen and the state, parents and children, husband and wife, as well as differing views of the relative importance of rights and responsibilities, liberty and authority, equality and hierarchy. These differences are the product of centuries. They will not soon disappear. (1993, 25)

The world "will be shaped in large measure by the interactions among seven or eight major civilizations. These include Western, Confucian, Japanese, Islamic, Hindu, Slavic-Orthodox, Latin American, and possibly African civilizations" (Huntington 1993, 25). These civilizations "obviously blend and overlap, and may include subcivilizations. Western civilization has two major variants, European and North American, and Islam has its Arab, Turkic, and Malay subdivisions" (Huntington 1993, 24). Huntington says:

> The fundamental source of conflict in this new world will not be primarily ideological or primarily economic. The great divisions among humankind

and the dominating source of conflict will be cultural. Nation states will remain the most powerful actors in world affairs, but the principal conflicts of global politics will occur between nations and groups of different civilizations. The clash of civilizations will dominate global politics. The fault lines between civilizations will be the battle lines of the future. (1993, 22)

Though Huntington's thesis is not accepted by all, in many ways this clash of civilizations has become a reality. The modern era has passed, and secular ideologies are viewed with suspicion, even in the West, where they originated. Religious fundamentalists in almost every major world religion have mobilized their followers to combat global perspectives in order to maintain their distinctiveness.

Islam: A Counter-Globalizing Movement

Islamic fundamentalists believe that Islam cannot be modernized. Rather, Islam must Islamize modernity (McVey 2003). Wherever Islam spreads, it attempts to reproduce a certain type of Arabic culture. This culture stands against the merging and mingling of ideas prevalent in globalizing Western countries and integrates the realms of both the natural and the supernatural. Generally, Islam is a counter-globalizing, noncontextualizing movement. Prince Hassan of Jordan said, "Globalisation ('awlanah) in our part of the world is held in deep suspicion" (Riddell and Cotterell 2003, 157). Many equate globalization with Americanization. Thus, Zafar Bangash writes, "Globalization means not merely uniformity but also conformity to the dominant, primarily American culture" (Riddell and Cotterell 2003, 158). Americans assume that democracy is the best form of government and that all people desire it. Muslim fundamentalists, on the other hand, perceive that form of government as ungodly, based on human initiatives rather than on the principles of Allah. This clash of civilizations is vividly illustrated in the terrorist attacks of September 11, 2001, and the American-led counterresponse resulting in the invasion of Afghanistan and Iraq and the deposition of their governments.

A major concern for Islam is whether Muslim leaders will be able to maintain their relatively cohesive, nonaccommodating—though not monolithic—religion in the face of spreading globalization. Stan Guthrie feels change is inevitable. He writes, "The driving forces of modern culture—science and humanism—have put even Islam, the most insulated of all the major world religions, next in line for significant change. . . . Muslim liberals from Iran to Bangladesh are seeking to link democracy and political pluralism with Islamic principles" (2000, 159). Some would argue that Guthrie's projections are based on the old secularization theory, which is now discredited. Yet it is likely that the rigidity of Islam will be questioned by cultural insiders until the essence of Islam is radically changed. This radical Islam will lead to either rejection by those seeking freedom from oppression or a revitalization movement from within that will change its essence.

As Christians minister in Muslim contexts, they must believe that "turning the other cheek" and "repaying good for evil" are the only Christian responses to opposition and persecution. They must learn how to suffer as Jesus himself suffered when he entered the human realm on behalf of humanity. Christians must realize who they are, disciples of the one who willingly died on the cross. While Islam has grown out of political and economic strength, Christianity has grown from the margins, from among the weak (McVey 2003).

Hinduism: Revitalizing and Reacculturating

More than any other world religion, Hinduism has been transformed and revitalized through encounter with Enlightenment and Christian thought from the West.

Traditionally, Hinduism (unlike Christianity, Islam, and Buddhism) has not been an organized, systematized world religion. According to S. Radhakrishnan, although Indian Hinduism was "a way of life characteristic of an entire people, it is a culture more than a creed. It permeates every aspect of the individual's public and private life" (Klostermaier 1989, 56; cf. Hiebert 2000, 48). Jawarharial Nehru writes:

> Hinduism, as a faith, is vague, amorphous, many-sided, all things to all men. It is hardly possible to define it, or indeed to say definitely whether it is a religion or not, in the usual sense of the word. In its present form, and even in the past, it embraces many beliefs and practices, from the highest to the lowest, often opposed to or contradicting each other. (1946, 75)

Hinduism's encounters with Western thinking and religion brought about major changes during the final decades of the nineteenth century. Neo-Hinduism grew out of these encounters.

> Indian scholars were inspired by the recognition given to the Vedas and Upanishads by the West. They created religious doctrines and institutions based on the old texts, long forgotten in traditional Hinduism, and organized Neo-Hinduism as a modern, formal "high religion." (Hiebert 2000, 48)

D. D. Pani describes the Christian missionary movement in India pejoratively because Christianity's failure over the last three centuries to engage Indian culture has brought devastating consequences. Rather than Christianizing India as intended, "the missionary movement has helped to re-ignite, reform, and revitalize Hinduism. . . . During the twentieth century, various elements of the nineteenth century Hindu renaissance movement evolved into militant forms of Hinduism. And these fanatical brands of Hinduism have merged into the most powerful political force in the country today" (2001, 23). Hindu nationalistic movements developed within the context of the Muslim invasions and Western imperialism. Thus, Islam and Christianity appear to be ideologies that seek political advantage. The Hindu attitude has been tolerant and nonviolent. However, Hindu militancy has developed to counter the perceived encroachment of foreign control (Hiebert 2000). Militants "publicly warn that soon most of India will be Christian and the great Indian civilization will be lost" (Hoefer 2001, 11).

Some Hindus are Jesus followers but reject the church as a product of colonialism, a vestige of Western culture. Herbert Hoefer, author of *Churchless Christianity* (1991), found through a random sampling that 200,000 people in Chennai identified themselves as "non-baptized believers in Christ" (NBBCs) but intentionally chose to remain separate from any church. These people call themselves *Jesu bhaktas*, "followers of Jesus." One itinerant *Jesu bhakta* described three principles he uses: acknowledge that you are a Hindu, never go to church (because church leaders "will come after you right to your home, embarrassing you and your family"), and do not go into full-time religious work (which limits your social responsibilities within your family) (Hoefer 2001, 11). While Jesus is appreciated by a portion of the population, "Christianity . . . is popularly viewed as repugnant in Indian culture. Baptism is viewed as an allegiance to a group and an organization allied with the West" (Hoefer 2001, 11).

While castes in India have been largely resistant to Christianity, the Dalits (the underclass, the untouchables) have increasingly become responsive. The 400 million people of India's lower castes (including 200 million Dalits) "are victims of Hinduism and have no reason to remain Hindus" (Mangalwadi 2001, 21). For them, Hinduism has been a religion of oppression. Bhimaro Ambedkar's famous declaration resounds in many hearts: "I was born a Hindu; I had no choice. But I will not die a Hindu because I do have a choice." He believed that "neither Constitution, nor democracy, nor political power is sufficient to liberate India's oppressed people from Hinduism. . . . India needed conversion" (Mangalwadi 2001, 20). Some Dalits are following Ram Raj into Buddhism, some are joining a new pantheistic Dalit religion of mother earth called Bhooshakti, and others are becoming Christians. Joseph D'Souza, president of All India Christian Council, challenges the Christian church to stand with those of the margins and not to bend to the political pressure of the fundamentalist Indian political leaders:

> If the Christian Church in India closes it doors to the Dalits because of the pressure of the Brahminical dominated RSS and its fundamentalist affiliates, the Dalits will turn to whoever offers them human dignity, equality and the right to spiritual salvation. The Dalits have come to the basic conclusion that their liberation will only come through spiritual salvation and that the Brahminical Social Order can be only challenged by a powerful spiritual ideology that encompasses social realities. (2002)

The church must stand with the oppressed and guide them to both spiritual and political liberation in the name of Jesus.

> The time has come for the Indian Church to openly offer and give the Dalits an equal place as the children of God in Jesus Christ. The time has come for the Dalits to appropriate the full spiritual rights available in Jesus Christ. The time has come to turn away from the Brahminical Social Order and to create a new humanity. The Gospel of Jesus has the solution to the caste problem because the Gospel deals with issues of the heart and soul and body and relationships. (D'Souza 2002)

The growth of the church has always come from the margins. Amazingly, the tension in India is between politically powerful religious leaders who seek to outlaw conversion and limit the freedom of religion and a reluctant church fearing to touch the untouchable. If the Indian church responds with compassion, thousands will come to Christ within the next decade.

Evangelicalism: Reformulating for a Postmodern Era

New emerging churches, frequently with little or no affiliation with traditional religious groups, are attempting to touch postmoderns, especially in urban North America. Seeker-sensitive churches appeared in the 1980s and exploded in the 1990s. They emphasize strategy and performance and, in some cases, tend to reduce the purpose of the church to a few simple commands such as the Great Commission and the Great Commandment. These worship-focused churches attract many to their services because of the impact of the services but have a hard time incorporating attendees into the community life of the church. Many members are drawn from small, struggling churches that have not adapted to a postmodern world. These seeker-friendly churches, because of a desire to accommodate prospective seekers, are tempted

96

to shape their messages to fit the felt needs of those attending rather than to draw people into the kingdom of God.

Recently, various voices have advocated a theologically sensitive, communally based kingdom-focus within churches. These so-called *missional* churches are biblically focused, Christ-formed, Spirit-led fellowships representing the purpose and reign of God on earth. As they receive the gospel, new Christians are equipped and sent into the world. Such movements are the Gospel and Our Culture Network, as represented by the book *Missional Church* (Guder 1998; cf. http://www. gocn.org and www.gospel-culture.org.uk) and reflecting applications of Lesslie Newbigin's thinking, and the Emergent Movement, reflecting the writings and thinking of Brian McLaren (emergentvillage.com/index. cfm?PAGE_ID=33) and characterized by his books *The Church on the Other Side* (2000) and *A New Kind of Christian* (2001).

The structure of North American missional churches varies depending on the context and the gifts of the evangelists. Some are simple house churches. We do not know yet if this is another fad or a simplification of the church for ministry in an intricate culture. Other missional churches meet publicly as a larger fellowship on Sundays and at other times during the week. Whatever their organization, these churches have four characteristics: (1) The church is understood as a community on a journey whose members help one another and encourage others to join them on the journey to heaven. (2) All members of the body are discipled to walk spiritually with God. (3) The story of God's mission is told and retold to describe a theistic worldview. (4) Leaders equip God's people for works of service and experientially model ministry.

Seeker-sensitive churches attract thousands to their assemblies, but simply because of their size, many attendees are merely spectators. Missional churches are smaller, focused fellowships seeking to be faithful to God. Those drawn into large seeker-sensitive churches—if not given adequate nurturing—may follow their hunger and eventually gravitate toward community-based, missionally focused fellowships of believers.

Developing a Theology of Religion

In light of the above, affirming the distinctive way of God in Jesus Christ has become the most important religious issue of our time. We must create a theology of religion that takes into account a developing pluralistic ethos.

In most urban contexts, Christians live in constant contact with those of other religions. This "pervasive exposure . . . to cultural and religious diversity, combined with the erosion of confidence in orthodox Christianity engendered by profound social and intellectual transformations, help to explain the current attraction of pluralistic views on Christianity and other religions" (Netland 2001, 24). On one level, religious pluralism is merely acknowledging the fact of religious diversity. "To relativists," on the other hand, religious pluralism is "an equalitarian and democratized perspective holding that there is a rough parity among religions concerning truth and soteriological (salvational) effectiveness" (Netland 2001, 12). This type of religious pluralism creates a pluralistic ethos, "a set of assumptions and values that celebrates diversity of religious experience and expression as something good and healthy, is deeply suspicious of attempts to privilege one tradition or teaching as normative for all, and while skeptical of claims that any particular religious tradition has special access to truth about God, nevertheless freely acknowledges that different people can find religious truth for them" (Netland 2001, 14). Within this multicultural, pluralist environment, the need for a theology of religion is apparent.

How should Christian theologians construct a theology of religion? Should Christian theologians compare world religions and prioritize what is common in all or what appeals to the contemporary cultural ethos? Or should finite humans depend on revelation from an infinite God, who desires to relate to his people? Where theological reflection begins will greatly determine the ultimate conclusion of the theologian. According to Harold Netland, an evangelical theology of religion must (1) be shaped "by the teachings, values and assumptions of the Bible and be faithful to the central confession of the church throughout the centuries" and (2) "be phenomenologically accurate in how it depicts the beliefs, institutions and practices of other religious heritages" (2001, 313).

The Bible consistently portrays the unique nature of the God of Israel compared with the gods of the nations. The first of the Ten Commandments is, "You shall have no other gods before me" (Exod. 20:3). God's exclusive nature is also seen in the Shema: "Hear, O Israel: The LORD our God, the LORD is one" (Deut. 6:4). Early Christians, living in a religiously pluralistic world, proclaimed a distinctive way to the creator God. In Athens, Paul was "greatly distressed to see that the city was full of idols" (Acts 17:16) and described the nature of "the unknown god" they ignorantly served. People of that age generally believed that there were "multiple ways to relate to the divine" (Netland 2001, 25–26).

Netland offers six general themes that are foundational to an evangelical theology of religion:

1. The one eternal God is holy and righteous in all his ways.
2. God has sovereignly created all things, including human beings, who are made in the image of God.

3. God has graciously taken the initiative in revealing himself to humankind, and although God's revelation comes in various forms, the definitive revelation is the written Scriptures.
4. God's creation, including humankind, has been corrupted by sin.
5. In his mercy, God has provided a way, through the atoning work of Jesus Christ on the cross, for sinful persons to be reconciled to God.
6. The community of the redeemed is to share the gospel of Jesus Christ and to make disciples of all peoples, including sincere adherents of other religious traditions, so that God is honored and worshiped throughout the earth. (2001, 313–25)

Ultimately, the distinctiveness of Christianity rests on the personal, holy nature of God, the reality of his mighty acts throughout history, and the authenticity of the incarnation and resurrection of Christ. Based on these biblical understandings, Ravi Zacharias asserts:

All religions are not the same. All religions do not point to God. All religions *do not say* that all religions are the same. At the heart of *every* religion is an uncompromising commitment to a particular way of defining who God is or is not and accordingly, of defining life's purpose. . . . Anyone who claims that all religions are the same betrays not only an ignorance of all religions but also a caricatured view of even the best-known ones. Every religion is at its core exclusive. (2000, 6–7)

The question, Will the church believe in Jesus Christ as the distinctive way to God in this culturally relativistic age? is the most significant question of the future.

An evangelical theology of religion, according to Netland, must not only take seriously God's revelation about himself but also authentically engage participants of other world religions. "Reductionistic and simplistic generalizations" must be avoided (2001, 325). For example, evangelicals who believe that the concept of

> *The Christian faith . . . is absolutely unique. There is no faith like it. No other god; no other Christ; no other Calvary; no other empty tomb; no other redemption; no other salvation; no other heaven.*
>
> David Hesselgrave (2004, 149)

grace is distinctive to Christianity are unaware that "certain forms of Hinduism and Pure Land Buddhism also acknowledge human inability to 'save' oneself and the need to rely totally upon the grace or merit of, for example, Vishnu or the Amida Buddha" (Netland 2001, 326). Truth must be upheld as truth wherever it is found and used as a bridge for deeper understandings of both the Christian gospel and other world religions.

ENGAGING THE TREND: MISSIOLOGICAL CHALLENGES OF A PLURALISTIC RELIGIOUS WORLD

The trend of multiple spiritualities creates a number of missiological challenges. Christian leaders must (1) communicate the gospel so that syncretism is avoided, and (2) contextualize the gospel for pluralistic, postmodern peoples.

Communicating the Gospel to Avoid Syncretism

A pervading syncretism, the blending of Christian beliefs and practices with those of a dominant culture, is a second missiological challenge of postmodernity. In such cases, Christianity loses its distinctive nature and speaks with a voice reflective of its culture.

A significant area of syncretism involves perceptions about the nature and character of humanity. As described earlier, modernity focused on human ability. Humans were understood to have rational abilities and to be capable of ordering their own world. Frequently, Christianity was attacked as illogical and superstitious. Christians were tempted to exclude the divine and to emphasize the human. This confidence in human ability tended to enthrone humans as masters of their own world.

A philosophical change regarding the nature of humanity has occurred during the postmodern era. Human understandings are thought to be culturally produced, formed by linguistic and social heritage rather than by cognitive, rational deduction. Reality is seen as being constructed arbitrarily and locally by participants of culture instead of having an ultimate, absolute essence. Life and experience are interpreted in terms of multiple narratives, each having its own meaning. Cultural meanings are thought to be formed by power struggles within culture rather than by humans seeking truth and searching for meaning. The use of mass media and the influence of consumer-driven technology have made it difficult for the postmodern mind to distinguish between truth and fiction. Since science and history are continually being reinterpreted, the postmodernist does not necessarily see them as truth-based. Thus, postmodernists live with ambivalence, supposing that objectivity and coherence in life can never be found.

How can this syncretism be overcome? First, church leaders and missionaries should be master teachers of the Word of God as well as effective cultural listeners. Rather than making cultural decisions

100

SIDEBAR 3.3
JESUS AMONG OTHER GODS

(Zacharias 2000, 6–7)

You hear it a thousand times and more growing up in the East—"We all come through different routes and end up in the same place." But I say to you, God is not a place or an experience or a feeling. Pluralistic cultures are beguiled by the cosmetically courteous idea that sincerity or privilege of birth is all that counts and that truth is subject to the beholder. In no other discipline of life can one be so naive as to claim inherited belief or insistent belief as the sole determiner of truth. Why, then, do we make the catastrophic error of thinking that all religions are right and that it does not matter whether the claims they make are objectively true?

All religions are not the same. All religions do not point to God. All religions do not say that all religions are the same. At the heart of every religion is an uncompromising commitment to a particular way of defining who God is or is not and accordingly, of defining life's purpose.

Anyone who claims that all religions are the same betrays not only an ignorance of all religions but also a caricatured view of even the best-known ones. Every religion is at its core exclusive.

REFLECTION AND DISCUSSION

1. Discuss the validity of the statement, Every religion is at its core exclusive.
2. How can God be known?
3. In what ways do we develop ideas about God in conformity with our own desires and feelings?

unilaterally based on their academic training and Christian experiences, church leaders and missionaries must partner with the body of Christ. They must work collaboratively with the Christian community to develop church patterns that are both theologically responsible and culturally responsive.

Second, church leaders must seek to communicate the gospel narratively, in broad strokes rather than piece by piece, so that it can be understood holistically. Gailyn Van Rheenen can testify from personal experience that narrative teaching is more effective than propositional teaching. He grew up thinking propositionally. His first sermons (and evangelistic lessons) dealt with topics, not stories. The typical sermon contained an introduction, three points centered around a topic, and an invitation that included an illustration. In Africa, he heard a young Christian, Jonathan Soe, preach using Bible stories. People loved to hear him tell these stories and learned from them. Van Rheenen learned that stories provide themes in real life, in living color, in flesh and blood. He realized that much of the Bible is a story and began to understand the narrative nature of Christian theology. He realized that the Bible was given to reveal not the lives of Abraham, Isaac, and Jacob but *the hand of God* in the lives of Abraham, Isaac, and Jacob. It was given as a revelation not of Mary and Martha and Lazarus but of *the Savior* of Mary and Martha and Lazarus. The work of Trevor McIlwain of New Tribes Mission also had an impact on his teaching: "We must not teach a set of doctrines divorced from their God-given historical setting, but rather, we must teach the story of the acts of God as He has chosen to reveal Himself in history. People may ignore our set of doctrines as our Western philosophy of God, but the story of God's actions in history cannot be refuted" (1987, 81). Van Rheenen found that receptor cultures already have existing categories of thought. When he taught topically, the listeners were forced to fit his categories into theirs, and the message was greatly distorted. Narratives provide the foundations for new, Christian categories of thought. Since the Christian message is inherently narrative, Christian leaders must become storytellers.

Finally, bringing Christ to postmodern culture involves comparing existing plausibility structures of the culture to the Christian worldview. Frequently, missionaries are so intent on finding common ground and communicating Christ in terms of this commonality that they do not contrast the culture with the Christian worldview. David Hesselgrave writes:

> Both philosophically and theologically, a communication approach that is over-dependent upon the discovery and utilization of similarities is open to question. *Dissimilarities* between beliefs and practices may, in fact, be more important and utilitarian in the long run. . . . If one's objective is to convert and disciple, both the number and importance of these differences will far outweigh the number and importance of supposed similarities. (2004, 147)

Christian evangelists must focus on both similarities and dissimilarities between Christianity and the recipient culture. Incorporating oils into Christian practice, for instance, does not necessarily help an aroma therapist understand the Christian message better.

Contextualizing the Gospel for Pluralistic, Postmodern Peoples

Frequently, syncretism develops because the Christian community attempts to make its message and life attractive, alluring, and appealing to those outside the fellowship. Over time the accommodations become routinized, integrated into the narrative story of the Christian community, and inseparable from its life. When major worldview changes occur within the dominant culture, the church has difficulty separating the eternals from the temporals. When it is swept along with the ebb and flow of cultural currents, the church loses its moorings.

Throughout the centuries, Christianity was significantly syncretized with Enlightenment and Constantinian perspectives. Enlightenment perspectives presupposed that humans are able to chart their own course through reason and human ingenuity with little reliance on God or spiritual realities. Christians, absorbing these viewpoints, tended to focus on the content of Christianity with too little focus on a spiritual relationship with God and personal morality. Constantinianism involved the shift of the church from a minority to a majority status. Whenever Christian faith became an official or established ideology, the lordship of Jesus was compromised. Power rather than servanthood was glorified.

Christians who syncretized in this way essentially became practicing deists. They limited the work of the Holy Spirit, demythologized spiritual powers (Satan, demons, gods, principalities, and powers), reduced Scripture to rational principles to be understood, and lived in the present with little regard for God's amazing work in the past and his designs for the future. Many, especially in the West, desired spirituality but were leery of organized religion.

A new contextualization of Christianity is needed—one that leads to the patterns of life and ministry of the early Christian, pre-Constantinian church. Christianity must once again look upon itself as a minority religion—"resident aliens, a pilgrim people, a caravan community" (Allen 1994). The church must be a distinct eschatological community formed by the calling and sending of God and reflecting the redemptive reign of God in Christ.

This distinctive community must then learn to communicate the gospel to those of other religions, including participants of both world religions and new religious movements. Because the gospel is innately narrative, Christians must become storytellers of God's mighty acts and work in the world since creation. Christians must continually demonstrate a prayerful, dependent, authentic relationship with God. In a practical age, cold, rational religion is rejected. Christians must teach with passion and emotion, expressing their brokenness before God and continual need for his grace. They can bear fruit only when they are like branches that are connected to the true vine because apart from Christ they can do nothing (John 15:1–5).

Postmoderns must not only understand the gospel narrative but also *feel* it. They must experience the emotion that artists feel as they look at a classic painting or that composers feel as they listen to an ageless composition. All parts fit together and sound intelligible to the rhythms and harmonies of life. Christian communicators, like musicians, must

---

CASE STUDY:
ENCOUNTERING RELIGIOUS PLURALISM

Adapted from Van Rheenen (2004a)

Patricia was highly educated and articulate, an attorney by occupation, and a Christian believer—and a fellow passenger on a flight from Dallas to Orange County. Noticing that I was reading the Bible, she asked, "Are you a preacher?" She told me that she was returning from her mother's funeral. Her mother was a Christian, she added. Over the next two hours we shared much about ourselves: our faith in God; how we felt about our parents' deaths, even though they were believers; and the maturing of our children.

In the course of our conversation, Patricia asked a question that she said had been bothering her for many months: "Will God save people of other world religions?" My sensitivity to this question had been greatly enhanced by reading Harold Netland's *Encountering Religious Pluralism* and Ravi Zacharias's *Jesus among Other Gods* and by discussing this topic with learners in various university classes. I was intrigued that this question came up so readily and was asked so urgently. I inquired, "Why do you ask this particular question?" She responded by saying that she had relationships in her community with many people from different world religions. These people, she added, were good and sincere in their beliefs. It was evident that she had been considering this question for a long time.

I asked her how she felt in her heart about this question. She was ambivalent, she said. She believed that Jesus is the way to God but objected to the strident, intolerant rhetoric of fundamentalists. She somehow perceived that God would accept people of all religions if they were sincere. Knowing that I would probably never see Patricia again and sensing that the time was right to plunge ahead, I breathed a quick silent prayer for wisdom and said …

---

place the content of the Christian message within appropriate cultural rhythms, which have both meaning and emotion.

Christians must address practical life experiences. This is best done through faith stories and testimonies that glorify God's work through frail humans. Public dramas, role-playing, and skits can also communicate this message. The relational thinkers who are so prevalent in our developing urban cultures are untouched by propositional categories. Above all, Christians must communicate that Christianity is as unique as the God who created this world and the Christ who died for our sins.

4

The Changing Basis of Knowledge

From Modernity to Postmodernity

MICHAEL POCOCK

As you stand on the bank of the Yukon River in northern Canada, in the old gold rush town of Dawson, the river appears to have two parts. The flow from the shore to twenty yards out is clear. Beyond stretches an immense current of silted, brown water. The clear current is coming from the fabled Klondike River, source of so many gilded dreams and from which millions of dollars in gold were mined more than a century ago. It joins the Yukon River just upstream of Dawson, struggles to retain its identity for some distance, then gradually disappears into the implacable flow. Which river enters which? It is hard to tell. Yet there is something in the Klondike and every other tributary that retains a distinct flavor in the larger Yukon. Migrating salmon with imprinted memories of their natal stream can taste it. After several years in the ocean, they enter the big river again and move inexorably to the waters they departed long before.

Modernity may be thought of as the silt-laden river in which we have been swimming for so long that we have become used to it. Pragmatically, it seems to be taking us somewhere. It solves so many of our im-

---

SIDEBAR 4.1
IMPORTANT TERMS USED IN THIS CHAPTER

---

empirical/empiricism: Generally, the concept that all knowledge is based on observation under the discipline of the scientific method.

epistemology: The study of the basis of knowledge or the approach to knowing utilized by a particular culture.

existentialism: A philosophical orientation that sees knowledge as the product of a personal search for meaning, yields a subjective grasp of reality that cannot be verified by scientific or solely objective means, and stresses the responsibility of individuals to be true to themselves and thus free from or at odds with conventional expectations.

modernity: The period beginning with the seventeenth-century Enlightenment in which knowing became based on

objective, rational observation and the scientific method. A modernist approach may be characterized by a quest for absolute truth using rational logic and scientific methods. It treats religion as unimportant in the quest. It values the individual, the material over the spiritual (e.g., industrialization), democracy, free-market economics, and universal truths.

postmodernity: Beginning in the 1980s, postmodernity is characterized by disillusionment with modernity as a system that claims certainty about its scientific conclusions but excludes spiritual realities. Postmodern people rely more on intuition, are more subjective in their judgments, do not trust systems and institutions, and treat most truth claims as personal or cultural.

---

mediate problems in scientific, rational terms. The method of modernity is the scientific method, marked by the use of hard data, rigorous and reproducible experimentation, and conclusions based on observation and logical deduction. Modernity has led to the exclusion of issues of transcendence, meaning, or metaphysics because these concerns cannot be studied using the scientific method. Modernity relegates issues of ultimate meaning to a realm outside science, making them unknowable or even "unreal."

How do people *know* what they know? What counts as an explanation? Those are the primary issues of what is called epistemology. Whether one ministers in North America, Europe, the Middle East, Asia, Africa, or Latin America, it is vital to know what counts to people as an explanation. In various parts of the world and in our own culture, people have different assumptions and use distinct approaches to knowing. Astrology, reading the intestines of sacrificial animals, casting lots, and dreams are often considered premodern ways of knowing. The modern era, usually considered to have begun with the Enlightenment in the seventeenth and eighteenth centuries, brought a more rationalistic, scientific approach to knowing and gave birth to an optimistic sense that all problems could be studied and resolved with good data and logic. The modern Protestant mission movement began in the modern era. Many missionaries adopted the findings of modern science as reasonable, but lately, both secular and Christian thinkers have questioned the capacity of modernity to address the deepest issues of humanity.

Postmodernism, by contrast, is characterized by an awakening to the limitations of modernity or, as some would say, its bankruptcy, particularly when it comes to providing final answers about existence or to resolving problems of human depravity and intractability. Postmodernity is a broad awareness of modernity's limitations with regard to attaining knowledge or absolute truth. Postmodernists are disenchanted with a system that represents its methods and conclusions as irrefutable but whose scientists modify their theories and conclusions as often as doctors reverse themselves about issues of health and nutrition.

Postmodern people have awakened to the fact that they have been taken for a ride. What do people do when they wake up to the reality of having been fooled, defrauded, or deceived? Should they have known better? Should they have fought it all along? Certainly, some knew what was happening, but perhaps they were beguiled by the benefits of modernity, from better transport to better health. Disillusioned postmodernists need answers to their questions. Modernity failed to deliver certainty about ultimate truth and meaning while posturing itself as the only way toward progress. Postmodernity offers no certainties or solutions but is open to transcendent realities and subjective, intuitive approaches to knowing.

The role of missions among people affected by postmodernity is to show them that Christianity can be understood through normal and even rigorous historical and literary study of Scripture. It can be experienced as a transforming reality through faith in Christ. Faith in Christ brings about a new relationship with God as believers become his children (John 1:12). Believers in Christ receive "the mind of Christ" (1 Cor. 2:16), giving them the capability to understand spiritual realities they could not otherwise have known. Missionaries can no longer rely on didactic, cognitive approaches, as if Christianity were a case that could be proven in a court of law or demonstrated by methods suited to the laboratory. Christians are still called to declare the truth of Scripture, but hearers are more likely to believe when the gospel is "storied," set in aesthetic, poetic, or dramatic fashion and lived out in relationships and concrete ways.

IDENTIFYING THE TREND: THE CHANGE FROM MODERN TO POSTMODERN WAYS OF KNOWING

Western Europe, much of North America, and peoples of the majority world who have been influenced by the modern Western worldview are today considered post-Christian. What was Christendom has become a mission field. Christian workers in Europe find that many consider religion simply irrelevant. To many, the decline of Christianity in the West is the logical product of modernity. Postmodernity, which expresses disillusionment with modernity, may look like a fresh possibility, since postmodernists are generally more open to spirituality. But will postmodernism help or hinder missionary work?

Both the modern and the emerging postmodern approach to knowledge constitute challenges to missionary ministry. Truth claims about transcendent issues in the realm of God and spirituality are not easily demonstrated by modern, data-based, rationalistic methods. However, absolute truth also cannot be found through the more postmodern emphasis on intuition and subjectivity.

Paul Hiebert traces postmodernity's latest and most apparent development to 1979 with the publication of *The Postmodern Condition* by François Lyotard (1984, English edition). Hiebert notes that others used the term in the 1950s and 1960s. Harold Netland indicates that the term *postmodern* was first used by Arnold Toynbee in *A Study of History* published in 1939 (Netland 2001, 57). Toynbee described the period beginning with World War I and recognized that the bright promise of modernity was not going to be realized on its own terms. That is to say, modernity was not leading to freedom from the insanity of war—war waged by totally modern and, presumably, rational people with all the tools of modern technology. Dissatisfaction with the empirical methodology of modernity has grown for over 150 years.

> *We are living in a world of quantum changes, of macro change. The whole world is changing. And we aren't?*
>
> Leonard Sweet (1999b, 76)

A constant stream of individuals and movements has resisted modernity or attempted to rescue Christian faith when it seemed threatened by the seemingly unstoppable progress of modernity. Opponents include Søren Kierkegaard (1813–55) and Friedrich Schleiermacher (1763–1840). The appearance of American religious fundamentalism and the Pentecostal movement of the twentieth century can also be considered either pre-postmodernist or antimodernist in nature. In America, these last two have been considered by writers such as Richard Hofstadter to be part of a wider stream of American anti-intellectualism (1963, 117–41). There has been a constant stream of criticism and discomfort with the epistemological method and the direction of modernity.

Can we trust a system of knowledge that speaks with arrogance about what it has discovered and promises more but that cannot resolve inter-tribal genocide, crop failures, or the global warming caused by its own technical advances? People, especially in the West, are retreating to a more independent, intuitive, and subjective system of knowing that they hope will be free of the presumptuous absolutism known as positivism, which characterized the heart of modernity. A postmodernist favors the present over the past, tending to live in the moment. Rather than try-ing to discern an overarching picture of reality, or metanarrative, the postmodern person gathers impressions from distinct experiences or momentary exposures.

When European Christians such as Richard Tiplady, Rose Dowsett, or Clive Calver speak of postmodernism, they speak with a history of confronting it. They live in postmodern cultures that are also manifestly post-Christian. At the same time, they are familiar with Bible-based evangelical churches and ministries that flourish against all odds in those cultures. Calver says that to a postmodernist "true truth" (a phrase coined by American Christian philosopher Francis Schaeffer in the 1960s) is dead. This, to Calver, is the essence of postmodernity. Post-modernists will not accept the superiority or correctness of a religious position beyond its value for the individual (Calver 1999, 430). "All truth is perspectival," as Josh McDowell puts it (1999, 611).

The difference between the modern and the postmodern perspective is sometimes likened to the difference between an analog clock, with a face and hands showing the sweep of time and the direction of the future, and a digital clock, which simply shows the time at a given moment, leading to a disconnected sense of being. The fragmentary, or digital, approach of postmodernism is most easily seen on MTV. Rapidly chang-ing scenes, generally too fast for older people to comprehend, leave a general impression extrapolated from the sum of the parts.

Postmodernists like to draw on multiple sources, even if they are disparate. They receive contradictory inputs from different religions, cultures, or peoples with no apparent problem. This was observable at the World Parliament of Religions in 1999 held at Cape Town, South Africa. There, in an atmosphere of pluralistic harmony, shamans, African traditional religious practitioners, Tibetan monks, and Bahais all led prayers, presentations, and dialogue. This was not merely pluralism; it was postmodernity on display. In postmodernity, there is no unified field of knowledge. There is no grand unifying theory (Hiebert 1999, 19, 32). Paradigms are not mutually exclusive if they differ from one another, nor can a theory or a plan (postmoderns would not use such terms) be rejected if some part of it is proven wrong. There is nothing like the law of noncontradiction (the idea that two contradictory claims cannot both be true in the same way at the same time) to which one might appeal to prove an assertion right or wrong. One simply agrees to disagree and lets people go their own way. Postmodernity has existed as either a rebellion against modernity or simply the orientation of many majority world cultures for a long while.

Richard Tiplady is an excellent observer of the people of postmodern culture who have been labeled Generation X. Tiplady recognizes that it is perilous to categorize the group born between 1965 and 1980. They do not like labels. He sees them as generally postmodern in outlook and very much worth dealing with as a special case for Christian outreach (2000, 463–75). Tiplady calls the trend toward postmodernity a "massive cultural transformation." It is not as much caused by the media as it is reflected in it. For Tiplady, postmodernity and the culture of Generation X are marked by intense individuality and the need for wage earners to adjust to the shift from mass production to information technology.

Consumerism forces producers into "mass customization" so that everyone can have just the car, clothes, or furniture that appeals to him or her. Lacking a deeper sense of personal identity, or perhaps even worth, postmodernists find identity in dress styles and the stuff they own. Because postmodernists have abandoned a metanarrative—large-scale unifying theories that explain or direct history, such as Marxism—they are marked by individuality, flexibility, and skepticism (Tiplady 2000, 468–69).

At the outset of this chapter, we compared modernity to the Yukon River: silty, wide, and unstoppable. But is the picture of modernity so unrelentingly bleak? Have we not all enjoyed huge benefits that we now consider indispensable? Don't postmodernists like to board trains that run on time, travel by airplanes that take them to their desired destinations, live in cities with a clean water supply, excellent sanitation, and public safety? Is it better, when charged with a crime, to have a judge who references case law (history) or the Constitution rather than simply using intuition? In fact, how could there be a just postmodern judge, unless that person were Solomonic in using God-given intuitive wisdom? The law, in postmodern frames, would become nothing more than a set of low-level communal agreements somehow collectively granted.

Positivism, the essence of modernity, was pioneered by Auguste Compte. Hiebert notes:

> Positivism has changed the world for good. It has a strong sense of truth and order, and a high view of nature. By focusing attention on careful

empirical research, it gave rise to modern science, which has contributed greatly to our understanding of the world, and to technologies that have benefited life on earth. It is hard for us today to imagine what life was like in the West before modernity.

But positivism is also flawed. It has divorced knowledge from morality and feelings, and in doing so it has unleashed modern technology with few moral constraints, and power without safeguards. In its materialistic forms it has absolutized scientific knowledge and relegated religion to private opinion, and it reduces humans to robots in a mechanistic world. Today, the certainty of positivism and the optimism that marked its early years, have been undermined from within and from without. Positivism is no longer accepted as universally true. (1999, 29)

Obviously, modernity brought enormous benefits. It also brought what postmodernists perceive as major deficits: (1) a crushing intellectual elite that manages education and general thought; (2) science, supposedly objective, corrupted by the businesses that pay for and use its results, often without consideration of environmental or human effects; and (3) political structures of the so-called free world wherein major corporations pay for the election of politicians who will advance and not obstruct their profit-making businesses.

Postmodernists do not like the arrogance of modernity's assertion that knowledge is the product of objective, empirical research. They simply

---

SIDEBAR 4.2
DIGGING DEEPER

The following authors and websites represent individuals and associations attempting to understand postmodern people and to engage them in meaningful ministry in Western and global contexts.

AUTHORS

Larkin, William J. 2004. "The Contribution of Luke-Acts to Missionary Moves of the Christian Religion in the Twenty-first Century Post-Modern Global Context," http://www.globalmissiology.net/docs_pdf/featured/larkin_contribution_of_luke_acts.PDF (accessed May 31, 2004).

McLaren, Brian D. 2001. *A New Kind of Christian*. San Francisco: Jossey-Bass.
Sweet, Leonard I. 1999. *Soul Tsunami*. Grand Rapids: Zondervan.
———, ed. 2003. *The Church in Emerging Culture: Five Perspectives*. Grand Rapids: Zondervan.

WEBSITES

http://www.beyondmag.com
http://www.christianityandrenewal.com
http://www.emergentvillage.com
http://tallskinnykiwi.typepad.com
http://www.the-next-wave.org
http://www.theooze.com

do not believe that so-called rational people can ever be completely objective. By giving the impression of finality, modernity has been used to manipulate and control the less powerful and less connected. Yet postmodernists are not all identical. They can be placed in four general categories: reluctant postmodernists, resentful postmodernists, reconstructive postmodernists, and reemerging postmodernists.

Reluctant Postmodernists

Reluctant postmodernists admit modernity did not deliver on its implicit or stated promises—but they wish it had. They hold on to a limited faith that rational thought processes and the sciences can solve many of the problems people face, but they admit that such things will not procure reliable answers to transcendent questions. Pauline Rosenau calls them hopeful postmodernists (Hiebert 1999, 51).

Resentful Postmodernists

Resentful postmodernists are angry that modernity became an exploitative culture- and individuality-crushing machine. They are antimodern and nihilist. They are deconstructivist, believing that the only way ahead is to dispense with the epistemologies of the past, but they have no replacement and do not believe one will be found (e.g., Jaques Derrida). Rosenau calls them skeptical postmodernists (Hiebert 1999, 51).

Reconstructive Postmodernists

Reconstructive postmodernists are hopeful that a new paradigm is out there. They are pluralistic and dialogue oriented. They are instrumentalists in that they are looking for what works. Some, such as secular existentialists, believe they must struggle to act responsibly or honorably, even though the world as they know it is incomprehensible (or even absurd) in terms of a reliable epistemology. They listen to every source to see what may emerge. There may be no final truth or grand paradigm, but there are helpful insights. These are represented by pluralistic religious practitioners such as those involved with the World Parliament of Religions or those who oppose exclusivism at every level because they believe it is dangerous to human coexistence.

Reemerging Postmodernists

Reemerging postmodernists are people who have been thoroughly immersed in postmodern belief and culture but have found it lacking. They may be represented by people such as Bono of U2, who is culturally at home with the music and much of the culture of the present generation but who often sounds like a person of faith (even Christian faith) and is ready to act on behalf of humanitarian values. Many in the environmental preservation movement may also be emerging from postmodernism. It is impossible for them to sustain passionate concern for anything that is not real. The environment is a reality for which they are ready to die.

EVALUATING THE TREND: WILL POSTMODERNITY CHANGE THE WAY WE DO MISSIONS?

Evaluations of postmodernism by evangelicals such as Clive Calver, Elizabeth Tebbe, and Jonathan Campbell range from hostile to empathetic in tone and scope, and their works range from critiques of culture to deeper philosophical responses. All agree that postmodernism is a serious challenge that confronts Christian faith and merits a clear and compassionate response.

Calver attests to both "the rampant progression of [the] New Age, the spiritual child of postmodernism, and the awful results of its ethical nihilism," yet he continues, "I have also seen the spiritual hunger it confesses. I have watched the rejection of the human self-aggrandizement of modernism, and I have listened to the desire to see a faith that works." He adds his belief that "postmodern thinking is totally non-Christian" (Calver 1999, 431). Tebbe says that postmodernism has become so mainstream that living as an evangelical today constitutes an alternative lifestyle (Tebbe 1999, 426).

Christians have to admit that they—even as Christians—are creatures of their culture. They want to be in sync with their culture because synchronization brings feelings of comfort and belonging. Believers need to be cognizant of this attraction.

Years ago, when Michael Pocock sensed God's call to ministry, he chose to attend a Bible college, believing that a solid grasp of God's Word was what he needed and wished to impart to others. In his context, this choice was countercultural. No one in his family had ever been to college, so they did not know how to advise him. His Christian friends were going to various secular universities. Almost no one he knew planned on attending a Bible college. Although he was glad to be studying the Bible at Washington Bible College, he was also relieved to be able to report, when asked, that he was taking courses in hamartiology (the study of sin), soteriology (the study of salvation), and eschatology (the study of the end times). No one asked him what those "branches of science" covered, but he felt vaguely pleased that his courses sounded scientific.

As he studied hermeneutics—principles for interpreting the Bible—he discovered that they were the same as for any piece of literature, with

SIDEBAR 4.3
CONCERNS ABOUT EVANGELICAL RESPONSES TO POSTMODERNISM

Jonathan Campbell feels that Clive Calver and Elizabeth Tebbe are too pessimistic about postmodernism and insufficiently critical of modernity. He voices four main concerns about many evangelical responses to postmodernism:

1. The assumption (by evangelicals) that modernity is somehow more biblically sound than its counterpart in postmodernity.
2. The failure to see the hope and positive opportunities to translate the gospel within the cultures of postmodernity.
3. The incognizance of many who do not realize how the church has succumbed to modernity.
4. The refusal to call the church to radical and systemic changes to recover its identity and missional purpose in order to engage postmodern cultures. Despite the dangers of the current culture shift, Christians can still discern and act on distinct opportunities for mission within postmodern cultures. (Campbell 1999, 432–33)

These concerns, particularly 1 and 3, are valid. It is not true that Calver and Tebbe have no hope for ministry to postmoderns. They and other evangelicals have issued calls for Christians to recover a missional identity (Guder 1998, 447–62). But when evangelicals adopted certain modern tools to counter the anti-biblical stance of modernity, with its exclusion of religious matters from the bounds of scientific investigation, they may have put too much confidence in those tools.

The use of the law of noncontradiction as a foundation for apologetics leaves little room for mystery, antinomy, or paradox—even though these forms of undisclosed realities and apparent contradictions are clearly present in Scripture (John 11:25–26; 2 Cor. 6:8–10; Eph. 1:9–10).

After Christians have done their best to prove God's existence, they have to admit that the fullness of his nature and ways evades purely rational proofs. God can be known only by special revelation and a subjective grasp of his reality aided by the illuminating work of the Spirit in a regenerated heart (1 Cor. 2:9–16).

REFLECTION AND DISCUSSION

1. What elements of postmodernism should a postmodern person reject to encounter Christ authentically?
2. What elements of postmodernism enable a more authentic encounter with Christ than possible in modernity?
3. If traditional evangelism directed at modern people often involved giving rational proofs that the Bible is true or that Christ is really God, how should the approach be changed for a postmodern person?

the exception that Scripture was divinely inspired. In seminary, as he studied Greek, Hebrew, and biblical exegesis, he learned how to apply careful grammatical analysis and to refer to the historical and literary forms in which the biblical passages being analyzed were written. He diagrammed sentences and made flowcharts of the Bible. There was little ambiguity to his theology, and everything was "schematicizable" with neat components that fit together. It all seemed so scientific and modern rather than archaic or outlandish. He did not see anything wrong with this. People who mastered the system became fine expositors of the Word, and their teaching seemed well grounded. What Pocock did not realize was that to the extent his Christian studies had a modern feel to them, he felt good. He was part of modern culture, comfortable with its categories and epistemology.

In recent years, however, he has become uncomfortable when a preacher has talked about the grammar underlying the teaching of a passage. He knows that such things matter but wonders if anyone reading Paul's letters for the first time to groups around the Mediterranean ever stopped in his reading to exclaim, "Did you see that folks? He just used a coordinate conjunction!" Certainly, they simply read the letter joyfully. Having discovered its profundity, someone among them may have said, "Let's hear that again" or "That was pretty convicting." But their focus would have been on the entire letter—the story line or narrative—rather than on finely dissected pieces. Those pieces belong in the study, not the pulpit. Perhaps the New Testament believers were pre-postmodernists! That is what Brian McLaren believes (see Sweet 2003, 24–25), and his thinking gave Pocock comfort that he is not the only one to feel as he does.

Having been influenced by modernity, is Pocock now quietly slipping into postmodernity with its love of stories, mystery, and subjectivity? He does not have less certainty, but he does have more awe. He accepts that God is not completely comprehensible. But God has shown Pocock enough so that he can sense him, relate to him, and know through Scripture that he is more than a subjective sense and bigger than a rational capacity to comprehend.

It is easy to be enamored with and to see the good side of both modern and postmodern trends of understanding. It is possible to be unaware and to drift to one side or the other, adopting not only these values but also the cultural values associated with them. Paul Hiebert states that Christians cannot simply move from one paradigm to another, especially when postmodernity:

- has no agenda of its own to solve the world's problems
- is reactive rather than proactive
- is opposed to modernity and all its fruits
- offers no criteria for right and wrong, true and false

- is primarily a Western concern—a luxury of those who already have plenty (Hiebert 1999, 65–66)

Postmodernism may affect missions in two significant ways: First, it may affect those who become missionaries, and second, it may affect the ways non-Christian postmodernists respond to missionaries. Christians are always influenced by the age in which they live, even when they scarcely realize it. Postmodernity has caused some Christians to become much more accepting of divergent religious opinions. It seems increasingly countercultural to hold to singular truth in an exclusive way. Christians who have lost the conviction that Christ is unique and the only hope for salvation and new spiritual life, however, may be less inclined to serve as missionaries or indeed to witness at all. On the other hand, an increased toleration of diverse viewpoints may make those who become missionaries more capable of understanding differences, more patient, and less peremptory than their predecessors.

Postmodernism has influenced the non-Christian world by creating a sense that no absolutes exist. Those (such as evangelicals) who make exclusive claims to truth are often viewed as dangerous fanatics. On the other hand, the postmodern appreciation for authenticity, warm relationships, and openness to spirituality may make it possible to minister to postmoderns in ways that lead to acceptance, trust, and ultimately belief in Christ's transforming power.

REFLECTING ON THE TREND: HOW DOES SCRIPTURE HELP US UNDERSTAND AND RESPOND TO POSTMODERNITY?

John R. W. Stott, in the 1988 Griffeth-Thomas Lectureship at Dallas Theological Seminary, reflected on the needs of what he called "modern man" but which had already become "postmodern man" in the West. He noted that people have three yearnings:

1. for transcendence—a sense of God or a connection with what is beyond immediate and material things and beings
2. for significance—a sense that they are meaningful, have purpose, and make a difference
3. for community—a sense that in a fragmenting world and society they belong to a family (1988, 123–32)

The following discussion uses these three yearnings of postmodernists to reflect biblically and theologically on postmodernity.

The Yearning for Transcendence

Postmodernists are skeptical of any unique claims about God, but they are keenly interested in spirituality. Some Christian observers have commented that in Europe discussions about spiritual matters are far more common today than in the past twenty years. This is echoed in North America by students from other countries and cultures. Students at Dallas Seminary have to make friends with an off-campus international student during the semester in which they take an introduction to missions course. These friendships, frequently pursued far beyond the class requirement, have surprised students because of the degree to which their counterparts from China, India, and the Middle East are the first to bring up spiritual issues. God and spirituality are of real interest to today's generation, whether they are postmodern Westerners or non-Westerners.

Babu Pimplekar, an outstanding Indian Christian and a student of Pocock, found Christ as a Hindu. He had an interesting answer when Pocock asked him how the Christian God had captured his interest. He replied that he had definitely been a spiritual seeker and had spoken widely with Hindu spiritual leaders. He read the great Hindu scriptures yet had remained unsatisfied. Someone told him that before he gave up his search he should also read the Judeo-Christian Scripture. He did and discovered two things: "The Bible," he said, "seemed like real history to me." In spite of great and wonderful miracles recorded there, it still seemed real rather than fanciful and fantastic. Second, he said, "The Scriptures seemed to know me." He found himself in the Bible. Even more importantly, he found Christ.

Though postmodernists may resist an appeal to authority like Scripture, they may sense God in nature and then in Scripture find God explained. And what a God! This is the God who shows himself in creation, truly transcending all creation, eliciting praise from the psalmist:

> The heavens declare the glory of God;
> the skies proclaim the work of his hands.
> Day after day they pour forth speech;
> night after night they display knowledge.
> There is no speech or language
> where their voice is not heard.
> Their voice goes out into all the earth,
> their words to the ends of the world.
>
> Psalm 19:1–4

Scripture indicates that unregenerate people do not independently draw correct conclusions about what they see in nature (Rom. 1:18–32). However, special revelation—Holy Scripture—is the Word of the Spirit (Eph. 6:17; 2 Tim. 3:16–17). In the hands of a believer, who is also an agent of the Holy Spirit (John 15:26–27; Acts 1:8), Scripture can be made understandable even to an unregenerate person, as evidenced in Philip's interaction with the Ethiopian eunuch (Acts 8:26–39).

In contrast with postmodernists, evangelical Christians proclaim God as a cognitive and knowable reality. Although no one may independently "guess" or discover God, knowledge of him is possible through the Spirit (1 Cor. 2:10). A key New Testament teaching on epistemology is Paul's treatment in 1 Corinthians 1:18–2:16. Paul is talking about knowing and communicating God in the context of diverse philosophies. He declares that God is not known through pagan philosophy (1:21). Rather, God is known paradoxically through the unsophisticated process of preaching, which proclaims Christ (1 Cor. 1:21–25). Is there agreement here with postmodernists who claim that no epistemological system can achieve a certain knowledge of absolutes? In this passage, Paul is saying, "You are right. Absolutes—like God as unique Creator and Sustainer of the universe and humans—are not learned through a process of deduction but instead are known only if revealed by the Absolute." Certainly, this curtails the pride displayed by modern positivist thinkers and disliked by postmodernists. In fact, this was the reason God arranged things the way he did. He wanted to use the lowly and despised things of the world so that "him who boasts boast[s] in the Lord" (1 Cor. 1:31).

There is a certain amount of mystery in biblical epistemology that is sure to appeal to postmodernists but is not capitalized on by many evangelicals, who spent the modern era minimizing the mystical. The transcendent, Triune God revealed himself in the greatest mystery of all: "Christ, in whom are hidden all the treasures of wisdom and knowledge" (Col. 2:2–3). This is indeed transcendent knowledge, because the Spirit is the only one who could have revealed it. This wisdom is Christ-centered and leads to a Christocentric way of knowing.

A mark of modernity is the distinction made between knowledge of natural things and knowledge of spiritual things. This duality goes back to Plato but was used by positivists to dismiss spiritual claims from the realm of scientific investigation, leaving theologians to work on what materialists held to be unverifiable claims. Modern evangelicals considered this unfair. They believed that what they knew of God could be demonstrated on the same grounds as any natural claim. They used pure rationality harking back to Aquinas and Anselm or an apologetic that began with establishing the historicity of New Testament claims about Christ recorded in the historically reliable New Testament documents.

Having established that point, they then built a case for the truthfulness of all Christ taught and the entire revelation of Holy Scripture. They made the claim that all Scripture is the Word of God because Christ, the self-proclaimed incarnate God, authenticated the existing Jewish Scriptures of his day (e.g., Mark 12:24; 14:49). He also promised that the Spirit would bring to the minds of the apostles all that they had heard him say and do (John 14:25–26; 15:26–27; 16:5–15)—referring to the production of the Gospel records.

Let's return for a moment to the dual level of epistemology noted above. Paul writes:

> The Spirit searches all things, even the deep things of God. For who among men knows the thoughts of a man except the man's spirit within him? In the same way no one knows the thoughts of God except the Spirit of God. We have not received the spirit of the world but the Spirit who is from God, that we may understand what God has freely given us.
>
> 1 Corinthians 2:10–12

This sounds like two levels of knowledge: (1) that which relates to people or at least to the subjective mind, and (2) truth about God. Without the Spirit, we can know only our own minds or possibly things that relate to human beings. This is said to be reliable knowledge. But unless the Spirit is in us, we will not comprehend truth about God. In these verses, Paul in effect said, "Modern one, you are right. You can know truth only at the level of human beings." But at the same time, "You can access transcendent knowledge through the Spirit of the living God, but only if you experience his regenerating work."

In contrast to postmodernists, Christians maintain that there is ultimate reality and a real world. This ultimate reality is the God of the Bible. He is knowable but not by any system devised by people. Instead, he is known by grace through faith in the person of Christ, revealed by the Spirit of God in the Word of God (1 Cor. 2:6–10; Eph. 2:8–9; Col. 1:15–23). The historically reliable New Testament documents, as well as fulfilled prophesy, attest to God and his self-disclosure in Christ, the Son. To experience a continuing relationship with the transcendent God, people can converse with him in prayer (Matt. 6:5–15), walk in his Spirit (Rom. 8:5–17), praise him in adoration (Ps. 22:3), and enjoy him in the community of Christ's body (Matt. 18:20).

The infinite, personal God of the Bible satisfies the yearning for transcendence that characterizes this generation. The catch for postmodern people is that this God, this amazing provision and possibility, is unique. To proclaim the gospel as the exclusive way of salvation will seem foolish to postmodernists, as it did to the Greeks who heard it in the first century. But today's postmodern hearers may go beyond laughter to rage over such a claim for exclusivity. Christians may be considered as dangerous as any other fundamentalist—whether Islamic, Hindu, or Aryan Nation. There may still be a cross to bear by those who follow seriously in Christ's steps. On the bright side, postmodernists are "interested in the eccentric, the marginal, the disqualified, and the subjugated" (Hiebert 1999, 53). Perhaps Christianity will constitute just the niche postmodernists need.

The Yearning for Significance

This chapter earlier referred to a postmodern person's need for personal identity and significance. Richard Tiplady says, "I believe that the issues of individuality and identity are at the core of the questions that contemporary culture is asking" (2000, 466). This is equal to the yearning for significance to which John Stott refers. Surely Scripture is clear that every individual is supremely important to God.

Why are postmodernists so concerned with identity, individuality, and significance? Identity and significance are taking a severe beating in today's world. The impersonal free-market forces of globalization move capital from place to place. Both labor and market can be liquidated in a moment. Companies collapse. Super-rich CEOs with inside knowledge of their corporations' weaknesses suddenly bail out, sell their stock options, and ruin the lives of faithful workers and investors. Dads leave their children and wives. Wives run away from their husbands. Single moms by the millions are trying to cope with limited time and income, seeing their children only a short time each day. Children are aborted, bartered, and abused. What does the individual mean anymore? For what does he or she count?

According to Scripture, human beings are the peak of God's creation. Appearing at the end of the creation process in Genesis 1, Adam is made in the image of God (1:26–27). So is Eve. Not only is she made in the image of God, but she is also the only living being appropriate as a mate for Adam (2:20–25). Together they have responsibilities and privileges; they walk with God. When they disobey, it is a vastly significant matter. There is no, "Just don't do it again" or "I told you a hundred times." This is not a petulant child and a harried parent in a grocery store. This is Adam and Eve and God. It matters supremely what they do. It may seem negative (and no one likes negativity in a postmodern world) to banish the couple from Paradise and to consider the entire race to come a fallen entity, but that is how much the actions of one couple meant to God (Rom. 5:12–20). Yet in every judgment of God, mercy and justice are also procured. Humankind's redemption begins to be spelled out by the third chapter of Genesis (v. 15), and we see that brokenness (sin) is fixable (redeemable) in the program of God.

The amazing thing about God is that he keeps track of so much. That is because people matter. Their actions can be earth shaking, or earth flooding. They are not a matter of indifference to God. As people multiplied, God knew the names of all the nations. Genesis 10 contains a catalog of them. In Acts 17, Paul mentions that God made all people and nations from one person, moving them around so that each is where God wants. To God, there are no inferior and superior people. None is any less human than any other, for all were made from "one man" (Acts 17:26).

Scripture focuses carefully on individuals and their worth. Abraham may have been a migrant nobody to others as he moved from Ur to Haran, but God made Abraham a somebody. He became not only the model of faith for Paul but also the foundation of a family and a nation through whom the entire earth was to be blessed (Gen. 12:1–3).

To God, evil people are as much a concern as those who love and serve him. Evil people are what God's redemptive program is all about; he takes "no pleasure in the death of anyone" (Ezek. 18:32). To a disgruntled Jonah, upset that God had spared the wicked city of Nineveh after the people repented, he said, "Nineveh has more than a hundred and twenty thousand people who cannot tell their right hand from their left, and many cattle as well. Should I not be concerned about that great city?" (Jonah 4:11). People living in a huge, depersonalizing, urban megalopolis such as London, Moscow, Mexico City, or Beijing matter to God.

Whether it was little children hoping for a blessing, a woman with vaginal bleeding, parents with an epileptic child, or a demonized madman, Jesus had time for them all. The best-known verse of the Bible says, "For God so loved the world that he gave his one and only Son, that *whoever* believes in him shall not perish but have eternal life" (John 3:16, emphasis added). This is not a generalized statement of humanitarian concern but a statement about the infinite value of each person, the objects of the life and ministry of Jesus, people for whom he gave his life. That's value. That's significance.

So what do we become if we believe in Jesus? Nothing less than a child of God (John 1:12). What if you have a despicable background? Do you still count? Were you an adulterer, a homosexual prostitute, a thief, a swindler, or an abusive alcoholic? Paul names them all and tells the Corinthians, "And that is what some of you were. But you were washed, you were sanctified, you were justified in the name of the Lord Jesus and by the Spirit of our God" (1 Cor. 6:11). It is wonderful to be accepted in the beloved. Postmodernists can be too.

The final miracle of significance for the individual is that God includes him or her in his work. Jesus sent out a group of ordinary men and put the program of world evangelization in their hands (Matt. 28:19–20). A number of women helped support Jesus in his ministry (Luke 8:1–3). Paul includes many women in a lengthy list of greetings and thanks to those who had done ministry well in Rome (Rom. 16:1–15). People matter in the program of God, and that is a significant fact to impress on the minds of postmodernists.

The Yearning for Community

As if it were not enough to be a significant individual in the sight of God, believers also become part of a new spiritual family. This is the church, also called a "a chosen people, a royal priesthood, a holy nation, a people belonging to God" (1 Pet. 2:9). Peter adds, "Once you were not a people, but now you are the people of God" (1 Pet. 2:10). Christians do not simply have personal identity and significance; they have acceptance in a community as well.

The creation of humanity began with a communal decision. "Then God said, 'Let *us* make man in *our* image, in *our* likeness, and let *them* rule'" (Gen. 1:26, emphasis added). God himself is his own community. As Scripture reveals, God was present and acting in creation, as was his Spirit (Gen. 1:2). Later we learn that the preexistent Christ was also at work in creation (John 10:25–38; Col. 1:15–18). The communal God created communal humanity. Adam received a partner in Eve, and they multiplied. When the nations showed the extent of their rebellion against the creation mandate, God created a new nation, Israel, to embody his praises and to grow *as a people*. The character of this people as a holy, priestly, and particular nation is seen in the Old Testament (Exod. 19:3–6) and is applied almost verbatim by Peter to the church (1 Pet. 2:9–10). Jesus worked with others, as did Paul. When people become believers, they become part of the family of God, the church. This is a worldwide, culturally diverse phenomenon. Its local expressions, especially in communities that are themselves diverse, should reflect that variety.

Henri Nouwen, a Roman Catholic whose work is appreciated by many evangelicals, became convinced during his ministry that no Christian work was designed to be done alone (1996, 6–7). He committed himself to working with others in ministry, even the severely disabled from his community at Daybreak in Canada. No believer should fail to be in a community of believers (Nouwen 1993, 40–41). David Howard has made the same point in regard to those who do God's work. Arguing for greater cooperation and fellowship, he says, "The Apostle Paul never conceived of himself as an army of one, even though he was often nearly alone. He fully recognized his need of the strength and help provided by others" (2003, 7). Paul Hiebert also maintains that theology and missiology must be done in community. There should be no lone wolves in either the doing of ministry or the enjoyment of the faith. It is a communal venture.

Churches and denominations that fail to live out the community love found in the New Testament (Acts 2:42–47) are part of the reason postmodernists are disinterested in institutional Christianity. Much of their disillusionment with the church or individual churches may come from a general distrust of all institutions rather than from direct experience. They read the newspapers. They see the multiplying cases of abuse by clergy. In 2002, director Peter Mullen produced a film dramatization of the brutality of the Magdalen Laundries in Ireland, where an estimated seventy thousand women accused of sexual immorality were incarcerated—most for life—under the Magdalen Sisters of Charity (Mullen 2002). Others have experienced disillusionment directly, leading to incredible anger, like that expressed by singer Sinead O'Connor. In 1992, she went public with harsh statements against the pope and the Catholic Church, even tearing up a picture of the pope on *Saturday Night Live* (Ankeny n.d.). When

> *They devoted themselves to the apostles' teaching and to the fellowship, to the breaking of bread and to prayer. Everyone was filled with awe, and many wonders and miraculous signs were done by the apostles. All the believers were together and had everything in common. Selling their possessions and goods, they gave to anyone as he had need. Every day they continued to meet together in the temple courts. They broke bread in their homes and ate together with glad and sincere hearts, praising God and enjoying the favor of all the people. And the Lord added to their number daily those who were being saved.*
>
> Acts 2:42–47

such stories emerge, it makes Christians realize how much they need to examine their churches and to repent of the ways they have not been a true community but a poisonous and dysfunctional one. Only then may they be able to offer the genuine community postmodernists seek.

Pocock has had the privilege of serving on the board of an openly Christian nongovernment organization (NGO) in China. The agency works for the well-being of the people of China in the name of Christ and in the spirit of a former missionary who is still remembered by local people and officials in Shanxi. This NGO has enlisted the assistance of many experts in medicine, public health, police work, and education, and it maintains a vibrant staff of committed workers on a long-term

123

> *I don't think you'll hear many people my age urging you to do what I'm about to urge you to do. But I will say it boldly: "I want you to invest your lives not in keeping the old ship afloat but in designing and building and sailing a new ship for new adventures in a new time in history, as intrepid followers of Jesus Christ. Thank you."*
>
> Neo (McLaren 2001, 21)

basis in China. Local officials are continually amazed by the relationships between the members of the expatriate team and local people. They are also amazed at the NGO's ability to bring in experts in almost any field to work on issues affecting the well-being of Chinese people. The ability to muster these experts comes from the fact that they are all part of the body of Christ. In our globalized world, of which postmodernism is a major component, NGOs are frequently more effective than nation-states, and there are key roles for the body of Christ to play, not as an organization or a corporation but as a community linked by spiritual rather than by economic or political bonds.

ENGAGING THE TREND: HOW SHOULD CHRISTIANS IN MISSIONS ENGAGE POSTMODERNISTS?

How are Christians to deal with the trend of postmodernity in regard to missions? Two areas of discussion are pertinent: recommendations about knowledge and recommendations about culture.

Recommendations about Knowledge

The way forward in the current context is neither insistence on the methods of modernity (positivism) nor the wholesale adoption of postmodern criteria. Paul Hiebert proposes a third way connected to both modernity and postmodernity that he calls critical realism (1999, 63).

> Critical realist epistemology strikes a middle ground between positivism, with its emphasis on objective truth, and instrumentalism, with its stress on the subjective nature of human knowledge. It affirms the presence of objective truth but recognizes that this is subjectively apprehended. . . . It challenges the definition of "rationality" in both positivism and instrumentalism that limits rationality to algorithmic logic. In doing so, critical realism offers a third, far more nuanced, epistemological position. (1999, 69)

Thus, Hiebert asserts that there is such a thing as objective reality but that empirical methods alone will not produce an exhaustive comprehension of it. This reveals his belief that all researchers bring subjectivity, including their cultural biases, to their task. But as he maintains elsewhere, personal and cultural subjectivity does not preclude arriving at real truth (Hiebert 1999, 73–74). He does not claim that objective truth is the result of an investigator's work but that a reliable *correspondence* between the object observed and its reality is possible. This means that in spite of the presence of subjectivity and cultural differences, truth is not simply cultural or relative. Such an understanding avoids the relativism of religious pluralism, which is a mark of postmodern thinking and culture.

Hiebert recommends the community of God's people as the safety net that enables people to avoid falling into subjective error when they strive to solve difficult problems. These problems may be the issues of a postmodern culture. God's people, as an "interpretive community," can come together to consider a given issue from both cultural and biblical perspectives. The meaning of Scripture and its application to the issue lead to a reliable, acceptable decision (1999, 102).

The issue of disputes between widows of diverse cultural background in Acts 6 is one such instance. The conference in Acts 15 dealing with the applicability of Mosaic law in the multicultural New Testament community is another. The checks and balances are theological, anthropological, and translational in nature. The church community is the best corrective to the unavoidable subjectivity found in any one person. As Jesus says, "Every matter may be established by the testimony of two or three witnesses" (Matt. 18:16). Multiple witnesses have historically been the best check on facts, and that continues to be true in the modern scientific and legal communities. It is also true as churches or missionaries try to resolve issues arising from misunderstanding or conflict in any culture, whether postmodern or simply culturally distinct.

Communities are not simply safeguards for correctness or orthodoxy. The church, as a worldwide, culturally diverse community, not only *corrects* but also can and should *contribute* to a more complete understanding of truth. We need to think of the separate cultures of the world as distinct corporate entities. Just as no single person can discover all there is to know about the truth, neither can a single society. The value of wider Christian community deliberation on major issues can be seen in the multinational and multicultural conferences held by the World Evangelical Alliance (WEA) and the Lausanne Committee for World Evangelization (LCWE). These organizations recently deliberated the future of missions at the Iguassu Dialogue (Taylor 2000b), the Nairobi conference on spiritual warfare (Moreau 2002), and the WEA conference on globalization (Tiplady 2003b). These conferences dealt with contemporary issues in mission ministry. The Iguassu Dialogue included significant papers and interaction regarding ministry in the postmodern context.

Cultural Considerations

Rose Dowsett (2000, 355–56) and Paul Hiebert (1999, 111–12) call for critical contextualization in ministry among other cultures—including the postmodern culture. Without ever leaving Europe or North America, Christians are in a missionary situation that requires intercultural insights and skills. What does critical contextualization look like? Essentially, it means helping people understand that the Bible relates to all areas of life. Missionaries must teach the whole of Scripture so that people grasp its entirety. Two ways to do so were developed in widely different cultural settings, but both can be used in the postmodern environment.

First is the chronological Bible teaching approach developed by New Tribes Mission and Trevor McIlwain (1991) called *Firm Foundations*. This approach was originally developed for use among nonliterate traditional peoples in tribal settings but has been adapted for wider use in more developed cultures. *Firm Foundations* starts with Genesis and works its way through the entire biblical story. The use of story is appropriate in postmodern settings in which people are more interested in story than in doctrine. Walk through the Bible (2004) was developed by Bruce Wilkinson initially for use in modern churches to help people obtain a thematic grasp of the sweep of Scripture. Like *Firm Foundations*, it enables participants to condense the entire biblical story, giving them the chance to see the sweep of Scripture and not get bogged down in the details. Its use of body motion, repetition, and story likewise appeals to postmodernists. Hopefully, these two methods will become springboards to new approaches specifically designed for postmodernists. Contemporary emerging church websites offer evidence that such methods are already being developed.

> *Some of the issues which haunt us in the postmodern world, such as responding to pluralism, or living without privileged place in our cultures, or dealing with pervasive pagan spirituality, or having no concept of absolute truth, are issues about which our two-thirds brethren have valuable wisdom. The question is "Are we willing . . . to listen? . . . Can we ask for the help we so badly need?"*
>
> Rose Dowsett (2000, 454)

Much of Europe today is in need of spiritual revitalization. European Christians know this. They have developed innovative evangelistic approaches such as the Alpha program, conceived by Nicky Gumbel (1999). The Alpha program is aimed at postmodern people in post-Christian cultures and capitalizes on the postmodern yearning for reality and the use of story and drama in settings that are relationally warm. Alpha has been used successfully in Europe, North America, and around the globe.

High impact churches have been established in several major cities of Europe, beginning with the Crossroads International Church of Amsterdam. These churches focus on global, English-speaking internationals. Church Associates founder Linus Morris, an American, envisioned churches established for Europeans who have come to believe that Christianity and the church are outdated, irrelevant, insignificant, and boring (Morris 1993). High impact churches attempt to prove the opposite, and they are growing. Begun in 1987, Crossroads now has a membership of over one thousand people, fifty small groups, and several off-site new churches. As the church's website states, "We're about pursuing genuine relationship with Jesus, reverently reaching out to our world, and building an authentic and genuine community. That's our story. We invite you to be a part of it" (Crossroads International Church 2004).

Missionaries cannot, as some postmodernists would like, treat history as if it never happened. Neither do they need to be prisoners of the past. This is a new globalized world. It has never been precisely this way before. Missionaries and ministers in postmodern cultures,

> Emerging churches don't typically look like church as we understand it. They are not "meetingcentric," but shape their "fellowship" around relationships, whether with each other or the people they seek to reach. Sermons, songs, and hymns won't necessarily feature. They may not meet on a Sunday. Their leader may not be called "pastor." The use of drama, multimedia presentations, or ancient symbols may feature. Some will meet in the workplace, café, or leisure center. The governing concern is living for Christ in a way that relates to and engages with the rest of the world and encourages greater interface with those outside the Christian community.
>
> Andy Peck (2004, 21)

realizing that they themselves are influenced by postmodernism, need to sit down with postmodern people and listen to and learn from them.

Christians must be concerned about postmodern people. Those of us who are not postmodernists must pray that we can get past their individuality, even when it seems strange to us. We can embrace—or at least understand—their music. We can rejoice with their love of the mystical. We can join in their tremendous diversity and weep about the brokenness all around them. One thing is certain: We cannot change anything or help anyone without the one for whom and by whom this planet was created, in whom are hidden all the treasures of wisdom

CASE STUDY:
PERPLEXED IN PARIS

Jim Newbar sat in a sidewalk café not far from the River Seine in Paris, France. It was a beautiful spring day, but Jim was feeling anything but spry. In fact, he could almost have cried. He had been in France for a little over two years, time enough to polish up his college French after a few years in seminary preparing for ministry in Europe. He had made some friends in Paris and had begun sharing the gospel with them, but they did not show much interest in what he had to say about religious matters. Jim wondered if the years of biblical and theological training really meant anything in the ministry he had felt so excited about starting.

Back in the United States, he had been quite effective in sharing the gospel. He had been a resident advisor in a secular university before seminary. He had gotten along with the guys in his dorm and had even led a well-attended Bible study every week. What had happened? Was he just in the depths of culture shock? Why did he feel so utterly useless in Europe when he had been confident and effective as a Christian in America?

All his early attempts to share the gospel among the Parisians flooded his mind, and the memories were not pleasant. He remembered asking a young French couple he encountered by the river, "What if you died tonight and were standing at the gates of heaven, and God asked you, 'Why should I let you in?' What would you say?" The couple had quizzical looks on their faces but quickly replied, "That would never happen. God does not exist, nor does heaven. The whole question is irrelevant. Besides, what are you doing bursting in with personal questions like that?" Jim knew a lot of French people were atheists, so he should have anticipated the couple's response.

He remembered another occasion when a neighbor had asked him how he knew God exists. Jim drew on what he remembered from his seminary apologetics class, giving all the philosophical arguments for God's existence. Each had drawn the same blank stares from his neighbor. No one cared about the evidence that meant so much to him.

As he pondered his failures, he realized he needed help. He called Mark, his field director, saying he needed to talk. They set a time, and now it had come. Jim, hunched over the small, round table, poured out his heart. Mark listened carefully, knowing from his own experience the difficulties Jim faced. Finally, Jim was silent. He looked expectantly at Mark. Uttering a quick prayer for wisdom, Mark began to share . . .

and knowledge. That is why, as always, we need a Christ-centered way of knowing in this postmodern generation. Christ's promise is certain: "If anyone is thirsty, let him come to me and drink. Whoever believes in me, as the Scripture has said, streams of living water will flow from within him" (John 7:37–38).

PART 2

The Missional Context

5

The Disappearing Center

From Christendom to Global Christianity

MICHAEL POCOCK

When the twentieth century began, Christianity was still predominantly a Western and Caucasian religion. It was embodied within major church structures and strengthened by its official or majority status in the West. Many evangelical Christians were praying for and expecting "the evangelization of the world in this generation." Colonialism was still strong, with European powers controlling most of Africa, the Indian subcontinent, and Southeast Asia. Advances in modern technology gave almost limitless confidence to its mostly Western possessors. What would the new century bring?

To the disillusionment of millions, two world wars were fought between countries at the heart of Christendom. Widespread defections from biblical faith and even from liberalism occurred among Westerners. The colonial empires of Christendom crumbled. Marxism institutionalized antireligious materialism in Russia, Eastern Europe, and later China. The detractors of Christianity, such as Marxists, believed that faith would die with the older generation. After all, religion was simply the "opiate of the people." Other skeptics thought that Christianity—as the religious arm of Western imperialism—would die with the retreat of the colonial powers. To their amazement, however, Christianity emerged at the end of the century as the largest religion in the world. Most Christians today live and thrive outside the former boundaries of Western Christendom, a development Philip Jenkins calls the next Christendom (2002).

IDENTIFYING THE TREND: GLOBAL CHRISTIANITY

Jesus promised that he would build his church and that the gates of Hades would not overcome it (Matt. 16:18). He also mandated that his disciples move worldwide to make disciples of all nations (Matt. 28:19–20) and that the gospel would in fact be preached in all the world before the end of time (Matt. 24:14). These should have been clues to the inexorable spread of the Christian faith, but nothing in Scripture predicts or explains why Christianity has established itself so strongly in certain areas of the globe. Sociologists of religion are studying that question with interesting results (Montgomery 2002, xi). For our present purposes, it is enough to note that there have been three major shifts in the geographic location of Christendom: (1) During the first one thousand years, Christendom was centered in the eastern half of the Roman Empire; (2) during the next millennium, Christendom was centered in the West; (3) in the third millennium, Christendom has shifted to the south (Buhlmann 1986, 6). Jenkins calls this emergence and growth of Southern Christianity the next Christendom, but it could just as easily be called global Christianity. In the current era of globalization, no phenomenon occurs that does not impact the rest of the world. This is the case with exploding Christianity in the majority world.

Samuel Escobar reflects on his own experience with the emergence of a global church:

> I have met with amazement, wandering prophets of independent African churches, native story tellers from Latin American Pentecostal movements, tireless missionary entrepreneurs spreading through the world from their Korean homeland, Orthodox priests regaining political weight in the lands of what used to be the Soviet empire. . . . They are . . . a living testimony to the remarkable variety of human cultures and the uniqueness of Jesus Christ, which is the one seed of a thousand different plants. (2000b, 27)

Escobar's sense of wonder at the global spread of Christianity has been the experience of many who have had the privilege of travel and ministry abroad. Michael Pocock met Korean Bible translators and Argentine church planters in Chad working with French, Swiss, and American missionaries. He ministered to and learned from believers at a conference of 1,800 Indian missionaries and their supporters of the indigenous Vishwa Vani movement, a group with church-planting ministries across the Indian subcontinent. At the opening of a Christian worship center

---

SIDEBAR 5.1
IMPORTANT TERMS USED IN THIS CHAPTER

evangelicals: In general, Christians who have a strong view of the Bible's authority and who hold to key doctrinal positions. These typically include the deity and virgin birth of Christ, the necessity of his atoning death on the cross and his resurrection for humanity's salvation, and so on (see, for example, the Lausanne Covenant at http://www.lausanne.org).

mainline denominations: The prominent denominations of the nineteenth and twentieth centuries in North America and Europe, including various branches within the Episcopal (Anglican), Presbyterian (and other Reformed groups), Methodist, Lutheran, and United Church of Christ traditions.

---

in a Middle Eastern country, he was struck by the national diversity of over 360 believers gathered to celebrate. He remarked that the congregation looked like a foretaste of Revelation 7:9 when people of every tribe, tongue, and nation will gather to sing God's praise. He invited the people to stand and call out in their own language, as we will all do one day, "Salvation belongs to our God, who sits on the throne, and to the Lamb." In groups of several or many, that cry went out in eighteen languages, from Arabic and Bengali to Swahili and Zulu. These were global Christians, expatriate workers gathered in the

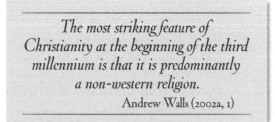

The most striking feature of Christianity at the beginning of the third millennium is that it is predominantly a non-western religion.

Andrew Walls (2002a, 1)

unlikely setting of a Muslim nation. As people from the majority world, they were representative of the new Christendom.

Demographers David Barrett, G. T. Kurian, and Todd Johnson (2001), historiographers Andrew Walls (1996) and Philip Jenkins (2002), sociologist Robert Montgomery (2002), and even the secular media have realized that, far from dying in the past century, the church is thriving at the global level in the third millennium. Patrick Johnstone, who has helped focus the prayer of thousands for world evangelization through *Operation World* (2001), appropriately titled his 1998 book *The Church Is Bigger Than You Think.*

Majority World Christianity Described

In the year 2000, Christians of all kinds constituted one-third of the world's 6 billion people (Barrett, Kurian, and Johnson 2001, 11). During the last decade of the 1900s, the Christian movement grew worldwide

---

SIDEBAR 5.2
WHO IS A CHRISTIAN?

A crucial issue for demographers who want to count adherents of the world's religions is how to define those adherents. The following definitions are used by those who provide the statistics.

1. "Followers of Jesus Christ as Lord, of all kinds, all traditions and confessions, and all degrees of commitment" (Barrett and Johnson 2001, 857).
2. "Those who claimed to be Christian, either by individuals themselves in a government census, or by the churches to which they are affiliated" (Johnstone and Mandryk 2001, xx).
3. "A Christian is someone who describes himself or herself as a Christian, who believes that Jesus is not merely a prophet or an exalted moral teacher, but in some unique sense the Son of God, and the Messiah" (Jenkins 2002, 88).

REFLECTION AND DISCUSSION

1. Given the definitions of a Christian given above, in what ways do the statistics of a particular country represent the true size of the Christian movement in that country?
2. Develop your own definition of a true Christian.

---

by 16.4 million people a year. At the same time, *Operation World* notes "an astonishing shift of the centre of gravity of Christianity in the non-Western world" (2001, 5). Majority world Christians made up 16.7 percent of all Christians in 1900 but 59.4 percent in 2000 (Johnstone and Mandryk 2001, 5).

The pendulum has swung from a majority of the world's Christians living in the West to a majority of them now living outside it. The balance between Western and majority world Christians changed around 1990, although the growth of the majority world movement was discernible starting in the mid-twentieth century. The defection of Western Christians from the faith was not the only reason for this shift. Rather, Christianity has grown outside the West and the North.

CHRISTIAN GROWTH IN AFRICA

Africa was only 25 percent Christian in 1950, but it was 48 percent Christian in 2001. If we consider only sub-Saharan Africa, the figure was closer to 60 percent (Johnstone and Mandryk 2001, 21). There are many indications of the vitality of Christianity in Africa. In Chad, churches of the Evangelical Church of Chad train and send believers for a month of evangelistic outreach among Muslims in northern Chad. In Nigeria, Christians number 58 million, roughly half the population of the country (though the number is hotly debated by Muslims, who maintain that there is a Muslim majority). The Evangelical Churches of West Africa, with 2.5 million members, have over 1,400 missionaries working cross-culturally in Nigeria and overseas (Johnstone and Mandryk 2001, 492).

Theological and pastoral training programs abound at every level in Africa, though more are needed to keep pace with the rapid growth of the Christian movement. At 3.2 percent annual growth, Christian growth outpaces Africa's overall population growth (2.7 percent) (Brierley 1998–99, 1.3). More than 17,000 expatriate missionaries are still present and needed in Africa, but increasingly their roles are in partnerships with Africans in education, relief, development, and theological education. Missionaries deal with AIDS victims, war-ravaged communities, child soldiers, and prostitution (Johnstone and Mandryk 2001, 26). Although expatriate missions played an undeniably large role in stimulating Christian growth in Africa, Andrew Walls suggests that African Christianity is no longer dependent on expatriate assistance for its growth. When he was asked over thirty years ago to found a department of religion at a Nigerian university, he and students surveyed an area about five miles in diameter around the university to discover the presence of churches there. There were 331 churches, and all of them had been started by Africans. Some resulted

> *With an estimated workforce of 25,000 African missionaries today, both in Africa and in the rest of the world, it can rightly be said that missions in Africa is approaching the epidemic level.*
>
> Tokunboh Adeyemo (2000, 266)

from urban migration within the country, others were founded by businesspeople who had been transferred from one part of the country to another, and still others were started by local churches with a church multiplication ministry. This, to Walls, showed the increasingly indigenous nature of the Christian movement in Africa (Walls 1996, xiv).

Philip Jenkins maintains that the growth of Christianity in Africa partly owes to the fact that it originated as and still is a fundamentally majority world religion (Jenkins 2002, 127). New Testament records reveal contacts with Africans who embraced the faith, such as those from Egypt and Libya (Acts 2). Acts 8:26–39 tells the story of Philip and an Ethiopian. Acts 13:1–3 mentions Simeon called Niger and Lucius of Cyrene.

Early church history testifies to the spreading of the faith across the Maghreb of Northern Africa. Africans such as Augustine of Hippo and Tertullian are unforgettable Christians. The faith ran early down the shores of the Red Sea to the Horn of Africa. These ancient North African church movements were nearly decimated with the rise of Islam, but they are proof that early Christianity took root and flourished in Africa.

Early African Christians such as Anthony (AD 300), a hermit monk of Egypt who began the monastic movement that became the characteristic form of deeper spirituality in Europe, and Augustine of Hippo (354–430), whose theological treatises are the foundation of the Roman Catholic Church, show that Christianity was strongest in North Africa before it assumed that status in Europe. Christianity is not a European and Western religion. That is why it should not surprise us that Christianity is once again thriving in Africa and other parts of the majority world. The African Independent Church movement, which sprang up in the twentieth century, is a form of Christianity that is more African than Western and closer in spirit to the earliest Ethiopian form of the faith, for which it was also named. Today, African Independent churches, or Ethiopic churches, have spread to Europe and may influence the direction of Christianity on that continent in the years ahead.

In the twentieth century, after Western missionaries arrived in Africa, some Africans began to see in Scripture practices and concepts that fit with their traditional African understandings of God and the spirit world. The dreams and visions of the prophets and the early church resonated with their own traditional understanding of supernaturally obtained knowledge. Demonization and exorcism, tongues and supernatural healing all seemed familiar, as did suffering for the faith. Missionaries did not need to convince Africans of the existence of God or the realm of the supernatural.

As some Africans read the Bible, however, they were puzzled that the missionaries did not seem to share the sense of readily available spiritual power that the Bible considered normal. Various Africans came to the conclusion that the Western missionaries were less supernaturally oriented than they should have been. Prompted by disappointments with missionaries and an understandable resentment of both colonial control of their society and missionary control of their churches, African Christians started movements collectively called the African Independent Churches (Barrett 1968, 44–63). This organization became African Indigenous Churches and more recently African Initiated Churches. Hereafter, we will simply refer to it as AIC, the most commonly used term.

William Wade Harris arose in 1913 as an early prophet of the AIC movement in the Ivory Coast (Cote d'Ivoire) (Shank 1994). Simon Kimbangu arose as a prophet and a healer in the Belgian Congo (Molyneux 1993; Martin 1978). In southern Africa, the Zionist movement spread (West 1975; Steyne 1978). The African Apostolic Church took root in Zimbabwe, and the Aladura or praise churches of the Seraphim and

Cherubim movement arose in Nigeria (see Anderson 2001 for a contemporary survey). In 2001, there were 9,603 African Independent Church denominations in Africa, with over 86 million followers (Barrett and Johnson 2001, 383).

The AIC found across the continent are vibrant and are growing annually at a rate of almost 4 percent. Many of them are characterized by messianic or prophet figures who provide guidance through supernatural visions, healing, and prayer. Members are often distinctive in their dress, particularly on days of worship, although it is not uncommon in Africa to find women of any church or women's society wearing clothes of the same color and design. As control by Westerners disappeared, some of the AIC became more open to biblical teaching from outside their groups, but they remain largely more supernaturally oriented than their evangelical and mainline counterparts in African Christianity.

GLOBAL IMPACT OF AFRICAN CHRISTIANITY

Many serious problems face Africa, some of which have prompted observers to call the continent not the third world but the "*n*th" world, referring to its chaos (Jenkins 2002). AIDS; wars in Congo, Liberia, and Sierra Leone; intertribal strife in Rwanda and Burundi; and nearly intractable strife in Somalia and Sudan cause many to throw up their hands. Yet African ministries exist that are directed toward healing the social and spiritual scars of these regions. One is ALARM, the African Leadership and Reconciliation Movement, led by Celestin Musekura of Rwanda. In South Africa, the potentially bloody transition to majority rule was ameliorated by Christian leaders such as Michael Cassidy and Bishop Desmond Tutu, who chaired the Truth and Reconciliation Commission following the advent of majority rule and the end of apartheid. African approaches to healing spiritual and social wounds have the potential for being replicated outside Africa where similar strife has torn populations apart, as in Northern Ireland and the Balkans, Southeast Asia, and parts of Latin America.

As the Christian movement in Africa has grown, so has scholarship in the region. John Mbiti, as early as 1970, introduced the world to African religions and philosophy (1970). Byang Kato of Kenya helped Westerners understand theological pitfalls in Africa (1975b). Kwame Bediako of Ghana wrote a book titled *Christianity in Africa: The Renewal of a Non-Western Religion* (1995). While much that is written by African scholars tends to be published in Africa and fails to attract the attention of Western readers, Orbis has made it its mission to bring majority world scholarship to English readers, and the World Evangelical Alliance (WEA) and the Lausanne Committee for World Evangelization (LCWE), through the publication of proceedings of conferences held in Africa and elsewhere outside the West, have brought African Christian reflection before the Western reading public.

Perhaps the picture painted here of Africa seems overly triumphalistic in terms of Christian expansion, but the fact that remarkable growth is occurring is undeniable. At the same time, Christianity in Africa faces major challenges as Islam expands from the north, around East and West Africa, across the Sahel, and down the east coast of the continent. It is estimated that 41.3 percent of the population of Africa is Muslim, while 48.4 percent is Christian. The growth rate of Christianity is only fractionally ahead of that of Islam (Johnstone and Mandryk 2001, 21), but the figures belie the earlier laments that the future of Africa would be Muslim (Jenkins 2002, 5).

CHRISTIAN GROWTH IN ASIA

Michael Jaffarian states that Christianity is the majority religion on five of the six continents of the world. Asia is the lone exception. While the percentage of Christians is small in comparison to the other continents, it has increased from 2.3 percent in 1900 to 8.5 percent in 2002 (2002, 16–31).

The presence of Christians in Asia varies from country to country. The Philippines is 93 percent Christian. South Korea is 31.6 percent Christian, and there are 12,000 Korean missionaries serving overseas. Indonesia, the world's most populous Muslim country, is 16 percent Christian and has experienced major movements to Christ since 1965. The People's Republic of China has the largest nonreligious population—almost 50 percent of 1.2 billion people. Christians make up as much as 7.25 percent of the population, which equals 91.5 million people. India, with 1 billion inhabitants, is 2.4 percent Christian, which is 25 million people. Most of these people live in the extreme southern and northeastern parts of the country, where they constitute between 20 and 30 percent of the population. This contrasts with the extreme north of Jammu and Kashmir, where Christians account for .16 percent of the population (Johnstone and Mandryk 2001).

As on the African continent, Christianity arrived early in Asia, having begun on its western fringes. Churches were established in India as early as the first or second century. The Mar Toma church of south India traces its founding to the apostle Thomas. He certainly could have arrived there by either land or sea routes known to traders at the time.

The Nestorians, a Syrian Christian movement, trace their roots to the fourth century. They fell from favor among Western Christians over differences in describing the relationship of Christ to the Father and Mary's status as the mother of Christ. They ministered in Mesopotamia, Persia, and India and traveled along the Silk Road, a trade route extending from Antioch in Syria to the heart of China before AD 650 (Gillman and Klimkeit 1999, 268). Chinese and Mongol emperors and later Indian Moguls all had Christian wives at one time or another.

There was considerable interaction between Christians from Asia Minor and those from East Asia from the earliest years of the Christian era, but Christianity never reached critical mass anywhere in East Asia before the sixteenth century, except perhaps in China between the seventh and the eighth century. Christians were present in Asia as traders, slaves, and wives and seem to have exerted some influence on rulers and even possibly on the religions with which they came in contact. Samuel Larsen has shown extensive early contacts between Christians and Buddhists in the area today known as Iran and Afghanistan. Mahayana Buddhism sprang up in the first century after Christ and contains a number of concepts similar to those of Christianity that were not present in older forms of Buddhism (Larsen 2002, 14). Today, Mahayana Buddhism predominates in Asia.

If Christianity originated in the Middle East and spread and became influential in Asia from such early times, as Samuel Larsen (2002) and Samuel Moffett (1998, 24–39) maintain, then it should not be considered or dismissed as merely a Western religion.

GLOBAL IMPACT OF ASIAN CHRISTIANITY

Though Asian Christianity is uneven in representation from nation to nation, it is remarkably strong, influencing many other parts of the world. The largest individual congregations of each of the traditional mainline denominations are in Seoul, Korea. The world's largest Pentecostal church, the Yoido Full Gospel Church of Pastor Paul Yonggi Cho, has over five hundred thousand members. The church's Prayer Mountain Retreat Center is visited by believers from all over the world. Its approach to ministry is constantly studied, and the cell group approach to church planting and church life pioneered by Cho (1981) has its champions around the world. Heterodox movements that consider themselves Christian, such as the Unification Church of Sung Myung Moon, have also become worldwide movements.

Evangelical Koreans such as Bong Rin Ro have helped both Asian and Western churches understand the contribution of Asians to theology through publication of the Asia Theological Association's series on Asian Christian theology. This series brought together the thinking of Asian Christians from Thailand, India, Taiwan, Sri Lanka, the Philippines, and Japan (Ro and Eshenauer 1984). Major mission consultations such as the Global Consultation on World Evangelization (GCOWE) held in Singapore in 1989 and Seoul in 1995 helped to set the agenda for reaching unreached peoples as part of the AD 2000 and Beyond Movement.

The Japanese church makes up only 1.56 percent of the population, but Japanese Roman Catholic author Shusaku Endo has written some of the most influential novels in Japan that are also recognized in the West. His *Silence* (1976) and *Samurai* (1982) ask deep theological questions about where God is when his people suffer and also recall the pivotal time when Christianity, after spreading widely in Japan, was crushed in the mid-seventeenth century. Although severe limitations have been placed on Chinese Christian writing in the past fifty years, the devotional life and writings of Watchman Nee are known worldwide.

The expansion of the house church movement in China is the fulfillment of what John Nevius recommended in his call for self-governing, self-propagating, and self-supporting churches as the key to growth in the Chinese context (1958). In the hands of the Holy Spirit and through the faithfulness of Chinese Christians, the three-self principle became the tool of amazing church growth in China. No wonder house churches have become the mode of choice for many agencies, including the International Mission Board of the Southern Baptist Convention (Garrison 1999), as they attempt to start not simply churches but church-planting movements around the world.

> *We Indian Christians are at a crucial and complex juncture in our history. Old categories of missiology and the latest fads from abroad won't do any good anymore. Any methodology that is one step removed from incarnational involvement in the life of our people just won't work.*
>
> Joseph D'Souza (2000, 404)

The church in India has produced its share of influential servants and communicators who have made an impact within and beyond the subcontinent. Voices from India resounded in the West as early as 1910 at the World Missionary Conference in Edinburgh, when the only Indian present called for friendship between majority world missionaries and their Indian counterparts (Walls 2003). Condescension had more frequently characterized relationships in what was still the colonial era. Evangelical Indians such as Samuel Kamaleson and K. N. Nambudripad addressed the first Lausanne Consultation in 1974 (Douglas 1975, 47–56, 790–97). Their dedication and scholarship were evident. Indians have continued to contribute regularly to international exchanges such as the Iguassu Dialogue of 1999 held in Latin America (Taylor 2000b). There K. Rajendran (2000) and Joseph D'Souza (2000) offered prophetic and penetrating analyses of Indian and world events and their effect on missions. Most importantly, they were not telling *Westerners* how to do missions; they were speaking to a *global* church. They are a part of missions in their own country, but, like Ajith Fernando of Sri Lanka, they also expound a missionary theology that challenges at the global level. These are not simply academicians but activists in leading ministries such as Youth for Christ, Operation Mobilization, and major Indian social and educational programs.

As proof that we have moved from Western to truly global Christianity, majority world Christians are present and ministering powerfully in the West. At the same time, they continue to influence their home countries. Ravi Zacharias is well known in the field of Christian apologetics. Ramesh Richard teaches at Dallas Theological Seminary and spearheads ministries that equip leaders and impact opinion makers worldwide. Sam George is typical of the growing category of middle-class Indian business and professional Christians who understand emerging, younger Indians and reach out in the often tense context of our global situation (2003a). K. P. Yohannan has mobilized thousands of Indian missionaries known as Non-Resident Indians (NRI), resourcing them from the West through Gospel for Asia. Together with outstanding leaders who live in India, such as Emil Jebasingh of Transworld Radio and Thinagaren Richard of Vishwa Vani, they are making a global difference because they link resources to needs inside and outside their local situations.

CHRISTIAN GROWTH IN LATIN AMERICA

Unlike Africa and Asia, Latin America knew no contact with Christianity until 1500. When contact came, it was through the Spaniards and the Portuguese, who had spent seven hundred years in conflict with Islam in their own countries. When they arrived in the New World, they were confronted with a continent of non-Christian yet highly developed peoples. They applied their method of relating to Muslims to the Indians. Such violence, combined with their lust for gold, land, power, and privilege, caused the Indians to be confronted with what Luis Rivera has called *A Violent Evangelism* (1992).

The Spanish and Portuguese crowns granted settlers land in the New World and with it the responsibility to evangelize and civilize the indigenous peoples. This put the principal exploiters of the indigenous peoples in charge of ministry to them, clearly a conflict of interest.

Thankfully, some of the Roman Catholic religious orders grasped the enormity of the problem. The saintly and insistent Bartolemé de las Casas, genuinely touched by the Spirit, documented the horrors visited upon the Indians by the *conquistadores* and landed gentry. He gained an appointment from Cardinal Jimenez y Cisneros as Protector of the Indies in 1520 (Tuck 2005) and began a new approach to evangelization and Indian relations. His work began a new era of Roman Catholic missions in Latin America that realized some major triumphs, such as the Jesuit work in the eighteenth century along the border of Brazil and

Paraguay, made famous, though portrayed as ultimately unworkable, in the movie *The Mission*.

Christianity, in its Roman Catholic form, captured almost all but the rain forests of Latin America by the twentieth century. Because of the Catholic Inquisition, which controlled the internal quality of Catholicism and excluded all non-Catholic influence from the sixteenth into the nineteenth century, there was no substantial Protestant presence in Latin America until the twentieth century. In the late nineteenth century, Catholic liberals grew tired of the isolation and antidevelopmental ideas institutionalized by conservatives through the Inquisition. Political liberals sided with Nicholas Penzotti, a Protestant Bible distributor, in Peru. A legal case had been brought against Penzotti by the authorities because of his Bible distribution ministry. Penzotti won the case, and the first legal foothold for disseminating evangelical ideas was established. Evangelical missions quickly became involved in Latin America.

Though Latin America is still overwhelmingly Roman Catholic (79 percent), non-Catholic Christians (Protestants, Anglicans, and Independents, often together called *evangélicos*) constitute almost 12 percent of all Latin American and Caribbean people (Johnstone and Mandryk 2001, 33). In many countries, evangelical numbers are even stronger. Guatemala and El Salvador each lead with 26 percent (including Pentecostals, Independents, and Anglicans). Chile has 16 percent, Brazil has 12.5 percent, and Venezuela has 11 percent. Paraguay and Uruguay are an anomaly with their secular orientation. They contain less than 50 percent Roman Catholics and 6 to 7 percent evangelicals. Over 25 percent of the people are nonreligious (Johnstone and Mandryk 2001).

The Pentecostal movement in Latin America began early in the twentieth century, almost immediately after its appearance at the Azusa Street revival in Los Angeles in 1906. Methodist missionaries present at the Los Angeles meetings took what would become the global spiritual phenomenon of the century to Chile in 1906. Today, almost 23 percent of the Protestant movement in Latin America is either Pentecostal or charismatic.

Evangelicals struggled in Latin America until the 1960s. Then began their astronomical growth, and missionary ministry was a key. In 1956, the martyrdom of five missionaries in Ecuador, including Jim Elliot, galvanized evangelical interest in Latin America. Elisabeth Elliot's books about the Aucas (now known as the Waorani) attracted thousands to ministries in South America. When Michael Pocock and his wife began their ministry in Latin America in 1971, most of the 150 missionaries in language school in Costa Rica had been at least partly motivated by reading Elliot's *Through Gates of Splendor* (1958).

The evangelical movement in Latin America grew from 1 percent in 1900 to 12 percent in 2001—from 700,000 people to 55 million. With an annual growth rate of 4 percent, evangelical numbers are increasing over twice as fast as the general population (Johnstone and Mandryk 2001, 34).

GLOBAL IMPACT OF LATIN AMERICAN CHRISTIANITY

The global impact of Latin American Christianity can be seen through five lenses: liberation theology, theological education by extension (TEE), Pentecostalism, Latin American evangelists, and Latin Americans in missions.

Liberation Theology

Latin American social and economic development has been plagued by conservatism, corruption, and the tendency of the Roman Catholic Church to guard the status quo and privileges of the elite. In 1968, at the Bishops Conference in Medellín, Colombia, Gustavo Gutiérrez, himself a priest, launched a searing critique of the church and its antidevelopmental stance. Gutiérrez had received part of his training in Europe and was attracted to the theology of Jürgen Moltmann and other existential theologians. Gutiérrez extolled the sacrificial model of Dietrich Bonhoeffer, who criticized the German church for failing to stand up to the Nazis and was killed by them. Gutiérrez was also influenced by the socioeconomic analysis of Marxism that attributed the poverty of the masses to oppression by the socially and economically elite. Gutiérrez put all this together in his influential work *A Theology of Liberation* (1973).

Across Latin America, socially concerned theologians, especially Catholics and liberal Protestants, flocked to Gutiérrez's ideas. Mortimer Arias, Juan Luis Segundo, Hugo Assman, Camilo Torres, and many others wrote and acted on the theme of liberation theology. Gutiérrez's ideas challenged the entrenched Catholic Church and became part of the ideological foundation of armed movements of liberation, even though few liberationists actually advocated violence. They did, however, create a climate in which a synthesis seemed possible between Marxism and Christianity. During the twentieth century, most of the revolutionary movements for social change in Latin America had a Marxist basis, and the yearning for a more equitable distribution of wealth in Latin America was clearly legitimate. Latin American liberation theology attracted a great deal of attention outside the continent, but after the collapse of Marxism worldwide in the late 1980s, it turned to concern over gender and sexuality issues.

Evangelicals were almost totally opposed to the ideas of liberation theology, but there were exceptions. Orlando Costas (1974), Emilio Núñez (1985), and William Taylor (Núñez and Taylor 1989, 19), together with

René Padilla and Samuel Escobar, came to grips with the legitimate question asked by liberation theology: What is the social responsibility of the church in a situation of oppression?

Theological Education by Extension (TEE)

Although evangelicals, Latino or expatriate, frowned on the liberationist trend, it did have an influence on them. The problem of the liberationists was how to educate the peasant *campesinos* they were trying to mobilize on behalf of their own improvement. Clearly, they were not to be taught in ordinary schools. Education would have to be taken to them in the villages and the fields. This was also the problem of missionaries. If evangelical leaders had to be trained in seminaries, usually located in big cities, how were there ever going to be enough trained leaders?

In Mexico, Ivan Illich had written a classic that became required reading even in secular education classes in North America: *De-schooling Society* (1970). He argued that the best and most crucial education does not happen in the classroom but in actual situations of life, the very point liberationists had made about learning theology. Brazilian Paulo Friere, another voice of liberation theology, wrote *Pedagogy of the Oppressed* (1986). In it he attempted to answer the question, How do poverty-stricken people learn? Again, this was the same question facing evangelicals in training largely poor Latin American believers and leaders. Out of this ferment, expatriate missionaries in Latin America such as Ralph Winter, Ross Kinsler, Kenneth Mulholland, and Sam Rowen developed the TEE approach. The Theological Education by Extension movement began in the 1970s in Central America as a response to the need of rural pastors and those without extensive formal education. These pastors needed to obtain preparation in ministry without leaving their homes, jobs, or churches to study in centralized seminaries or Bible colleges. TEE enabled them to receive training otherwise unobtainable. TEE spread rapidly to Africa and Asia, where similar challenges faced leadership trainers.

Pedagogy was not the only level at which liberation theology challenged Latin America and the world. Liberationists' concerns for God's action in the concrete historical situation forced evangelicals to think about the holistic element inherent in the idea of God's shalom (peace) but that had become marginalized in their effort to maintain the priority of evangelism in missions. Evangelicals feared that social concern, if ever raised to the level of structural change, would cause them to lose their emphasis on evangelistic ministry. This was admittedly something to consider since many evangelicals believed the liberal social gospel had caused many mainline denominations to lose their missionary fervor.

Beginning with Lausanne 1974, Latino evangelicals such as René Padilla, Emilio Núñez, and Samuel Escobar (Douglas 1975) challenged other evangelicals to see evangelism in its biblical wholeness. Salvation is certainly liberation from sin, but it is also liberation from the kingdom of darkness and entrance into a life distinct from the sinful patterns of the world. The voices of these Latino brothers and others caused John Stott to think, write, and speak more openly about the social dimension of Christian responsibility (Stott 1975).

Pentecostalism

As mentioned earlier, Pentecostalism had a large impact on Latin America, but Latin America's Pentecostalism and later charismatic movements have also influenced the world. Pentecostals and charismatics have always felt that their influence has to do with recognizing the Holy Spirit's place in empowering life and ministry. They clearly believe that what God did in the New Testament he can do today. They live in daily expectation of divine intervention in their lives and service. They are evangelistically oriented, and their churches are growing.

Peter Wagner, former professor at Fuller Theological Seminary and a key North American exponent of the church growth movement, became greatly interested in Pentecostal gains in Latin America. Although he earlier prefaced statements about the Pentecostal movement with "I am not a Pentecostal," he was clearly appreciative, and it shows in books such as *Look Out! The Pentecostals Are Coming* (1973). He later reflected on his debt to Pentecostalism in "Contemporary Dynamics of the Holy Spirit in Missions" (1997, 107–22). It was not Wagner's exposure to Pentecostal writers in North America but his research into Pentecostal growth in Latin America that opened him to supernatural factors and dependence on the Holy Spirit in matters of church growth. Wagner has been an influential exponent of prayer walks, spiritual mapping, and related missiological issues worldwide, and it was a Latin American movement that prepared the way.

Latin American Evangelists

In the realm of evangelistic ministry, Luis Palau was perhaps the first Latin American to gain a wide hearing outside the continent of his birth. Beginning in the late 1960s, he launched evangelistic campaigns in both South and North America and eventually in Europe, Asia, and Africa. Luis Bush likewise enjoyed a worldwide hearing. Perhaps his greatest contribution was focusing the evangelical world's attention on completing the Great Commission when he took over leadership of the AD 2000 and Beyond Movement (Bush 2000). Whether traditional evangelicals such as Palau, Bush, and Padilla or charismatics such as

Juan Carlos Ortiz and Carlos Annacondia, Latin evangelists are making an impact at the global level.

Latin Americans in Missions

In the realm of missiology, from COMIBAM I (Missionary Conference of Iberian-Americans) in Brazil in 1987 to the Iguassu Dialogue held in Brazil in 1999, Latin American and other majority world missiologists have been helping to guide the world mission enterprise. Latin America is no longer simply a missionary *receiving* continent. It is also a *sending* continent. Six thousand Latin American missionaries work cross-culturally within the continent, and almost four thousand work outside its borders (Johnstone and Mandryk 2001, 34). Missiologists such as Valdir Steuernagel, Samuel Escobar, Alex Araujo, Antonia Van der Meer, Norberto Saracco, and Rudy Girón, all natives of Latin America, made valuable missiological contributions at Iguassu.

Samuel Escobar called missiologists to a deeper trinitarian understanding of the missionary task (2000a, 114–20). He criticized Western "managerial missiology" (2000a, 109–12), in which business and corporate work styles eclipse spiritual dynamics, and he called for more holistic and incarnational approaches (2000a, 112–14). He envisioned an approach to missions that allows for local initiatives and does not wait for proclamation and directions from the perceived centers of missiological endeavor. Valdir Steuernagel (2000, 123–32) agreed with Escobar, adding that missions should be involved in issues of justice and the political process on behalf of the poor and marginalized. Norberto Saracco (2000, 357–66) called for the mobilization of every member of every church across entire nations as a way to saturate a people with the gospel. In this he followed the pioneering work of Kenneth Strachan, who as a missionary of the Latin America Mission launched the strategy of "Evangelism in Depth" (1968). This missionary approach was applied across the continent by Latin Americans and inspired other networking ministries that have been implemented around the world such as DAWN (Discipling a Whole Nation). They were joined by mission mobilizers from new mission organizations in Latin America such as Fraternidad de Apoyo Misionero (FAM), led by Abel Morales from Guatemala.

EVALUATING THE TREND: MAJORITY WORLD CHRISTIANITY AND GLOBAL MISSIONS

Global Christianity Is a Testament to Missionary Faithfulness

The ultimate explanation of any spiritual success is God and his Holy Spirit. The Lord Jesus Christ sends people into the world, and he deserves the glory for whatever progress is made in spreading the gospel. But missionaries are the instruments God uses. Philip Jenkins has recognized and catalogued the tremendous reality of Christian expansion in *The Next Christendom*. Speaking of the earlier stage of missions from the West, Jenkins writes, "Whatever their image in popular culture, Christian missionaries of the colonial era succeeded remarkably" (2002, 56). K. Rajendran summarizes the contribution of missionaries—from the early Jesuits to William Carey and others—in India: "They revolutionized India by preaching the gospel, winning people for Christ, discipling, establishing churches, igniting social changes and even influencing the Freedom Movement. These missionaries had much to do with building modern India and with developing a new ethos in the country through their many social endeavors" (2000, 308).

Rajendran emphasizes that the regeneration of lost people was the single most significant missionary accomplishment, but he also cites Kushwant Singh, a secular journalist, who says:

> More far-reaching than the number of converts it [Protestantism] made was the influence of Protestantism on Hinduism. Protestants took active part in the suppression of *sati* [widow burning], ending female infanticide, and suppressing the thugs; alleviating the condition of Hindu widows and temple prostitutes and raising [the level of] marriage. (2000, 308)

Similar positive evaluations can be found throughout the literature summarizing the missionary endeavor, which has led to the phenomenon of a strong and vibrant church more centered in the Southern Hemisphere than in the Northern.

There were, no doubt, failures among missionaries. They assumed too readily that their Western culture was linked to Christianity and that therefore Western culture needed to spread with the faith. Jenkins has noted that as Christianity spread in Europe, it actually mixed with existing pagan culture, melding the church's festivals with established pagan celebrations and pagan deities with Christian saints. Even church buildings reflected cultural norms (2002, 109–11). The Christianity of the North and the West continued to transmute itself, yet after two thousand years, the emerging Southern Christianity is fundamentally identical to the New Testament roots from which it sprang. Ralph Winter reflects on the contribution of missionaries, saying, "When I reflect on the sacrificial service of these early missionaries, I ask myself if I, or any of my colleagues, would be willing to do the same today, knowing for certain that it would take me to an early grave" (Winter and Hawthorne 1999, 255).

Global Christianity Is a Testament to Majority World Christians

Western missionaries and the churches that send them are certainly one key to the modern spread of the gospel around the globe. But as already shown, Christianity spread outside the West early, and many communities of Christians survived throughout the ages. Now that the faith has achieved critical mass in the majority world, it is clear that indigenous believers are also key to the growth of the movement. This is true in China, India, Africa, and Latin America. National believers constitute part or all of evangelistic teams, Bible translation teams, church leadership, and theological training programs. Christians from majority world churches now send thousands of the world's cross-cultural missionaries. Even though many of these work within their own countries, they do so in other cultures and languages.

Missionary activity at the global level is robust and growing. Majority world churches and their missionaries are fully involved. This is wonderful news, but it is still tempered by the fact that, on the whole, missionaries go where it is legally possible, relatively safe, and bearable to live. This means that most are not deployed to unreached peoples in Muslim, Hindu, or Buddhist cultures or among the very poor. More cross-cultural missionaries from Western and majority world churches are needed who will find ways to live sacrificial lives among the unreached (Jaffarian 2002, 28). At this point, such missionaries are more likely to come from majority world churches. This is because many unreached poor people live in culturally diverse countries like India. Missionaries from these countries can legally move within their own national boundaries to live and witness among those without Christ.

MAJORITY WORLD CHURCHES ARE THE HOPE OF THEIR NATIONS

Nations such as Japan, Singapore, South Korea, and Taiwan are prosperous and stable countries, but many people live in chronic crisis situations. Chaos and disorder reign in large parts of Africa, Asia, Latin America, and southeastern Europe. Despite being reviled by Muslims and Hindus, Christians are the only speck of light. As indicated in chapter 1, assistance for communities in need often comes not from governments but from or through churches in needy communities and churches in other countries. After being in Mozambique, *New York Times* columnist Nicholas Kristof (2003b) explained that, while he disagrees with evangelical doctrines and is not in fact a Christian, he had to admit that the only hope among the poorest of the poor in most of Africa was the Christian churches and missionaries and their health programs. In the Middle East, Jordanian Christians of Manara Ministries distribute food relief and books in both Iraq and the Palestinian West Bank. They have helped over 1,850 families in Baghdad, Mosul, and Kirkuk (Reapsome 2002, 1).

In addition, nongovernment organizations, frequently Christian, provide more services in many majority world countries than governments are able to deliver. Many of the hospitals established by Western mission agencies now function effectively under national Christian direction and staffing. As Steven Fouch says, "Today there are thousands of hospitals, clinics and healthcare projects around the globe set up and run by various Christian groups. India alone can boast over a thousand Christian hospitals, now run almost exclusively by the national church" (2003, 125). He offers encouraging case studies of churches and communities that have linked up to solve major health challenges in Africa and Asia.

Whether it is basic education, protection of children, community organization, reconciliation following wars, empowerment of women, enhancement of family solidarity, or help in forming sustainable small businesses, Christianity in majority world areas provides hope and care for communities. It is time the secular world and Muslim, Hindu, and Buddhist majority governments recognize this reality and rejoice with those who are being helped. Thank God, some of them already do.

MAJORITY WORLD CHRISTIANITY RESTORES SUPERNATURAL EXPECTATION TO THE CHURCH

"If there is a single key area of faith and practice that divides Northern and Southern Christians, it is the matter of spiritual forces and their effects on the everyday human world" (Jenkins 2002, 123). Jenkins is not referring simply to what Paul Hiebert has called "the excluded middle" of demons and spiritual forces (1982) but to a heightened sense of expectation of God's intervention in daily affairs. This has clearly been a part of all three waves of the Spirit in the twentieth century, which have influenced the global church and missiology. But it also characterizes biblical Christians throughout the majority world church. This supernaturalism makes a lot of Western Christianity look like the Deism of the Enlightenment, in which it was thought that God, if he existed, had started the world and left it to run by immutable natural laws. God is a more distant God in the West than in the rest of the world.

The supernatural orientation of majority world churches manifests itself in more fervent, frequent, and lengthier prayer. Koreans are famous for it, but one can see it elsewhere. Michael Pocock vividly remembers the start of a drive to a distant town in Chad. He normally begins journeys with a word of prayer, asking God for safety. The Chaddian believers and missionaries got down on their knees in the sand for ten minutes, fervently imploring God to keep him safe. The greater the exposure to danger, the clearer the knowledge that the mercy of God is needed. He weeps when he recalls the faith and kindness of missionaries and the president of the national church in Chad, who traveled all the way to where he lay miserable with dysentery and sang:

> He is able, He is able,
> I know God is able,
> I know God is able
> to carry you through.

That is the God the majority world church and those who work among them know. It is the God with whom many of us need to be reacquainted. And, by the way, he *did* carry Mike through.

MAJORITY WORLD CHRISTIANS MAY SAVE WESTERN CHRISTIANITY

Global migrations have brought people from the former European empires to Western Europe. The United Kingdom has 1.2 million Muslims and many ethnic groups and other world religions. Germany has 1.6 million Turks, half a million Kurds, and over a quarter of a million Arabs. Overall, more foreign-born Muslims live in Europe than any other group (Johnstone and Mandryk 2001). Latin America has substantial populations of foreign-born people, including Japanese, Chinese, and Europeans. North America, likewise, has an immense immigrant population. All this migration brings millions of non-Christians from the majority world into contact with Westerners, who in many cases are living in post-Christian situations. All of them need to be reached for Christ.

The good news is that the growth of majority world Christianity combined with migration fired by the globalization process has brought a vibrant Christianity back to areas where faith of any kind was hard to find. J. A. B. Jongeneel says that the Christian migrants in Europe are not

> just an appendix to the established congregations and churches in Europe. They have their own identity, take their own initiatives, and show leadership: their enthusiasm and experiential knowledge of the non-Christian religions and ideologies pave a new way in missions and evangelism. . . . Migrant Christians . . . can help established Christianity in Europe to renew its mission and evangelism. (2003, 29–33)

Samuel Escobar, who ministers in Spain, asserts, "Spain has moved beyond secularism to paganism" (2003, 21). In recent visits to Spain, Michael Pocock met African believers who are respected elders in Spanish Brethren assemblies. They bring a new joy and enthusiasm to the church. With a team of students, he attended a gospel music concert in which a choir of 250 Spaniards sang marvelous African American and Swahili gospel songs. Over 2,500 people from the community attended. Churches established by the Evangelical Alliance Mission in France some time ago were able to draw big crowds when they advertised a Christmas pageant in which children of 14 nationalities played the parts. All the children lived in the local community.

Virtually every continent in the world participates in the modern migratory "dance." It should be our prayer that the fervor of majority world believers will be infectious and will reignite the lost passions of the Western world. There are solid indications that this is already happening.

The Majority World Christian Movement Should Be Alert to Syncretism

Syncretism is the attempt to mix two otherwise incompatible elements in a single new reality. It is usually unintentional, a by-product of two or more distinct movements rubbing against each other and coming to a blended compromise. It is manifest in every religious movement. At the individual level, it is much like Christians who attempt to live partly according to God's way of doing things and partly according to their own or the world's. Westerners are just as guilty of syncretism as anyone else. We have tried to mix Enlightenment versions of modernity with biblical truth.

Majority worlders can do the same in their environments. Majority world believers need to recognize that the prevalence of spirit orientation in some of their cultures does not necessarily mean that those cultures have rightly understood the powers.

Do majority world Christians understand the danger of syncretism as it relates to spiritual warfare? Many do, and their perspectives are being shared. Escobar looks at evangelical missiology in the future and calls us all to the statement of the Lausanne Committee of 1992 (repeated and enlarged at the LCWE 2000 Consultation at Nairobi; Moreau 2002b), which recognized the reality of spiritual warfare but noted, "There is a danger that we revert to think and operate on pagan worldviews or on undiscerning application of Old Testament analogies that were in fact superceded in Christ" (Escobar 2000a, 115).

The urge to make Christianity understood and accepted among those of other world religions must not lead us to compromise major elements of the faith, such as the uniqueness and full deity of Christ; the finality, authority, and sufficiency of the canonical Scriptures; and the reality that Christ died for the church (Eph. 5:25). We must always seek to live in community. No Christian's life should be lived alone. As the majority world church finds itself in the midst of sometimes hostile communities, majority world Christians must find ways to exalt Christ, study the Word, and fellowship with one another as God intended.

REFLECTING ON THE TREND: HOW DOES SCRIPTURE HELP US UNDERSTAND AND RESPOND TO GLOBAL CHRISTIANITY?

Jesus Said It Would Happen

The emergence of a truly global church, at this point growing strongest in the South and the East, is integral to the promises of God. Not only did Jesus send his disciples out to make disciples of all peoples, promising that he would build his church against all odds, even hell itself, but the entire Bible is a record of this movement. God promised that out of Abraham he would make a nation that would be the channel of blessing to every nation (Gen. 12:1–4). This promise was of such transcendent importance that it was repeated five times in Genesis and served as the basis for Paul's understanding of his cross-cultural missionary endeavor (Gal. 3:6–29). We expect God to fulfill his promise, and he is doing so.

> *Looking at Christianity as a planetary phenomenon, not merely a Western one, makes it impossible to read the New Testament in quite the same way ever again.*
>
> Philip Jenkins (2002, 220)

Although 2 billion people still do not have a church among them, God's salvation in Christ has been preached among the majority of the world's peoples, offering hope that the Great Commission will be completed, perhaps in our own day. The body of Christ is forming in every part of the globe and in agreement with the promise to Abraham (Gen. 12:1–3): God is *blessing* the peoples of the world through his people. Global Christians are sharing the gospel, binding up wounds, and providing stability to communities in need. Those who were dead in their sins and to their Creator are being raised to new life in Christ. It sounds similar to what Jesus told John's disciples when they asked if Jesus was the real thing (Matt. 11:1–11).

We Have Some Things to Learn

There are three important lessons we can draw from the work God is doing in raising up the majority world church with such force in the modern context.

First, God works in mysterious ways. Although the growth of Christianity should be almost self-evident, many Christians seem unaware of the extent of what God is doing. This can be true even of missionaries. When Michael Pocock served in Venezuela, he was not a global Christian. He disobeyed Paul's injunction, "Each of you should look not only to your own interests, but also to the interests of others" (Phil. 2:4). He did not concern himself with what was going on in Japan, China, or Nigeria. His task was to reach Venezuela. He has since awoken to what God is doing and has made it his mission to produce Christian workers at Dallas Theological Seminary who will be nothing less than global Christians.

If Christian missionaries can be myopic, what about the rest of the world, Christian or secular? Jesus exhorted his disciples to look at the fields because they were white and ready to be harvested (Matt. 9:38). But many of us have not noticed that the fields are ready. It took the exhortation of George Verwer of Operation Mobilization to help the Interdenominational Foreign Mission Association executives in the late 1970s realize that God was doing something truly amazing in China. He implored those at a meeting in New Jersey to beg God every day to continue that work and to open up that great nation. The massive house church movement in China took many by surprise. Is this a commentary on our blindness, or is there a spiritual dynamic we have not understood?

Jesus said that the growth of his kingdom would be quiet, sometimes imperceptible. He used metaphors such as the mustard seed, the hidden pearl and treasure, and the quiet and variable growth rate of seeds to help his hearers understand the way God works (Matt. 13:1–52). This is a point we need to understand: Jesus was not simply describing the kingdom of heaven. We would better understand these parables if we heard Jesus saying at the beginning of each one, "Let me tell you how God works." As Western Christians wake up to the movement of God at the global level, we need to ask if he is telling us something we do not know. Do people redeemed in circumstances of poverty, violence, and chaos have anything to tell us?

Second, God is triune and transcendent yet close to his creation. Missiologists should carefully peruse the work of Sri Lankan Ajith Fernando. He lays afresh the foundation of mission in Scripture and biblical trinitarianism (2000, 189–256). Many missiologists have traced God's work back to the call of Abraham (e.g., Kaiser 1996, 1999, 2000), and rightly so. They have shown that the missionary enterprise flows from the way God is. He is a *missionary* God. But Fernando shows what it means that this God of Scripture is a *Triune* God. How, for example, does God's trinitarian nature affect the body of Christ and cause ordinarily hostile groups to get along? This is a real issue wherever cultures are in conflict. Fernando shows that God is himself a community of three. This community is reflected in the universal human desire of people to relate to one another. But only through the work of Christ can a redeemed community, the body of Christ, achieve what sin among unregenerate people stops them from becoming. Paul mentions the role of the Father and the Spirit in addition to that of Christ in Ephesians 2:18. The trinitarian nature of the Godhead is the ground, model, and means of the community that exists among believers from diverse cultures.

The twin attributes of God, his transcendence and his immanence, his greatness and his immediate presence and involvement with humankind and his creation, are more clearly grasped by majority world Christians than by many in the West. Westerners such as Francis Schaeffer emphasized the "infinite-personal" nature of God in an attempt to correct the distant, almost deistic stance of many Westerners (1969). Many theologians, however, generally have a tendency to emphasize the transcendent aspect of God, while ordinary people are concerned with whether God acts today on behalf of those he loves.

> *He [Christ] himself is our peace, who has made the two one and has destroyed the barrier, the dividing wall of hostility. . . . His purpose was to create in himself one new man out of the two, thus making peace, and in this one body to reconcile both of them to God through the cross, by which he put to death their hostility. . . . For through him [Christ] we both have access to the Father by one Spirit.*
>
> Ephesians 2:14–18

The God of the Bible is not only the Lord of all creation, the one who is incomprehensible unless he reveals himself to people. He is also the God who has even the hairs on our heads numbered. He is the God who helps barren women conceive and heals those who are sick in answer to prayer. He sends his Spirit to guide and comfort those who believe. He knows all the nations and even puts people where they are—which is never far from God himself. He is the one of whom pagans said and Paul affirmed, "In him we live and move and have our being" (Acts 17:28). This is the God to whom people of the majority world are turning.

Third, and finally, God helps his children who suffer. The rapid expansion of the Christian movement in the majority world has brought suffering for those who take a stand with Christ. Western missionaries such as Graham Staines and his sons and Martin Burnham have paid the ultimate price, as have thousands of majority world Christians who die every year—people whose names we will not know until we

154

SIDEBAR 5.3
A WORD OF ADVICE ABOUT SHORT-TERM MISSIONS

When you plan a short-term mission trip in another culture, be sure to set aside a day simply to listen to local believers tell how God helps them cope with their circumstances. Let them be your teachers. You will learn a great deal about God and also about the kind of faith it takes to live where they are. Here are three questions to consider asking local believers. We encourage you to add several more of your own.

1. How did God convince you to accept and believe the gospel?
2. What have been your greatest trials as a Christian, and how did God help you face them?
3. What are the greatest needs your community and country face?

---

meet them in eternity. What do people from these areas have to tell us about suffering? On mission trips, are we so intent on delivering *our* agenda that we do not listen to what believers have to tell us about God's faithfulness and how he helps them cope? We may need those insights sooner than we think.

Samuel Escobar points out with prophetic insight, "The world in which missions will take place in the coming decades will be cruel, cold and desperate" (1994, 49). Having faced this reality already, majority world Christians are developing deep biblical and experiential insight into suffering (Ro 1989). They are currently the ones most affected by persecution as well as natural disasters and wars. Numerous websites (http://www.persecution.org; http://www.mislinks.org/practical/persecuted.htm) document a tragic, seemingly endless list of recent horrific acts against Christians in Africa, Asia, and even Latin America. What does Scripture say about suffering?

Jesus emphasized the similarity between his own mission and ours. In John 20:21, he tells his disciples, "As the Father has sent me, I am sending you." Like Jesus, we are sent into the world. There will be similarities between his mission and ours. Jesus lived a vulnerable life. Evil people tried to kill him, from the cowshed where he was born to Calvary, where he gave up his life. He lived close to people, experiencing the joys of weddings and the despair of funerals. He told his disciples, "In this world you will have trouble. But take heart! I have overcome the world" (John 16:33). Believers who take a stand for Christ, especially in hostile societies, will pay a price, as did first-century Christians. They survived by persevering in light of eternal perspectives.

Christians in communities hostile to Christianity do not speak lightly of their troubles. However, as Panya Baba admits, persecution has a cleansing and invigorating effect: "We have seen that without persecution the church in Nigeria was lacking lots of spiritual strength and boldness. But it's a new experience, bearing much fruit, since our churches started to be bombed by Muslims" (White 1998, 167).

ENGAGING THE TREND: MISSIONS IN LIGHT OF GLOBAL CHRISTIANITY

As the body of Christ expands to include more and more peoples and nations, it is only natural that it shows great diversity. The church is an organism. It is not a corporation like McDonald's that seeks to deliver a uniform product with uniform quality in every outlet worldwide. Like so many things God makes, the body of Christ exhibits diversity in the way it worships, fellowships, passes on knowledge, organizes for tasks, and relates to cultures. The marvelous thing is that the body of Christ is identifiable everywhere it is found. Leaves differ in shape and color from plant to plant, but they are all clearly leaves. Christians differ from nation to nation, but as part of the body of Christ, they are a single entity with one Lord, one faith, and one Scripture.

Christ said that his disciples would always be identifiable by their love for one another (John 13:35). The apostle Paul enjoined his readers to "make every effort to keep the unity of the Spirit through the bond of peace" (Eph. 4:3). He told the Philippians, "Each of you should look not only to your own interests, but also to the interests of others" (2:4). All of this points toward living the Christian life interactively. Mutual respect and appreciation, sincere love, and a desire to benefit from what we have all learned about the Lord in each of our cultures should characterize Christians.

The spiritual realities just mentioned also make partnerships in ministry possible. Near the beginning of the modern era of missions, in 1848, William Carey called for a conference of all those doing mis-

> *Remember those earlier days after you had received the light, when you stood your ground in a great contest in the face of suffering. Sometimes you were publicly exposed to insult and persecution; at other times you stood side by side with those who were so treated. You sympathized with those in prison, and joyfully accepted the confiscation of your property, because you knew that you yourselves had better and lasting possessions. So do not throw away your confidence; it will be richly rewarded.*
>
> Hebrews 10:32–34

sionary work in order to coordinate them in the spirit of Christ's call to "show we are Christians by our love." It took a while, but by the end of the nineteenth century, mission coordinating conferences were held. The World Council of Churches was formed in 1948, grounded in the concerns for unity expressed at the 1910 World Missionary Conference in Edinburgh.

During the last part of the century, great evangelical mission conventions such as those in Berlin in 1966 and Lausanne in 1974 witnessed an increase in participation by Christians from the global church, the majority world areas of Latin America, Africa, and Asia. As the majority world Christian movement grew larger in proportion to its Western expressions, Christians from these areas were in greater evidence at global conferences on world evangelism such as the Global Consultation on World Evangelization (GCOWE) conferences held in Korea, the Philippines, and South Africa. This was exemplified at the 1998 Anglican Lambeth Bishops Conference in the United Kingdom, when major-

> *As the church has become increasingly global, as technology has made cooperation more and more feasible, as Christians have become more sophisticated about the presence and gifts of overseas churches, and about mergers and strategic alliances in the business world, they are increasingly demanding that the agencies they support become involved in partnerships.*
>
> Stan Guthrie (2000, 94)

ity world bishops outnumbered their Western counterparts and outvoted them on crucial issues related to same-sex marriage and the ordination of homosexual priests (Jenkins 2002, 202–3). Whether for fellowship, partnerships, or mutual correction, the global church is now an undeniable reality, one not to be feared but to be understood in terms of its implications for ministry in the new millennium.

Interest in partnerships has grown a great deal over the past ten years. Some are global and others are regional. In 1994, the Missions Commission of the World Evangelical Alliance (WEA) issued a guide to partnerships in missions titled *Kingdom Partnerships for Synergy in Missions* (Taylor 1994). As a product of international Christian thinkers on partnership, it reveals what the global church needs. Ongoing international associations of evangelicals such as the WEA, the Lausanne Committee for World Evangelization, and the GCOWE help to network and coordinate ministry concerns. The four thousand Latin Americans working cross-culturally outside their continent are linked through the COMIBAM network. Mission organizations across India are linked through the India Missions Association.

CASE STUDY: TRAINING IN SPAIN

Several years ago, Francisco and Edgardo and their families left their homes in Latin America and moved to North Africa and Spain respectively. They were among the earliest wave of Latin American missionaries to respond to God's call to preach the gospel outside their own continent. Their churches were thrilled to send them.

Soon after they arrived, they discovered that other Latin Americans had experienced the same calling. Quietly in North Africa, and more openly in Spain, Francisco and Edgardo began their work. God blessed their efforts, and soon Francisco saw several Muslims come to the Lord in North Africa. Edgardo also saw response in Spain. The new North African converts experienced intense persecution, and some of them, along with Francisco, found themselves in prison.

God intervened, and after some months, all were freed, but Francisco and his family were expelled from North Africa and left for Spain. There they were helped by Latin American missionaries like Edgardo and eventually discovered many Muslim North Africans to whom they could minister. As Francisco and Edgardo compared notes with other Latino coworkers, they discovered they had something in common. Although they had all been biblically trained and were experienced in ministry, they had never been trained to work cross-culturally. Neither had they been trained to face the kind of opposition Francisco had just experienced. They began to think about how to help other Latin American missionaries understand cross-cultural ministry in Spain, North Africa, and the Middle East.

In educational work, the globally organized International Council for Evangelical Theological Education oversees seven regional groups, including the Asia Theological Association, the Accrediting Council for Theological Education in Africa, and the Association for Evangelical Theological Education in Latin America.

Opportunities to serve overseas in an international partnership abound. Groups such as Devcorps network specialists in many fields who serve as tentmakers. Although one would think that the more than eight hundred mission agencies and boards working out of North America would make for a hopeless competitive mess around the world, they actually work together in associations and local partnerships. Partnerships involve many international and indigenous workers. A synergism develops that accomplishes more than any one group could by itself.

Interdev, though now no longer functioning, facilitated a partnership called the Albanian Encouragement Project (AEP) in Albania beginning in 1991. The Marxist national government of Albania had been hostile

Francisco, Edgardo, and other Latino missionaries decided to start a training program in Spain. In Spain, there were tremendous ministry needs, and the presence of Muslims in Spain and its proximity to North Africa made it possible to accompany and mentor new workers in cross-cultural ministry.

Soon after the Latino missionaries started their training program, it attracted the attention of a large American church that wanted to participate in the new school. But the Americans found that the Latinos did not work in the same ways they did. The Latinos were more spontaneous, and the Americans were more businesslike. The more the Americans pressed for a business plan, the more the Latinos felt they might be victims of "Gringo" domination, just as they had experienced in Latin America. The Americans decided to start a training school of their own.

Francisco and Edgardo felt wounded by the American church's decision.

They sensed that their missionary training venture, almost unmatched by any earlier Western venture, had been disregarded and was about to be duplicated by the Americans. Not wanting these strained feelings to persist between believers from different continents, Edgardo asked Derek, a trusted American friend, what could be done to resolve the misunderstandings.

When he got the call, Derek had to sit down and think a while. He knew everyone involved and respected them greatly. How could things have gotten to this point? Now that innovative initiatives were being advanced by workers from different countries, how could they be coordinated in ways that showed mutual respect?

Derek continued to think and pray and then began to make some calls of his own. Eventually, he sensed what he needed to say. He called Edgardo, and, with a prayer for wisdom, he said . . .

to any religious group. At the time, there were only five known Albanian Christians. With the general collapse of Marxism in Eastern Europe, Christian agencies worldwide entered Albania for ministry and practical assistance and formed the AEP partnership to avoid duplication and competitive confusion. By 1998, believers numbered eight thousand. Still, the evangelical church constituted only .2 percent of the population. During the Balkan crisis of the 1990s, however, this small group, together with the AEP, was able to help seventy thousand Kosovar refugees (primarily Muslims) who fled to Albania (Shubin 1999, 28–29).

As the church grows globally, the diversity and numbers of believers doing ministry "from all nations, to all nations" require cooperation, consideration, and consultation. This is the only way to bring the incredible resources of the international Christian community to bear on the challenges and opportunities abounding today.

6

Changing Motivations
for Missions

From "Fear of Hell" to "the Glory of God"

GAILYN VAN RHEENEN

The following four illustrations reveal that core motivations for missions are changing. Once people preached and responded to the gospel out of fear of hell or because of the lostness of humanity. These motivations have waned in the postmodern context. Motivation for missions is frequently defined by postmodern Christians as "giving glory to God" or "an overflowing of thankfulness."

The movie *Luther* contains a graphic scene depicting how the Dominican monk Johann Tetzel used fear of hell to extract money for indulgences. People bought these indulgences to save themselves or their loved ones from eternal punishment. Tetzel believed that he had "grace and power from the Pope to offer forgiveness even if someone had slept with the Holy Virgin Mother of God, as long as a contribution would be put into the coffer" (Hillerbrand 1964, 41).

Jimmy Allen, a former teacher at Harding University, had a significant influence on Gailyn Van Rheenen during his undergraduate studies. During the 1960s and 1970s, Allen, mimicking Jonathan Edwards's famous 1741 speech "Sinners in the Hands of an Angry God," gave his powerful sermon "What Is Hell Like?" Thousands responded in various crusades as they contemplated their sins and the impending judgment if they did not repent. Some were motivated to become missionaries to save people from hell.

Van Rheenen has also personally been touched by human lostness without God. If Jesus came to seek and to save the lost, should that not also be our motivation? He felt a burden, an obligation, to preach. He had been saved from his sins. It was his responsibility, therefore, to teach others about salvation in Jesus Christ. He felt like Paul, who wrote, "I am compelled to preach. Woe to me if I do not preach the gospel!" (1 Cor. 9:16). Those of Van Rheenen's generation feel an affinity to this biblical understanding of personal lostness.

Van Rheenen and his wife recently shared fellowship with a vibrant church planter and his wife who radiated love and passion for God. They had learned to glorify him as God, and Van Rheenen and his wife were touched by their joy. It was apparent to them that the church planter and his wife ministered out of a relationship with God. A couple weeks later, Van Rheenen heard this evangelist commission a mission team with the words, "We get to do the thing we were made to do, that is, give glory to God! God desires that his name be glorified in all nations. Both Christ and his church are representations of this glory. This team is going to give God glory."

> *And let every one that is yet out of Christ, and hanging over the pit of hell, whether they be old men and women, or middle aged, or young people, or little children, now hearken to the loud calls of God's word and providence.*
>
> Jonathan Edwards (1741)

In focusing on the trend of changing motivations for missions, this chapter answers a number of central questions. First, what motivates Christian leaders to leave behind family, friends, and culture; head to unfamiliar places; and dedicate their lives to serving peoples of an entirely different language and culture? Further, what motivations enable missionaries to persevere while learning languages, working through culture stress, learning to minister in a foreign culture, and raising a family in a new environment? What cultural and historical trends have shaped the changing motivations for missions? What are scriptural motivations for missions? Finally, how do these changing motivations influence the growth, stagnation, or demise of the worldwide mission movement?

IDENTIFYING THE TREND: DEFINING MOTIVATIONS FOR MISSIONS

Motivations for missions and ministry are shaped not only by Spirit-guided responses to God's revelation but also by cultural and historical

162

perspectives. At times the revealed glory of God stirs hearts and leads disciples of Christ to reflect the nature of their Creator. At other times the divine shines only dimly, radiating principally from secluded sanctuaries like monasteries. The divine never ceases to shine, however, even when societies choose to follow their own gods or erect self as god. God's glory is simply marginalized by busy schedules, challenged by secular perspectives, and disfigured by cultural misunderstandings of God and his mission. Paradoxically, when Christianity appears to be strongest from a human standpoint, the divine impulses forming Christian motivations can be dimmed as people trust in human impulses rather than God's Spirit.

This section briefly overviews Christian motivations throughout the generations, revealing that past motivations continue to ripple through the ages and influence people in unexpected ways.

Early Christian Motivations

In broad terms, the early Christians were motivated by the eschatological glory of God—the glory that would be revealed when Christ returned—and thereby were able to survive as a people not allowed to participate fully as citizens in the larger culture. They had seen God's glory in Jesus Christ, and in the midst of many struggles and even sinful inclinations, they survived and grew as people who reflected the glory of God. C. S. Lewis writes, "There is no getting away from the fact that this idea [of glory] is very prominent in the New Testament and in early Christian writings. Salvation is constantly associated with palms, crowns, white robes, thrones, and splendour like the sun and stars" (1949, 8).

> *Motivations become heart allegiances that lead missionaries and ministers into action and sometimes result in inaction. Most frequently the human psyche is made up of impulses which battle against each other. Prayerful consideration of motives enables those who carry the mission of God to overcome or at least compensate for defective motives and deepen the foundations of fundamental Christian motivations.*
> Gailyn Van Rheenen (1996, 37)

The prologue of John describes how the world, although created by Christ, did not recognize and receive him when he came (1:10–11). Nevertheless, God's glory was demonstrated by God's Word becoming flesh, tabernacling among humanity, and revealing "the glory of the One and Only, who came from the Father, full of grace and truth" (1:14). Christ's purpose was to make known God's fullness of grace (1:16–18) so that all might be transformed into his nature.

163

Likewise, Paul wrote that "Christ has become a servant of the Jews on behalf of God's truth, to confirm the promises made to the patriarchs *so that the Gentiles may glorify God* for his mercy" (Rom. 15:8–9, emphasis added). Christ was a servant to the Jews so that they might fulfill God's long-desired purpose and become God's lights, illuminating his glory before the nations.

> Christ was on a mission to magnify God. He came to show that *God* is truthful. He came to show that *God* is a promise-keeper. And he came to show that *God* is glorious. Jesus came into the world for *God's sake*—to certify *God's* integrity; to vindicate *God's* word; to magnify *God's* glory. Since God sent his Son to do all this, it is plain that the primary motive of the first great mission . . . was God's zeal for the glory of God. . . . Zeal for the glory of God motivates world missions. (Piper, 1993, 29)

Early Christian martyrs exhibited this zeal for the glory of God. For example, Polycarp, a convert of the apostle John and bishop of Smyrna, was commanded to accept the Roman emperor as God but replied, "For eighty-six years I have been his servant, and he has never done me wrong: How can I blaspheme my king who saved me?" He was then burned at the stake (Tucker 1983, 33). Acknowledging the glory of God led the early church not only to survive persecutions but to proclaim the ultimate allegiance of their lives. God reigns. This is his world. He is "majestic in holiness, awesome in glory, working wonders" (Exod. 15:11).

Foundational motives for missions that reflect the will of God include God's love and compassion, God's sovereignty over time, and an outpouring of thanksgiving to God (Van Rheenen 1996, 38–41). These three descriptions, however, are only items under a broader rubric, *the glory of God.* The early Christian church, when faithful to God, glorified God as God.

The early Christian period, however, should not be idealized. The Pauline and Johannine writings reflect mixed motives. Paul writes that "some preach Christ out of envy and rivalry, but others out of goodwill" (Phil. 1:15). John encourages early Christians to "not believe every spirit, but test the spirits to see whether they are from God, because many false prophets have gone out into the world" (1 John 4:1). Early Christian motivations were not always pure.

Christendom Motivations

When Constantine proclaimed Christianity an acceptable religion in AD 313 and the official religion of the Roman Empire in AD 375, the many Christian communities in the empire rejoiced. Truly the kingdom of God had displaced the kingdom of men. Christ was victorious. God

Most High, however, must have grieved, knowing that when everyone considered themselves Christian, Christianity would quickly accommodate to the political and cultural impulses of the world.

The alignment of Christianity with the state, forming what today is called *Christendom,* has had a radical and lasting impact on Christian motivation. The church grew to rely on political power to enforce sanctions. The state, in turn, expected the church to give credence to its decisions. Thus, during this period, the motivation of God's consuming mercy and compassion changed to coercion and constraint, eschatological expectations were superseded by contemporary demands, and thanksgiving was more readily given to earthly benefactors than to God. The church used many devices to obtain money, including the selling of important positions within the church and indulgences, which corrupted its spiritual influence. The sacraments were celebrated meaninglessly, sometimes as rituals to obtain spiritual power. The message of "God's mercy was weakened by an emphasis on man's good works" (Spitz 1972, 188).

> *The church's final word is not "church" but the glory of the Father and the Son in the Spirit of liberty.*
> Jürgen Moltmann (1977, 19)

During the Middle Ages, the church used fear of hell to maintain the allegiance of its people. Hell was portrayed as a place of turmoil, chaos, pain, despair, and wretchedness. Dante's *Inferno* graphically described the state of souls after death with sins punished according to their severity. Sinners were traitors who rebelled against God and the church. The Catholic Church held "the firm conviction . . . that those outside the church were eternally damned—a stance that has been associated with the formula *extra ecclesiam nulla salus* (outside the church no salvation)" (Netland 2001, 26). Johann Tetzel, using fear of hell to extract money for indulgences during the time of Martin Luther, illustrates how the threat of eternal punishment can induce response.

In many ways, the Enlightenment was a reaction to the state's malicious use of religion to control the people. The life of René Descartes (1561–1626) exemplifies this reaction. As a student, Descartes became disenchanted with medieval religious paradigms. He anticipated Henry IV of Navarre being crowned king of France and believed that he would bring peace and unity to a Europe torn apart by religious wars. But Henry was assassinated. In actions reflecting medieval paradigms, Henry's head was displayed throughout France as a religious relic and was eventually enshrined at La Fleche near Paris, where Descartes was a student (Brueggemann 1993, 3–4; cf. Toulmin 1990). Knowing that magical practices were employed by the church to control the people,

165

Decartes rejected religion and advocated an alternative paradigm based on human objectivity. This "self" was able to use reason and observation to determine one's way in life (Van Gelder 1996, 117).

Enlightenment philosophies increasingly amplified perceptions of human potential, which resulted in the decentering of God and religion and the enthroning of humanity as the center of life. "Rather than starting with revelation and the God-hypothesis to understand life, Descartes constructed a different epistemological method for discovering truth by starting within himself as an autonomous individual. By employing reason and assuming objectivity, he developed a type of knowledge different from that derived from revelation and tradition" (Van Gelder 1996, 117). The rift that occurred between science and religion is only now reconverging. As a result, modern "Christians" focused on the present, attempting to live a happy life, with little time for religion.

In the meantime, Protestant Reformers challenged not only the Catholic Church's use of indulgences but also its belief that salvation exists only within the traditional church. Reformers declared that salvation is "found only in the person and work of Jesus Christ. All those who die without the saving gospel of Christ face an eternity apart from God" (Netland 2001, 22). This Protestant theology also absorbed concepts of modern individualism. Individuals, according to these conceptions, are saved by faith separate and apart from the traditional church, family, or government. Luther wrote in *The Freedom of a Christian* that "a Christian man is the most free lord of all, subject to none; a Christian man is the most dutiful servant of all, and subject to every one" (Luther n.d.).

Although early Reformers held to Scripture as their sole guide for life, they believed that the Great Commission, "to make disciples of all nations," had been fulfilled by the apostles. There was thus no need for missions (Netland 2001, 27). Only the countercultural movements of the believers' churches, such as the Anabaptists, challenged these perspectives. Members of such churches asserted that most Catholics and Protestants had never made a kingdom-level commitment to God and were therefore in need of conversion. Because the believers' churches challenged the state-church affiliation of Christendom, they were persecuted by both Catholics and Protestants.

A world missions movement emerged as European explorers discovered new worlds that had never heard of Jesus Christ. This movement must be understood within the context of both Christendom and colonialism. Christendom assumed a partnership between the state and a nationally recognized church. This church "served as the protected and privileged religion of society" and "its legally established institutional form" (Guder 1998, 6). In at least the initial stages of colonialism, missionaries of Catholic orders went wherever Catholic nations established their colonial empires, and Protestant missionaries were likewise commissioned to follow in the footsteps of their explorers, colonists, and companies. Generally, missionaries, even though they stood against slavery and the social excesses of colonialism, viewed the world from a Western mind-set. They assumed the superiority of Western culture, believing themselves to be civilized and others to be barbarians or savages. As a consequence, they deemed it unnecessary to contextualize the gospel message and Christian forms; they were literally translated in colonial lands. Christianity, civilization, and commerce were considered "the threefold flag under which the missionary ship sailed" (Shenk 1980, 36). Motives were generally benevolent but within Christendom and colonial models of thinking.

The Protestant assumption that those apart from the gospel of Jesus Christ were forever lost inspired early missionaries to take the gospel of Christ to the peoples of China, Africa, Latin America, and the islands of the Pacific. Hudson Taylor, the great missionary to China, vividly expressed this perspective in his challenge to the Student Volunteer Movement in Detroit in 1894: "There is a great Niagara of souls passing into the dark in China. Every day, every week, every month they are passing away. A million a month in China they are dying without God" (Netland 2001, 27).

The desire to save those in pagan lands was encased within understandings of individual salvation. "Missionaries tended to focus upon proclamation of salvation to individuals and to look upon majority world cultures as obstacles in their way" (Netland 2001, 29). This individualistic approach was expressed by D. L. Moody in his often-quoted statement, "I look upon this world as a wrecked vessel. God has given me a lifeboat and said to me, 'Moody, save all you can'" (Netland 2001, 29). Individuals were to be pulled into God's lifeboat one by one. The motivational appeal was to save individuals who were eternally lost without Jesus Christ.

Paradoxically, as Christianity spread throughout the world, secular thinking eroded Christianity in the West, particularly in Europe. The secularization process was hastened by Christendom. The church had too long tied itself to earthly, political power to maintain its support rather than promoting Christian assumptions, values, and behaviors. Christendom thus ultimately eroded Christianity.

During Christendom, Christianity was frequently used to enforce the political and economic designs of the powerful, thereby subverting God's holiness and compassion. Religion became a tool to constrain the masses. However, authentic Christianity continued, as illustrated by the devotional and theological literature written throughout the generations. Frequently, God-glorifying, Christ-following, self-denying Christianity survived on the fringes, within monasteries, in mission areas, and in minority communities distinct from the principalities and powers that pervaded popular cultures.

EVALUATING THE TREND: POST-CHRISTENDOM MOTIVATIONS

Christendom sees the church standing in the city square next to the offices of government officials. Civil and religious authorities exist side by side and give authenticity to one another. We have, however, entered a new time of history. Although church structures continue to be prominent in many cities and towns in Europe and North America, the church has been culturally marginalized. What formed the center of the old Christendom model has been displaced. The church has become one of many options in an increasingly complex world in which world religions, new spiritualities, and secular therapies compete in a multicultural marketplace. The cathedrals and church buildings are considered by some, especially in Europe, to be relics of the past.

This marginalization of Christianity is not surprising to those who understand that the authentic way of Christ, even during Christendom, has always existed on the periphery of popular culture. The church, by its very nature, is composed of those called out of the world, "aliens and strangers in the world" (1 Pet. 2:11; cf. 1:1), those walking in the earthlies while dwelling in the heavenlies (Eph. 1:20–21; 2:6). This colony of God in a strange world has always realized that "the Most High does not live in houses made by men" (Acts 7:48; e.g., 1 Kings 8:27; 2 Chron. 2:6). The church during Christendom frequently projected the myth of strength and power without reflecting the glory of God.

The post-Christendom world has not only displaced the church but also questioned modernity's enthroning of humanity. Humans are no longer considered the center of their world, able to determine their own way by empirical knowledge and their own ingenuity. The world seems to have no foundations. According to philosopher Thomas Kuhn, one paradigm of reality takes the place of another so that the world seems to be one of impermanence (1970). There is less and less optimism.

In the post-Christendom era, a number of factors have combined to erode the Christian faith. These include not only "the cumulative influences of the disestablishment of Christianity in Western societies" and "the increased marginalization of traditional religion in modern life" but also "a deepening skepticism about the claims of orthodox Christianity, and the existential awareness of cultural and religious diversity engendered by globalization" (Netland 2001, 15). These factors, enhanced by a naive tolerance of intellectually competing postmodern options, have led many to ask, Don't all religions lead to the same God? Will God not save people of other world religions?

Within the current postmodern, pluralistic cultural context, Christian teaching on hell, while never particularly popular, is increasingly unacceptable. As early as 1932–33, in preparation for the International Missionary Council in Tambaram, India, William Hocking wrote in the infamous Layman's Foreign Missions Inquiry, "There is little disposition to believe that sincere and aspiring seekers after God in other religions are to be damned: it has become less concerned in any land to save men from eternal punishment than from the danger of losing the supreme good" (1932, 19). Tim Keller tells of a successful thirty-year-old businessman with only loose connections to a mainline church and little knowledge of Christianity who was searching for spiritual answers. His spiritual interest grew so that he was ready to embrace the gospel—except for one obstacle. "You've said that if we do not believe in Christ," he said to Keller, "we are lost and condemned. I'm sorry, I just cannot buy that. I work with some fine people who are Muslim, Jewish, or agnostic. I cannot believe they are going to hell just because they don't believe in Jesus. In fact, I cannot reconcile the very idea of hell with a loving God—even if he is holy, too" (Keller 1997).

This ambivalence toward hell was reflected in Ryan Shaw's study of the mission focus within campus fellowships. The problem of universalism and the reality of hell were the most frequently noted problems hindering student involvement in world missions. Shaw writes:

> There are many in the body of Christ who quietly are not sure what to make of hell. Though most Bible believing churches assert that apart from Christ people will suffer eternally in hell, some believers have a hard time bringing themselves to accept this truth deep in their hearts. In our pluralistic, politically correct society it is especially frowned upon. A leader in Colorado commented, "To adhere to something which cuts out such a large segment of society for such a horrible demise is seen as narrow and arrogant." (N.d., 38)

Thus, "belief in heaven and damnation is routinely dismissed today as a vestige of a less sophisticated era. The atheist philosopher Bertrand Russell, writing half a century ago, captured the ethos of the times when he quipped, 'Hell is neither so certain nor so hot as it used to be'" (Netland 2001, 151).

Since 1988, the respected evangelical theologian John Stott has tentatively embraced annihilationism, the "view that unbelievers are finally annihilated and thus do not experience torment that is eternal in duration" (Peterson 2000, 30). Since then, a debate has raged among evangelicals over the nature of hell. Do sinners live eternally in hell, or do unbelievers merely cease to exist? Are humans created inherently mortal, or do they take on immortality by God's grace and their relationship with him? Is hell a literal place or a metaphor? Robert Peterson (2000) gives an extensive summary of evangelical discussions about the nature of hell. Authors advocating annihilationism include Philip Hughes (1989), John Wenham (1992), and Edward Fudge (1994). Authors advocating the traditional approach include J. I. Packer (1990), John Gerstner (1990), Larry Dixon (1992), Kendall Harmon (1992), Robert Peterson (1995), and Donald Carson (1996). This discussion of hell, reflecting postmodern tolerance and acceptance, has a direct bearing on missionary motivation. As Peterson aptly states, "Evangelicals historically have understood hell as a spur to evangelism. Recently, however, some have debated how prominent a place hell should have in Christian witness" (2000, 35).

Wade Clark Roof writes that postmoderns increasingly feel uncomfortable with the language of *religion* and prefer instead the language of *spirituality* (1999, 3–4). "*Religion* connotes rigid, authoritarian, oppressive institutions; dogmatism and lack of openness to alternative perspectives; and cold formalism or ritualism. *Spirituality*, by contrast, suggests flexibility and creativity; tolerance and respect for alternative insights from all peoples and cultures; room for doubt and searching; and an emphasis upon personal experience" (Netland 2001, 152). Robert Wuthnow approaches this new way of thinking in terms of "place" and "journey" (1998, 4, 41). The church has traditionally defined itself as a place to meet, a gathering place of the faithful, and faithfulness has been related to attendance. Truth is a commodity agreed upon by the faithful. Postmodern boundaries, however, are blurred. God is seen as working in unexpected places in unanticipated ways. Freedom of choice and competing options provide a menu from which to choose. "Spirituality . . . is more ambiguous with vague and open boundaries and loose connections, if any, with religious institutions" (Netland 2001, 153). A traditional spirituality, which occurred in sacred places, has given way to a new spirituality of seeking.

The change in terminologies described by Roof and Wuthnow is more than semantics. It is a new way of looking at the world. Christians, influenced by postmodernity, are uncomfortable making statements about the eternal lostness of humanity. The question How can we as humans judge eternal consequences for living without Christ? continually arises in discussions about human lostness. Saying that people are going to hell or will be lost eternally is considered abrasive and intolerant.

How then should Christians look at biblical perspectives of hell and lostness? Should a theology of the glory of God as a motivation for missions include or exclude elements of past motivations?

REFLECTING ON THE TREND: THEOLOGICAL ISSUES

A Theology of Hell

A biblical understanding of hell is fundamental to a Christian world-view and therefore cannot be negated. The concept of "perishing" in John 3:16 does not mean "extension of being," as some propose, but, as interpreted in the context of other passages, an eternity of suffering without God. The account of the rich man and Lazarus indicates continual pain and punishment (Luke 16:19–31). Jesus, teaching about compassion for the culturally disenfranchised, describes two destinies: *eternal* punishment and *eternal* life (Matt. 25:46). Jesus indicates that the reality of hell is a stimulus to pure living. If one's hand, foot, or eye causes sin, it would be better to have the part cut away than to "be thrown into hell" (Mark 9:42–47). "Whatever in one's life tempts one to be untrue to God must be discarded, promptly and decisively, even as a surgeon amputates a hand or a leg in order to save a life" (Lane 1974, 348). Radical discipleship requires costly sacrifices. Temporary impairments are trivial compared to sins that carry eternal consequences.

The fire of hell is "not quenched" (Mark 9:48). Likewise, Satan and those who collaborate with him will be thrown into the "lake of burning sulfur," where they will be punished "for ever and ever" (Rev. 20:10; cf. 14:9–12). Thus, Aquinas insisted that "sins against an infinite God deserve infinite recompense" (Peterson 2000, 35). Christian leaders must, therefore, affirm the reality of hell and the need to save the lost as a biblical motivation.

Teaching on hell, however, must be understood within the broad historical context of a holy God seeking to reconcile his creation to himself in Jesus Christ. God is our loving Creator, always seeking to relate personally to us. He is like a father caring for his children (Prov. 3:11–12; Hosea 11:1–5; Heb. 12:5–11) or a husband loving his wife (Hosea 1:2). A loving God sent the Israelites into Assyrian captivity never to return (2 Kings 17:14–18) and the Jews into Babylonian captivity (Jer. 17:1–4) for seventy years. But God's punishment (Hosea 11:6–7) was accompanied by great grief (Hosea 11:8–9). The "tears of God" passage in Hosea expresses God's great compassion even as he punishes Israel. He says, "How can I give you up, Ephraim? How can I hand you over, Israel? How can I treat you like Admah? How can I make you like Zeboiim?

My heart is changed within me; all my compassion is aroused. I will not carry out my fierce anger, nor will I turn and devastate Ephraim. For I am God, and not man—the Holy One among you. I will not come in wrath" (Hosea 11:8–9). "God gave them over to shameful lusts, . . . to a depraved mind" because they "exchanged the truth of God for a lie, and worshiped and served created things rather than the Creator" (Rom. 1:26, 28, 25). He could not do otherwise. Holiness and idolatry cannot coexist.

The fact that God is angered by sin and will ultimately condemn unbelievers to hell must stand beside other Christian truths. The tension between God's saving love and his expectation of holiness must never be lost. God's compassion, resulting in his desire to save, is frequently seen in Scripture. God used five phrases to describe his eternal nature to Moses in Exodus 34:6–7: He is "compassionate and gracious," "slow to anger," "abounding in love and faithfulness," "maintaining love to thousands," and "forgiving wickedness, rebellion and sin." The description concludes, however, with the reality that God "does not leave the guilty unpunished; he punishes the children and their children for the sins of the fathers to the third and fourth generation" (v. 7). Sin ramifies through the generations, and, despite his graciousness, God punishes as a father who disciplines his child (Prov. 3:11–12; Heb. 12:5–11). The binary descriptions of conversion—from darkness to light, from the dominion of Satan to the kingdom of God, from the power of Satan to that of God, from old to new self (Acts 26:18; Eph. 4:22–24)—illustrate the transformation from hell to heaven, from lostness to savedness through the gracious hand of God (Eph. 2:1–10).

Fear of hell is often used as a guilt-inducing knife piercing the heart of the naive and producing a fear-laden response. Gailyn Van Rheenen recently heard an evangelist describe his spiritual journey. He was baptized at age 12 after hearing a sermon on hell and seeing that many of his friends were also responding. Nothing, however, occurred to change his heart, and he lived for many years as an immoral, self-indulging pagan. Only when he was older did he come to know Christ and live in relationship with him, giving glory to God. Likewise, many have become missionaries hoping to assuage the guilt of battered, broken consciences. Sometimes good comes out of these poor motives and battered lives because Christ is preached (Phil. 1:15–18). Frequently, however, the demons within surface, creating guilt and fear. Godly motivations flow from a basic theology of the glory of God that leads new converts to enthrone God as their Lord and to walk with him as Lord and Savior.

A Theology of Lostness

The related perspective of lostness is also fundamental to a biblical view of reality. Jesus "came to seek and to save what was lost" (Luke 19:10). In Luke 15, Christ responds to the criticism that he "welcomes sinners and eats with them" (v. 2) by illustrating the joy of finding something that was lost. The emphasis is that *finding* the lost sheep, the lost coin, and the lost son brings joy. The parable of the lost son reveals that some of those apparently saved may in fact be lost. The Great Commission recorded in Mark illustrates that the goal of world evangelization is in finding the lost: "Go into all the world and preach the good news to all creation. Whoever believes and is baptized will be saved, but whoever does not believe will be condemned" (16:15–16). Lostness is inherent in many passages. For instance, Paul, in Ephesians 2, describes how the dead in sin are made alive by God's grace so that Christians are elevated into the heavenly realms to be seated with Christ, who has himself been raised to be seated with God in the heavenly realms (Eph. 1:20–21). Thus, D. L. Moody's statement, "I look upon this world as a wrecked vessel. God has given me a lifeboat and said to me, 'Moody, save all you can'" (Netland 2001, 29), has a biblical foundation.

There has always been a subtle temptation to relate the concept of lostness to fear. Robertson McQuilkin begins an otherwise excellent chapter titled "Lost" with the question, "Have you ever experienced the terror of being lost—in some trackless mountain wilderness, perhaps, or in the labyrinth of a great, strange city?" (1999a, 156). Such fear-based analogies are more harmful then helpful. *Lost* has meaning only when describing what is missing, which in a Christian definition is a relationship with God. People without God cannot discover their ultimate identity, that they were created to live in a relationship with God. Humans living without God have lost their created identity. They are operating by human initiative or under the varying influences of Satan.

A Theology of God's Glory

As stated earlier, Christians are called to taste the glory of God, enabling them to reflect God's glory to the world. This desire for God—to be with him, to reflect his glory, and to perceive life beyond these human bounds—is the core of Christian motivation. Glory is "a quality belonging to God" and can be recognized only in relationship to him. Glory "radiates from the one who has it" (Aalen 1971, 44). Christians, therefore, must first perceive God's glory and then participate in it.

The words of David Brainerd, seventeenth-century missionary to the Native Americans in New Jersey, graphically depict the profound impact that giving glory to God has on missionary life:

> My soul was, this day, at turns, sweetly set on God: I longed to be "with him" that I might "behold his glory. . . ." Oh, that his kingdom might come in the world; that they might all love and glorify him for what he is in himself; and that the blessed Redeemer might "see the travail of his soul, and be satisfied. . . ." Oh, "come Lord Jesus, come quickly. Amen." (Linn 2000)

These were the last words he wrote before he died at age twenty-nine. They illustrate the power God's transforming glory can have on missionary motivation.

Many Scripture passages emphasize God's glory as a motivator for missions. One that merits focus is 2 Corinthians 3:7–4:18. Here, Paul compares the fading glory of the Mosaic covenant, which brought condemnation, to the glory of God's never-fading covenant in Jesus Christ. The first was of letters, the second of the Spirit. The first was glorious but led to condemnation and death; the second, of greater glory, produced grace and mercy leading to life. God's glory in the first was concealed; in the second, God's glory was unveiled and open in the person of Jesus Christ (2 Cor. 3:7–11). Paul then aptly connects the concepts: *God's glory* generates *hope*, which produces *boldness* (3:12). This Pauline process illustrates how boldness for God's purposes flows from the resources of his glory.

Under the old covenant, a veil concealed God's glory. As a result, people's minds became dull (3:14). This same veil remains even today and can be removed only in Christ: "Whenever anyone turns to the Lord, the veil is taken away" (3:16). Paul continues, "Now the Lord is the Spirit, and where the Spirit of the Lord is, there is freedom" (3:17). The Lord in this passage is Christ, the source of light and life, the remover of the veil, the giver of freedom. Freedom results from the veil being lifted: "The Jews were in bondage to the letter that kills, but Christians have entered into the liberty of Christ—the dynamic liberty of the spirit as opposed to the mere letter" (Hughes 1962, 116).

Christians now have a special relationship with God in Christ. The veil has been lifted. God in his Son Jesus has become immanent. "The Word became flesh and made his dwelling" among human beings (John 1:14), thus raising the veil and enabling Christians to look at God himself. God's action in Jesus enables Christians to "reflect the Lord's glory" with "unveiled faces" (2 Cor. 3:18). As Christians look at Christ, they are changed into his divine nature. Philip Hughes writes:

> To contemplate Him who is the Father's image is progressively to be transformed into that image. The effect of continuous beholding is that we are continuously being transformed "into the same image," that is,

into the likeness of Christ—and increasingly so: "from glory to glory."
(1962, 117–18)

As Moses on Mount Sinai reflected God's radiance, Christians under the
new covenant begin to reflect the nature of God as they look to Christ.
Paul says that they "are being transformed into his likeness with ever-
increasing glory" (3:18). This transformation, which results from looking
upon Christ, who is the image of God, leads to ministry.

Second Corinthians 4:1–18 describes the nature of ministry under the
new covenant (v. 1), a ministry formed by Christians perceiving God's
glory and thereby being transformed into his likeness. Ministry formed
by covenant transformation is not manipulative or deceptive. The Word
of God is not distorted. Rather, the truth is spoken plainly with the realization that the power lies not in the teacher but in the gospel itself.
The gospel must never be veiled by human embellishment or ego (vv.
2–3). While unbelievers are helplessly blinded by the god of this age and
cannot see the light of the gospel (v. 4), the glory of God is unveiled in the
hearts of believers to give them "the light of the knowledge of the glory
of God in the face of Christ" (v. 6). Creation is compared to re-creation.
The God who said, "Let there be light," is the same one who makes light
shine out of darkness in conversion (v. 6). This ministry is not of self for
the glory of self but of God for the glory of God. Ministers are merely
servants who preach Jesus Christ as Lord rather than a message of self-
esteem and self-proclamation (v. 5; Hughes 1962, 132). They are merely
earthen vessels, lamps of clay through whom the light of God shines (v. 7).
Paradoxically, the treasure (v. 7), referring to "the light of the gospel of
the glory of Christ, who is the image of God" (v. 4), is placed in fragile
clay lamps to demonstrate God's all-surpassing power (v. 7). There is
"no contrast more striking than that between the greatness of the divine
glory and the frailty and unworthiness of the vessels in which it dwells
and through which it is manifested to the world" (Hughes 1962, 135).
In the new covenant, God's glory is fully evident, unveiled by Christ,
reflected by fragile human servants who are "being transformed into
his likeness with ever-increasing glory" (2 Cor. 3:18).

Even when undergoing various trials (2 Cor. 4:8–11), believers who
have seen the glory of God cannot be silent. They are compelled to
speak. They have witnessed the light of the glory of God. They "believe
and therefore speak" (v. 13). As a result, God's grace reaches more and
more people, causing "thanksgiving to overflow to the glory of God"
(v. 15). Those who have been transformed into his likeness lead others
to give glory to God.

Becoming like God has always been the ultimate motivation for missions. Understandings of hell and lostness are secondary to seeing God's

glory and incarnating this glory in Christian ministry. C. S. Lewis says that Christians not only see the beauty of God but also become beautiful: "We want something else which can hardly be put into words—to be united with the beauty we see, to pass into it, to receive it into ourselves, to bathe in it, to become part of it" (1949, 12–13). We are called to taste the infinite glory of God and thereby become finitely glorious ourselves.

ENGAGING THE TREND: PRACTICAL IMPLICATIONS

The contemporary world is in the midst of chaotic change. Modernity is being swallowed up by postmodernity. The Enlightenment enthroned humanity as the center of the universe. Humans could determine their own way in life by ingenuity and reasoning. The world, as outlined by Newtonian physics, was orderly and predictable. Scientists optimistically predicted that they could solve most human problems if given the time. This optimism, however, is waning. People increasingly feel that they are unable to determine directions in life merely by human reasoning and ingenuity. The new world is less predictable, more mysterious, somewhat antireligious, more spiritual. Einstein's theory of relativity and the quantum theory of physics cast doubt on the predictability of the universe. This has led some to say that the world is characterized by chaos rather than by order.

Science and human rationality have been used not only to better humankind but also to create weapons of mass destruction that are used in the massive slaughter of innocents. Left to their own devices, people are unable to make moral decisions based merely on human reasoning. Many scholars question the truth of metanarratives (grand theories or stories that make sense of everything) and assume that life can only be interpreted locally. Others assume that cultural perspectives result not from a searching for and a discovering of truth but from the use of power and persuasion. Truth is relative to the cultural situation. Old foundations—and even the belief that foundations exist—are called into question.

Missionary recruiting and training during this time of cultural transformation is a colossal paradox. Moderns are training postmoderns. In postmodern language, rationals are teaching emotionals; cognitivists are mentoring experientials; propositionists are equipping narrativists. Consequently, many of the old models are being challenged publicly and privately. New mission agencies, more attuned to contemporary issues of culture and Christianity, are growing, and older agencies are declining.

Four practical guidelines may help as we transition from one age to another.

SIDEBAR 6.1

THE SUPREMACY OF GOD IN MISSIONS THROUGH WORSHIP

(*Piper 1993, 11–12*)

Missions is not the ultimate goal of the church. Worship is. Missions exists because worship doesn't. Worship is ultimate, not missions, because God is ultimate, not man. When this age is over, and the countless millions of the redeemed fall on their faces before the throne of God, missions will be no more. It is a temporary necessity. But worship abides forever.

Worship, therefore, is the fuel and goal of missions. It's the goal of missions because in missions we simply aim to bring the nations into the white-hot enjoyment of God's glory. The goal of missions is the gladness of the peoples in the greatness of God. "The LORD reigns; let the earth *rejoice*; let the many coastlands *be glad!*" (Ps. 97:3–4). "Let the peoples praise you, O God; let all the peoples praise you. Let the nations *be glad and sing for joy!*" (Ps. 67:3–4).

But worship is also the fuel of missions. Passion for God in worship precedes the offer of God in preaching. You can't commend what you don't cherish. Missionaries will never call out, "Let the nations *be glad!*" who cannot say from the heart, "*I rejoice* in the LORD. . . . *I will be glad and exult in you,* I will sing praise to your name, O Most High" (Ps. 104:34; 9:2). Missions begins and ends in worship.

If the pursuit of God's glory is not ordered above the pursuit of *man's* good in the affections of the heart and the priorities of the church, *man* will not be well served and *God* will not be duly honored. I am not pleading for a diminishing of missions but for a magnifying of God. When the flame of worship burns with the heat of God's true worth, the light of missions will shine to the most remote peoples on earth. And I long for that day to come.

When passion for God is weak, zeal for missions will be weak. Churches that are not centered on the exaltation of the majesty and beauty of God will scarcely kindle a fervent desire to "declare his glory among the nations" (Ps. 96:3). Even outsiders feel the disparity between the boldness of our claim upon the nations and the blandness of our engagement with God.

REFLECTION AND DISCUSSION

1. Piper contends that "missions is not the ultimate goal of the church. Worship is." What assumptions undergird this statement?
2. Worship is the fuel and the goal of missions. What are some practical ways that worship ignites people's passion for missions?

Return to the Core

Many mission leaders are frightened because the new generation feels uncomfortable emphasizing lostness and salvation from hell as motivations for missions. "How can this new generation of missionaries," they ask, "effectively carry out missions *without* emphasizing human lostness?" This leads them to ominously predict the demise of the North American missionary movement. They fail to see the reformulation of missionary motivations because they are blinded by the negation of what they consider to be the core motivation for missions.

Contemporary trends, however, are more positive than negative. Preaching that reflects the glory of God is a return to the core of the gospel. Proclaiming good news is an announcement of God's in-breaking glory, an opening of eyes, a turning from darkness to light, a revolution from "the power of Satan to God" (Acts 26:18). Paul writes to the Ephesians that Christians who dwell in the heavenlies while still living in the earthlies (1:20–21; 2:4–6) reflect "the praise of [God's] glorious grace" (1:6). They live "for the praise of his glory" (1:12; cf. 1:14).

> God is calling us above all else to be the kind of people whose theme and passion is the supremacy of God in all of life. No one will be able to rise to the magnificence of the missionary cause who does not feel the magnificence of Christ. There will be no big world vision without a big God. There will be no passion to draw others into our worship where there is no passion for worship. (Piper 1993, 40)

The glory of God is the essence of the kingdom of God and therefore can stimulate missions like no other motivation. Rather than complain that lostness is not a part of present theology, mission leaders must seek to redefine lostness within the broader theological motif of giving glory to God.

Emphasize the Positive

Within the postmodern context, no one, not even Christians, likes to think in terms of lostness. The Western freedom orientation also discourages preaching out of obligation or debt. For too long the negative has been substituted for the positive. When the lostness of humanity is substituted for honoring the glory of God as the source of missions, then the negative is promoted and the positive is relegated to the periphery.

It is mercenary to live the Christian life to get to heaven. Heaven should be seen as a place to commune with God and to share in his glory forever and ever, not merely as a reward for a life well lived.

Focus on the Spiritual

During modernity, Christian leaders focused on religious beliefs, anxiously seeking to differentiate truth from error. Theological debates were prevalent and appreciated. The emphasis has drastically changed during the postmodern period. What is negatively connoted as *religion* is being swallowed up by *spirituality*. What is considered rigid, authoritarian, and dogmatic is giving way to what is considered spiritual, creative, and tolerant. People who live spiritual, holy lives reflecting their relationship with God are looked upon as authentic Christians by their non-Christian peers. They are living righteously because they love God, not merely because they will receive a reward. Unless mission agencies rethink the theological emphases that draw the postmodern generation to missionary service, recruiting and maintaining missionaries will prove extremely difficult.

Gailyn Van Rheenen has had to learn to teach young postmodern searchers. Cold, rational religion is rejected. Postmoderns hearing the Christian message must not only understand the gospel narrative but also *feel* it. They must experience the type of emotion that artists feel when they perceive the meaning of a classic painting or composers feel when hearing an ageless musical composition. All parts fit together and sound intelligible to the rhythms and harmonies of life. Christian communicators, like musicians, must place the content of the Christian message within appropriate forms that have both meaning and emotion. Within this cultural climate, Van Rheenen has learned to teach with greater passion and emotion, expressing his own brokenness before God and continual need for his grace. This age is a practical age. We can bear fruit only when we are like branches connected to the true vine because apart from Christ we can do nothing (John 15:1–5).

The Christian communicator must also address practical life experiences. This is done most easily through faith stories and testimonies that glorify God's work through frail humans. Public dramas, role-plays, and skits also perform these functions. Postmoderns are bored with propositional categories.

Recognize Receptivity

It is amazing that Christianity survived the modern age in North America, while secularism eroded much of the Christian influence in Europe. During this period, the secular, naturalistic mentality declared God to be either nonexistent or irrelevant to human affairs. The natural realm was segmented from the supernatural, and many secularists declared that the natural world operated autonomously without interference from the supernatural. People increasingly lived for the here and now; were absorbed by material, this-worldly concerns; were extremely busy with earthly distractions; and were consumed by careers.

When taught empathetically, emotionally, and passionately, postmodernists tend to be much more receptive to Christianity than modernists.

179

CASE STUDY:
TWO CHURCHES

Two churches of the same denomination exist in close proximity in the same city. Both churches reach out to unbelievers and are growing, each in its own way.

Central Church focuses on the content of the gospel and the human response to it. Christians are trained to teach the gospel to unbelievers one at a time. They present the gospel in clear, understandable terms, being careful to include the major themes of grace, humanity, God, Christ, faith, response/commitment, and follow-up. Members of the church are trained to start conversations by using the two diagnostic questions developed for Evangelism Explosion (Kennedy 1983): (1) "Have you come to a place in your spiritual life where you know for certain that if you were to die today you would go to heaven?" and (2) "Suppose that you were to die tonight and stand before God and he were to say to you, 'Why should I let you into my heaven?' What would you say?"

Perimeter Church draws people into the church through fellowship, children's ministry, and Bible teaching. They focus on drawing people into the church, where evangelism can take place in natural, relational settings. They try to put living the Christian life over teaching about it. They think of themselves as God's people on a journey through life, glorifying God, helping one another as fellow disciples of Christ, and encouraging others to join in the journey to heaven. The members want to be living models of truth rather than people who prepare and organize propositions about truth.

Both churches focus on the Bible, are growing, and express Christianity in a saving, godly way. Both have asked you to evaluate their outreach ministry in a joint meeting. What would you say?

As God's creatures, they intensely feel a spiritual emptiness, a spiritual vacuum created by the heritage of Christendom. They feel disconnected from churches who give cognitive answers but have not been nurtured as spiritual communities on a journey with God. As a result, they tend to reject "religion" while seeking spirituality. Many are entering new spiritualities that borrow elements from the East and from folk religions and intertwine them with contemporary cultural beliefs and customs. They are highly responsive to Christianity, however, when a spiritual connectedness with God and a community is present.

Churches experience renewal when they relate personally with God rather than merely learning about God. The church, which has been marginalized by busy schedules and fragmented lives, must be recentered as a distinctive community formed by the calling and sending of God and reflecting the redemptive reign of God in Christ. Churches must accept the challenge to become spiritual communities that relate more intimately with God in this generation.

Ultimately, Christians must be aware of the truth that though our ways seem innocent to us, "motives are weighed by the LORD" (Prov. 16:2). "For the praise of God's glory" (Eph. 1:12, 14) is at the heart of Christian motivation. All other motivations are subcategories expressing the inward content of how God's people relate to the King of kings and the Lord of lords. During our few days on earth, we live to give glory to God while anticipating an eternity with him. The kingdom of God has come—we now perceive his glory. But with Christ's second coming, the kingdom will be consummated, and we will stand eternally in his glory. The majestic scene in heaven comes to mind:

> After this I looked and there before me was a great multitude that no one could count, from every nation, tribe, people and language, standing before the throne and in front of the Lamb. They were wearing white robes and were holding palm branches in their hands. And they cried out in a loud voice: "Salvation belongs to our God, who sits on the throne, and to the Lamb."
>
> Revelation 7:9–10

7

Increasing Awareness of Spiritual Power

The Spiritual Warfare Orientation to Missions

MICHAEL POCOCK

> The people at the World Prayer Center describe their sleek new building as a base for waging spiritual warfare. They aren't exaggerating by much.
>
> They've got prayer warriors battling Satan. They've got a combat plan for saving souls. They've got a situation room full of data and computers. They've even got a director who sounds like a general.... The World Prayer Center ... is expected to become the nerve center of an emerging worldwide evangelical prayer movement. Using phone, fax and Internet, evangelicals are trying to link 50 million Christians in 120 nations in targeted prayer. (Caldwell 1998, 26A)

The World Prayer Center, dramatically described in the *Dallas Morning News*, is an example of a spiritual warfare orientation to missions that has gathered strength during the past fifteen years. The center began out of a 1983 conversation between Ted Haggard, pastor of New Life Church—which houses the center in Colorado

Springs—and C. Peter Wagner, a missiologist then at Fuller School of World Mission. A 1998 campaign to target the "100 Gateway Cities" of the 10/40 Window was part of a movement to "Light the Window" with prayer, praise, and worship visits to key cities among unreached peoples. New Life Center, the Christian Broadcasting Network, and the AD 2000 Prayer Track of the AD 2000 and Beyond Movement were all involved.

IDENTIFYING THE TREND: SPIRITUAL WARFARE AND MISSIONS

At the international, local church, and personal levels, there has been a growing emphasis on overcoming what is viewed as satanic resistance to the program and people of God through focused prayer, power encounter, mapping of territories deemed to be under the control of particular demonic entities, binding "strong men," and identificational repentance for societal sins. How much of this is biblically sound? Why has this emphasis emerged, and what are its roots? Furthermore, in what ways should a spiritual warfare orientation guide missionary activity in the years ahead?

Toward the end of the twentieth century, mission thinkers and missionaries focused on completing the Great Commission. After almost two thousand years, it seemed the task Christ had given to his disciples and the church should be finished, and to a few it seemed within reach. At the beginning of the century, John Mott, a leading statesman of the Student Volunteer Movement (SVM), had challenged Christian university students with the phrase "the evangelization of the world in this generation" (Howard 1979, 91). The SVM did not accomplish all it had hoped to, but in one generation, it sent out over twenty-one thousand missionaries (Howard 1999, 283, citing Rouse and Neill 1967, 138).

In 1974, Billy Graham organized the Lausanne Conference on World Evangelization. The conference has been called "the most historic watershed in the development of evangelical Christianity in our generation" (Wagner 1996, 15). Mission speakers from around the world addressed the conference. Donald McGavran and Ralph Winter pleaded for setting mission priorities regarding unreached peoples. McGavran described the remaining situation that faced missions (1975, 94–107), and Winter called for cross-cultural evangelism as the only way to finish the task (1975, 213–41).

Winter then envisioned the creation of a closure-oriented movement, similar to the 1910 World Missionary Conference in Edinburgh, which was focused on completing world evangelization in that generation. In 1980, Winter gathered the World Conference on Frontier Missions, again in Edinburgh, Scotland. The old SVM challenge was renewed, this time as "a church for every people by the year 2000" (Butler 1995, 1). With just twenty years to go, it was clear that without a new vision and worldwide mobilization of Christians, neither the Great Commission nor the SVM goal would be fulfilled before the end of the century. Christianity had already spread worldwide by 1960, yet 2.4 billion people were still unreached, and they were out of reach of most existing Christians. The challenge was huge. Mission agencies and missionaries needed to freshen their focus and reexamine the way they worked. In 1985, Thomas Wang and Luis Bush amplified the rallying cry: "A church for every people and the Gospel for every person by the year 2000" (Winter 1993, 2). Bush, Wang, and others went on to head the AD 2000 and Beyond Movement. The stage was set for a great deal of reflection on factors that could speed up world evangelization and the barriers to overcome.

One of the questions being asked focused on the extent to which the perception of Christianity as a Western religion deterred majority world people from believing in Christ. Perhaps the answer was to indigenize the faith, making it appear to be of the soil of each culture in which it was proclaimed. Was communication the source of the problem? Perhaps contextualization, putting the message in verbal forms relevant to the target cultures, was the answer. Did mission organizations or churches not know where the unreached peoples lived? Bush made it easy for them by coining the term *10/40 Window*. Was it a failure to focus on actually finishing the task of world evangelization? Following Winter's lead, the main emphasis of the AD 2000 and Beyond Movement was on closure—completing the Great Commission. Under the leadership of Bush and others, this movement mobilized people, planning, finances, and prayer for world evangelization.

As mission strategists struggled to identify and overcome the barriers to bringing closure to the task of world evangelism, some concluded that a loss of biblical moorings, on the one hand, and of spiritual power, on the other, were primary problems (Peters 1975, 181–91; Lindsell 1976). In some cases, the emphasis on evangelism and missions that characterized many Western churches in the early years of the twentieth century faded as mainline denominations joined the World Council of Churches. Even the SVM began to lose its commitment to the authority of Scripture and ceased to exist in 1969 (Howard 1999).

But from Lausanne 1974 onward, there was a growing concern that many missionaries lacked spiritual power and that one of the principal limiting factors in finishing world evangelization was the opposition of Satan, the archenemy of God. After all, "The god of this age has blinded the minds of unbelievers, so that they cannot see the light of the gospel of the glory of Christ" (2 Cor. 4:4), and "Our gospel came to you not simply with words, but also with power, with the Holy Spirit and with deep conviction" (1 Thess. 1:5). Some mission thinkers began to focus more intently on the issues of satanic opposition and spiritual power.

The concern to recapture Holy Spirit power had been the major impetus of the Pentecostal and charismatic movements, beginning in the 1900s. However, even non-Pentecostal Anglicans such as Roland Allen drew attention to the role of the Spirit. His books *The Spontaneous Expansion of the Church* (1962b) and *Missionary Methods: St. Paul's or Ours?* (1962a), which reentered circulation in the 1960s long after their original appearance in 1912 and 1927, focused attention on doing missions, not simply with Pauline *doctrine* but with New Testament *patterns*.

Peter Wagner, with mission experience in Latin America, researched and taught for years on the theme of church growth. Like Winter, he was an early disciple of McGavran at the Fuller School of World Mission. Wagner wanted to see churches growing and multiplying among the receptive peoples of the world, which McGavran strongly emphasized (1979). Wagner, though not a Pentecostal himself, could see that Pentecostal and charismatic churches were growing the fastest (*Look Out! The Pentecostals Are Coming*, 1973). He identified the Pentecostal emphasis on the power of the Holy Spirit as the basis for ministry effectiveness. He could see that Pentecostals were people of prayer and that they believed God has power over Satan, disease, poverty, and alienation. Although this chapter takes issue with some of the distinctive emphases of Wagner's thought, there is no doubt that he made an indelible impact on thousands of Christian workers who learned from him how to start and grow multiplying churches.

Wagner was not alone in sensing the need for spiritual power in missions (1996, 13–14). By the 1980s, the charismatic movement was followed by what Wagner called the Third Wave (Wagner 1988; see sidebar 7.1). Leaders included Wagner and John Wimber of the Vineyard Church. Together they taught a class titled "Signs and Wonders" at Fuller Seminary beginning in 1983. Other Fuller School of World Mission faculty, including cultural anthropologists Allan Tippett and Charles Kraft, interacted with Wagner and Wimber. Tippett and Kraft brought a deep awareness of the worldviews of traditional tribal peoples sometimes called animism. As missionaries and anthropologists, they had witnessed rites of possession and exorcism. They had observed that among traditional folk religion, power, the ability to effect outcomes, was the primary factor in conversion and that power was an integral part of Jesus' and the apostles' ministry of word and deed (Kraft 2002b).

By the mid-1980s, Pentecostals, charismatics, and Third Wavers had people advocating a spiritual warfare approach to ministry and missions. Among these were Juan Carlos Ortiz of Argentina, Edward

---

SIDEBAR 7.1
IMPORTANT TERMS USED IN THIS CHAPTER

---

animism: A once-popular term that expressed the belief that spiritual forces and spirits animate the universe and determine most earthly and heavenly events and that these can be influenced or appeased by magical acts, incantations, ritual activity, or avoidance of objects and activities that are taboo.

binding Satan or spirits: A process of stopping satanic or demonic opposition to the spread and receptivity of the gospel by identifying the demons in control of an individual, group, or area and commanding them to stop interfering with God's purposes. Advocates claim as a basis the binding of the strong man (Matt. 12:22–29).

closure strategy: An orientation toward finishing the task of the Great Commission, a situation in which a biblically sound, culturally relevant, and growing body of Christians is found in every people group on earth, and all have heard the gospel.

identificational repentance: When a representative group repents on behalf of a larger group, with an emphasis on corporate repentance for corporate sins (see Moreau 2002b, 262).

prayer walks: The practice of going to areas resistant to the gospel and walking in prayer for the people and against whatever forces may be opposed to the gospel. Prayer walks usually are also worship centered. Advocates claim as a basis Israel marching around Jericho (Josh. 6) and Jehoshaphat's victory over his enemies through worship (2 Chron. 20:1–29).

Strategic Level Spiritual Warfare (SLSW): "Describes confrontation with high-ranking principalities and powers such as Paul writes about in Ephesians 6:12. These forces are frequently called 'territorial spirits' because they attempt to keep large numbers of humans networked through cities, nations, neighborhoods, people groups . . . or any other form of human society in spiritual captivity" (Wagner 1996, 22).

territorial spirits: Demonic beings said to control geographic areas or groups of people. These spirits limit the ability of people in the group or area to respond to the gospel. Advocates claim as a basis events depicted in Daniel 10:10–20.

Third Wave: Evangelicals who embraced the ongoing nature of the gifts of the Spirit without agreeing to the Pentecostal or charismatic position on the baptism of the Holy Spirit. It was often associated with the signs and wonders movement led by such figures as John Wimber and Vineyard churches.

Silvoso of Brazil, John Dawson of Youth with a Mission, and Cindy Jacobs of Generals of Intercession. Several faculty members from Bible colleges and seminaries—including C. Fred Dickason (1975), Merrill Unger (1957, 1977), Mark Bubeck (1991), Neil Anderson (1990), and Timothy Warner (1991)—also realized that they were failing to prepare men and women for ministry in a world in which real satanic opposition existed and introduced spiritual warfare courses into their curricula.

Many others have wrestled with the issue, though from a variety of stances. They include Clinton Arnold (1992, 1997), David Powlison (1995), Robert Priest (Priest, Campbell, and Mullins 1995), Michael Pocock (1997, 2001), Douglas McConnell (1997b), Gailyn Van Rheenen (1991), and A. Scott Moreau (1995, 1997, 2002b). Most of them have had numerous occasions to minister to those facing severe spiritual conflict, sometimes of a demonic nature. As a result, they are aware that their basic theological training, while biblical and sound, did not give them sufficient pastoral or ministry preparation for dealing with extreme spiritual conflict. They found it necessary to initiate courses to prepare their own students for spiritual warfare or conflict.

Out of this general awakening, the trend of an increasing awareness of spiritual power arose within evangelical ranks. It grew to such importance that the Evangelical Missiological Society, made up of professors and practitioners of missions, devoted two of its annual volumes to spiritual warfare and spiritual power (Rommen 1995; McConnell 1997b). A third book dealt with other factors in overcoming resistance to the gospel (Woodberry 1998).

Robert Priest, Thomas Campbell, and Brad Mullins offered a sharp critique on the emergence of the spiritual warfare orientation to missions (1995). This was compiled with responses by Kraft and Johnstone (Rommen 1995), creating perhaps the best scholarly evaluation of the issue (see also Lowe 1998). However, it is lacking in prescription for actual ministry.

The most recent work that integrates reflection from majority world writers is *Deliver Us from Evil: An Uneasy Frontier in Christian Mission* (Moreau et al. 2002). Containing the papers delivered by people from every continent at the "Deliver Us from Evil" LCWE conference (Nairobi, Kenya, August 16–20, 2000), it offers truly global perspectives. The consultation statement, produced by the international body at the consultation, is helpful (Moreau et al. 2002, xvii–xxviii; Moreau 2002a).

Many spiritual warfare advocates focus on the identification of spirits that they believe control areas where there is resistance to the gospel. The research involved is called spiritual mapping, and the confrontation that results is called Strategic Level Spiritual Warfare (Wagner 1996, 42). Proponents believe that once spirits are identified, proponents can bind or limit their effectiveness in opposing the gospel. Many also believe and practice identificational repentance, which involves a representative group repenting on behalf of a larger group for sins done in the past. Examples include Southern Baptists repenting on behalf of their ancestors for the slave trade and Christians retracing the route of the Crusades to repent on behalf of the church to descendents of Muslim victims. The foundational idea is that it is possible and even necessary to break down resistance to God or to speed answers to prayer by recognizing the sins of self and others and repenting of them (Dan. 9; Neh. 1; see Moreau 2002b, 262–65).

Understanding the Christian life as one lived in a context of conflict is neither unbiblical nor new. It is the classic stance of Scripture and believers throughout the ages. Present circumstances require a renewal and an awakening of this understanding, but Christians should also be aware of aspects of novelty and concern.

EVALUATING THE TREND: THE FUTURE OF SPIRITUAL WARFARE AND MISSIONS

A spiritual warfare orientation toward missions includes an understanding that the chief factors involved in the spreading of the Christian faith are spiritual in nature. God, human beings, and angels (good and evil) are in conflict with one another. Each of these is fundamentally spiritual in nature. God works in spiritually powerful ways—sometimes dramatically, more often quietly—to make himself and his salvation known to people. He works through people as well as angelic beings, orchestrating circumstances to accomplish his will.

God is the transcendent or ultimate being in the universe. He is in sovereign control of all that exists. In Christ his Son, he has broken the chief dynamic of opposition to himself and his purposes, which is sin, and by this has also destroyed the work of Satan. The forces that oppose God were defeated through the life, death, and resurrection of Jesus, who took on himself the sin of the world. All people who receive this atonement, with the regenerating presence and power of the Holy Spirit, are free from bondage to sin. They are also free from Satan, who works on people through their own sinful patterns of living.

The gospel is the good news of what Christ has accomplished. People who receive the gospel change kingdoms from that of darkness to that of God's Son. Evangelism is, therefore, a deliverance ministry. Christian ministry is the application of the results of Christ's finished work. Christians, who are forgiven of their sin and freed from Satan, may nevertheless be troubled by their sin or Satan's emissaries to the extent that they fail to walk in the truth of God's Word. They may believe Satan's lies about themselves, their circumstances, or God.

Satan, though defeated, is not confined. He seeks to blind those who have not heard, received, or understood the gospel and to block all attempts to evangelize the lost. He controls those who think they have no alternative but to serve him or the institutions, false religions, or obligations he uses as principalities and powers, of which the apostle Paul and others spoke.

SIDEBAR 7.2
EVALUATING STRATEGIC LEVEL SPIRITUAL WARFARE

(Adapted from Moreau 2002b, 265–69; Engelsvíken 2001, 59–61)

Perhaps no area in the discussion of spiritual warfare has been more controversial than the practice of engaging territorial spirits put forth in Strategic Level Spiritual Warfare (SLSW). The following lists provide negative and positive aspects of the approach.

POSITIVE ASPECTS

1. SLSW advocates take Satan and the powers more seriously than has occurred in previous Western mission approaches. The emphasis on prayer is a good corrective to planning and strategizing along the lines of Western management-oriented missiology.
2. SLSW advocates emphasize that divisiveness weakens prayer. They stress the unity of the church and cooperation over competition in missions.
3. SLSW advocates focus on the ultimate goal of saving the lost.
4. Cultures do have evil spiritual dimensions in which various elements work together to trap people and keep them blinded to spiritual realities.
5. SLSW attempts to discern areas in which churches need to repent, expressing this in corporate ways. This is a positive help in unleashing the power of God.
6. Advocates see themselves as experimenters, understanding that the approach of SLSW is new. They seem open to dialogue and correction.

Christians, therefore, understand that they are free but in a struggle to live for God's glory and to spread the gospel. Victory over sin, the influence of the world, and the efforts of Satan rests on the following: daily dependence on the Spirit of God and the truth of the Word of God; constant, fervent prayer that signifes a conscious dependence on God; and a life of joyful worship, fellowship, and service with a community of God's people.

With this in mind, how are we to evaluate this trend? As noted previously, a good starting point is the statement of the "Deliver Us from Evil" conference—all the more so because of the global makeup of its participants and the variety of their perspectives on spiritual conflict.

Questionable Elements Do Not Nullify a Legitimate Movement of God

While many find the spiritual warfare trend to be a mixed bag of positive and questionable features (e.g., Moreau [2002b]; Powlison [1995]; Priest, Campbell, and Mullins [1995]), we dare not dismiss the trend

NEGATIVE ASPECTS

1. A number of SLSW distinctives are not found in the Bible.
2. An emphasis on discerning the names of demons in order to control them approaches a form of Christian animism or magic.
3. Prayer was not intended to be a sophisticated spiritual weapon but a means of fellowship, growth, and strength.
4. Seeking information about the spirit realm as a means of overcoming evil powers does not appear to be necessary (or significant) in the Bible.
5. The strategy of SLSW may ultimately demean Scripture when it is presented as a key to effective evangelization that is not found in Scripture.
6. An emphasis on territorial spirits detaches demons from people and thus deemphasizes participation of humans in their rebellion against God.
7. The ideas of serving notice, evicting, and binding spirits do not have biblical warrant and place too much emphasis on technique and effectiveness, especially when the people themselves continue to invite control by the way they live.

REFLECTION AND DISCUSSION

1. SLSW advocates encourage prayer walks and also praising and worshiping God openly in areas where there has been spiritual opposition to the gospel. Can you think of instances in Scripture when this was done?
2. Look up Joshua 6; 2 Chronicles 6:1–29; and Nehemiah 2:7–20. These are Old Testament passages. Do you think their examples apply today? Why? Why not?
3. Who is really in charge of affairs in this world? How do you reconcile the statements found in Psalm 96:1–13 and 1 John 5:19?

as inconsequential, illegitimate, or even bereft of the blessing of God. Movements of God often have a certain untidiness that is not attributable to God but to the fact that limited human beings are involved.

For example, the founding of the Antioch church (Acts 11) was a spontaneous movement to the Lord in response to the witness of Jewish-background believers fleeing from Jerusalem. Gentiles began to flock to the faith. Gentile response to the gospel seemed to puzzle the Jewish believers in Jerusalem, so they sent Barnabas to investigate. It did not take long for him to realize he needed help in teaching this growing flock, so he invited Paul to lay down some systematic teaching of Scripture.

New Testament churches such as those at Corinth, Galatia, and those mentioned in the book of Revelation experienced excesses and misunderstandings. They needed correction, but the believers were still called saints. They still made up the church of God. This reality was also observed by Puritan preacher Jonathan Edwards during the First Great Awakening in America (1832, 108). Winter (1996) points out

191

that many genuine movements of God, like Protestantism itself, were considered heretical at their inception. The point is not that we should tolerate error but that we should be patient with fresh movements in missions that do not fit our expectations of how God works. They may very well be of God.

Is the Spiritual Warfare Orientation to Missions Effective?

Quantification of the results of the growing spiritual warfare orientation is difficult. Perhaps it is only an American who would demand hard data about spiritual issues. But it is worth asking whether the spiritual warfare orientation to missions has made a noticeable impact on the progress of world evangelization.

> *Even rash acts that are contrary to the Word of God do not disprove the presence of revival. . . . The Spirit who works sanctification in the believer does not do it all at once. There is dross with the gold, tares with the wheat.*
>
> Jonathan Edwards (Parrish and Sproul 2000, 28)

There is no doubt that the gospel has spread widely and has penetrated many previously unreached peoples during the same period in which the spiritual warfare orientation to missions has been growing (from the early 1980s to the present). Christianity as a percentage of the world population dropped slightly from 33.2 percent in 1990 to 33 percent in 2002, but that still represents a numerical increase of 253 million people—a 14 percent growth rate in the 1990–2000 decade (Jaffarian 2002, 19).

The question remains: Was this attributable to the spiritual warfare trend? That would be difficult at best to establish. However, as Philip Jenkins shows, the growing edge of the church worldwide is attuned to "a very strong supernatural orientation" (2002, 7). The newest Christianity, the Christianity that is growing in Latin America and Africa, he maintains, is most like the oldest Christianity of the New Testament, complete with dreams, prophesy, healings, and spirit exorcisms. He notes:

> These signs of power usually imply the concept of spiritual warfare, of confronting and defeating evil demonic forces. For African Christians, one of the most potent passages of the New Testament is found in the letter to the Ephesians, in which Paul declares that "Our struggle is not against enemies of blood and flesh, but against the rulers, against the authorities, against the cosmic powers of this present darkness, against the forces of evil in the heavenly places." However superstitious and irrelevant it appears to mainstream Northern Christians, the passage makes wonderful sense in most of Africa as it does for believers in Latin America or East Asia. (Jenkins 2002, 129)

Jenkins's careful research squares with Michael Pocock's own experience in ministry where the church is growing at the edges of its frontiers. In Nepal, where known Christians numbered 25 in 1950, there are today over 440,000 (Johnstone and Mandryk 2001, 470). In 1991, Pocock had the opportunity to interact with first-generation believers there who had previously been Hindu in faith. He inquired as to how they had been drawn to Christianity. The most frequent response was that they had experienced difficulties with demons and had tried many remedies, even exorcism attempts by Hindu priests, all to no avail. In response to their desperation, people recommended that they "go to the Christians; they know what to do." They were introduced to Christ and had no further difficulties with evil spirits.

In 2003, Pocock was also impressed by God's work in new believers in India. A number of these testified to rescue from demon possession and physical healing as the key factors in coming to faith. All of them emphasized that it was not so much the act of a person casting a demon out of them that brought them to faith as the message of the gospel, which they believed in their desperation. Having believed, they had no further difficulties with demons. Others who were sick had gone to Christians to pray for them, and when these believers prayed and they were healed, they trusted in the Lord Jesus Christ. Several times Pocock and his wife found themselves in the midst of humble, sick people asking for them to anoint them and lay hands on them in prayer, which they did. It felt as though they were living in the New Testament. This is the experience of Christianity at its growing edges.

The question is, did the spiritual warfare orientation cause the growth in the Southern and Eastern hemispheres over the past twenty years, or is the North American phenomenon a reflection of what was happening elsewhere? As noted near the beginning of this chapter, Latin American Christians such as Juan Carlos Ortiz, Ed Silvoso, Luis Bush, and Rita de Cabezas have been influential in the growth of the spiritual warfare trend, and they have always been in touch with their North American counterparts. Globalization, as shown in chapter 1, is a two-way cultural, commercial, communicational, and even spiritual exchange. There is no way that a growing, more supernaturally oriented faith would not influence the West in the same way that Western technology and culture have influenced the rest of the world. This is particularly true at a time when a great deal of Western Christianity, particularly in Europe, seems to have stalled. It needs the help of majority world Christians because, in many ways, Western Christianity has become indistinguishable from the secular culture that surrounds it.

The spiritual warfare orientation to missions parallels the amazing growth of Christianity in the majority world. We may not be able to establish a direct relationship between the growth of the trend among North Americans and the success of outreach among unreached peoples achieved by North Americans, but the people most involved in the spiritual warfare orientation are also among the most active mobilizers for missions, raising both prayer for and personal involvement in cross-cultural missions.

John Dawson of Youth with a Mission (YWAM) is a proponent of the spiritual warfare orientation to missions. YWAM now has 12,000 workers in 135 countries. It is one of the largest and fastest growing mission movements originating in North America and draws workers from around the world. Steven Hawthorne is a spiritual warfare advocate, coeditor with Ralph Winter of the immensely influential *Perspectives on the World Christian Movement* text (1999), and teacher of an introductory class in missions that has been taken by over 40,000 students. Luis Bush headed the AD 2000 and Beyond Movement, which focused attention on engaging unreached peoples. Rick Love, international director of Frontiers, a leading and rapidly growing ministry to Muslims, finds that the spiritual warfare approach fits with the folk expression of Islam found around the world (Love 2000, 112).

Apart from rapid Christian growth worldwide in the past twenty years, there are indications in some countries that the employment of spiritual warfare techniques has led to greater evangelistic success. Charles Kraft notes that those who take a spiritual warfare approach in Argentina, particularly Carlos Annacondia, Omar Cabrera, Claudio Friedzon, and Victor Lorenzo, "have been very successful in winning people to Christ." He adds, "The conversion records of Annacondia and the other Argentine evangelists are truly impressive" (2002a, 193–94).

David Garrison identifies ten church-planting movements that are sweeping areas of Latin America, Africa, and Asia. These movements are vibrant and unmistakably Christian yet at the same time contain elements that differ from standard Western orthodoxy. They are "untidy" and depend more on workers from inside the cultures than those from outside. Among these movements are people who still read the Quran, who gather on Fridays rather than on Sundays, who meet in houses rather than in church buildings, and for whom spiritual conflict and power encounter are daily realities (Garrison 1999, 29). Expatriate Christian workers are present in many of these movements. They have a catalytic effect but do not control the spread of the movements nor the manner in which their adherents live.

During the twenty-plus years of the growth of the spiritual warfare orientation to missions, the Joshua Project has taken on the challenge of identifying unreached people groups and encouraging others to engage these peoples with a Christian witness. The Joshua Project report of 1995 showed 1,739 unreached people groups around the world. This number was reduced to 539 groups by 2000. Joshua Project workers acknowledge the encouragement they have received by those in the spiritual warfare movement.

It seems evident that God is doing a wonderful work in the world. Christian faith at the edges of its expansion shows many marks of New Testament Christianity, including a keen awareness of situations of spiritual conflict and evidences of the power of God to challenge and overcome demonic strongholds. People who work cross-culturally among unreached peoples or in situations of rapid Christian growth must be knowledgeable about biblical teaching on spiritual power, have confidence in their authority to minister in Jesus' name, and have Christ's power to confront and overcome spiritual opposition.

Michael Pocock has been in overseas ministry or has taught missions during the entire period the spiritual warfare orientation has been growing. He considers many of the people cited his friends, brothers and sisters in Christ. Yet he knew little about dealing with demonic issues when he had his first encounter with a demonized person in Wheaton, Illinois. He was in the same position John Nevius observed regarding fellow missionaries when they encountered demon possession in China in the nineteenth century. They were unprepared and knew nothing but to dismiss possession as a phenomenon of prescientific cultures (Nevius 1968). Thankfully, in Pocock's case, another missionary was able to help, and he learned a lot about dealing with demonically affected people through the use of Scripture, prayer, and solemn confrontation.

> *The mission and passion of the Joshua Project is to identify and highlight the peoples of the world that have the least exposure to the Gospel and the least Christian presence in their midst. Joshua Project uses this information through data sharing and networking to encourage pioneer church-planting movements among every ethnic people group.*
>
> http://www.joshuaproject.net

Gradually, it became clear to Pocock that many missionaries and Christian workers either lacked insight into spiritual warfare or had simply never been prepared. They generally felt that whatever problems they encountered in themselves or others were a product of the flesh or the world culture. He came to realize he was inadvertently sending the message to anyone troubled with demons that he did not believe they could have the problem. About the same time, Wagner and others were beginning to consider the role of spiritual power in understanding cultures around the world. They sensed that many Western missionaries

195

and thinkers were less supernaturally oriented than people in other parts of the world. Pocock did not move into the Third Wave of the Spirit, as many spiritual warfare advocates did, but he did become much more aware that Satan "prowls around like a roaring lion looking for someone to devour" (1 Pet. 5:8). He also began to look more closely at what Scripture says about the activity of Satan, the triumph of Christ over him, and the application of these truths to people in need.

Then graduates of his seminary began writing and asking why it had not prepared them for dealing with the spiritual warfare they encountered in their ministries. Typically, an evangelical school offers courses in Christian life truths, systematic theology courses in which the activity of angels is only a subset of a larger treatment of another theological category, and counseling courses to help Christians deal biblically with emotional struggles. The focus in all these is on describing biblical teaching or handling the "normal range" of Christian life. Not a great deal is taught about applying biblical truth or ministering in a pastoral way to those with purported demonic difficulties. Pocock's experience was not atypical. In fact, many evangelical schools have responded to a perceived lack in ministry preparation by introducing courses on spiritual warfare. The multiplication of classes and texts reinforced the sense that the spiritual warfare orientation was a growing trend, but actually the courses supplied a need that in many cases had been there all along.

Worldview Implications of the Trend

The chapter on the changing basis of knowledge dealt with the movement from modernity to postmodernity. This change has a great deal to do with those involved in the spiritual warfare trend, who are far more ready to accept and deal with what Paul Hiebert called "the flaw of the excluded middle" (1982). He and others who have dealt with this phenomenon (Love 2000, 70–74) contrast the Western worldview with the majority world orientation. Hiebert argued that during the Enlightenment period (1750–1850), which led to the era of modernity (1850–1980), Westerners separated reality into two distinct compartments. They formed an upper-level category of the transcendent or religious and a lower level of the immanent or mundane world of nature (1982, 82; see also Love 2000; Moreau 2000b).

For Westerners, little or nothing exists in the space between the upper and the lower level. The upper level cannot be known except through empirically unverifiable faith. It is therefore not susceptible to scientific investigation, and what cannot be demonstrated verifiably may not exist. The lower level, nature, can be investigated and known through empirical means, namely, the scientific method. Although Bible-believing Western Christians knew that the middle area contained activity of angels or demons, they paid little attention to it. Many from the majority world, however, possess a worldview in which a great deal of activity takes place in the middle realm that affects life. In the postmodern world, there is considerable interest in the middle sphere.

Western missionaries tended to present Christianity as an intellectually understandable truth about the transcendent God revealed in his Word. This knowledge, when embraced, would change the eternal state of the believer and would gradually transform the believer's lifestyle. As the new believer progressed, he or she would also experience positive changes in life circumstances, what Donald McGavran called "social lift." Western missionaries also felt that their civilization, which owed much to Christian influences, when embraced, would bring positive change to cultures that theretofore had suffered from what was perceived as superstitious or magical worldviews (Kraft 1995, 93).

The orientation of Western missionaries was less supernatural than the worldview of those they were trying to reach. Most Western missionaries simply did not take the middle realm seriously enough to understand it. They believed that all difficulties stemming from what they regarded as either wrong belief and practice or possibly demons would disappear when new converts realized they were fearful of forces that did not exist or played a minor role in life.

What Western missionaries did not realize was that they were unconsciously syncretizing their faith with the secular worldview of modernity. Though modernity produced many physical benefits, it was also spiritually bankrupt. It offered no way of dealing with ultimate meaning in life, which is why a general rebellion against modernity, or secular materialism, occurred between 1980 and 2000. Many people could see that Marxist materialism had failed to provide a better life in the areas controlled by it, and Western materialism had no answers to transcendent questions. While parading as the irrefutable way, secular materialism could not solve problems like those in Bosnia and the Balkans or the genocidal intertribal conflicts of Rwanda and Burundi, Ireland or the Middle East. Frustration with the failure of modernity brought on the rebellion of postmodernity. Postmodernity has not necessarily solved the problems of modernity, but it has unleashed a search for meaning and understanding in life, the key to which is not rationality or empirical investigation but intuition and subjectivity. This is why so many forms of spirituality are thriving today and undiluted supernaturalism has grown in older religions, including Christianity, which are manifesting themselves with new vigor.

As shown in chapter 4, dissatisfaction with modernity had been growing since the days of Søren Kierkegaard in the nineteenth century. Both religious and secular existentialism are really "pre-postmodernism" rebellions against modernity. To combat the secularizing and faith-destroying elements of modernity, many in the evangelical movement attempted to contextualize the faith by setting it in more empirical language and approaches to biblical studies. Evangelical Christians did not want to look unscientific, antiquated, irrelevant, or anti-intellectual. In many ways, their efforts succeeded. However, the result was often the minimizing of supernatural elements clearly present in Scripture. Majority world Christians intuitively and practically knew of the existence of good and evil spirits as well as the mighty power of God, who can and does manifest himself today.

The spiritual warfare orientation to life and ministry is a part of postmodernity. It is understandable and needed as a corrective to a Christianity overly influenced by modernity, but those who follow it can make as many mistakes in observing and coming to conclusions about spiritual phenomena as unregenerate people have about general revelation. People of majority world traditional cultures can fail to comprehend correctly what God has shown in nature (Rom. 1:18–32). They can draw incorrect conclusions about the nature and the extent of spirit control in their lives and how to deal with it. That is why Christians must subject their thinking even more carefully to Scripture. The Bible speaks adequately about the so-called excluded middle. Evangelicals have long recognized the "perspicuity" of Scripture—that the Bible both is understandable and deals as fully as God deems necessary with every area on which it touches (2 Tim. 3:16–17). The result is that missionaries can be confident that Scripture instructs us about every area of ministry and Christian life for every culture. It is unnecessary and unwise to formulate understandings of spiritual realities that do not square with Scripture or to conduct ministries based on less than scriptural foundations. We must listen to the advice of A. Scott Moreau when he urges us "not [to] let the flaw of the excluded middle become the flaw of the expanded middle" (2002b, 270).

> *Both the disenchanted world of modern rationalism and the charmed world of pre-modern spiritism are wrong. . . . The deliverance mentality often grafts Christian elements onto an underlying demonic and superstitious world-view, creating a hybrid perhaps acceptable to pre-modern minds. But the biblical Christian faith needs to stand alone; it should not be grafted onto other world views.*
>
> David Powlison (1995, 25)

REFLECTING ON THE TREND: SCRIPTURAL REFLECTION ON SPIRITUAL WARFARE

This section does not reflect on the historical continuity of spiritual warfare thinking from the New Testament era to the present. Clinton Arnold and others have shown abundant evidence that the church has always seen itself in a conflict with the powers of darkness (Arnold 1992, 1997; Pocock 1996b). The church's response to satanic influence, however, has not always been biblical and balanced. People suspected of demonic involvement have been treated terribly in Europe (Joan of Arc), Latin America (Pizarro's treatment of the Inca Atehualpa), and North America (the Salem witch trials). But these failures do not negate the reality of satanic opposition; they simply call for more biblical and balanced approaches.

The main point is that we should not dismiss the current spiritual warfare trend simply as a contemporary fad but instead recognize it as a renewal of old and legitimate concerns. Those engaged in the present trend, nevertheless, need sound biblical and theological grounding and some correction. The question is whether spiritual warfare, while clearly a part of scriptural and historical testimony, is an overarching theme or motif in Scripture. Does spiritual warfare deserve to be elevated to the dominant place it holds in the emphasis and orientation of some people and movements?

The Pilgrimage Motif

The spiritual warfare orientation tends to present conflict as the key motif of Scripture and the Christian life. This is not reasonable—at least not as the dominant motif of Scripture. Some would argue that pilgrimage or journey is a more dominant theme. After all, the events of the exodus and journey through the wilderness occupy a great place in the Pentateuch. They are referred to throughout the Prophets and poetic books, are memorialized in Jewish feasts such as Passover and Tabernacles, and brought to the minds of New Testament believers in 1 Corinthians 10:1–13.

The concept of developing spirituality progressively over a long period, like a pilgrimage, is indisputably a major biblical theme. It is an antidote to the quick fixes that spiritual warfare advocates have sometimes been accused of using when they practice deliverance ministry (Powlison 1995, 148–52). The idea of pilgrimage really is about sanctification—it is more about people than about God. It has to do with how people grow and mature spiritually. Nevertheless, it may reflect something about the way God works, which should be understood by his people. Kosuke Koyama must have realized this when he wrote *Three Mile an Hour God* (1979). His contention is that when God wanted to accomplish his greatest work, he did it through Christ, who never traveled faster than three miles an hour yet fully accomplished his Father's will.

The Glory of God Motif

In 1993, John Piper wrote *Let the Nations Be Glad!* In it he emphasized worship, declaring that worship of God is the main objective of missions. He stated, "Worship is the fuel and object of missions" (1993, 15). The book was widely read and used in mission classes. Students enthusiastically embraced global ministry as an opportunity to declare God's glory and to raise up what Piper called "white-hot worshippers of the Lamb" (1993, 11).

Piper was not new in his emphasis on God's glory. InterVarsity Christian Fellowship used "Declare His Glory" as the theme of the 1961 Urbana Missionary Convention. They were drawing, as Piper did, on Psalm 96:3, which quotes 1 Chronicles 16:24. Declaring God's glory is a major theme of the most "internationalist" of the prophets, Isaiah. He continually calls the peoples of the earth to worship the Lord (55:1–13; 56:3–8) and prophesies that they will indeed come to worship him and "revere his glory" (59:19). As history merges into eternity in Revelation 7:9, we see people from every tribe, tongue, people, and nation worshiping the Lamb, and angels are singing, "Amen! Praise and glory and wisdom and thanks and honor and power and strength be to our God for ever and ever. Amen!" (7:12).

> *Let me tell you something wonderful that happens when you draw near to God in praise and worship. It gives the devil an allergy. He's allergic to the praise of God. Satan is hypersensitive to prayer. When the air is filled with prayer and praise, it chokes Satan up and makes it hard for him to function.*
>
> Tony Evans (1998, 338)

The glory of God is clearly a major theme of Scripture, and spiritual warfare advocates have never maintained that their chief aim is other than to glorify God. But if the "excluded middle" becomes the "expanded middle," then focus on the glory of God may suffer. Amazingly, Paul tells the Colossians that *because* of Christ's supremacy, he aims to teach the glorious riches of Christ among the Gentiles, "struggling with all his energy, which so powerfully works in me" (1:29). The struggle or conflict of ministry is related to and finds its logic in the glory and supremacy of God.

SIDEBAR 7.3
THE CHRISTIAN WORLDVIEW

We glorify God when we consider him the sovereign ruler of the universe, for that is who he is. The LCWE statement (Moreau et al. 2002, xxi) and contributor Hwa Yung (2002, 9) spend a good deal of time on this fact. A Christian worldview must include the following:

1. God is the creator and sustainer of all that exists, both seen and unseen.
2. People were made in the image of God and are whole beings with their parts inseparably connected.
3. God remains sovereign over all creation.
4. A dualistic worldview must be rejected.
5. Teaching on spiritual warfare that leads people to fear the devil to such an extent that they lose confidence in Christ's victory over him and in God's sovereign power must be rejected.
6. Spiritual conflict must be viewed in terms of a relationship to and faith in God, not simply in terms of techniques that people must master.
7. The return of Christ and the ultimate consummation of his victory over Satan provide confidence today in dealing with spiritual struggles and a lens through which to interpret the events in the world today.

REFLECTION AND DISCUSSION

1. Discuss how Satan and demons fit in a world in which God is sovereign.
2. Describe your level of confidence in your ability to be successful in a world in which Satan and demons are clearly at work.
3. If you were teaching new believers in a traditional or animistic culture, what would you emphasize about the causes of the fortune and misfortune they face?

The Kingdom Motif

The significance of the person and glory of God fills the pages of Holy Scripture, meaning that God's glory is indisputably a motif, or organizing theme, of the Bible (see McClain 1968). God is the sovereign ruler of the universe, and what he controls is his kingdom. In one sense, nothing that exists is outside his rule or kingdom, and yet there are kingdoms within the kingdom, somewhat like spheres of interest. God expresses his kingdom rule at various levels and in various ways, and he progressively reveals the nature of it in Scripture. Humans at any period in history have had only a partial understanding of the kingdom of God, partly because we are constitutionally incapable of grasping its immensity. This is why Jesus, in teaching about his kingdom, actually hid it from those who were not disposed to grasp it while revealing it to others through parables and other explanations (Matt. 13:10–17).

SIDEBAR 7.4

GOD'S KINGDOM IN THE OLD TESTAMENT

The idea of God's kingship and his possession of a kingdom is beautifully expressed by David in 1 Chronicles 29:10–13. Read the following passage and reflect on the questions that follow.

> Praise be to you, O LORD,
>   God of our father Israel,
>   from everlasting to everlasting.
> Yours, O LORD, is the greatness and the
>   power
>   and the glory and the majesty and
>   the splendor,
>   for everything in heaven and earth
>   is yours.
> Yours, O LORD, is the kingdom;
>   you are exalted as head over all.

> Wealth and honor come from you;
>   you are the ruler of all things.
> In your hands are strength and power
>   to exalt and give strength to all.
> Now, our God, we give you thanks,
>   and praise your glorious name.

REFLECTION AND DISCUSSION

1. Has there been or will there ever be a time when God is not in control of everything?
2. When you consider how you handle difficulties, who gets the most attention, God or Satan?
3. What is the appropriate response to God's rule and power?

David grasped the comprehensive nature of God's kingdom, which, as Daniel said, is an eternal kingdom (Dan. 4:3). This kingdom cannot be shaken, though adversaries revolt against it and reject it in favor of personal autonomy. This is, of course, what happened with the rebellion of Satan (Isa. 14:12–20; Ezek. 28:11–17) and the fall of humankind in Adam (Gen. 3:1–24; Rom. 5:12–19). With these rebellions, a different sphere of operation came into being—a kingdom of darkness (John 12:31; Col. 1:12–13).

There is a kingdom sphere into which God's people are invited. Early in Scripture, God spoke to Abraham, promising to make him into a great nation through which he would bless the entire world and every clan or extended family in it (Gen. 12:1–3). Through Moses, God promised Israel that "although the whole earth is mine, you will be a kingdom of priests and a holy nation" (Exod. 19:5–6).

The concept of God's people as a special kingdom is developed throughout the Old Testament. That development continues in the New Testament, where Jesus is presented as the king (Matt. 2:2, 6) whose kingdom is near (Matt. 3:2). Jesus speaks of himself as the one who brings the kingdom of God (Matt. 12:25–28). The nation of Israel rejected Jesus as the Messiah and king. Yet even this attempted thwarting of God's plans for Israel was turned into victory when Christ secured on the cross and through his resurrection the salvation of all who believe (1 Cor.

15). Those who trust in Christ become, by faith, part of the family of Abraham (Gal. 3:26–29), "A chosen people, a royal priesthood, a holy nation, a people belonging to God, that you may declare the praises of him who called you out of darkness into his wonderful light" (1 Pet. 2:9; citing Exod. 19).

Israel represented an intermediate yet real version of the kingdom of God. Believers today are also part of the kingdom of God. The kingdom has only shown signs or hints of itself. It is real, just not complete. Christ showed the power of the kingdom in the signs and wonders he performed. Believers are part of and signs of the kingdom that will one day manifest itself in fullness when Christ comes to reign on earth (Rev. 20) and afterward ushers in the totality of fullness in the eternal state. Then all the kingdoms and realms of earth and even the heavenlies will "become the kingdom of our Lord and of his Christ, and he will reign for ever and ever" (Rev. 11:15).

A few paragraphs cannot do justice to the motif of the kingdom of God dealt with so consistently throughout Scripture. One thing is clear, however: This kingdom is unstoppable, and the kingdom of darkness is not. Satan's rebellion and rule in the world receive serious treatment, but Satan is always presented as the ultimate loser. From Genesis 3:15, where the adversarial relationship between Satan and God and his people begins, it is clear that Satan will be crushed. God works out his purposes in spite of everything the adversary does to hinder the program and people of God. Though the gods of the pagans are demons (Deut. 32:17; 1 Cor. 10:19–20) and lead Israel astray, the idols portraying the demon gods are nothing. They receive no respect; they can do nothing—as Isaiah mockingly declares (Isa. 44:6–23). Satan opposes Christ but is thwarted in the desert through Christ's use of Scripture (Matt. 4:1–11). Demons who confront Jesus are cast out (Luke 10:17). Demonized people oppose the apostles in their ministry in Acts but cannot stop the progress of the gospel (Acts 16:16–18). Those who believe the gospel escape from the kingdom of darkness and are transferred into another realm, the kingdom of the Son God loves (Col. 1:12–13).

Clearly, the focus of any treatment of Satan, demons, and the kingdom of God must be on the victorious rule of God. None who follows Christ needs to fear the control of the evil one. Ministry today is a matter of proclaiming and applying the results of God's victory in Christ. Nonbelievers need to understand this victory and how it frees them from a sense of obligation to any other spirit, demon, or god. They need to understand what embracing and acting on the truth can do to release them from doing Satan's will.

Indications are that even believers need to have these truths reiterated and applied, for even they may be controlled by Satan, though they do not belong to him (2 Tim. 2:24–26). No wonder that the final verses portraying Paul's ministry in the book of Acts declare that even in the conditions of prison, "boldly and without hindrance he preached the kingdom of God and taught about the Lord Jesus" (Acts 28:31). That is where the emphasis should lie.

The nature of Satan and of evil is mysterious. It is "the secret power of lawlessness," and it is definitely at work (2 Thess. 2:7). But those who operate in a humble relationship of faith toward God, resist the devil in God's power, and minister the gospel can and will be victorious (1 Pet. 5:6–11; Rev. 12:11).

There is no doubt that conflict between God and Satan and Satan and the people of God is a recurring theme in Scripture from Genesis 3:15 to Revelation 20. Christians can expect opposition from Satan in their walk with God and their ministry for him. Scripture shows that Satan and demons, though judged and limited in power, nevertheless cause nonbelievers to reject the gospel and are in fact the spiritual realities behind the gods and idols of pagan religions. Missionaries and all Christian workers must be alert to these realities and ready to help those who are in spiritual bondage. But other themes also exist in Scripture, such as the sovereign power and glory of God and the spiritual journey of sanctification. The emphasis in ministry should be on proclaiming the victory of Christ over sin and Satan, which is the gospel. People are set free from besetting sin when they believe and embrace the truth of God's Word. This is the approach made popular by Neil Anderson's Freedom in Christ Ministries (1990).

Spiritual warfare advocates have helped Christians to see more clearly the reality of satanic activity. Yet in some cases, they may have led people to focus on the extrabiblical activities of locating, identifying, and binding demons thought to control people who are resistant to the gospel. This emphasis cannot be seen in apostolic ministry. There is no biblical prescription for ridding an area of demonic influence. There is only the bold proclamation that Jesus has triumphed over them all (1 John 3:8).

ENGAGING THE TREND: MISSIONARIES AND SPIRITUAL WARFARE

We have identified the trend, evaluated it, and reflected on it. The rest of the chapter examines what people should do in regard to spiritual warfare and whether there are models to follow. Ten points are presented in that regard.

First, it should be clear that no one involved in pastoral or missionary ministry today disagrees with the notion that we are in spiritual conflict. Some may not wish to call it "warfare" because it sounds histrionic or threatening, but the New Testament descriptions regarding the struggle frequently use terminology reflecting warfare. We have the peace of Christ, which he promised, but we are not in a peacetime situation. "In this world you will have trouble" (John 16:33). "The sinful mind is hostile to God" (Rom. 8:7). In God's strength and by the sword of his Spirit, we can "extinguish all the flaming arrows of the evil one" (Eph. 6:16). This certainly sounds more like war than peace—but it sounds like a war Christ has already won, and we are on the winning side.

Second, the detractors or critics of spiritual warfare need to take more seriously the reality and activity of Satan and demons. We should not assume that demonic interference is less likely than difficulties resulting from our sinful nature or the world.

Third, every person is accountable for his or her responses to impulses, temptations, or harassment—whatever the source. We are not responsible for the impressions that are thrown at us daily in the media, in public, by our enemies, and sometimes by our friends. But we can respond in truth and love, and we can remove ourselves from situations that threaten our spiritual well-being or integrity as people of God.

Fourth, we must live truly, being who we say we are and not hiding from the struggles we know we have. Living transparently and in the light of Scripture truth, we can be properly confident and relatively free from anxiety and inner conflict.

Fifth, there is no quick fix for struggle in this fallen world. It is possible for a troubled person, Christian or non-Christian, to wake up to a new reality and to take a quantum leap forward in terms of spiritual well-being. This may be truly transforming. Yet the Christian life is a pilgrimage. We will not be free of challenges and difficulties until we see Christ face-to-face. Detractors of spiritual warfare therapies that can accomplish great progress in a relatively short period of time should understand that breakthroughs are possible, all the more so when an individual is highly motivated to change because of the God-given discomfort he or she feels. We all have teachable moments.

Sixth, at the ministry level, it is not important to discover the precise source of each difficulty or obstacle in evangelism or life in Christ. There is no scriptural teaching about the identification of demons that would suggest a spiritual mapping or SLSW approach. Study and understanding of the worldview and local situation where evangelism is to take place help focus prayer. Focused and fervent prayer is probably what God is honoring among Christians who practice SLSW. At the personal level, we must identify whether an idea or a notion is embraceable or not.

CASE STUDY:
WHO CONTROLS CARACAS?

Lauren sat up in her chair and took a deep breath. She faced a difficult task at tonight's meeting and wanted to make the best of the opportunity it presented for her ministry among her Venezuelan friends.

Before coming to Caracas, she knew it was considered by missionaries to be a difficult place to minister. Competent workers assigned there encountered more resistance to evangelism and church planting than they did in other parts of the country, and after years of work in Caracas, Lauren felt a weariness that reflected her own struggles.

Even though some evangelical churches were flourishing, many were still small and lethargic compared to their counterparts in other large Venezuelan cities. In the preceding months, as

Lauren and the Venezuelan believers from her church had struggled to understand why Caracas was so difficult, they had repeatedly talked about several issues. Caracas certainly was more sophisticated as the capital city, and that meant some of the more rural-based evangelistic approaches were looked down on here. It was also true that historically evangelical missionaries had focused more on the other cities and were simply not used to Caracas.

What had recently moved their thinking in a new direction was a combination of two things. First, several of her friends had attended a spiritual warfare workshop that had left them excited and energized. They had started talking with Lauren about whether the city was under a particular spiritual "cloud"

The key to this kind of discernment is prayer for wisdom (James 1:5) and using the filter suggested by Paul: "Finally, brothers, whatever is true, whatever is noble, whatever is right, whatever is pure, whatever is lovely, whatever is admirable—if anything is excellent or praiseworthy—think about such things. Whatever you have learned or received or heard from me, or seen in me—put it into practice. And the God of peace will be with you" (Phil. 4:8–9).

Seventh, the recognition of societal sins, even by those who were not the perpetrators, together with expressions of abhorrence and sorrow for the hurt caused, may do much to open the hearts of hitherto resistant people. This type of identificational repentance is appropriate.

Eighth, optimum communication depends on understanding the receptor culture as well as one's own. Too often we have failed to look deeply at our own culture and to take seriously the details of other cultures, especially spiritual and occult beliefs. We have assumed too readily that there are standard versions of the world's religions when in reality the version we know is limited to certain sectors of that religion's of demonic influence. What had really gotten them going, however, was the unexpected cracking of the fifty-year-old statue of the popular Venezuelan witchcraft figure Maria Lionza. Maria Lionza had thousands of devotees across the country, and the statue was an important icon for their devotion.

Through some background research, Lauren learned that a previous Venezuelan president had dedicated himself to Maria Lionza, promising to build a national park in her honor if she would only help him keep power as a dictator. Thus, he ordered a bronze statue of Maria Lionza cast in Europe. Prior to its delivery, however, he had been forced to flee Venezuela. When the statue finally arrived, the new leaders decided to place it in the center of a traffic circle near the congressional building and presidential mansion. Eventually, however, it was transferred to the center of the median of the main superhighway into Caracas. The statue portrays Maria Lionza as a robust, naked woman astride a tapir (an animal common in the plains of Venezuela) and holding a woman's pelvis over her head.

Local spiritists took the cracking as an omen indicating that the current president's time in office would be shortened. Lauren's Venezuelan friends, however, saw it as an opening to end Maria Lionza's maleficent influence over the city. They were convinced by the events that Maria Lionza, by whose power many spiritists work, was actually the ruling demonic spirit over Caracas who caused the spiritual resistance of the Caraquenos.

One week ago they had called a meeting to talk and pray about the issue. They had asked Lauren as the missionary to give them biblical guidance. Lauren had spent the week wrestling in prayer and biblical research and had come fully prepared. Whispering one final prayer for the right words, she looked out at the expectant group and said …

adherents. We typically know about formal religious teachings but not enough about the various folk expressions of the people among whom we minister. Fortunately, that lack is remediable (Van Rheenen 1991; Hiebert, Shaw, and Tiénou 1999; Love 2000)

Ninth, Christians who experience overwhelming or besetting struggles should take a careful inventory of what they believe and practice and compare it to biblical truth. In prayer and humility, they should invite fellow believers to help them identify areas of sin and error. Further, they should express repentance for wrongs done, anger cherished, or forgiveness denied. Finally, they should be open to the possibilities that Satan or his emissaries have had reason to harass a believer because of his or her apparent willingness to live in a sinful pattern.

Tenth, we should always be suspicious of convoluted solutions. All things being equal, the best explanation is often the simplest. Some who advocate a spiritual warfare orientation to ministry have been guilty of overcomplicating understandings and procedures.

So what about the World Prayer Center "Light the Window" campaign, the AD 2000 and Beyond Movement, and the other spiritual-warfare-oriented ministries cited at the beginning of this chapter? They may smack of Western marketing theory and even seem overly dramatic, but to the extent that they are focusing attention, mobilizing prayer, and leading many to engage the lost among unreached peoples, we can only thank God for them.

8

Innovation in Mission Operations

Creative-Access Platforms

MIKE BARNETT

In a one-week period in February 2004, the following crossed Mike Barnett's desk. First was a quarterly report from a ten-year-old kingdom-minded international trade company that connects customers and vendors around the world. Second was an invitation to attend Global Spectrum's 2004 EDGE Conference in Houston, Texas, where the theme centered on the intersection of marketplace professionals with global missions in mind. Third was a reminder to attend the "Kingdom Business Forum," a three-day gathering of business and mission CEOs, professors, and business practitioners in Atlanta, Georgia, for the purpose of discovering best practices in the entrepreneurial world of business and missions. Then there was an email from a former student celebrating the privilege and challenge of serving on a new non-government organization relief and community development team in Iraq. The same day, an email from a former colleague from the Horn of Africa connected Barnett with a U.S.-based mission network dealing with platforms—the means for access to a particular area. The next day he received an email reminding him of the June meeting of tentmaker

---

SIDEBAR 8.1
IMPORTANT TERMS USED IN THIS CHAPTER

---

church-planting movement (CPM): A rapid multiplication of indigenous churches planting churches that sweeps through a people group or population segment (Garrison 2004, 21).

creative-access: The term evolved in the 1990s from the earlier "restricted-access" once missionaries discovered alternative opportunities for accessing peoples isolated from the gospel. Creative-access methods are used in countries in which access by traditional missionaries has been restricted for some reason.

platform: Derived from a 1980s computer term that referred to the general

operating system of a computer and/or network. It is used today in secular and mission worlds to indicate the primary base or foundation of operation, employment, vocation, or avocation.

restricted-access: An older term referring to the same thing as creative-access.

strategy coordinator: A missionary who takes responsibility for developing and implementing a church-planting-movement strategy for a people group or population segment (Garrison 2004, 345).

practitioners in a Southeast Asian capital city. Later in the week there was a telephone call from a prospective doctoral student who wanted to do a study on creative-access platforms in missions. That same day the faculty at Barnett's school approved a new intercultural studies elective course on creative-access, tentmaking, and platform development. Next was a call from a mentor who had just returned from a university consortium trip in East Asia seeking to develop student, faculty, and research exchange programs. That same week Barnett purchased two books, *Great Commission Companies* (2003) by Steve Rundle and Tom Steffen and *On Kingdom Business* (2003) edited by Tetsunao Yamamori and Kenneth Eldred.

All these contacts share a common theme, a mutual concern. How do we evangelize and establish the church among the unreached peoples of the world where vocational missionaries are not allowed? How do we equip and connect marketplace Christians to carry the gospel and establish churches in and through the markets and industries of the world? These individuals, organizations, events, and strategies reflect a persistent and steady trend to deliver the gospel and establish the church of Jesus Christ through today's global markets and marketeers. As teachers and educators, Christians communicate eternal truths of Scripture through the schools, universities, and training institutes of the world. As workers in nongovernment organizations, they demonstrate the love and mercy of Christ through the relief and community development channels of a world in need. As businesspeople, they trade concepts of discipleship through the commercial networks of a global economy. They strive to bridge the gap, to connect with those who are isolated from the truth of the gospel. Most focus on least-evangelized peoples. All are part of a vast company of ambassadors, tentmakers, envoys, and kingdom professionals being raised up, trained, and sent out to disciple all peoples on earth. They are creating the future of a church that will not take no for an answer when it comes to global evangelization. They are living out a model of evangelization and church planting that depends on everyday disciples of Christ for witness, teaching, mentoring, and community. They are part of today's world of creative-access platforms.

Creative-access platforms are the practical means for providing mission workers the opportunity and relational basis for effectively accomplishing their main goal. For some the word *platforms* is negatively associated with illegitimate attempts to establish a reason for living or working within a given country in order to provide a "cover" for missionaries. Yet an increasing number of missionaries consider platforms essentially good. They are a definitive part of believers, an intrinsic aspect of the call to be witnesses of Christ. God provides each believer with a platform from which to serve him and to communicate the gospel. Platforms are a product of God's calling, equipping, and gifting. They provide a legitimate reason and right for sharing the faith among the nations. They are not a cover for covert activities but a basis for living among, interacting with, and communicating the gospel to those around us.

All Christians have one or more platforms from which to serve as witnesses for Christ. Some serve as equipping ministers from vocational ministry platforms as pastors, church staff ministers, denominational or agency workers, and missionaries. Others serve as God's people of the church who witness in the marketplace as teachers, caregivers, skilled workers, or businessmen and women. Creative-access workers are both witnesses and equipping ministers, but they go as God's people through the marketplace, and they take the gospel to peoples who live where vocational missionaries are not allowed or well received.

The main objective of most missionaries involves some aspect of evangelism and church planting—that is, the communication of the gospel in a way that results in biblical, indigenous, reproducing congregations of disciples of Jesus Christ. Platforms vary according to tasks. If a mission worker's main task is to translate Scripture, then his or her creative-access platform should provide the opportunity and the relational basis for connecting with resources, people, and means for effectively translating Scripture. If the objective is to train indigenous church planters, then the platform should serve that purpose. If the mission is to facilitate church-planting movements, then the platform should serve those specific needs. The platform should be built to fit the objective or task and not the other way around.

Though a broader application is warranted, today's creative-access platforms generally are used only where the objective or mission cannot be accomplished through official Christian organizations or by those identified as vocational missionaries. Where a missionary visa is unavailable due to prohibitions of governments or cultures, creative-access platforms offer a strategic solution. Though the trend has increased over the past twenty years, creative-access platforms still stand on the leading edge of mission strategies. It is a high-risk, entrepreneurial venture with ample failures to inspire skeptics, but it is a strategic approach to missions with a strong biblical basis and an impressive historical heritage.

The goal of this chapter is to survey and analyze creative-access platforms of today in a way that facilitates those of tomorrow. To do that, it first identifies today's trend of creative-access platforms by tracking the emergence of the trend in the twentieth century. Then it asks the ethical questions surrounding creative-access platforms and evaluates their effectiveness. Next it reflects on the trend in light of its biblical basis and historical precedents. Finally, it engages the trend of creative-access platforms by discussing strategic rationales for effective platforms and potential industries for platform development.

The reader must be warned that there is no silver bullet, no single model or foolproof approach to creative-access and platform development. There is no perfect platform, no flawless strategy. God's designs are diverse and so are his strategies for reaching all peoples on earth. Hopefully this chapter will stimulate the thinking of those involved in creative-access platforms and will provoke dialogue regarding this remarkable trend in missions.

IDENTIFYING THE TREND: FROM MAKING TENTS TO DEVELOPING PLATFORMS

Though the practice of tentmaking has existed since the beginning of the church, its reemergence in the last few decades as a preferred strategy has been significant. Most church members with a mind for missions today are aware of the term *tentmaker,* and an increasing number is seeing the strategic viability of creative-access platforms. This section identifies the primary motive for the recent emergence of the trend, defines its basic meaning, and highlights key people and events that blazed the trail for creative-access platforms in the twentieth century.

Motive for the Trend

Like most mission strategies, the concept of creative-access platforms grew from the grassroots of the mission fields themselves. The most fertile grounds were found in the 10/40 Window. In the wake of the Lausanne conferences of the 1970s and 1980s, many in the evangelical mission community focused on reaching hidden or unreached peoples of the world (Reapsome 2000; Wilson 2000). This resulted in the launching of numerous teams and strategies to identify, engage, and evangelize thousands of these unreached peoples.

With this new approach to the task came new challenges. The colonial age of missions was gone. "Professional" missionaries were no longer welcomed in many parts of the world. Missionary visas needed to access most of these unreached peoples were simply not available. How could unreached peoples be accessed if they lived in a part of the world where vocational missionaries were not allowed? How were Christians to preach and teach the gospel behind the iron and bamboo curtains of communism? How could they plant churches in the heart of the Islamic world? What were they to do in these lands that became known as restricted-access countries? The goal was clear—to take the gospel to all peoples on earth. Now, however, new methods had to be developed.

From Restricted-Access to Creative-Access

As the mission community faced the challenges of restricted-access countries, it developed innovative approaches of tentmaking. This was really nothing new. The practice of tentmaking as modeled by Paul (Acts 18) had survived throughout the ages of missions. Paul was a tourist, philosopher, tentmaker, lecturer, fund-raiser, and even prisoner. In response to the new mandate to reach the least-reached peoples on earth, tentmaking was simply moved from the bottom of the tactical toolbox of missionaries to the top.

Veteran mission workers such as J. Christy Wilson and Tetsunao Yamamori documented tentmaking strategies (Wilson 1979; Yamamori 1993), and an entire industry of tentmaker facilitators and sponsors emerged. Business delegations traveled to restricted-access nations to find opportunities for entry and access. Intercultural and educational exchange agencies initiated projects in hopes that doors to the restricted-access world would open. Humanitarian relief and community development alliances were formed in hopes of meeting needs and adding value in lands where Western missionaries were unwelcome but Western aid was well received. Reports from these restricted-access fields began to trickle in, and a pattern emerged.

As Western mission workers prepared to engage restricted areas, they expected insurmountable barriers. One mission agency even developed a new category of missionary service called the nonresidential missionary (Garrison 1990) as a strategy for engaging unreachable peoples. The nonresidential missionary became the prototype for the current role known in some circles as strategy coordinator. Nonresidential missionaries were assigned a specific unreached people group in a restricted-access area and asked to initiate a strategy to reach them. They often established a residence in an "outside" city with a significant population of their people group where natural networks in and out of the restricted-access world existed. Nonresidential missionaries researched their people group, mobilized prayer, developed a strategy, traveled in and out of their unreached region, and facilitated others with access to communicate the gospel and plant churches.

> *What is clear is that every Christian was a witness. Where there were Christians, there would be a living, burning faith, and before long an expanding Christian community. . . . Nothing is more notable than the anonymity of these early missionaries.*
>
> Stephen Neill (1964, 22)

But as these nonresidential missionaries returned from their initial travels "inside," they emerged with remarkable reports. Much to their surprise, they found many opportunities for long-term residency and access among their unreached peoples. They merely had to be creative in developing legitimate means or platforms from which to serve. What had been considered restricted areas simply required some ingenuity on the part of the missionaries. It was not a question of restrictions but of creativity and determination. Mission workers simply needed to get out of their vocational missionary mind-set and enter the real world of marketplace witness—the modern-day version of the world of the apostle Paul. The term *restricted-access* gave way to *creative-access*, and the strategy of developing creative-access platforms took root.

Trailblazers

Of course, most of the creative-access trailblazers remain anonymous. This is a fitting legacy for those who often served from their platforms in a land where professional or vocational missionaries were not allowed. However, two of the many that could be presented are J. Christy Wilson and Ruth Siemens, both of whom were willing to be creative long before the needs we see today arose.

SIDEBAR 8.2
CREATIVE-ACCESS CHALLENGES

(Adapted from Wilson 1979, 68–70)

Much progress has been made in equipping and connecting tentmakers with viable opportunities overseas. Yet serving as creative-access workers still has its challenges.

- Tentmakers' employers may restrict their witness or freedom to express their faith.
- Demands on the tentmakers may limit their ability to learn the local language.
- Terms of overseas employment are often limited to a couple years.
- Time demands of the job may limit time for witness and ministry.
- Some will accuse tentmakers of being missionaries in disguise.
- Christians back home do not support tentmakers with prayer and member care because they are not seen as missionaries.
- Expatriate workers are often isolated in compounds or are limited to working with only fellow expatriates.
- Tentmakers may not receive adequate orientation for crossing culture and being effective witnesses or church planters.
- Tentmakers may lack Christian fellowship and accountability for their mission work.

REFLECTION AND DISCUSSION

1. Choose three of the obstacles and brainstorm ways to overcome them.
2. What other obstacles would you add to the list?

J. CHRISTY WILSON

It was the same motive—to take the gospel to all peoples on earth—that led J. Christy Wilson and his wife, Betty, to go as tentmakers to Afghanistan. Caught up in the spirit of excitement surrounding the InterVarsity headquarters on Chicago's Lake Street in the winter of 1947, Wilson felt led to go to Afghanistan, one of the restricted or closed countries of Central Asia (Wilson 1979, 11). Though it took four years to get there, he and his wife served for twenty-two years as teachers and medical and educational workers in the city of Tabriz. They worked alongside many tentmakers of their day and learned by experience how to be marketplace witnesses among some of the least-evangelized peoples on earth. After their overseas service, Wilson taught at Princeton and Gordon-Conwell seminaries. He authored various books, including an official biography of Samuel Zwemer, the missionary to Muslims, and he served as a leader in organizations such as Near East Relief and Near East Council of Churches (Anderson 1998, 741). But Wilson's greatest legacy is based on his contributions and reputation as "the father of the modern-day tentmaking movement" (Cox 1997, 116). His ground-breaking work as a tentmaker in Afghanistan, his unceasing advocacy for tentmaking among student-missionaries around the world, and his classic primer—*Today's Tentmakers*—clearly identify him as a trailblazer in the world of creative-access platforms.

RUTH SIEMENS

Meanwhile, another tentmaker was blazing trails in Latin America. Born in California, one of ten children from an immigrant Mennonite family, Ruth Siemens did not choose to go as a tentmaker; God called her into the tentmaking business. As a young college student seeking to serve Christ, she signed a commitment card at an InterVarsity Christian Fellowship (IVCF) student meeting pledging to go abroad as a missionary if God would open the door (Siemens 2004, 1–2). First she thought she would be a Wycliffe translator, but that door did not open. Then she was stricken with an illness that closed the doors to serving in remote areas through a mission board. She assumed she would not serve as a foreign missionary after all. She changed her plans, enrolled at a nearby secular university, and began an English and education degree in hopes of becoming a teacher. There is where she found her first mission field, at a secular university in California. Later, God provided a job for Siemens in Peru. With little training in Spanish or in crossing culture, she learned on the job how to be a tentmaker, and God blessed her ministry. Siemens led many to Christ through her relationships at school.

> *People often ask me if it wasn't frustrating to have so little free time left over for God, but I considered all of my time to be God's. Soon I realized that tentmaking is "full-time" ministry. . . . It was important for me to put a great deal of effort into my [secular] job, because God expects all Christians to serve their employer as though he were Jesus Christ.*
>
> Ruth Siemens (2004, 4)

After twenty-one years of tentmaking ministry in Peru, Brazil, Portugal, Spain, and Austria, Siemens became one of the most effective advocates for creative-access platforms and tentmaking. She returned to the States in 1975 and continued to blaze trails, only this time as a tentmaker equipper and mobilizer. Her organization, Global Opportunities, was the first of its kind and focused on connecting tentmakers with employment opportunities overseas. Based in the U.S. Center for World Mission in Pasadena, California, Siemens was in the middle of a cohort of mission trailblazers. Her organization is still the starting point for hundreds of tentmakers today.

The Networks

Perhaps the best indicator of the degree to which this trend has developed is a survey of today's creative-access networks. They focus on two terms: *tentmaking* and *kingdom business.*

TENTMAKING

Tentmaking research and advocacy networks began to emerge in the mid-1980s. Siemens's Global Opportunities was a prototype for tentmaking advocates. TMQ Research, established in 1985 by Don Hamilton, began practical research on preparation and best practices for tentmakers. In 1987, two seminal books on tentmaking were published. Hamilton's book *Tentmakers Speak: Practical Advice from Over Four Hundred Missionary Tentmakers* provided a readable query of critical issues for tentmakers based on testimonies and responses from tentmaking practitioners around the world. *God's New Envoys: A Bold Strategy for Penetrating "Closed Countries"* by Tetsunao Yamamori, intercultural scholar and president of Food for the Hungry International, proposed the raising up of a generation of special representatives or envoys of the gospel to reach restricted people groups. He introduced the viability of humanitarian and community development opportunities through the nongovernment organization industry as a means for meeting both physical and spiritual needs of those without the gospel.

Meanwhile, overseas employment opportunity databases popped up all over North America, to the extent that some expressed confusion and concern regarding overlap and duplication of effort. New organizations such as Crista, Issachar, and Tentmakers International (Cox 1997, 114) suggested the emergence of a kind of tentmaker cottage industry. Even denominational mission agencies were talking about tentmaking. For example, the International Mission Board (IMB) of the Southern Baptist Convention started a tentmaker category of service in 1988 and began to recruit and establish covenants with marketplace witnesses abroad. Though the IMB program itself was short-lived (five years), covenants were established with over fifty tentmakers, and over eight hundred prospects were developed. After the home office discontinued the program because of staff downsizing, responsibility for creative-access strategies, including tentmaking, shifted to the field, where such strategies continue to play a primary role today, especially among 10/40 Window teams.

The real turning point or catalyst for the tentmaking movement came at the Lausanne II Congress in Manila in 1989 (Cox 1997, 114). Manila's Tentmaker Track produced a concise "Tentmaker Declarative Appeal" for the church to lead in the mobilization, preparation, placement, and

---

SIDEBAR 8.3
TENTMAKER DECLARATIVE APPEAL

(Adapted from Tentmaker Track, Lausanne II Congress 1989, 1–2)

1. To encourage Christian laypeople to seize opportunities for cross-cultural positions to extend God's kingdom.
2. To recognize the key position of church congregations in mobilizing and equipping the laity for world evangelization.
3. To identify and enlist people for cross-cultural witness among unreached people groups.
4. To produce training materials and programs for tentmakers involving Scripture, interpersonal relationships, and time management.
5. To involve home churches in assisting in the placement and orientation to cope with culture shock successfully.
6. To nurture tentmakers through faithful pastoral care, including prayer, backing, good communication, and visits.
7. To assist in reentry culture shock, and to use tentmakers efficiently in challenging and recruiting others.

---

nurture of tentmakers (Tentmaker Track, Lausanne II Congress 1989, 1–2).

The church responded, and over the next few years various tentmaker agencies and networks were developed on an international scale. By the mid-1990s, the topic of tentmaking permeated most mission journals. Ralph Winter's U.S. Center for World Mission included tentmaking in its frontier missions focus. Their *International Journal of Frontier Missions* dedicated two entire volumes (14, no. 3 [1997] and 15, no. 1 [1998]) to the subject. Mission conferences and training courses around the world included tentmaking tracks. Creative-access task forces, partnerships, and alliances multiplied. Platform consultants were added to strategy support teams. The expanding network rode the technology wave of the 1990s with its web-based databases and information links. By the end of the decade, a global network of tentmakers and their advocates was in place.

KINGDOM BUSINESS

On June 30, 1997, the Global Consultation on World Evangelization (GCOWE 1997), an initiative of the AD 2000 and Beyond Movement, convened in Pretoria, South Africa, with roughly five thousand in attendance from around the world. A new emphasis in the creative-access trend coalesced through the Business Executive Track. Roughly five hundred businessmen and women with a serious interest in world evangelization met, worshiped, prayed, and dialogued together. They produced a consultation declaration that called for a commitment to "stimulate cooperation among existing businesses, market place ministries, churches, para-church organizations, missionary societies, and service groups of all kinds" to work toward fulfilling the Great Commission of Matthew 28 (GCOWE 1997). The conference was worthwhile in and of itself, but perhaps its significance is seen more in the events of the years following the South Africa meeting.

Since 1997, there have been numerous initiatives to engage business professionals in the unfinished task of world evangelization. Again, the books tell the tale. In 2001, David Befus, president of Latin America Mission (LAM), published *Kingdom Business: The Ministry of Promoting Economic Activity*, a practical handbook for mission workers who want to apply "economic development . . . as a tool in evangelism and discipleship" (2001, 13). Befus proposes that, like the mission hospitals and schools of the previous era of missions, business and economic development can be an effective tool for the gospel. He describes five paradigms, each of which focuses on a function: ministry service, endowment, tentmaker support, business incubators, and micro-credit. His book reflects the growing trend of developing viable platforms that add value to a community and serve as bridges for witness and evangelization.

In October 2002, a consultation on kingdom business was held in Virginia Beach, Virginia. The following year *On Kingdom Business: Transforming Missions through Entrepreneurial Strategies* was published as a collection of the presentations of the consultation. In the preface, coeditor Tetsunao Yamamori posits the question and the answer of the consultation and book. Question: How do we communicate and demonstrate the gospel to a growing population of globalized people focused "more on finding a job and attaining economic development than on investigating the claims of Christ?" Answer: "In a word, the answer is 'business,' or, to be more precise, 'kingdom business'" (Yamamori and Eldred 2003, 7). The book provides case studies, essays, and conclusions that focus on kingdom business entrepreneurs who develop their own businesses with world evangelization in mind. Such an approach differs from classic tentmaking, in which a mission worker seeks employment for support and strategic engagement. The kingdom business network is about kingdom entrepreneurs, that is, "cross-cultural business owners, called by God, to do ministry through business in restricted-access countries" (Yamamori and Eldred 2003, 8–9). This is another stream of the trend of creative-access platforms. If tentmakers use the apostle Paul as their model, then perhaps kingdom entrepreneurs use Aquila and Priscilla (Acts 18).

The most recent title on kingdom business activity is *Great Com-*

SIDEBAR 8.4
ASSESSING THE VIABILITY OF A GREAT COMMISSION COMPANY

(Rundle and Steffen 2003, 94–95; used by permission of InterVarsity Press, P.O. Box 1400, Downers Grove, IL 60515)

The following are just a few of the questions that should be asked when assessing the viability of a Great Commission company.

ECONOMIC VIABILITY

1. Is there a clear statement of the purpose and goals for the company?
2. Does the management team have the appropriate experience and training?
3. Can the business create and maintain a competitive advantage?
4. From a financial perspective, is the business an attractive investment?
5. Is there a clear path from start-up to financial sustainability?
6. Are there investors and other advisers committed to helping the company reach financial sustainability?
7. Is this a business concept that has worked in other contexts?
8. What are the risks?
9. Is the business model flexible enough to allow for expansion, changes in direction, or alliances with other companies?
10. How will the net earnings be distributed?
11. How and when can the investors expect to be repaid?

MISSIONAL VIABILITY

1. Is the business concept consistent with the missional focus and objectives?
2. Is there adequate potential for making a significant kingdom impact?
3. Does the company have a multicultural, multigenerational team of kingdom professionals in place that has a track record of effective ministry inside and outside the workplace?
4. Has the management team identified other mission organizations working in the area, and are they open to partnering with them?
5. Does the plan demonstrate an understanding of and respect for the legal and ethical boundaries between for-profit and nonprofit activities?
6. Does the business create socially beneficial "backward linkages" with local firms?
7. Is the net impact on the host economy's balance of payments positive?
8. Is there a plan to turn over as much authority and responsibility as possible (missions and business) to local professionals?
9. Is the management team committed to serving under the local church (if one exists)?
10. Is the management team committed to communicating regularly with other stakeholders so that they know how to pray and what things they can do to benefit the work (for example, short-term trips)?

mission Companies: The Emerging Role of Business in Missions (2003) by Steve Rundle and Tom Steffen. The authors deliver an integrative analysis of the economic and missiological methods, structures, and results of businesses that are intentional agents of God's fulfillment of the Great Commission. They cite globalization as a driving factor for utilizing Great Commission companies, and they provide an assessment tool for determining both their economic and missiological viability (Rundle and Steffen 2003, 6, 94–95).

Platform Development

As creative-access became a necessary part of doing missions, especially among the unreached peoples of the 10/40 Window, the practice of planning for effective platforms evolved. In the early 1990s, the term *platforms* began to be used in training sessions for nonresidential missionaries, strategy coordinators, and team leaders. The term was probably borrowed from the computer industry, which was creating competing operating systems for personal computers (e.g., Macintosh vs. IBM/Microsoft). The idea was that a creative-access platform served as the primary base or foundation for mission operations. The simultaneous call for mission workers to penetrate the least-reached peoples on earth along with the devolution of the Soviet regime and the opening up of communist China undoubtedly accelerated the need for platform development.

Platforms seemed to fall into one of two major categories, individual or corporate, depending on strategic objectives, abilities, and inclinations of the mission workers. Individual platforms such as the direct-hire teacher, medical worker, nongovernment organization consultant, field worker, or agriculturalist were generally seen as preferable because they did not require significant infrastructure or human and financial resources. Perhaps the best example of this streamlined individual platform approach was the direct-hire English teacher. A state school or university offered an invitation to a foreign teacher, obtained a work permit or visa, and usually provided housing and a small stipend. English teachers or "foreign experts" frequently found themselves immersed in the ethnographic center of their chosen people group. What better way to impact a people group with the gospel than to share it with their brightest and potentially most influential citizens?

In some cases, however, these individual tentmaker platforms were not sufficient for engaging and influencing a people group for Christ. For example, in many 10/40 Window countries, the activities of Westerners were highly restricted. If a direct-hire contract was obtainable, the job was of such intensity and the freedom to interact with locals was so restricted that the platform was ineffective. In these cases, larger-scale corporate platforms were developed that met various felt needs of communities. These generally required significant infrastructure and investment of human and financial resources. At the same time, they often offered a more stable, long-term option for large numbers of mission workers.

Some of the best examples of these corporate platforms were seen in the former Soviet Union. Russia and its former Central Asian republics emerged from the fall of the communist regime starved for information and relationships with the outside world. Several service-oriented organizations were developed for the purpose of connecting former Soviet governments, companies, and individuals with everything from nonprofit cultural exchange programs to for-profit business development opportunities. These early years of the 1990s provided a wild and reckless environment for platform development. The lack of infrastructure in the former Soviet society was problematic. For example, platform representatives often carried tens of thousands of dollars of hard currency into a country because there was no banking system for transfer of funds. Business contracts and memorandums of understanding were seldom enforceable because legal systems in this new free world were nonexistent. Mission workers found themselves doing business with newly appointed government and business representatives who were former KGB representatives, the management and leadership legacy of the U.S.S.R. But mission workers were creative, persistent, and providentially guided through the minefields of the era. Someday historians will reveal the critical role these pioneer creative-access mission workers played in the redevelopment and globalization of these long-isolated societies. Meanwhile, seeds of the gospel were being sown along with the seeds of cultural and commercial development.

By the end of the 1990s, platform development had been built into the training and operating structures of most mission agencies working in creative-access regions. The four 10/40 Window regions of the IMB each had platform consultants who advised team leaders on platform development strategies. One regional team reported sixty-four distinct corporate platforms in existence in 1996. The building block of "platform construction" was added to the strategic planning process pyramid of the IMB alongside other strategic issues such as team building, resources, networking, security, and updating of planning (Myers and Slack 1999, 1.11). In 1993, then director of Frontiers, Greg Livingstone, addressed strategic questions regarding tentmaking and creative-access options for working among Muslims (Livingstone 1993, 49–50). Patrick Johnstone, director of research for WEC International and developer of the various editions of *Operation World* (see, e.g., Johnstone and Mandryk 2001), recognized the growing cooperation among like-minded 10/40 Window teams working in areas where "missionary visas are not readily given" (International Mission Board 1995). He was referring to joint platform development efforts among various agencies and their mission teams. Today, regional mission strategy conferences regularly include seminars on platform development. In fact, regions beyond the 10/40 Window are finally taking a look at creative-access platform development as a viable means of effectively engaging unreached peoples in areas where vocational missionaries are allowed but often marginalized. By the turn of the millennium, platform development was an established component of strategy planning in the world of missions.

The trend of creative-access platforms is clearly a reality in the world of global evangelization today. Spawned from the challenge of unreached peoples and the Lausanne movement and inspired by modern trailblazers such as Wilson, Siemens, and anonymous tentmakers, the creative-access approach has rightly regained its place in the theory and practice of missions. The global network of tentmaker and kingdom business advocates, equippers, and facilitators is operative. The persistent presence of creative-access thinking and platform development among parachurch and denominational mission agencies alike bodes well for the future of this trend.

EVALUATING THE TREND: ETHICAL QUESTIONS

Before reflecting on the various rationales for employing creative-access platforms, we must address some critical issues. First, is it ethical? Second, does it really work?

Is It Ethical?

The first question that often comes to mind when discussing creative-access platforms is, Is it ethical? In other words, is it right, is it honest, is it fair to enter a country and work as a marketplace person when your real motive for being there is to convert people to Jesus Christ? Isn't that being deceitful, dishonest, and untruthful? In many cases, this is the most critical question facing creative-access mission workers. If they cannot clearly answer this question, they will face the perils of self-questioning, identity crisis, and ethical doubt throughout their lives and work as mission workers.

MARKETPLACE MISSION WORKER?

If the question is whether it is ethical for a missionary to also work in the marketplace in order to gain access to and to build witnessing relationships with those who do not know Jesus Christ, then the answer seems simple enough. Of course it is ethical. There are many biblical and historical examples of the effectiveness and legitimacy of such bi-vocational missionary tentmakers (see below). Any hesitancy regarding this aspect of the ethical question is probably a result of Western church culture. The tendency for hundreds of years has been to separate the divine life from the real world, the religious from the everyday, the clergy from the laity. This has resulted in a kind of division of vocational consciousness among Christians. In the Western church, pastors and ministerial staff members are professional, ordained specialists. We put them on the apostolic pedestal of highest calling. The act of clergy and missionaries returning to the world of the marketplace seems ill conceived and even wrong.

In fact, much of the rest of the world does not think like this about their religious leaders. Buddhist priests often hold jobs in the marketplace. Many are simply itinerant or interim priests serving their term in the temple only to return to their full-time occupations. Muslim imams are generally marketplace members of their community called to a special Islamic office and service. The same applies to the traditional Jewish rabbi, trained in a trade for purposes of self-support and no doubt community relationships. More importantly, for much of the rest of the world, faith and everyday life and work are not separate realms but equal parts of the whole of life. In comparison, Western church culture teaches us that clergy cannot and should not take the role of a teacher, farmer, or business person. They are paid solely by the church to do the work of the church. Of course, this philosophy does not reflect the biblical model for ministry in Ephesians 4:11–13 and throughout Acts, which clearly assigns the ministry of the church to its members rather than to its equipping ministers. We know better, but old habits are hard to break. The Western church culture blinds us to the sensibility and normalcy of marketplace mission workers. This question of whether a missionary can also work in the marketplace, therefore, is not really an ethical one at all. It is more a question of church practice.

ILLEGAL MISSIONARY?

If the question is whether it is ethical to practice evangelism or church planting in a country where it is illegal, the answer is clear, though not as simple. David Barrett and James Reapsome contend that "from the Christian perspective, legality is not an ethical matter, but it is a purely de-scriptive term describing the secular government's requirements, which may well be arbitrary, harsh, cruel, unjust, ephemeral, inconsistent, unstable, or even impossible to comply with" (1988, 29). In other words, creative-access mission workers may be illegal, but that does not mean they are unethical. Though Christians normally make every effort to obey the laws of the government, when those laws prohibit them from obeying the Great Commission of Christ to share the gospel with those who have not heard, they may decide to act illegally. After all, time after time the apostle Paul preached, witnessed, taught, or wrote from prison. He did not get there by civil obedience. Strategic questions, not ethical ones, are critical in such cases. Mission workers must ask, Will civil disobedience jeopardize future work in the area? Will we be evicted from the land? Will our platform(s) be vulnerable? Will it threaten the well-being or lives of locals with whom we work? Will our lives be at risk? If so, they must weigh the risks against the potential for accomplishing their objectives, and they must be prepared for the consequences. The question whether to be legal or illegal may be a tough one, but it is not an ethical one.

> *Across the centuries, Christians ministering in closed or difficult areas have usually sought to obey the laws of the ruling regime, and to minister within them. But they have not hesitated to operate illegally, or secretly, in situations where their basic rights and roles as believers or Christian workers have been denied.*
>
> David Barrett and James Reapsome
> (1988, 29)

COVERT WITNESS?

If the question is whether it is right to hide an evangelistic purpose from those to whom you plan to witness, the answer is more personal. On the one hand, it may be a moot question. If you are going to hide your purpose of witnessing from the one to whom you were sent by God to be a witness, you will fail in your mission. Paul may have served regularly as an illegal witness, but he was seldom if ever a secret or covert witness. A missionary who hides his witness is not a missionary. A marketplace Christian who hides her witness is not a discipler on a mission with God. Once again, the real questions seem to be strategic. When and how will you project your witness of Jesus Christ? Will your faith in Jesus become an immediate part of your identity (see below) as you live and work in the marketplace? Will you light your lamp and let it "shine among men, that they may see your good deeds and praise your Father in heaven," or will you hide it "under a bowl" (Matt. 5:15–16)?

Again, Western thinking invades at this point. The issue is not whether to hide the fact that you are a vocational missionary who also works in the marketplace. The issue is who are you as a marketplace mission worker? If you do not separate your life of faith from your life of work, your witness for Christ will permeate every meeting, every conversation, every act among your new community. People from majority world cultures seldom have a problem with this kind of personal witness. If you are a person of faith, they expect you to say so. Seldom can you have a conversation with a religious Muslim, Jew, Hindu, or Buddhist without a conversation on faith and religion. So should you hide your witness? Should you be a covert missionary? Not if your purpose is to share Christ. But be a marketplace person who is overtly a faithful follower of Jesus more than a covert professional missionary who happens to work in the marketplace.

A Case in Point

The example of Heather Mercer and Dayna Curry illustrates the challenges of working in a creative-access situation. These two young women went to Afghanistan as workers with Shelter Now International, a German-based relief agency (CNN.com 2004b). They went to help the physically and spiritually desperate peoples of that land. On August 3, 2001, they, along with other foreign and national workers, were arrested by the Taliban and held pending charges of preaching Christianity—an unlawful act in the Islamic state, punishable by death in some cases. They were held for over three months until their remarkable rescue on November 13 in the midst of the post-9/11 war in Afghanistan. In a series of television interviews after their heralded return to the States, they were challenged about their reason for being in Afghanistan. In a feature story broadcast on *Dateline NBC* on June 11, 2002, Heather's mother went public and announced that their primary motive was to convert Muslims and to plant churches. Her mother had protested to Heather and even government authorities before she had left for Afghanistan. She could not understand how Heather and Dayna could knowingly violate the laws of the Taliban against spreading the Christian faith. Though Heather's mother was primarily concerned for her daughter's safety, her protest questioned the ethics of the girls, their church, and all such humanitarian creative-access mission workers. Heather's response was clear:

> For most people religion is a compartmentalized part of life. For me and many aid workers who are out there and are people of faith, the two are integrated. . . . If I can have an opportunity to serve people and share this love that brings hope and life, then . . . to me, that was something worth spending my life on. . . . When I read about the life of Jesus, the two went hand-in-hand, loving the poor and giving a verbal testimony to who God is. I can't do one without the other. I can't separate the two.

Did Heather and Dayna go as creative-access workers through the marketplace of humanitarian aid in order to build witnessing relationships with the people of Afghanistan? Yes. But they clearly were committed aid workers. In a follow-up story on the next morning's *Today Show*, Dayna pointed out that the overwhelming majority of their time was spent helping the poor. She added, "I went to address the physical needs of the people as well as the needs of the heart." As Heather put it, "It is a both/and thing." Were they aware that it was illegal to share their faith under the Taliban regime? Yes. But this was not a question of ethics but of a willingness to serve God and the people of Afghanistan. They knew the consequences and were prepared to suffer them. Did they hide their witness from those they served? No. As they earned the right through personal relationships based on their humanitarian service and care, they shared Christ through their words, the *Jesus* film, and other literature. They were overt witnesses, and for this reason, they were arrested and imprisoned for months. Would they do it again? Absolutely.

Does It Really Work?

The second critical issue is whether creative-access platforms really work. The two greatest critiques of the tentmaking approach to missions come from extreme ends of the mission world. Missionaries who work where the fields are most ripe for the harvest—such as China—claim that platforms are unnecessary. They depend on quick and easy means for access and shun anything that slows down the rapid pace of responsiveness and indigenous church-planting movements. Such missionaries still use the roles of English teacher and traveling salesman for temporary access, but they rely most heavily on tourist visas. Why bother to establish a nongovernment organization or a commercial venture when the church-planting movement facilitator will only be staying for the short period required to mobilize and equip the emerging church? In the midst of rapid church growth, creative-access platforms are unnecessary and may even be counterproductive.

The criticism from the other end says that where a long-term presence is necessary to build relationships, sow gospel seed, and prepare for the time when God begins to move, the kinds of platforms required usually do not allow sufficient time for mission work. In other words, in places like the Arab world, where tentmakers need to establish a substantial long-term foundation, most of their time is spent on their marketplace venture, leaving no time for seed sowing, relationship building, and witness. Remember Ruth Siemens's comment that tentmaking is a full-time job? Remember Heather and Dayna's testimony that a person cannot separate faith from work? The question of time is surely a strategic concern, but it is often a red herring—an excuse for those who do not really understand creative-access platforms or are unwilling to use them.

Throughout the 1990s, case studies and evaluations trickled out of the creative-access world. Perhaps failures from the field were more readily cited by mission agencies, since successes were kept at a low profile by mission workers. Today, it is clear that hundreds of mission workers *are* effectively engaging people with the gospel through creative-access platforms. The *Mission Handbook* reported 3,220 agency-supported tentmakers in 1999 (Moreau 2000f, 34), a growth trend that occurred at the same time the number of "full-time traditional missionaries actually declined" (Yamamori and Eldred 2003, 8).

Though momentum for the house church movement in China is not dependent on outside influence, hundreds of English teachers, community development workers, and businesspeople add spiritual fuel to the fire of this most remarkable movement of churches planting churches. In Central Asia, creative-access platforms played a key role for mission workers throughout the 1990s. According to David Garrison's report, a church-planting movement of over thirteen thousand new Kazakh believers and three hundred churches was built firmly on the establishment of legitimate platforms that added value to the communities of Kazakhstan over the past fifteen years (Garrison 2004, 108).

In the most difficult mission fields, where access to the gospel is least available, creative-access platforms play a pivotal role. In North Africa, both international mission workers and those from cultures similar to the ones in which they work are able to travel or live in-country through their legitimate marketplace ventures. These itinerant evangelists and church-planting facilitators serve as catalysts for the gospel seeds sown through decades of radio broadcasts and supported by one hundred years of prayer for the peoples of North Africa. Reports of new churches made up of Muslim-background believers are flowing in from the Arab world. Teachers, community development workers, business developers, and technology consultants are living and working in every capital city from Morocco to Kuwait in order to share the gospel and assist emerging churches.

So do creative-access platforms really work? Yes. Where creative-access methods are necessary to achieve the purpose of missions and when platforms are developed to fit that purpose, they work. They may be unnecessary in the midst of a church-planting movement. They may become ineffective when a platform becomes the end more than the means. But they are proving to be pivotal throughout the least-reached world. The last section of this chapter addresses strategies that will improve the effectiveness of creative-access platforms, but first we need to reflect on the biblical and historical bases for creative-access platforms.

REFLECTING ON THE TREND: BIBLICAL AND HISTORICAL PERSPECTIVES

This chapter verified and defined the trend and evaluated it in terms of ethical questions and strategic viability. Before proceeding to strategic considerations, we need to identify biblical and historical foundations for effective creative-access platforms. Does a biblical model exist for engaging unbelievers through the marketplace? Is there historical precedence for creative-access methods?

A Biblical Basis for Platform Development

When you think of Abraham, Joseph, Moses, Ruth, Daniel, Jesus, and Paul, do you think of vocational ministers or marketplace people of God? Part of the problem when we discuss creative-access platforms is that we see missionaries as professional witnesses or vocational clergy. We tend to think of platforms as a necessary evil, a last resort. We wish people and governments would just let missionaries in so that they could spend all their time doing missions, and we could avoid talk of creative-access platforms. But what does the Bible teach about engag-

---

SIDEBAR 8.5
SO GOD USES . . .

(Wilson 1979, 20–21)

Adam was a cultivator, Abel was a sheep farmer, Abraham was a cattle raiser, Hagar was a domestic worker, Isaac was a farmer, Rebekah was a water carrier, Jacob was a roving rancher, Rachel was a sheep herder, Joseph was a premier, Miriam was a baby-sitter, Moses was a flock-grazer, Bezaleel was a skilled artificer, Joshua was a military commander, Rahab was an innkeeper, Deborah was a national deliverer, Gideon was a military leader, Samson was a champion fighter, Ruth was a gleaner, Boaz was a grain grower, David was a ruler, Asaph was a composer, Solomon was an emperor, the Queen of Sheba was an administrator, Job was a gentleman farmer, Amos was a sharecropper, Baruch was a writer, Daniel was a prime minister, Shadrach, Meshach, and Abednego were provincial administrators, Queen Esther was a ruler, and Nehemiah was a governor. . . .

Also in the New Testament our Lord's stepfather, Joseph, was a carpenter, Martha was a housekeeper, Zacchaeus was a tax collector, Nicodemus and Joseph of Arimathea were supreme-court councillors, Barnabas was a landowner, Cornelius was an officer, Luke was a doctor, Priscilla, Aquila, and Paul were tentmakers, Lydia was a purple-dye seller, Zenas was a lawyer, and Erastus was a city treasurer.

229

ing and evangelizing people? The heroes of the faith usually were not professional witnesses but real-world marketplace men and women of God (see sidebar 8.5). God uses real-world marketplace witnesses to reach the world. He provides each of them with a viable platform for engaging people who do not know God. It seems that we can learn from the pattern God used and apply it to today. Indeed, tentmaking and creative-access platforms are biblical.

OLD TESTAMENT

An extensive study of the Old Testament reveals that all but a few of the primary human instruments of God's mission were people from the marketplaces of the ancient Near East. In other words, few were from the priesthood, vocational ministers if you will. Many were people of influence—rulers and leaders such as Joseph, Joshua, Gideon, and David. But they came from all walks of life—farmers, craftsmen, ranchers, soldiers, and servants.

The case of Daniel and his colleagues Shadrach, Meshach, and Abednego is an excellent example. Though they did not choose the time and place, God used them to influence the minds and hearts of King Nebuchadnezzar and his Babylonian kingdom. The king selected these four Israelites and had them educated, trained, and prepared for his service in the palace. Daniel and the others stood out as people who would not compromise their faith even for the king. God blessed them and influenced the king and his administration so that these four rose to a level of high influence in the government. Daniel, as "ruler over the entire province of Babylon" (Dan 2:48) and a member of the royal court, was able to lead that kingdom in a way that fit into God's long-term plan. As provincial administrators, Shadrach, Meshach, and Abednego also served as witnesses to the power and position of the God of Abraham. Of course, their miraculous survival in Nebuchadnezzar's fiery furnace resulted in the king praising "the Most High God," the "God of Shadrach, Meshach and Abednego" (Dan. 3:26, 28).

NEW TESTAMENT

The New Testament is full of examples of creative-access methods. The incarnation of Jesus himself is a model. God chose to cross the divine/human cultural boundary and to come to earth as a child born in a livestock feed trough. He soon became a refugee to Egypt, was raised the son of a carpenter, was followed as a radical rabbi, was crucified as a traitor, and was raised as the Messiah. The platform was strategic. It provided access and identity among a strategic people group at the center of God's plan to reach all peoples on earth. It allowed Christ to live out his sacrificial mission of atonement. God incarnate was able to establish a lasting, witnessing relationship with the marketplace people of the world through this platform in Israel. He did not come as a high priest housed in temple dwellings but as the son of a craftsman who became an itinerant teacher from Nazareth. The creative-access platform of Jesus Christ laid a foundation for the launching of a global movement of churches planting churches that continues to this day.

The apostolic actors of the book of Acts are almost all marketplace witnesses. Lydia is a great example. Paul's first Macedonian convert was a businesswoman, a trader in the high quality and well-known cloth of her region. As the head of her household (a widow?) she held a position of influence in her family and community. As the missionary/tentmaker doctor Luke writes, this woman from Thyatira, already "a worshiper of God" (Acts 16:14), responded to Paul's message by being baptized as a believer along with the members of her household. Evidently, the church that likely met in her house became a base of operations for the church-planting activities of that region. God led Paul to a successful businesswoman, not an established rabbi or religious priest. He led Paul to a marketplace person of influence and means to facilitate the birth of a new church and the spread of the gospel in that region. Lydia became one of many New Testament tentmaker church planters.

Romans 16 introduces us to a sampling of first-century creative-access mission workers. As Paul commends his coworkers, he lists names, their households, and the churches that meet in their homes. These are the marketplace witnesses of Asia Minor. They include people like the trans-regional merchants Aquila and Priscilla, who take their leather-working trade with them as they move from city to city, always leading a church that meets in their home (v. 5). Workers for the faith come from all walks of life, men and women, young and old. Some, like Erastus, hold offices of power in the community (v. 23). Others are family members, like the mother of Rufus. All are key to Paul's mission work, yet none are professional ministers or vocational missionaries.

The best New Testament model for the creative-access approach is the apostle Paul. Paul's call was to preach to the Gentiles, especially where there was no access to the gospel and where there were no churches (Rom. 15:20). He focused on training disciples so that through them the gospel would spread far beyond his own reach (Acts 19:10). Wherever he went he focused on starting churches and empowering leaders. Then he moved on to start new works. He knew how to access people at their point of need and interest—to "become all things to all men so that by all possible means [he] might save some" (1 Cor. 9:22). In Athens, "he reasoned in the synagogue . . . [and] in the marketplace" (Acts 17:17) and was eventually asked by the fraternity of philosophers to speak at the meeting of the Areopagus, a most influential body of learned leaders. There Paul contextualized the gospel by referring to the altar to the "unknown God" as an introduction to the one, true Creator God.

The best example of Paul's creative-access platform approach was his work as a leather worker or "tentmaker" in Corinth and Ephesus as a platform for preaching and teaching (Acts 18:1–4). In Corinth, it appears that the tentmaking opportunity serendipitously presented itself in the persons of Aquila and Priscilla, but in Ephesus, this tentmaking approach was an intentional strategy. Paul wanted to avoid the identity of one who "peddle[s] the word of God for profit" (2 Cor. 2:17). International trade cities like Corinth and Ephesus were full of religious peddlers selling everything in the name of some god or goddess. Paul wanted to separate himself from these cheap ideological hawkers.

But Paul wanted to make another point. By modeling a strong and honest work ethic for his disciples, he set the pace for living a life of integrity and Christian compassion for the needs of others. He pointed this out to the elders of the church in Ephesus: "You yourselves know that these hands of mine have supplied my own needs and the needs of my companions" (Acts 20:34). In other words, he established the pattern for believers to become not professional religionists—"who work in the temple [and] get their food from the temple" (1 Cor. 9:13)—but mission workers who lead the work of preaching the gospel, equipping the saints, and starting new churches from their positions in the marketplace. Paul admonished them not to extract themselves from their communities and to isolate themselves within the cultural confines of institutional religion but to remain in, though not of, the real world for the sake of witness. For Paul it was strategic. For us it is biblical.

Historical Precedence

Time and again disciples of Christ have followed the model of Paul. We have already established that the first-century church fit the creative-access mold. Church historian Stephen Neill wrote of "the anonymous and unchronicled witness of all the faithful" during these early days of "greatest glory of the Church" (1964, 22, 23). Surely the pattern of anonymous marketplace witnesses has been continuous throughout the history of the church. Even today we know that untold success stories abound. But a few of these moments in creative-access mission history have been recorded.

ACROSS ASIA

The spread of the gospel across Asia took place through a movement of merchant missionaries who traveled the silk road trade routes from China to Persia and Europe (Moffett 1998, 291, 297, 461). These Nestorians represent another example of how God uses marketplace witnesses to accomplish his mission. Matteo Ricci led the Roman Catholic work in China from 1582 until his death in 1610 (Latourette 1939, 339–42). He targeted the educated class of Peking and combined his highly contextualized missionary tactics with his marketplace skills as a mapmaker, translator, watchmaker, author, and general scientist. Today, Ricci, known as Li Matou in Chinese, is recognized as a great teacher, scholar, and scientist who came from the West and made his home in China. His contribution is still taught in the government schools of communist China. The legacy and lasting influence of missionary tentmakers like Ricci and the Nestorians are being evaluated today, especially in light of the phenomenal growth of churches in China.

MORAVIAN BRETHREN

Perhaps the best-known example of a mission movement of tentmakers is that of the Moravian Brethren or United Brethren. This group of refugee Anabaptists from eighteenth-century Eastern Europe migrated to Germany and found a benefactor and protector in Count Nikolaus Ludwig von Zinzendorf. At the peak of their mission activity, one out of sixty Moravians was an international missionary. At the same time, only one out of five thousand European Protestants was a missionary (Danker 1971, 16).

Moravian missionaries were required to support themselves and generally worked alongside the common people, even as slaves in some cases, wherever they took the gospel. They were trained at the home-base community of Herrnhut as evangelists and church planters as well as craftsmen, farmers, or tradesmen. When missionaries were unable to support themselves financially, they called on the Herrnhut community for relief. But their overall tactic for missions was to establish and support themselves as evangelists and church planters through the marketplace of the local community. They took care "not to carve out a kingdom for [themselves] overseas" but to contribute their profits for the work of the mission—"to seek profit for Jesus Christ and not for themselves" (Danker 1971, 34).

The first Moravian international missionaries were sent in 1732 to the West Indies. By 1760, the Moravians had deployed 226 missionaries in over 16 regions on the continents of North America, Europe, Africa, and Asia. Many of these missionaries reached thousands of new converts and helped start hundreds of churches. For example, in the West Indies, it is estimated that 13,000 African slaves were converted and became members of various churches primarily through the work of Moravian missionary tentmakers (Spaugh 1999). The Moravian Brethren are often remembered for their influence on the lives of church and mission lead-

233

ers such as John Wesley and William Carey (Pierson 2000), but their greatest distinction may be the successful practice of self-supporting creative-access platforms in carrying out their mission.

WILLIAM CAREY

William Carey is another historical example of a creative-access missionary. Most students of mission history know Carey as the pioneer or father of the modern mission movement. His *Enquiry into the Obligations of Christians to Use Means for the Conversion of the Heathens* (1792) is still used in missionary training classes today. What is not recognized by many is that this bi-vocational shoe cobbler/pastor was a creative-access missionary whose mission was built on various marketplace platforms. Throughout his thirty-two years (1792–1834) as a missionary to India, Carey worked as a translator, factory manager, farmer, agriculturalist, author, social activist, scientist, medical worker, and educator. These marketplace ventures provided financial support and the relational basis for the establishment of the Serampore mission that resulted in translations of Scripture into dozens of Indian dialects, preaching of the gospel, the planting of churches, and the establishment of Christian schools and a seminary (George 1991). Some forget that Carey entered the country without legal papers and served much of his time in India as an illegal missionary immigrant. Yet he laid the groundwork for generations of missionaries to follow.

The biblical and historical evidence for the use of creative-access platforms in mission work is overwhelming. God's method of engaging the unreached peoples on earth has, from the beginning, been one that uses real-world, marketplace laypeople. The pioneers of the gospel have been and still are the Daniels, Shadrachs, Meshachs, Abednegos, Riccis, Moravians, and Careys of today. This recent trend of creative-access platforms is returning us to the cutting edge of God's global mission.

ENGAGING THE TREND: THE WHYS AND HOWS OF CREATIVE-ACCESS PLATFORMS

Obviously, a trend for using creative-access platforms exists in the world of global missions today. This section addresses some practical issues by asking two basic questions.

Why Do We Need a Platform?

Ask an experienced strategy consultant what is the most frequent mistake made by organizations, businesses, or teams that prevents them from accomplishing their goal, and you will usually get the same answer. They do not have a clearly defined purpose. In other words, they do not really know what their goal is. Some are focused on the details of implementing the plan and have lost sight of the overall objective or end result. Others are just along for the ride and never really caught the vision; they never saw the big picture in the first place. It happens in the mission world as well. One of the best ways to define a purpose is to ask the "why" question. For the creative-access missionary who wants an effective plan that capitalizes on the potential and avoids the pitfalls of platform development, the most critical question is, Why do we need a platform in the first place? (Barnett 2002).

> *Those who in that day sneered that England had sent a cobbler to convert the world were the direct lineal descendants of those who sneered in Palestine 2,000 years ago, "Is not this the carpenter?"*
>
> Frederick W. Farrar, Westminster Abbey, March 6, 1887
> (George 1991, xxii)

ACCESSIBILITY

The first answer is the most obvious. Creative-access platforms are needed to provide accessibility. As Paul declared in Romans 10:14–15, "How, then, can they call on the one they have not believed in? And how can they believe in the one of whom they have not heard? And how can they hear without someone preaching to them? And how can they preach unless they are sent?" Here we might add, "And how can they be sent unless they have a way to gain access?" In other words, mission workers need a reason for entering a region to live or travel among the unreached peoples they seek to reach. This was the driving force behind the reemergence of tentmaking in the twentieth century: to gain access to the restricted peoples on earth. For mission workers seeking to engage a least-reached people group, the platform is their reason for being there. It provides an entrée into a previously inaccessible region. It serves as a starting place for future possibilities. It answers the question, Why are you here?

A case in point. A relief worker we will call Anna obtains permission to travel to the most remote corners of a region where tribal peoples live. Though the government seldom allows outsiders access to these isolated peoples, Anna is given permission based on her role of researching relief and aid needs. She is a qualified and experienced relief worker and consultant. She has extensive contacts with subsistence farming experts in-country and in the outside world. She is representing one of these organizations as she travels. Anna is also an experienced cross-cultural communicator of the gospel. She wants to verify the existence of a specific least-reached people group, identify their felt needs, and design a plan to catalyze a movement of churches planting churches among this people. She is prepared to reside in the remote region if this is determined to be strategic. She spends several months learning about the people, their language, culture, religion, and worldview. The decision whether to locate inside the remote region follows her research. As a relief and development consultant, she gains access. When asked why she is there, her natural response is, "I am here to help you."

In Anna's case, there is no need for her to create a new nongovernment organization in the country. She does not require an extensive budget, office, staff, capital investments, or projects. She is a relief and development consultant. Does she need to be legitimate regarding her credentials, intentions, and behavior? Absolutely. But this platform allows her to conduct mission research and strategic planning. Her platform matches her purpose. Anna's objective drives her platform.

Legitimacy

Often the objective of a mission worker or team requires more than initial access for a few months. Frequently, mission workers need a long-term base from which to carry out a mission strategy. In these situations, the platform must provide more than accessibility. It requires long-term legitimacy or a credible activity or endeavor that validates the reason for staying in a region. Relief workers may gain permission to enter a city or region, and they may even research potential projects, but if no real relief services are provided, they will not be allowed to stay or return. If, on the other hand, the workers actually provide relief for the community under duress, then they will be allowed to remain. Relief services provide a value added to the community or government. The platform not only provides access and a reason for being there but also answers the question, What do you do here?

A case in point. After a major war in an Arab country, the United Nations imposed a protective zone for a large population of historically persecuted peoples. Tom and Linda went as volunteer workers on a water resource development team directed by a respected international organization. Tom was a middle-aged recently retired civil servant. Though he had training and experience in crisis management and team building, he knew virtually nothing about well drilling or irrigation. Linda was a former school teacher and stay-at-home mother. They learned about this two-year opportunity through their church. The organization approved their application based on Tom's experience in crisis management, their age and maturity, and the reputation of the charitable organization that sponsored them. They gained access, but would they be able to stay for the two years? They needed legitimacy.

In spite of their struggles with language and culture, this capable couple learned on the job. Before long Tom was leading a drilling crew of national workers. He led them on three-day projects in the remote villages, repairing old water wells and drilling new ones. He worked with a translator and began to learn enough of the trade language to gain the respect and love of the nationals he served. He planted seeds of the gospel through his life's witness and through literature and Bible portions that the team distributed upon request. Linda settled into an administrative job at the base of operations in the regional capital. She established lasting relationships with the local women. She was able to lead several to Christ and even mentor a young leader who spoke English and started a Bible study group. Tom and Linda became known as hard-working, honest, compassionate workers who were committed followers of Jesus. Their commitment to do the work and do it well added value to the community and gave them the legitimacy they needed to remain in the country for longer than their original two-year commitment.

IDENTITY

One of the most strategic advantages of a platform is that it provides an identity for a mission worker, which naturally provides a right to be heard. A local resident knows why the worker is in the land and what the foreigner docs. As the resident encounters the worker, the resident is able to answer the question, Who are you? Are you an American? Are you a husband, a father, a family man? Are you a professional woman, a mother, a sister? As the worker lives and works from the platform, the locals observe who he or she really is. This opens the door for the worker to be heard. It lays the foundation for bridges to be built between cultures and worldviews.

A case in point. Moira was a young British believer just out of college who felt called to give two years of her life to serve the Lord overseas. Like thousands of native English speakers around the world, she took a three-month TEFL (Teaching English as a Foreign Language) course through a local community college, and she applied for various English teaching jobs in a Central Asian country. While she was waiting for confirmation of a job, she took a course on how to disciple across cultures. Her purpose for the two years was to evangelize and disciple university students so that they could start their own churches. Moira secured a teaching contract and moved to a regional capital city.

Her two-year term was successful beyond her dreams. The teaching was rigorous work, and the schedule was intense. She lived on campus in the faculty dorms with modest accommodations. Crossing culture was a challenge, and she was not able to learn much of the language, since her students always insisted on speaking English. But she was able to lead a small group of students to Christ and to disciple them. She then saw them lead others, and the beginning of a movement of house churches began. By the time she left Central Asia to return to the UK, she had witnessed the planting of over twenty house churches in the city.

As she evaluated her experience, it was obvious that TEFL was an excellent platform for evangelism and discipleship. The open environment of education set the tone for sharing and discussing profound concepts. The rigorous work schedule and the close quarters she shared with students provided a visible test of Moira's character. The students saw something different in this teacher. The light of Christ shone through Moira's life and work. Her identity as a follower of Jesus impressed her students, and she earned the right to be heard. God used her as an instrument for transforming lives and establishing his church among the people of Central Asia. There are hundreds of Moiras around the world today who lead students to become disciples of Jesus—the greatest teacher of all time.

STRATEGIC VIABILITY

Effective platforms can also provide strategic viability for mission workers and their teams. Well-thought-out platforms offer a basis for relationships between workers and locals. Strategically viable platforms lead to life-changing relationships. Again, the concept of adding value to the lives and communities of locals is vital. Humanitarian aid, schools, hospitals, and the like often result in goodwill and favor among locals, which leads to an openness to the worker and the gospel. Such a platform answers the question, What do you have for me?

A case in point. Some platforms are more viable than others. A platform that provides a job for an international accountant to crunch numbers in a high-rise office building surrounded by English-speaking expatriates sixty hours a week may not allow the worker to connect with an unreached people group. A job may provide a Christian access to a country, it may be legitimate and even add value to the community, and it may even project a clear and positive identity in Christ, but it still may not be a strategically viable platform. Why not? Because it does not provide a basis for relationships with the people he or she intends to reach with the gospel.

On the other hand, a platform that allows that same international accountant to travel throughout the region to train local non-English-speaking businesspeople in practical business accounting practices may be extremely viable. Such a platform facilitates the development of multiple, meaningful relationships within the unreached people group. It even sets the pattern through business for a mentoring or discipling relationship outside business. This is strategic viability at its best.

INTEGRITY

Finally, an effective creative-access platform provides the opportunity for a worker to demonstrate integrity or character. The apostle Paul took advantage of this aspect of platforms when he refused to become another peddler of the gospel in Ephesus, a city rife with profiteers of religion. Paul says he supported himself and others through the labors of his own hands. He modeled the principle that true disciplers should care for their disciples out of a sense of love and obedience to Christ, not for profit. He reminded the elders, "In everything I did, I showed you that by this kind of hard work we must help the weak, remembering the words the Lord Jesus himself said: 'It is more blessed to give than receive'" (Acts 20:35).

In the same way, mission workers model the lifestyle of a disciple of Jesus through their daily life and work. This aspect of creative-access platforms answers the question, What kind of a person are you? and therefore, What kind of a person is a follower of Jesus?

A case in point. Rusty was an athlete in college who met the Lord and accepted God's call to go to China to teach the gospel to those who had never heard it. Convinced that the best way to penetrate the bamboo curtain was through the business world, Rusty learned the sales business working for a world-class retailer in Seattle, Washington. Next, he spent two years in Taiwan as a professional athlete learning the Mandarin language and the culture of the Chinese people. He was hired by one of the major international manufacturing companies that entered China in the early 1980s. Rusty was a hard worker and an experienced salesman who spoke Mandarin. He quickly advanced himself through the company and became the lead representative of the company in Beijing.

After living and working for fifteen years in China, today Rusty is one of the best-known and most respected Christian businessmen in China. He has witnessed to thousands of Chinese businessmen and women and has led many to Christ. He has been a supporter of the Chinese church and has assisted hundreds of mission workers and Chinese believers in establishing themselves in business and ministry in China. A newspaper article about Rusty in one of the Beijing newspapers highlighted his contributions to the Chinese people and characterized him as an honest and trustworthy businessman. His business platform provided the basis for a reputation of integrity, which opened the minds and hearts of many.

TABLE 8.1
SUMMARY OF PLATFORMS

Why Platforms?	Strategic Advantage	Answers the Question
accessibility	reason for entering	Why are you here?
legitimacy	reason for staying	What do you do here?
identity	right to be heard	Who are you?
strategic viability	basis for relationship	What do you have for me?
integrity	witness for discipling	What kind of a person is a follower of Christ?

What Types of Platforms Are There?

We have seen why we need creative-access platforms, but what exactly do they look like? Platforms come in all shapes and sizes, and selecting the right platform for the task at hand is critical (Barnett 2002). Some are individual platforms based on the credentials and networks of a mission worker. Some are a part of the strategy for a team of mission workers seeking access, legitimacy, identity, strategic viability, and integrity among a specific people group or population segment. Some are simple and streamlined. Some require the establishment of a registered organization or company.

STUDENT

One of the most frequently used and most effective platforms is that of the student. Mission workers spend several years in another culture as full-time or part-time students. Hundreds of student-missionaries study the language and culture of their host nation in state universities. This enhances the bonding experience of mission workers with the people group, familiarizes them with the worldview of their host culture, and facilitates the development of witnessing and discipling relationships among the crème de la crème of their host society. From the fertile and open environment of a university, missionary students model the life of a disciple of Christ as they live, study, and work alongside fellow students. This platform often paves the way for future platform opportunities.

A student platform can provide access, legitimacy, identity, strategic viability, and integrity all in one. Of course, the legitimacy and integrity aspects require hard work and much time. Every waking moment for the student is ministry.

TOURIST

Sometimes the best way to access an unreached people is as a tourist. For example, one strategy coordinator in Asia is able to maintain a ten-year multi-entry visa as a tourist. This kind of platform has advantages and disadvantages.

Since tourists are key contributors to the economy, this platform can provide a positive starting point for building relationships. Tourists also find open doors for in-country travel, sometimes to remote areas where a people group resides. At the same time, a tourist platform may fall short of providing a real reason for staying. After all, few tourists stay for long. The short-term nature of a tourist platform may limit the potential for long-term relationships.

The primary downside of the tourist approach concerns the issue of integrity. Few mission workers have the time and money to be real tourists for long. So you say you're a tourist? Why aren't you touring? Does this create an ethical problem? Yet many governments issue a general tourist visa to all foreign visitors who live temporarily in their country regardless of the nature of their visit. Therefore, it may not be an ethical issue at all. For some governments, the status of tourist simply means legal, temporary visitor.

Even if the tourist platform does not create an ethical or legal issue, it still may not provide an answer to the questions of identity, strategic viability, or integrity. In that case, a bit more creativity may be called for. For example, the strategy coordinator mentioned above uses the tourist platform for accessibility but has another role or platform for establishing long-term viability. He is an active and highly respected volunteer worker in community development and education projects. He has discipled new believers and planted churches among his people group through a combined tourist and community development platform.

EDUCATOR

Thousands of English-speaking mission workers have responded to the universal demand for English teachers. Teaching English as a second language (TESOL) is a viable platform that allows for long-term employment (Snow 2001). TESOL adds value to the host culture and provides a solid basis for relationships. The role of teacher is transcultural and universally recognized and respected. Good teachers demonstrate strong character and earn the right to share their faith. But there are other opportunities for creative-access via education.

One U.S.-based nonprofit agency provides various educational and vocational training services at centers around the world. Mission workers with appropriate credentials and skills represent the agency. They promote faculty/student exchange networks among major universities from every continent. Another company provides application and orientation services for students seeking overseas admissions and education: seminars on how to complete an application, how to interview, how to write entrance essays, and so on. Yet another organization specializes in cutting-edge business management and entrepreneurial seminars for junior executives in the Middle East. It partners with venture capitalists and business development companies in Central Asia.

The industry of education is a fertile field for creative-access platforms. Opportunities abound for individual educators or providers of education services.

SPORTS DEVELOPER

One of the exciting platform options of recent years is that of sports developer. Sports is a natural bridge for crossing cultures. People connect with one another when they talk, view, or play sports together. The platform industry of sports is being approached from all angles. One of the most effective and viable strategies is that of the sports development company. Every country wants a sports hero. The world-famous long-distance runners of Kenya and Ethiopia have become supreme ambassadors for their countries. A sports development company connects interested organizations, schools, clubs, and even governments with the rest of the sports world. Sports figures are frequently given the opportunity to tell their life stories and to challenge others with the gospel. The sports developer serves as a broker for sports contacts, events, sports personalities, training clinics, equipment companies, and so on. Such an approach results in stable, long-term platforms for missions. This platform industry works for individual consultants or direct-hire coaches as well as for teams or sports development companies.

BUSINESSPERSON

Perhaps the most effective but least developed platform option is that of the businessperson. When you do business with people, you get to know them at their most basic point of need. As a legitimate businessperson, a mission worker enters the real world of an unbeliever, where the gospel is uniquely relevant. The personal testimony of a Christian businessperson often has a tremendous influence on an unbeliever. Accessibility, legitimacy, identity, and viability are givens for a businessperson. Integrity depends on the quality of work and the character of the worker.

We have already mentioned the "Kingdom Business Forum" and the growing emphasis on kingdom entrepreneurs. This approach focuses on equipping and connecting mission workers to be effective business developers. Kenneth Eldred, well-known business leader and venture capitalist, calls us "to do the outrageous," to think of business as "an opportunity to win many to Christ, reach an entire city, and possibly influence the thought process and views of those who lead the country"

CASE STUDY:
MARY'S DILEMMA

Mary, an experienced educator with a Ph.D. in nursing education, was in a quandary. She was ready to return and pick up her work in a country where visas for missionary work were regularly denied. Mary was told that the agency intended to request a tourist visa for her return. The previous year Mary had served six months under a tourist visa at the hospital and had heard several warnings that a tourist visa was not correct for what she was doing. While Mary appreciated her sending agency's support base and wanted to maintain the relationship with the agency, she did not feel she could work with a tourist visa.

At the same time, the hospital needed to improve its medical staff, and

Mary's level of education and teaching experience made her an asset for the hospital. Her teaching was deeply appreciated, and the national staff requested that she return and continue her teaching. The hospital administrator was prepared to send a formal letter of invitation to Mary. Of course, the hospital would not be able to pay her a living wage, and so it was counting on her to continue as a missionary medical teacher.

Mary was in a quandary. How could she fill the position where she was needed and where she wanted to serve if the mission agency could not secure her a visa?

(Yamamori and Eldred 2003, 20). This side of the platform of business may be on the verge of tremendous growth and success.

Though business platforms offer much, they are still one of the most challenging options for today's mission workers. Why? Some contend that mixing the unethical world of mammon with the world of faith is risky business. Others point out that some of the least-reached parts of the world do not offer prospective markets for good business practice. Others suppose that a business platform that is unable to support the life and work of a mission worker without outside support is invalid or unethical (Guthrie 2000, 117). The bottom line may lie in the fact that most mission workers today still come from a culture that has a professional witness or clergy mentality. The challenges are formidable, but the potential of legitimate business platforms is huge.

By simply asking the question, Why do we need a platform? a mission strategist can assess the type of platform best suited for the task at hand and can periodically evaluate the viability of the platform. For example, if a platform is needed solely for accessibility to a given city or region for a few months of initial research and networking, then a tourist platform may serve best. If, on the other hand, the objective requires viable, long-term mentoring relationships among a specific people group, then the legitimacy, identity, and integrity provided through a businessperson's platform may be the best strategy. By regularly returning to the basic question of why a platform is needed, mission workers ensure that a platform does not become the end rather than the means.

Creative-access platform development is one of the most vital and challenging aspects of twenty-first-century missions. The trend continues to increase and is driven by the passion of the church to engage all peoples on earth with the gospel. Though it has been a part of mission history since Abraham, a fresh rediscovery of its biblical and historical bases is necessary and inspiring. Old habits are hard to break, and the modern tendency to rely primarily on vocational missionaries to complete the task will not get the job done. The case study on page 243 demonstrates the value and the challenges of creative-access missions in the twenty-first century. Hopefully, this chapter provides a basis for an informed and strategically focused dialogue regarding the trend.

PART 3

The Strategic Context

9

Working Together

Beyond Individual Efforts to Networks of Collaboration

DOUGLAS MCCONNELL

In the second half of the twentieth century, the parade of flags was a common feature of annual mission conferences in local churches and colleges across the United States. Typically, flag bearers would march down the aisles toward the platform at the front of the sanctuary, where the flags were placed in stands for all to admire. Each flag represented a country where a missionary was serving. Speakers would then tell stories of great opportunities and challenges from the far reaches of the globe. These ceremonies provided tangible evidence that the Great Commission was alive and well.

As the new millennium drew closer, the effects of globalization began to change the significance of these vicarious mission experiences. Short-term missions increased the number of Christians who had firsthand experiences to share at annual conferences. Mission pastors were added to the staffs of churches, colleges launched summer mission trips, and mission societies were drawn into the action, albeit reluctantly, by engaging in formal short-term mission programs. The emergence of groups that specialized in mobilizing people, particularly the young, became household names among dedicated Christians. Youth with a Mission (YWAM) and Operation Mobilization (OM), specialists in mobilizing young people, have two of the best-known acronyms in the world of missions.

As the twentieth century closed, a dramatic shift had taken place. Missionary service was no longer restricted to a career option. Mission trips often were short-term experiences. In the midst of this shift, traditional agencies and churches on the mission fields of the world scrambled to integrate the new wave of volunteers. Simultaneously, majority world missionary movements emerged as a significant force for the global spread of the gospel. An important element of the new paradigm is recorded in the closing statement from Lausanne II: "Our manifesto at Manila is that the whole church is called to take the whole gospel to the whole world, proclaiming Christ until he comes, with all necessary urgency, unity and sacrifice (Luke 2:1–7; Mark 13:26, 27; 13:32–37; Ac. 1:8; Matt. 24:14; 28:20)" (Lausanne Committee for World Evangelization 1989).

Globally, there is a movement toward greater collaboration among agencies, churches, and other mission-minded organizations. This trend is the result of efforts to expand the impact of the gospel by building on the strengths of shared resources, ideally through commitment to a common purpose. This chapter focuses on the change from isolated efforts to collaboration that has taken place in missionary service.

IDENTIFYING THE TREND: THE CONNECTIONS OF LIFE

In the years following World War II, people around the world poured into cities. Between 1970 and 2000, the population of urban dwellers grew from 1.3 billion to 2.8 billion, while the number of cities with over 1 million inhabitants grew from 161 to 402 (Barrett and Johnson 2004, 25). This new urban world presented agencies and churches with tremendous challenges on every front. The popular view of a Western missionary as an intrepid adventurer with a pith helmet, hiking boots, and a Bible was slowly transformed into the image of a minivan-driving apartment dweller with even greater traffic problems than the supporters back home. A second picture began to emerge as well, that of the bi-vocational pastor who spends the day working in a "secular" job and the evenings and weekends sharing the gospel among migrants in the city.

One of the immediate challenges of this new reality was to mobilize missionaries for the multicultural world of neighborhoods and slums. Traditional mission stations, which were centers of Christian outreach, gave way to apartment complexes filled with the people to whom missionaries were sent. Doug McConnell's experience mirrors this change. In the late 1970s, his family served in the isolated highlands of Papua New

Guinea. The people were clearly delineated by their culture, clothing, language, and residential patterns. The McConnells lived at a mission station with other expatriates separated from the local tribal people. In the 1980s, they moved to the capital city, where their apartment was on the ground floor. The crowded neighborhood was made up of people from all over the country plus expatriates from all over the world. No longer could the behaviors of the residents be categorized as those of "the people" and "the missionaries."

The interconnected world of cities and the rural areas that surround them provide a framework for the trend of moving from individual efforts of missionaries to networks of collaboration in global missions. This section identifies three major elements shaping the trend: (1) social networks, (2) team efforts, and (3) companies and collaboration. These elements emerged in stages that roughly paralleled the rapid growth of urban populations in the last three decades of the twentieth century.

Social Networks

Urban centers affect far more than housing and traffic patterns. At the heart of urbanization is a change in the structure of society itself, seen clearly in the social upheaval of the 1960s. Tribal people and peasant villagers migrated to urban centers in search of a new life, and cities became centers of cultural diversity rather than melting pots as predicted by sociologists (Fischer 1984). Naturally, a generation of young social scientists began to study the culture and structure of cities to explore better ways of understanding the urban reality. Out of these studies came the term *social networks* to describe the interconnectedness of urban dwellers (Mitchell 1974).

CONNECTING

The crowds of humanity in a city are striking even to the casual observer. On further observation, it appears that while these crowds share a common space, they do not necessarily share common relationships. Not surprisingly, one characteristic of the urban world is the presence of multitudes of familiar strangers. People may share a bus stop or a checkout line at the grocery store, but there is an absence of personal relationships. So we are faced with a critical social network question: How do we build relational worlds?

Due in part to urban migration, extended families play a smaller role in the lives of urban dwellers. To replace the loss of more traditional social relationships, people tend to build their worlds among those with whom they share significant involvement. Coworkers, classmates, members of the same church, neighbors, and/or members of a health club make up the world of people who move from familiar strangers to friends. From the standpoint of structure, social relationships are the building blocks of society.

These personal networks can be defined as "the set of people who are most likely to be sources of a variety of rewarding interactions e.g., discussing personal problems, borrowing money or social recreation" (Burt and Minor 1983, 78). As Claude Fischer notes, each person within a network may choose to be connected to others or not (1982, 4). On the positive side, the urban world allows for greater opportunity to form relationships. Negatively, giving and receiving support are choices that must be made on a regular basis.

> *In general, we each construct our own networks. The initial relations are given us—parents and close kin—and often other relations are imposed upon us—workmates, in-laws, and so on. But over time we become responsible; we decide whose company to pursue, whom to ignore or to leave as casual acquaintances, whom to neglect or break away from. Even relations with kin become a matter of choice; some people are intimate with and some people are estranged from their parents or siblings. By adulthood, people have chosen their networks.*
>
> Claude S. Fischer (1982, 4)

Individuals in a personal network tend to be connected to one another relationally, and the strength of the relational connections creates a supportive network. Members share many things in common, including access to the resources of the individuals. To illustrate, a group of students at a college may share everything from classroom experiences to textbooks, study halls, dorm rooms, and youth groups. Such significant social support forms the basis for a feeling of belonging within a community.

A corollary is that the absence of a supportive network leads to isolation or loneliness, which is a common experience among migrants or those newly arriving in a city. Seldom do networks remain constant. Over time people move on. Life changes resulting from marriage, children, career demands, and a host of other realities put pressure on networks. In most cases, building new networks is an important part of moving on.

Personal networks tend to draw on the same pool of resources. This often leads to a shortage of specific types of resources, particularly when it comes to money. For example, a church youth group may be able to draw on the money of their families to sustain regular activities such as weekly gatherings or special outings to a local theater or restaurant. However, if the same group decides to participate in a short-term mission trip, wider fund-raising will inevitably be necessary to support the individual members. Strong social ties consume the limited available resources as part of normal social interaction.

An interesting contrast may be found among people who are less connected to one another. Mark Granovetter, in a theory known as "the strength of weak ties," observed that even though ties may be weak, such relationships may still be crucial in connecting two important groups together in a new way (1982, 106). This is especially important in helping people on the margins by providing them access to vital resources. For example, a missionary taught English to refugees. As part of her ministry to these new acquaintances, she introduced them to the health care system and to places to acquire the goods and services necessary to live in the city. Although the teacher and her students had only weak ties, she was a bridge to vital resources previously unknown to them.

As these insights spread among churches and agencies, a new method of helping emerged known as networking. In short, networking is a means of intentionally connecting people to other people beyond the realm of their known contacts. The practice of networking was not so much a new discovery as it was a helpful way to think about an age-old practice. These insights, however, enabled new developments in the way networking can be used more strategically by Christian missions.

PROMINENCE

Within any social network, various people may be more connected and even more helpful than others in the networking process. These individuals have prominence within the network. Typically, we equate network prominence with prestige, which is based on a person's important position or wealth. Prestige often determines the degree to which others within a network seek to connect with a person. For example, a young leader will often seek opportunities to relate to an older, more visible leader in order to build his or her reputation by association. Newly formed groups or associations establish a board of directors comprised of well-known individuals for the sake of building credibility for the group and its cause.

A lesser-known form of prominence relates to an individual's broad base of relationships. This type of prominence within a network is known as centrality. A person with centrality is typically one who can be depended on to help a cause, through either communication or introducing people to one another.

Whereas prestige is often acquired through an important social position, centrality is more a product of a person's relational skills. In research conducted in the 1980s, Doug McConnell found that centrality was a critical component of the success of networking among ministers. Centrality was particularly evident in cooperative ministries such as evangelistic crusades or social service efforts because of the capacity of these individuals to build trust and distribute vital resources within the network (1990).

Both elements are important for effective networking. In the early stages, people with prestige provide credibility. As relationships strengthen, individuals emerge who are central to the network and, therefore, more likely to have the capacity to facilitate networking.

For missionaries and church workers, cities demand more dynamic skills in adapting to multiple cultures, languages, and worldviews. Thus, during the 1980s and 1990s, networking emerged as one of the primary approaches for advancing beyond the individual efforts of agencies. While networking is an important type of collaboration, it places new demands on individuals. One practical method of meeting the challenges is to engage in teamwork.

Team Efforts

While teams were not new in any sense, the major emphasis on teams in the workplace and in missions emerged as a dominant approach by the 1990s. In the field of business, the leading researchers on teams, Jon Katzenbach and Douglas Smith, compiled their studies in the book *The Wisdom of Teams* (1993). It rapidly became a national best seller with over one hundred thousand copies sold in the first year in the United States and subsequently over four hundred thousand copies worldwide. By the turn of the century, the proliferation of research and literature on teams had strongly influenced the way people approached work (e.g., Katzenbach 1998, 2000; Katzenbach and Smith 2001; Lipman-Blumen and Leavitt 1999; Lencioni 2002).

> *Social networks have important consequences for the ways that we behave, the information we receive, the resources we exchange, the communities in which we are involved, the opportunities that we try to pursue . . . how we think. . . . Social networks are the strings that simultaneously constrain our freedom and provide us with opportunities to take initiatives.*
>
> Barry Wellman
> (Wellman, Berkowitz, and Granovetter 1997, xiii)

Typically, organizations, institutions, and even mission agencies have hierarchical structures. These organizations have clearly defined job statements and formal lines for accountability. In contrast, teams involve a more relational approach. While both forms require disciplined participation, teams are made up of peers who must cooperate with one another. Thus, a team is "a small number of people with complementary skills who are committed to a common purpose, performance goals, and approach for which they hold themselves accountable" (Katzenbach and Smith 2001, 7).

Ideally, teams will have fewer than ten members, among whom there are complementary skills. Apart from the obvious difficulty of group dynamics in larger teams, there is a tendency in large groups to assign fixed roles that focus on specialized tasks to be achieved. Inevitably, formally appointed leaders in larger groups develop a bias toward efficiency, stability, and subdividing tasks that tends to reduce the capacity of the group to respond to rapidly changing situations (Katzenbach and Smith 2001, 89–92). In contrast, members of smaller teams, assuming they have all the necessary abilities to get the work done, have the advantage of immediate access to one another because of interdependence. Interestingly, research indicates that the more demanding the goals, the stronger the team (Katzenbach and Smith 1993, 3).

Beyond size and skills, a team that functions well possesses individual commitment to a common approach that fits the specific goals set by either the organization or the team. This can be extremely difficult in situations in which the team faces political, social, and even environmental challenges. For example, mission teams working in the war-torn Balkans during the 1990s found it difficult to set realistic long-term goals. Yet even with the challenges of setting clear goals, teams can flourish in most settings when the members are willing to hold themselves accountable. One reason is that mutual accountability builds trust. Research in the business world points to the foundational principle of trust as a basis for moving from individual interests to teamwork (Katzenbach and Smith 2001).

Anyone who has worked on a team can testify to the fact that teamwork is not easy. One of the most helpful analyses of the weaknesses of a team approach focused on five common dysfunctions: absence of trust, fear of conflict, lack of commitment, avoidance of accountability, and inattention to results (Lencioni 2002). Patrick Lencioni suggests that "these dysfunctions can be mistakenly interpreted as five distinct issues . . . but in reality they form an interrelated model, making susceptibility to even one of them potentially lethal for the success of the team" (2002, 187).

Despite the potential for dysfunction, teamwork is a trend that has influenced the worlds of business and missions. Building on the role of networking, teamwork is a model that has broad appeal within societies where globalization has the greatest effect, particularly in big cities.

Companies and Collaboration

In the corporate world, at the close of the twentieth century, two related but opposite practices helped set the stage for identifying the trend toward collaboration. The first practice was a global move toward acquisitions and mergers, leaving the average consumer unsure who owned a company and how long a product would be available. Among the underlying pressures was the growing problem of maintaining a competitive edge in the rapidly changing marketplace of a global economy. A readily identifiable solution was either to merge with a compatible company or be acquired by a company with a stronger economic base.

Inevitably, mergers and acquisitions raise concerns about the compatibility of purposes among the partners. In some cases, incompatibility can be in the form of an ethical dilemma. For example, take someone who worked for Kraft Foods, a well-known company that started by processing cheese. When Philip Morris, a conglomerate with its origins in the tobacco industry, acquired the Kraft Foods Corporation, this person had to decide whether working for the tobacco giant was in line with his personal integrity.

The second practice was a proliferation of new start-up companies that targeted a particular market niche. Among the many corporations that became legendary during this period are the software giant Microsoft and the personal computer companies Dell and Gateway. The enormous success of these rags to riches start-ups tempts even the most cautious investor or inventor. However, as many discovered, the proliferation of new technology companies hurt the long-term success of many start-ups. Scores of young entrepreneurs made millions during the technology boom, but in the vast majority of cases, those small companies are now part of larger companies that diversified their interests in an effort to remain solvent. Others busted as quickly as they boomed, leaving the rich soil of Silicon Valley full of highly educated but unemployed technology people.

In the midst of these well-known practices, a trend emerged that had a significant impact on the world of nonprofit and mission organizations, namely, collaboration through strategic alliances. Harvard Business School professor James Austin documents the trend in a book titled *The Collaboration Challenge*. As Austin states, "The magnitude and complexity of our social and economic problems are . . . outstripping the institutional and economic capabilities of individual nonprofits and business organizations to deal with them" (2000, 9). Thus, an alternative to mergers and acquisitions is collaboration, especially between businesses and nonprofit organizations.

Research identified a collaboration continuum of three stages of growth in the relationships among participants (Austin 2000, 20). The first is well known in the nonprofit sector, the philanthropic stage. At the heart of this stage is a desire on the part of businesses or foundations to distribute a share of the profits to worthy causes. Among the most visible philanthropic investments are those of Microsoft cofounder Bill Gates. The Bill and Melinda Gates Foundation made the staggering donation of $200 million to increase Internet access in public libraries, primarily aimed at lower-income areas (Rothman 1997). Overall, philanthropic giving in the United States in 2002 totaled $240.92 billion (Sinclair 2003). The largest portion of the giving, $84.28 billion or 35 percent, was given to religious organizations (Sinclair 2003).

The second phase of the collaboration continuum is the transactional stage (Austin 2000, 22). This type of collaboration moves from the distribution of funds to the exchange of resources through coordinated activities. This is a common approach in the nonprofit and sporting worlds. For example, two students were preparing to run the LA marathon sponsored by Honda and Bank of America. A portion of the proceeds of their fund-raising efforts, $1,600 each, went to the Leukemia and Lymphoma Society. A characteristic of the second phase is a clear agreement between the partners with clearly specified transactions. One of the most critical variables in establishing these transactions, therefore, is to identify "overlapping missions and compatible values" (Austin 2000, 24).

The third phase of the collaboration continuum is the integrative stage. This stage goes beyond finances and activities to a level of collaboration that benefits the participants in ways unexpected at the outset. For example, CARE and Starbucks began to collaborate in 1992 with a line of coffee from which a percentage of each sale was donated, generating $62,000 for the year (Austin 2000, 30). The relationship built in this collaboration grew over the decade, as did the giving, making Starbucks the largest corporate donor to CARE, $1.2 million by 1998 (Austin 2000, 31). One unexpected benefit of this collaboration was the establishment of the Starbucks Foundation in 1997, which increased the company's capacity to work with others. The northwest regional director of CARE was appointed to head the foundation, and the CEO of Starbucks was appointed to CARE's board (Austin 2000, 31).

After reviewing a range of examples of collaboration, Austin developed what he called the seven C's of strategic collaboration (see sidebar 9.1). This set of guidelines provides a practical view of the elements contributing to successful collaboration. In the increasingly changing world, the concept of a single group, company, or mission society possessing

---

SIDEBAR 9.1
GUIDELINES FOR COLLABORATING SUCCESSFULLY

(Austin 2000, 173–83)

The following guidelines are relevant for effective collaboration between corporations and nonprofit organizations.

1. Connection with purpose and people. Alliances are successful when key individuals connect personally and emotionally with the alliance's social purpose and with each other.
2. Clarity of purpose. To help ensure clarity of purpose, prospective partners should jointly prepare a written collaboration purpose statement.
3. Congruency of mission, strategy, and values. As an extension of clarifying purpose, partnering organizations should identify areas of alignment between their missions, strategies, and values. Engaging early in conversations about alignment is essential to building a solid foundation for collaboration.
4. Creation of value. High-performance collaborations are about much more than giving and receiving money. They are about mobilizing and combining multiple resources and capabilities to generate benefits for both partners and social value for society.
5. Communication between partners. Good communication is essential to building trust, and trust is the intangible that makes a collaboration cohesive.
6. Continual learning. Collaboration must be viewed as dynamic. Although systematic analysis and planning are desirable, a partnership's evolution cannot be completely planned or entirely predicted.
7. Commitment to the partnership. Because partnerships increase in scope, scale, strategic importance, and operational complexity as they advance along the Collaboration Continuum, partners must be prepared to ratchet up their personal, institutional, and resource commitments accordingly.

REFLECTION AND DISCUSSION

1. What are some of the reasons for clarifying the purpose of collaboration in a formal document?
2. Discuss some of the primary reasons for maintaining open communication between partners in a collaborative venture.
3. Give examples of mission partnerships that demonstrate the application of the guidelines for successful collaboration.

---

the needed human, financial, physical, and spiritual resources may be immediately dismissed as a hollow claim.

This section identified the broad elements shaping the trend from individual and group efforts to collaboration. A common factor in all three elements is the force of urbanization, which brings increasingly diverse populations into close proximity and thereby creates new alliances and methods. In each case, these strategic new alliances can be viewed through the relationships formed among those who share similar visions and values.

EVALUATING THE TREND: NETWORK INITIATIVES IN MISSIONS

On the last evening of a three-week trip to Vietnam, Doug McConnell's hosts decided to give him and his group a farewell at a restaurant atop one of the newest and tallest buildings in Ho Chi Minh City. Standing on the rooftop patio at dusk, he could see the expanse of this growing city of 5 million inhabitants. It was a beautiful sight, yet it was also perplexing in that globalization and communism seemed to share the same streets. The shifting political position had opened the door for greater collaboration between local initiatives and international groups. As a result, leaders from three of seventeen new private universities had invited the visitors from a Christian agency to form a cooperative venture of faculty and student exchange in an effort to escalate the development of their academic programs. As McConnell looked out on the city that night, he saw the formidable challenge created by the scope of this opportunity. The question that lingered in his mind was, Can we rise to the challenge by employing some of the newer collaborative approaches?

In an effort to answer this question, this section evaluates the trend toward collaboration by using the major elements identified in the previous section.

Networks

Central to the network perspective is a focus on relationships. Rather than the more traditional views of location and kinship, the interconnections of people living in a city facilitate greater understanding of the social worlds in which we find ourselves. The implications for missionary engagement are far reaching. Concepts such as connectedness, the strength of weak ties, prominence, and subcultures are useful tools in assessing the most productive ways to engage in missions within a city. In practical terms, by applying the insights gained from the study of networks, agencies and churches can identify not only new vistas for ministry but also a greater range of resources through the connections of their various constituencies.

For example, Kevin, a bi-vocational missionary, arrived in the city hoping to engage in ministry among the urban poor. While attending a church that served the international community, he met a young missionary who had contacts in several of the settlements populated by

257

migrants to the city. A relationship was formed that allowed Kevin to visit the poor communities with a person who already had the trust of the local population. In the months that followed, Kevin built relationships that led to the establishment of a small congregation. From their congregational base, Kevin and his new friends began to network with people and like-minded groups from around the country and internationally. Within a couple years, the community had a clinic, a preschool, and a multipurpose building. These services provided an example for many other settlements.

A network approach to missions has grown beyond local initiatives. Building on the same insights, missions and church leaders have discovered a multitude of opportunities to network with those who share similar concerns in a broad response to world missions. To evaluate the contribution networks have had on the trend of collaboration, the following sections examine three types of networks commonly employed in mission practice at the beginning of the twenty-first century: (1) local network initiatives, (2) specialized network initiatives, and (3) global network initiatives.

LOCAL NETWORK INITIATIVES

A characteristic of local network initiatives is the necessity to respond to problems facing a community beyond what a single ministry is equipped to handle. These local responses range from the approach Kevin took in a single locale to much broader responses that tackle problems with an urban or regional effort, such as responding to the needs of recently arrived refugees.

An example of a local network initiative is Love INC, or Love in the Name of Christ. Launched as an effort to help the poor and vagrants in a small town in Michigan, Love INC has grown into a volunteer ministry sponsored by World Vision US. Built on the concept that each church has limited resources and time to contribute, Love INC serves as a clearinghouse with no direct services. A group of network volunteers identifies local resources within a community. This is achieved through contacting ministries and social service agencies while also recruiting local churches to be participants in the Love INC network. In some cases, a church distributes a "talent tithe inventory" to its members to determine the types of goods and services available within the congregation. These can range from financial assistance (e.g., $500 per month) to practical skills in mechanics, carpentry, or transportation. These lists are then compiled to create a profile of services and assistance available through the Love INC clearinghouse.

The impact of local network initiatives is readily observable to those who are committed to missions in a given place. People who are con-

---

SIDEBAR 9.2
A TESTIMONY OF LOVE INC

(World Vision n.d.)

Jeff and his nine-year-old son needed a place to live. His wife had kicked them out of the apartment. Love INC put them up in a motel near the boy's school so he could continue school uninterrupted. The cost for one week, plus food and some utensils, was provided by a Love INC church. Jeff filed for AFDC benefits [government assistance] but couldn't get them immediately. A church volunteer helped find him and his son an affordable apartment in the area while Jeff found himself a part-time job. Their new landlady was very much taken with the boy and treated him as a grandson. The church volunteer invited them to worship, and they are now members of that church. Jeff accepted Christ as his Lord and Savior. Soon, Jeff obtained a full-time job and got off welfare.

REFLECTION AND DISCUSSION

1. Discuss the dynamics of the Love INC network in meeting the needs of Jeff and his son, particularly the volunteer network necessary to supply the variety of needs.
2. Are there other examples of networks that provide vital intervention on behalf of the poor? If so, identify the key elements in their successful intervention.
3. How might this form of networking apply to a ministry situation in which you are currently involved?

---

nected to other Christians in a city are often the best initiators for these responses. Prominence in the form of prestige or high visibility can help to establish credibility for the network. In time, however, the greatest assistance to the cause comes from those who have strong relationships that can facilitate the flow of information and resources. Sustainability is not so much dependent on resources available as it is on volunteers with a vision to supply the specific needs addressed by the network.

SPECIALIZED NETWORK INITIATIVES

A second type of network is formed with a specialized ministry or mission in focus. Examples of specialized network initiatives include church training programs, congregational associations, educational programs, mission associations, and specialized ministries. Building on the same principles as local network initiatives, advocates of the ministry pull together people who can provide both financial support and prominence. The prestige of the support network is important for broader acceptance over a long period of time. Until the network is established, people are likely to ask about the credibility of the ministry and for references.

The Alpha Course was developed in the social context of secular England, where the tradition and the social convention of going to church had long passed. In an effort to reach those who knew nothing about the Christian faith, the Alpha Course was designed around a typical evening get-together. It consisted of a series of talks that related the Christian faith to life questions. Each gathering began with a meal to provide time to get acquainted, followed by a talk on a specific topic that helped to develop an understanding of the faith. Participants were encouraged to ask questions and to share opinions in response to the talk. The evening gatherings concluded with a time for coffee and small-group discussion. The format, while developed in a particular context, has proven effective worldwide.

The second example of a specialized network initiative is the Willow Creek Association (WCA). Launched in 1992 by the Willow Creek Community Church, which is located in a suburb of Chicago, WCA links churches that share a commitment to offering a church environment that is sensitive to those who are seeking a place to meet God. The purpose of WCA is to "inspire, equip, and encourage Christian leaders to build biblically functioning churches that reach increasing numbers of unchurched people—not just with innovations from the Willow Creek Association or the Willow Creek Community Church, but with God-given breakthroughs with widespread potential from any church in the world" (Willow Creek Association 2004). Indicative of the wider scale of the specialized network initiative is the phrase "breakthroughs with widespread potential from any church in the world." These networks are not limited by a specific location but rather are characterized by their specialized appeal. The global impact of these specialized initiatives is illustrated by the fact that WCA now involves more than ninety-five hundred churches around the world.

Specialized networks are dependent not so much on marketing as on the felt need of people in ministry. Attracted to the clarity and accessibility of the model, these networks spread along relational lines, reinforcing the basic premise that networks are not bounded by location or membership. The rise of global transportation and technology-driven communication has created an environment in which specialized networks flourish.

GLOBAL NETWORK INITIATIVES

Building on the structural elements of the local and specialized network initiatives, the third type of network is characterized by a global focus intrinsic to its purpose. Global networks bring together churches, agencies, and individuals with a broad vision to affect the entire world through alliances and partnerships. Global network initiatives often begin with either the selection of delegates to participate or broad invitations.

DAWN Ministries began as a network initiative with a view to multiply church-planting efforts among every group of people in a nation. Hence, DAWN is an acronym for Disciple a Whole Nation. The initiative was predicated on Donald McGavran's church-growth strategy, which affirms that the best way to achieve world evangelization is through the multiplication of churches (1979). Following this strategy, DAWN networks churches to engage in saturation church planting. From the beginning, DAWN committed itself to a strategy that could be replicated. The DAWN approach has been replicated in 148 nations (DAWN Ministries 2004).

Another example is the Lausanne movement that grew out of the World Congress on Evangelism held in Berlin in 1966. Participants from the congress caught the vision for a global movement committed to world evangelization. Subsequently, an active group of influential evangelicals emerged as the driving force behind the movement. Building on their considerable global influence, they convened the International Congress for World Evangelization in Lausanne, Switzerland, in 1974. Working together, the delegates developed a document, the Lausanne Covenant, that set out a representative position of evangelicals worldwide. During the next fifteen years, meetings were convened around an increasing number of relevant topics, thus building momentum for the movement. The second international gathering of the movement took place in Manila in 1989. Building on the momentum from the first Lausanne Congress, the Manila event brought together over 4,300 Christians from 173 countries (Ford 1990, 11). In September 2004, the Forum on World Evangelization was held in Thailand to continue the tradition, further demonstrating that a truly global network is at least possible as a mission strategy.

All three types of network initiatives emerged as a major force in missionary practice at the end of the twentieth century. Local and global network initiatives tend to foster voluntary participation for the sake of achieving a stated purpose based on the open participation of like-minded people. In contrast, specialized networks tend to require either membership or subscription in order to access the materials produced by the group. Strengths of network strategies are their accessibility and their broad-based participation. Weaknesses include a varying degree of commitment and the difficulty in creating a sustainable identity. On the whole, from the perspective of network initiatives, it is possible to mobilize a variety of groups and individuals to participate in a strategy to influence a city or even the globe.

Mission Teams

It is difficult to isolate missionary methods as unique to a particular period of history. In the case of mission teams, small groups of believers were the "missionary teams" of the first century. Jesus sent out his disciples in teams (Mark 6:7; Luke 6:12–16; 10:1), believers scattered by persecution witnessed as they fled (Acts 11:19–20), and the apostles formed teams to spread the gospel (Acts 10:23; 13:2–4; 15:39–41). Throughout mission history, small groups of believers have been a potent force in the expansion of Christianity (Mellis 1983).

Another characteristic of the missionary movement was the move toward more permanent settlements as the gospel message took root in a given context. Along with forming local churches or parishes, missionaries often built mission stations from which to continue the work of establishing the ministry. The goal was to disciple churches to maturity so that they could take over the work with all its complexities. Although necessary, these stations tended to move away from team dynamics to more institutional approaches. The missionaries occupied particular roles, such as pastors, teachers, health care workers, and administrators. A popular view of missionary success became working oneself out of a job by training a national to take over. By 1970, mission stations and institutions were the norm among Western missionaries.

Paralleling the trend toward network initiatives was a shift away from mission stations to a variety of approaches, among which was the rediscovery of mission teams. This shift toward teams challenged the popular view that agencies and missionaries had to work themselves out of a job. Growing out of the Lausanne movement and the work of leading missiologists such as Ralph Winter, new emphases arose that stressed reaching every unreached people group through global strategies, partnership, and more holistic understandings of the mission of God. Naturally, new strategies required rethinking approaches to the missionary role.

In the final three decades of the twentieth century, not only did established mission societies change their approaches, but new agencies that embraced the new methods were launched in the 10/40 Window. Among the best known are three that built teams into their organizational DNA: International Teams, Pioneers, and Frontiers.

Earliest among the new agencies to begin with a team approach was International Teams. Begun in 1960 as a short-term literature ministry, International Teams developed into a mobilizing mission focusing on teams committed to building transforming communities (International Teams 2004). In 1979, Pioneers was launched to focus on the remaining unreached peoples of the world. From the outset, the new mission was committed to teamwork as an approach to mobilizing missionaries. The mission statement demonstrates its commitment to the approach: "Pioneers mobilizes teams to glorify God among unreached peoples by initiating church-planting movements in partnership with local churches" (Pioneers 2004). The third example is Frontiers, founded in 1982 to concentrate on the Muslim world. Like the other two, Frontiers chose to adopt the teamwork approach as its operational strategy throughout the world. The vision and practice are built into its mission statement: "Our passion is to glorify God by planting churches that lead to movements among all Muslim peoples through apostolic teams in partnership with others who share this vision" (Frontiers 2004).

> *The world is rapidly changing, and these changes are having a profound effect on today's mission enterprise. Even as modern missiology identifies more people groups, which have little relevant access to the Gospel, it is apparent that many of these same people groups will not be accessible by traditional mission methods. Most of these new methods find their focus in the concept of a mission team.*
>
> Eric Adams and Tim Lewis
> (1990, 22)

Many other mission societies have adopted teamwork or a variation of it as their modus operandi. At the heart of such an approach is the willingness to affirm that each member of the team makes a significant contribution to the mission. Such an affirmation moves away from filling roles, typical of institutional approaches, to using gifts and skills within the team. Matters of trust and commitment are foundational to the success of mission teams.

Mission leadership structures have adapted to the specific needs of teams. In most cases, area or regional teams are appointed to provide oversight or shepherding, primarily for team leaders. Teams are then entrusted with greater degrees of member care. The locus of influence, such as decision making and team member selection, has moved from a headquarters to the teams themselves.

Parallel to formal mission societies is an informal movement toward teamwork. Typically, those who find themselves in a given location reach out to other believers for fellowship and ministry. Increasingly observable are teams of lay leaders who serve in international churches in cities worldwide. This lay movement has been powerful in creating a missional church in areas where diversity results in greater challenges than can be met by a single mission society.

The impact by teams both formally through agencies or churches and informally through lay movements is increasing around the world. The contribution of mission team approaches is that teams can minister to diverse needs by bringing together various gifts into an organic unit. As a team, people reside in a given place and are connected to one another in ways that allow their ministry efforts to be multiplied through focus on a shared purpose.

Strategic Collaboration

A third significant element in the shift in the missionary paradigm from individual efforts to networks of collaboration was the emergence of a variety of specialized organizations. In the entrepreneurial style of Western society, major new initiatives emerged to supplement the more traditional activities of evangelism, discipling, and church planting. Facilitated in part by technological advancements and the fact that Christian foundations handled much of the wealth of the post–World War II economies, particularly in North America, new specialized ministries provided an amazing range of support for the missionary cause. In most cases, the organizations were expressly committed to serving other ministries by contributing particular specializations. Consider the following short list of organizations and their expressed purpose in regard to the wider mission community:

- Overseas Ministries Study Center (OMSC) began as a retreat center for missionaries in 1922. It expanded its work by offering seminars and workshops for leaders from churches and missions globally in 1967.
- Missionary Aviation Fellowship began in 1945 to provide air transportation for missionaries to isolated locations. It took the next step in technological service by offering help with satellite communications in 1994.
- World Relief, the social concern arm of the National Association for Evangelicals in the United States, began in 1945. It provided relief and development assistance to the efforts of evangelical churches and agencies.
- World Vision began to assist in relief and development, particularly among orphans in Asia, in 1950.
- Evangelical Missions Information Service began to publish *Evangelical Missions Quarterly* in 1964, a journal that explored topics relevant to the missionary community.

- Link Care Center, providing counseling and pastoral care, began in 1965.
- Perspectives on the World Christian Movement, an extension course in missions offered around the world, began in 1974.
- U.S. Center for World Mission, the vision of Ralph and Roberta Winter that began in 1976, was dedicated to producing and publishing resources for world mission.
- Global Mapping International, committed to providing the mission community with an accurate profile of the "harvest fields" and the "harvest force," began in 1983.
- STEM Int'l, which specialized in helping to mobilize and provide resources for short-term missions, began in 1984.

Organizations such as those listed above were initiated as a response to a growing need felt in the mission community. Characteristic of specialized organizational responses was the nature of their calling to serve other mission organizations. Whether through voluntary associations or partnerships, the provision of services was geared toward participants who belonged to a wider recognized body, such as the World Evangelical Alliance or one of the national mission associations, such as Evangelical Fellowship of Mission Agencies (EFMA) or Interdenominational Foreign Mission Association (IFMA) in the United States.

Missionary Aviation Fellowship (MAF) provides a good illustration of the nature of these specialized organizations. MAF describes itself as "a non-profit team of aviation and communication specialists overcoming barriers in support of more than 300 Christian and humanitarian organizations around the world." With more than 71 aircraft flying out of 41 bases, MAF pilots fly more than 40,000 flights per year in 24 countries (MAF 2004).

Like MAF, other organizations provide services that draw on their unique calling and abilities. In essence, this generation of cooperation tended more toward formal partnerships conducted on contractual lines in which each participant subscribed to the same rules of conduct, providing one another with the validating purpose of their individual charters. A second generation of collaboration involved mission associations. For example, EFMA came into being to bridge and even broker partnerships. In its own words, "EFMA was established to increase the effectiveness of agencies and their leaders in worldwide, cross-cultural mission by providing spiritual fellowship, the exchange of ideas and the building of skills and cooperative relationships, thereby creating mission synergy" (EFMA 2004).

Instead of inviting agencies to join an association, as was the case with EFMA, Interdev established active partnerships among agencies and churches internationally, offering training in collaboration. In the words of a press release of November 2003, "Arriving on the missions scene twenty years ago with an innovative strategy for collaborative ministry, Interdev has brought together 500 partner agencies and churches, and has invested time and resources in almost 300 partnerships working to birth the Church among the world's least reached peoples" (Simmons 2003). Even though the original purpose of Interdev remains a worthy and less than realized goal, the ability of the organization to foster collaboration ceased to be viable in 2003. Again in their own words, "Having analyzed the organization's vital signs, the Board moved prayerfully and courageously to hand off the partnering ministry to the next runners" (Simmons 2003). Despite the termination of Interdev as an organization, its efforts set the pace for a new generation of collaboration.

From colonial compounds to urban neighborhoods, the dramatic changes at the end of the twentieth century raised new questions about collaboration. In part because of changes in the sociopolitical climate, missionaries responded to the need to expand their efforts at collaboration to new levels. As the missionary force became multicultural, the understanding of interconnectedness opened the door to cooperation based on relationships rather than on organizational partnerships. Collaborative efforts will similarly diversify in the years ahead. Doubtless formal partnerships may decline due to economic factors. However, the creation of new forms of collaboration that network human and material resources appears to be escalating. Such networks of collaboration are creating mutual benefit through shared missions and values (Austin 2000, 37–38).

Although it is still too early to predict the outcome, an initiative known as World Inquiry—launched by mission collaborator Luis Bush—illustrates these less formal aspects of collaboration. Bush initiated World Inquiry after a period of sabbatical in which he studied the nature of networks and collaboration, writing a dissertation on the topic at Fuller Seminary (Bush 2002). The process of inquiry involved listening to the burdens, visions, and dreams of more than twenty-five hundred Christian leaders in focus groups from sixty-five countries and over four hundred cities (Luis Bush, personal correspondence, December 7, 2002). Among the goals is the establishment of transformational focus groups that study significant areas of concern with a goal of bringing together twenty-five influential leaders, with at least 75 percent coming from the majority world, to study and consider collaborative action to guide missional response.

Irrespective of the outcomes of World Inquiry, it provides an example of the trend toward networks of collaboration that transcend the natural organizational boundaries of Western mission efforts to reach a globally inclusive approach. It is difficult to predict the variations that may arise as new forms of collaboration emerge, but one thing is clear: Traditional barriers are dissolving in the wake of new participants in the global movement of the Christian faith. Those called to share their gifts with the entire church must be reminded that spreading the gospel is in fact the mission of God, not the domain of a single human grouping.

Now the answer to the question McConnell asked that evening in Vietnam takes on new meaning and, thankfully, a note of promise. Based on the trend toward networks of collaboration, creative new ways exist for missionaries and agencies to respond to the complexities of the world emerging at the beginning of the twenty-first century.

REFLECTING ON THE TREND: RELATIONSHIPS AND GOD'S PURPOSE

A rare joy that belongs to those who travel internationally is found upon attending Christian services in new places. Apart from language difficulties, a visitor is immediately reminded of the joy of belonging to the global family of God. Shortly after the end of the open conflict in the Balkans, Doug McConnell joined others at a gathering of the Evangelical Alliance in Sophia, Bulgaria. The event was held in a large church building in the city. As part of the celebration of faith in Christ, a large banner hung over the stage that read, "All one in Christ Jesus." On the final evening, internationally known missiologist Peter Kuzmic led the meeting. Calling three pastors to the platform to join him, Kuzmic asked each in turn to give his name, home country, and local church affiliation. The three men were from Serbia, Bosnia, and Croatia. At the end of the short introductions, the four of them embraced one another as a living symbol of the truth of the words over their heads.

When Jesus gave his disciples the new commandment recorded as part of the upper room discourse, he made a clear statement of purpose for the kind of unity seen in Sophia. "By this everyone will know that you are my disciples, if you have love for one another" (John 13:35 NRSV). There is no shadow of uncertainty in his words or contradiction in the testimony of his life. In both the Gospels and the Epistles, it is hard to overestimate the importance of Christ's command to love one another. The call to unity in love is as profound at the beginning of the twenty-first century as it was in the first.

The previous two sections discussed the trend of collaboration and the emerging methods of missionary practice. As with every trend, there

267

are more theological issues raised than space available to address them. This section limits the discussion to two theological concerns related to the trend of collaboration: (1) the nature of our relationships and (2) our mission in God's purpose.

The Nature of Our Relationships

As those who have been redeemed by God's divine plan of salvation found in Christ Jesus, we are commanded to love one another on the basis of God's love for us. It is difficult to dismiss this fundamental aspect of Christian theology. When asked about the greatest commandment, Jesus stated first that we are to love God above everything else and second that we are to love others (Matt. 22:37–39). The reality of putting God above all else should be primarily observable in our relationships with other believers (John 13:34–35; 15:12) and, shockingly, with even our enemies (Matt. 5:44; Luke 6:27, 35).

Scripture repeatedly correlates our commitment to God with the manner in which we act toward others. Two cases illustrate this. The first example is found in a letter of John to the faithful in Christ. While the entire epistle sounds the call to communion with God and one another, it is expressly articulated in the words, "Those who say, 'I love God,' and hate their brothers and sisters, are liars; for those who do not love a brother or sister whom they have seen, cannot love God whom they have not seen" (1 John 4:20 NRSV). The reality of our love for God is made known through the observable love we have for others, in this case for believers. The idea is again captured in the epistle in the words, "We proclaim to you what we have seen and heard, so that you also may have fellowship with us" (1 John 1:3). The Greek word used for "fellowship" here describes "the living bond that unites Christians" (Bromiley 1985, 450). Our relationship with Christ at once brings us into relationship with other Christians.

The second example is Jesus' parable of the sheep and the goats (Matt. 25:31–46). In making the point of the parable, Jesus said the king would reply, "I tell you the truth, whatever you did not do for one of the least of these, you did not do for me" (v. 45). Jesus brings into focus the behavior toward those who are weak and marginalized as an indication of the heart toward God. The principle is set in the context of demonstrating genuine love for God through loving service to those who cannot repay. There is no direct reference restricting the demonstration of love to those in the household of faith. Such love should be given to others without reservation.

In the New Testament, it is striking how many times "one another" occurs in the English translations. In addition to the phrase "love one another" spoken by Jesus to the disciples, "members one of another," "fellowship with one another," "encourage one another," "welcome one another," "serve one another," "show hospitality to one another," and "honor one another" are used to reveal guidelines for our life together.

It is apparent that those redeemed through the grace of God are called to live it out in relationship with others who are equal recipients of the grace.

The nature of our relationships with one another, therefore, is that of interdependence. Because we are dependent on God in Christ, in whom all things are held together (Col. 1:15–20), we cannot absolve ourselves of the bond to others, who are also dependent on God. The picture in the Epistle to the Ephesians is one of being "one new humanity," "members of the household," and "built together spiritually into a dwelling place for God" (Eph. 2:15–22 NRSV). The interdependence of our relationships has a significant bearing on our service to the mission of God.

Realizing the interdependence of our relationships as Christians clarifies the importance of the trend of collaboration. As the gospel spreads throughout the world, bringing people into communion with the Lord, it calls them into fellowship with one another. In these newfound relationships, there is increasingly a pull to work together in service of God's purpose. To frame any further reflections, we must look carefully at our mission in God's purpose.

> *We affirm our belief in the one-eternal God, Creator and Lord of the world, Father, Son and Holy Spirit, who governs all things according to the purpose of his will. He has been calling out from the world a people for himself, and sending his people back into the world to be his servants and his witnesses, for the extension of his kingdom, the building up of Christ's body, and the glory of his name. We confess with shame that we have often denied our calling and failed in our mission, by becoming conformed to the world or by withdrawing from it. Yet we rejoice that even when borne by earthen vessels the gospel is still a precious treasure. To the task of making that treasure known in the power of the Holy Spirit we desire to dedicate ourselves anew. (Isa. 40:28; Matt. 28:19; Eph. 1:11; Acts 15:14; John 17:6, 18; Eph 4:12; 1 Cor. 5:10; Rom. 12:2; 2 Cor. 4:7)*
>
> Lausanne Committee for World Evangelization (1974)

Our Mission in God's Purpose

In 1974, the participants of the International Congress of World Evangelization in Lausanne adopted what has become known as the

Lausanne Covenant. It was the conviction of those who framed the covenant that the place to start in any call to greater levels of collaboration is the central purpose of God. Based on the trinitarian belief in one true God, the writers acknowledged that God governs all things "according to the purpose of his will" (Lausanne Committee for World Evangelization 1974). Such an acknowledgment is clearly in line with a declaration of our dependency on God alone. Given that we are dependent on God in all things, we must understand our task in relation to his purpose.

The statement of God's purpose in paragraph 1 reminds us further that God continues to call people out of the world and to send them back into the world as part of his overall redemptive purpose. We are called out to be his people and sent back to be his witnesses. Clearly, this acknowledges the love of God for us, by calling us out to be his people, and for the world yet to hear and receive, by sending us back as servants and witnesses. The call seeks to transform our purpose and our very beings (Rom. 12:2). Hence, our response as sent ones is not so much an act of our will as an act of obedience to God's will.

Called and sent as servants of the kingdom of God and witnesses to the gospel of Jesus Christ, we are specially gifted to serve (Van Engen 1991). In two epistles, this fact is recorded specifically in light of the urgent mission. "Like good stewards of the manifold grace of God, serve one another with whatever gift each of you has received" (1 Pet. 4:10 NRSV). The task of "faithfully administering God's grace in its various forms" (1 Pet. 4:10) is central to our mission and requires the humble service of all. The Epistle to the Ephesians records the same truth: "But to each one of us grace has been given as Christ apportioned it" (Eph. 4:7). This grace given freely by God is administered by believers through the amazing diversity of gifts within the equally amazing unity of his purpose. God's mission is to be done in God's way by God's missionary people (Van Engen 1991).

A corollary to the unifying purpose of God is the divisive nature of human competition in regard to the mission of God. In reviewing the impact of the Lausanne movement twenty years later, John Stott offered a few of his personal reflections. While still committed to the cause, he questioned the level of unity clearly called for in the covenant. In paragraph 7, the covenant expresses penitence, for "our testimony has sometimes been marred by a sinful individualism and needless duplication." Stott asked the question, "I wonder what has become of our penitence and our pledge?" (1995, 1). He then proceeded to cite examples of offensive practices of "individualism and empire-building" seen in many parts of the world, particularly in Eastern Europe (1995, 1). It does not take the mature reflections of a leader like John Stott to see evidence of individual efforts that disregard the work of others.

Despite the glaring examples of disunity, over the past three decades, agencies and churches have moved closer together in many tangible ways. However, if we are to forge ahead in a manner that honors God's purpose, we must consider carefully the basis of our collaboration. While acknowledging our God-given unity, we must also acknowledge our tendency toward sinful responses. Based on both Scripture and the human practice of collaboration, we must move toward a more clearly articulated theological understanding as a basis for our shared commitment to the purpose of God. This was at the heart of the Lausanne Covenant. The challenge as we move forward into the twenty-first century is to revitalize the momentum for a truly global movement.

The joy of discovering new members of the body of Christ is not the exclusive domain of those who travel. It is the growing realization of people who grasp the nature of our unity as followers of Christ. The encouraging signs of a growing commitment to collaboration invite all of us to act globally with the assurance that we are dependent on God and interdependent as his servants. Yet to be effective beyond the boundaries required by the establishment of new organizations will require higher degrees of trust and more creative approaches to strategic engagement. With that observation in mind, we now turn our attention to engaging the trend of collaboration.

ENGAGING THE TREND: BUILDING NETWORKS FOR COLLABORATION

Gathered with the delegates from eight West African countries and two Western nations, Doug McConnell and his colleagues listened as speakers reported on the growth of the church among the unreached peoples of the southern Sahara Desert region. Each missionary shared the joys and struggles of life among peoples who were yet to hear the gospel of God's grace. As one of only seven non-Africans present at the conference in Accra, McConnell was challenged to look at his limited view of God's mission to the world. Thankfully, he had the opportunity to sit again with many from this group at an international gathering in Pattaya, Thailand, twelve months later. In this larger gathering of the mission, he again heard the testimonies of African missionaries blended with those of missionaries from three other continents. As each day of this second conference passed, the singing and praise seemed to increase in its intensity. They were not only giving thanks for those who were coming to faith but also enjoying fellowship that foreshadowed the picture of "saints from every tribe and language and people and nation" (Rev. 5:9 NRSV).

SIDEBAR 9.3
DIGGING DEEPER

The following websites are useful for further study of the variety of responses to networking, teamwork, and collaboration. The websites are a rich source of specific approaches to the challenges facing missions today.

Alpha Course: http://alphacourse.org

DAWN Ministries: http://www.dawnministries.org

EFMA: http://community.gospelcom.net/Brix?pageID=7115

EMIS: http://www.wheaton.edu/bgc/EMIS

Frontiers: http://www.frontiers.org

IFMA: http://www.ifmamissions.org/home.htm

International Teams: http://www.iteams.org

Global Mapping International: http://www.gmi.org

Lausanne Congress on World Evangelization: http://www.gospelcom.net/lcwe

Link Care Center: http://www.linkcare.org

Love INC: http://www.worldvision.org/worldvision/wvususfo.nsf/stable/loveinc

Missionary Aviation Fellowship: http://www.maf.org

Overseas Ministries Study Center: http://www.gospelcom.net/omsc

Perspectives on the World Christian Movement: http://www.perspectives.org

Pioneers: http://www.pioneers.org

STEM International: http://stemmin.org/aboutSTEM.shtml

U.S. Center for World Mission: http://www.uscwm.org

Viva Network: http://www.viva.org

Willow Creek Association: http://www.willowcreek.com/wca_info

World Relief: http://worldrelief.org

World Vision: http://www.wvi.org

Knowing that our destiny is to join together with such a great multitude, we are well served to begin the songs of praise in our generation. There is no more visible indication of this sense of unity than when we as diverse peoples join in the single purpose of world evangelization. Having introduced the trend in the context of Christian mission, this chapter now looks more closely at how best to engage the trend using the same three elements identified earlier: (1) networks, (2) teamwork, and (3) collaboration.

Engaging the Networks

Where do we start as we consider collaboration in our missionary efforts? A good place to start is to take personal responsibility by reaching out to those who are already within our network. Missionaries supported by our local church provide such a starting point to expand our personal network. Even if we do not know the missionary personally, our affiliation with him or her by virtue of our local church membership is sufficient to tie us together in faith and practice. As an introductory exercise, connecting with a missionary serving cross-culturally will facilitate an opportunity to establish new contacts.

For example, a missionary has a group of people that he or she is working with in a given location. Getting to know this group of people builds a profile of the scope of the work supported by the local church. Adding the various agencies or churches represented by the missionary's network will further develop the profile of the work. From that point, it is important to examine not only the workers and the organizations but also the types of work involved in the mission context. Again, the goal of this exercise is to build a profile to understand better the network that is already in existence. Before long, a broad base of work emerges that will either encourage us by its magnitude or call us to action in our desire to impact the location for Christ. This simple yet effective approach can open doors for service that has previously eluded us.

Once we have an understanding of the beginning point, we can undertake the more significant prospect of networking beyond our current levels of involvement. This has the capacity to involve all three types of network initiatives previously evaluated: local, specialized, and global. Determining the focus of our efforts should, therefore, build on the interests and skills already in place. For example, if a person is committed to children, it is logical to seek out a network of people who are similarly concerned, such as the Viva Network. Established in the mid-1990s to bring together people and projects concerned about children at risk, Viva Network now connects thousands of people in an ever-widening network of care. Engaging with others who share the same passion for children widens the scope of influence through collaboration, enhancing both individual efforts and those of the wider network. Beyond personal networking, churches and agencies also have a growing role in initiating networks of collaboration.

Those who have a vision for impacting the world can see the immediate benefits of networking. Perhaps one of the overlooked benefits is the refining of our own understanding of the issues. Based on the insights gained from social network analysis, we are always in danger of creating a tight social world that excludes anything that does not agree with our own likes and dislikes (Fischer 1982). In contrast, networking allows us to expand our perspectives through new relationships and moves us toward a deeper understanding of the prayer in Ephesians 3: "And I pray that you, being rooted and established in love, may have

273

power . . . to grasp how wide and long and high and deep is the love of Christ" (vv. 17–18).

Engaging in Teamwork

For those who are observant, the love of Christ lived out in the context of a local community provides an agenda for both ministry and personal growth. As such, teamwork is a source of blessing as well as frustration. When we read through the list of "one another" passages, we are reminded of both. "Love one another" (John 13:34) may be seen in the encouragement to "accept one another" (Rom. 15:7) and the challenge to "carry each other's burdens" (Gal. 6:2). Relationships are never dull or easy. To live in community the way Christ requires demands a deep-seated commitment to the transformation of our sinful selves. As Patrick Lencioni noted, the potential for dysfunction is present in all teams (2002). Thus, for those open to work together as a team, the task is one of building and maintaining trust.

One of the foundational issues that thwart efforts of teamwork is the problem of cultural distinctives. On the practical level, it takes time to overcome the barriers of culture in a way that builds community. If a team is willing to work together, there are positive steps that can assist in the process. The first is to accept the fact that differences are the norm, not the exception. While this sounds obvious, it is interesting to watch people relax when they accept differences between themselves and others. Giving one another the freedom to disagree without losing favor with the group has a liberating effect on all team members.

Second, identify the favorite food of each member of the team, within the limits of available ingredients. Then take turns preparing food for the group. During the meal, tell the stories that surround your memories of your favorite food. The power of fond memories can bond people together. Then plan a time when all the members of the team can reflect on the various types of food, including preparation, ingredients, and presentation. For example, it can be very revealing to compare a Japanese meal with a barbeque prepared by an American from the South. Just a comparison of the presentation styles is enough to open the doors of cultural understanding: chopsticks versus fingers, small tea cups with green tea versus large glasses of sweetened iced tea, raw fish versus large amounts of cooked meat covered in barbeque sauce. If participants adhere to the first suggestion, differences are acceptable, and the evening will result in a new level of understanding.

A third suggestion involves the celebration of special days from each culture represented, whether a national independence day or a special religious or social celebration. If all members of the team can be represented by and participate in these events, a greater degree of appreciation will be fostered. The main objective is to be creative in affirming one another while allowing space to be different.

On the negative side of things, the disparity of resources, particularly wealth, is one of the most potent divides in any teamwork situation. When teams commit to a lifestyle that is inclusive of all members, the teams prioritize their identification with those to whom they are called to minister, leading to greater influence. When disparate lifestyles are the norm, team longevity is often threatened because of the inevitable problems associated with jealousy or greed. It is disheartening to watch material possessions and comfort hamper the integrity of the message that is preached.

> *The most visible and profound way in which the community gives physical expression to its fellowship is the common meal. Paul writes about the common meal in only two places, and Acts associates him with it once.... [Yet] this meal is vital, for as the members of the community eat and drink together their unity comes to visible expression. The meal is therefore a truly social occasion.*
>
> Robert J. Banks (1994, 80, 83)

We must never forget Jesus' words to the disciples in the upper room: "I give you a new commandment, that you love one another. Just as I have loved you, you also should love one another. By this everyone will know that you are my disciples, if you have love for one another" (John 13:34–35 NRSV). In a world that is torn by ethnic rivalries and racist wars, we dare not overlook the power of unity as a testimony for Christ.

Engaging in Greater Collaboration

Between 1970 and 2000, two practices in the mission world paralleled those in the corporate world. The first was new partnerships resulting from the joining of two or more mission agencies into one. While in most cases the rhetoric used carefully highlighted the positive blending of the individual organizations, the act was similar to the mergers and acquisitions of their business world counterparts. The overall result was the growth of larger groups such as World Vision, SIM, and others who moved forward in formal partnerships.

In the case of many smaller agencies, a new lease on life is gained by joining their supportive memberships and constituencies with a broader group in agreement with their mission. For example, two agencies in Australia, Asia Pacific Christian Mission and South Pacific Partners, agreed to join ranks with the Florida-based group, Pioneers,

CASE STUDY:
THE COST OF REPRESENTATION

As Peter Walker and Nguyen Van Nam waited for their steaming bowls of pho, the conversation naturally recounted the time spent with the chairman of the Government Liaison Office. At that meeting, Peter discussed openly the purpose of his visit. As the director of education for International Service Group (ISG), Peter was empowered to negotiate an agreement with the private universities emerging in the new Vietnam. The chairman listened politely to Peter's description of the work of ISG. After hearing from him, the chairman asked Nguyen Van Nam if he supported the organization. Pausing to think through the issues surrounding such a claim, Nam said, "Yes, Mr. Chairman. I serve as the local representative of ISG."

ISG, like so many other nonprofit organizations, began as an evangelistic mission. As the opportunities for entering new areas grew, so did the problems associated with obtaining visas. Few countries were open to missions and fewer still to those specifically targeting their populations. For months, the leaders of ISG researched the best approaches for serving internationally. They were committed to integrity in both their calling and their claims. After considering a number of options, they decided to move in the direction of bi-vocational workers who could

make credible contributions to the development of the nations in which they worked. Generally, they would do so in the areas of education, business, and health care.

Peter, a half-time professor of intercultural studies at an accredited graduate school, acted as an educational consultant for ISG. As part of his teaching duties, he organized teams of graduate students and faculty to teach intensive courses in various countries in which ISG was working. The work in Vietnam had been a particular joy since Peter, like many others of his generation, had a long history with the country. Given this chance to influence the spiritual and educational development of the country, Peter was working to negotiate a long-term agreement.

Vietnam was experiencing a number of changes as relations between the West and Vietnam improved. Among the changes most affecting Christian organizations were the 17 private universities that had opened in the previous 5 years, a move toward English as a second language, and the government's recognition of a coalition of 245 Protestant churches. For more than 25 years, there had been no formal training schools for pastors and church workers. The combination of the three changes was attractive to Christian groups from around the world. As a

to form Pioneers of Australia. The overall result was that the mission movement was strengthened by the presence of the Aussie missionaries, while a fresh wind of missions swept back into the Australian landscape as a new generation of young people caught the vision for result, traditional agencies and groups such as ISG were entering Vietnam with a view to working with or establishing churches and assisting in areas of development for the country.

Nam had completed a doctorate at an American university during his years living as a refugee. A strong Christian leader among the Vietnamese populations scattered around the world, Nam had the reputation of being an excellent informant on the state of the church in Vietnam. Having taught in schools and pastored churches, he was the kind of leader that many groups sought out for assistance. Nam had served as an instructor in English and Western civilization studies at one of the larger new universities since his return five years earlier. Peter and Nam had become friends through their mutual involvement with ISG over the past decade.

Through their mutual efforts, Nam and Peter knew other Christian groups who would be strong partners in an official venture. Apart from the logistic problems of negotiating a partnership, they were well aware of the risks of overzealous groups making extravagant claims or sending ill-prepared workers. Yet at the same time, collaboration was the most promising means of fulfilling the requirements of the government while simultaneously addressing the range of needs in this developing nation.

As they sat together over dinner, Nam began to reflect on the current state of negotiations with the government. To demonstrate a genuine commitment on the part of ISG, they would be called upon to provide a significant number of professors, ESL instructors, medical personnel, and exchange possibilities for Vietnamese students to study at colleges and universities in the West. Peter remembered well the instructions from the chair of the board of ISG: "We want to establish the work, but do not commit us to financial or exchange conditions." Both Nam and Peter recognized the difficulty of proceeding with a unilateral agreement.

Before they finished eating, Nam asked his friend Peter the question they both knew was inevitable: "Can you sign the memorandum of agreement tomorrow?" Peter contemplated his responsibilities and the importance of this move for the future. Nam, as the local representative, and Peter, as the international representative of ISG, had the status to formalize the relationship. On what basis should they take this step of faith and commit to an agreement that would surely require collaboration to fulfill? Was this the right path to take, even if it required going farther than their authority allowed?

Peter leaned over the table to be heard clearly in the noisy restaurant. "Nam, you know that I value our friendship and look forward to sharing in the work of the gospel in Vietnam. Based on our understanding of an appropriate response to this opportunity, tomorrow I will ..."

missions. The wonderful synergy of the merger was a joy to all who observed it firsthand.

The second practice that paralleled the business world was the launching of many start-up missions around the globe, from those started by visionary young missionaries in Kenya and Nigeria to initiatives started by people leaving established work to launch uniquely focused ministries. As with the move toward mergers, this trend should be met with enthusiasm when there is a commitment to work together to avoid competition. Equally active should be a commitment by established organizations to act cooperatively with start-ups in areas where mutual benefit is gained through sharing resources to achieve greater economies of scale. Examples include business services, information systems, accounting and business practices, missionary children's schools, and insurance for members.

The broader areas of collaboration covered in the previous sections must be carefully assessed with a deep-seated commitment to join ranks in greater levels of strategic collaboration. We must look seriously at the level of integrative collaboration that will not only create stronger partnerships but also give rise to new forms of engagement beyond those currently known. Without a doubt, if we are to take seriously the challenges examined in this volume, we must give up our small visions to grasp the broader perspectives of global strategies. We must continue to look to the Lord for guidance in reaching above and beyond our own worlds.

10

The Changing Uses of Money

From Self-support to International Partnership

GAILYN VAN RHEENEN

Money is a two-edged sword—it can either empower or hinder missionary efforts. It can empower missions by enabling effective missionaries to open new areas of the world to the gospel, helping national churches train and oversee effective national leaders, and providing media and materials to strengthen specific local ministries. However, it can hinder missions by creating patterns of dominance of givers over receivers, jealousy between those supported by the West and those not supported, and parasites whose only desire is for the opportunities wealth brings, such as employment, social power, and authority. Inappropriately used, it can even cause missionaries to separate themselves physically from the people among whom they hope to minister because of economic disparities (Van Rheenen 2000a, 2001a).

IDENTIFYING THE TREND: AUTHENTIC PARTNERING IN INTERCONNECTED WORLD CONTEXTS

Soon after writing and posting on the Internet a reflection titled "Money and Mi$$ion$" (2000b), Gailyn Van Rheenen received letters from two Christian leaders. A long-term missionary coworker challenged him for rejecting the self-support principles learned in his mission training and consistently employed during the first twenty years of his mission work in Africa. At about the same time, a dedicated Abilene Christian University graduate student from Africa wrote Van Rheenen saying that the article was biased in favor of the support of American missionaries and largely excluded the possibility of American churches sending money directly to support national leaders. He felt that Van Rheenen was racially prejudiced.

Many missionaries were trained to believe that money would create "an ecclesiastical welfare system" in which local churches and Christian ministries would be financially dependent on Western finances. Local ministries, therefore, would not be sustainable without outside help (Elder 2003). National Christian leaders, on the other hand, felt that these perspectives limited the growth of the church and were rooted in paternalism and prejudice. Advocates of each view frequently indict the motives of the other. The issues then become so emotional and personal that effective communication is impossible.

> The Western temptation is to conceptualize and organize the missionary task on an economic level that can only be sustained by Western support and oversight. Effective missional patterns, however, reflect the economic and social realities of the local context.
>
> Gailyn Van Rheenen (2000b)

This issue has also surfaced in the pages of *Christianity Today*. Robertson McQuilkin, president emeritus of Columbia International University and past executive director of the Evangelical Missiological Society, wrote, "Stop Sending Money: Breaking the Cycle of Missions Dependency" (1999b, 57–59). In it he quotes national leaders, such as Bishop Zablon Nthamburi of the Methodist Church of Kenya, who said, "The African Church will not grow into maturity if it continues to be fed by Western partners. It will ever remain an infant who has not learned to walk on his or her own feet" (McQuilkin 1999b, 58). McQuilkin suggests that standards for the use of money in missions should be measured against four biblically based principles: Does the giving (1) win the lost? (2) encourage true discipleship? (3) honor the role of the local church? (4) nurture generous givers? He concludes that the New Testament specifically says that the poor are to be the primary recipients of money and that the support of preachers, construction of church buildings, and creation of institutions emerged only when the church was able to afford them (1999b, 58–59).

McQuilkin's self-support perspectives were challenged by Bob Finley, chairman of the Christian Aid Mission of Charlottesville, Virginia (1999b, 73–75). Finley agreed with McQuilkin that "churches, by their very nature should be self-supporting" and that "the most effective indigenous missions organizations are those independent of foreign control and not affiliated with foreign denominations or missions organizations" (Finley 1999, 73). He stated the belief, however, that "providing financial support to indigenous ministries is effective *if* a clear distinction is made between directly supporting individual workers . . . and . . . supporting such workers indirectly through indigenous missions boards that give oversight to the handling of funds" (Finley 1999, 73). He encouraged mission leaders never to support individual missionaries directly, to hold local mission boards accountable for decisions made, and to require financial accountability (Finley 1999, 74).

McQuilkin and Finley provide a glimpse of one area of missiological tension over the use of money in missions. McQuilkin represents the traditional self-support view and Finley the more recent partnership perspective.

EVALUATING THE TREND: AFFLUENCE AS A WESTERN MISSIONARY PROBLEM

Roger Greenway relates how "stuff" can get in the way of incarnational ministry. Upon arriving in Colombo, Sri Lanka, he and his family moved into a house rented for them by the national church and bought everything they needed in local shops and markets. For the first four months, they effectively built relationships with the people of their new community. Neighbors viewed the Greenways very much like themselves: They were "young parents trying to raise a child, solve everyday problems, and meet basic needs." Then the Greenways received word that their shipment was being off-loaded at the dock. Soon five bullock carts delivered eighteen barrels and two big crates to their new home. They acknowledged, "We were discovered to be what some probably suspected all along filthy rich Americans who could fill their home with every conceivable comfort and adornment. A thousand sermons could not undo the damage done that day" (Greenway 1992, 126–27).

This story illustrates one of the countless dilemmas concerning the use of money in missions. It correlates with the great disparity between the rich, mission-sending churches of the West and the poor, mission-receiving churches of the majority world. Other dilemmas include the following.

First, missionaries possessing great wealth tend to build walls and barriers around themselves for privacy and security. Paradoxically,

---

SIDEBAR 10.1
MONEY AND SHORT-TERM MISSIONS

As noted by A. Scott Moreau, Gary Corwin, and Gary McGee (2004, 279–82), short-term missions have arisen in part because of the increase of disposable income for North Americans and the relative low cost of airfare to almost anywhere in the world. Further, those who go on such mission trips can bring with them wealth that dwarfs local resources. This has positive and negative implications. The following questions address important issues of money and short-term missions.

REFLECTION AND DISCUSSION

1. How might short-term mission trips cultivate dependency on foreign visitors rather than on Christ? What can be done to avoid inappropriate dependence?

2. How would you respond to a proposal from someone on your church's mission committee that they funnel the majority of the church's mission funds into sending people from your church on short-term projects?

3. Considering that church-planting movements originate from long-term mission efforts, how would you prioritize the use of funds in your church's mission budget?

---

wealth creates isolation from the very people missionaries hope to reach. Jonathan Bonk notes:

> Prosperity, while enabling the Western Church to engage in numerous expensive, efficient, and even useful activities, overseas, has an inherent tendency to isolate missionaries from the cutting edge of missionary endeavor, rendering much of their effort either unproductive or counter-productive, or sometimes both. (1991, xix)

He later adds:

> There is something both ironic and tragic in the specter of a supremely relational gospel being proclaimed by an isolated community of segregated whites. . . . Since biblical faith is above all a relational faith, it is not only sad, but also sinful, when personal possessions and privileges prevent, distort, or destroy missionary relationships with the poor. But this is the almost inevitable price of affluence. (1991, 48)

Bonk is correct. Too frequently, comfort takes priority over incarnational ministry.

A second dilemma is that "mission done in the North American way is exceedingly costly" (Bonk 1991, 7). For example, schools, hospitals, administration, and salary levels are developed in line with Western economy and thus create built-in dependency. Such projects can require massive funding, often well beyond local church-supported means.

A third dilemma is seen when national Christian leaders expect to be supported at the level of the missionaries rather than at the economic level of their own people. There has been and still is a move by national leaders to displace missionaries holding to self-support perspectives. These national leaders, having established their own connections with churches and individuals in the West, now control the dispensing of wealth. Frequently, they use wealth and authority in a worldly way. Wealthy elitism is thus passed from missionaries to national leaders with a mutation toward enhanced control.

> *The effectiveness of the gospel is hindered by insensitive affluence that makes social relationships not only difficult but embarrassing; for as long as there is an economic gap between missionaries and their converts, fraternal fellowship is difficult to maintain. In the end, the gospel that the missionary tries to proclaim is watered down, not intentionally but watered down nonetheless.*
>
> Zablon Nthamburi (1991, xv)

These highly volatile issues concerning the use of money in missions frequently undermine core Christian values. A desire for influence, money, and power undermines servant leadership, thereby allowing the dominion of Satan to infiltrate the kingdom of God.

REFLECTING ON THE TREND: OPTIONS IN PLACE OF TRADITIONAL PATERNALISM

There is little biblical content that directly addresses the financial issues faced in churches and missions today. Christians in New Testament times were certainly not the wealthy elite. They were not participants in an economy that provided them with large disposable incomes. Nor did they have well-established administrative bureaucracies or institutions—such as schools and hospitals—that needed large capital outlays to start and stay afloat. However, the Bible does contain examples and principles that can offer guidance for today's mission agencies, missionaries, and churches.

As a general orientation, the reality that the love of money is the root of all sorts of evil (1 Tim. 6:10) should remind us that money should always be handled carefully. Scripture is also quite clear on our responsibilities toward the ever-present poor (Matt. 26:11; Gal. 6:10): "When we defend their cause (Jer. 22:16) or help them (Prov. 14:31), we walk in his ways" (Moreau 2001c, 932). Any guidelines designed to help missionaries, agencies, and churches should be framed in light of these two foundational truths.

Scripture also provides examples of financial sharing in relationship to missionary and church work. Five approaches apply on an individual level. The first was simply to trust God to supply (Phil. 4:19). The second was generous hospitality toward those who traveled, bringing the gospel (3 John 5–8). A third was the use of a professional vocation to support ministry. Paul's tentmaking is the classic example (Acts 18:3; 20:34; 1 Thess. 2:9). Fourth, at least one church (in Philippi) sent financial support to Paul as a traveling missionary (Phil. 4:10–19). Fifth, as ecclesiastical offices began to develop, Paul instructed the Galatians that those who are taught God's Word should provide for their teachers (Gal. 6:6). He reminded Timothy that because those who work deserve payment for their work, church elders are worthy of wages (1 Tim. 5:17–18).

Scripture also contains examples that apply to the corporate level. The earliest believers in Jerusalem shared all things in common so that no one was in need (Acts 2:44–45). When churches in one area suffered, money was collected from churches in other areas and sent as relief to the suffering churches (Acts 11:27–30; 1 Cor. 16:1–4; 2 Cor. 8:1–9:15). Paul's concern was such that he postponed a trip to Spain to personally deliver funds that had been collected for the poor in Jerusalem (Rom. 15:23–29). It appears that these relief efforts were limited to specific events such as famine, even though these events may have lasted for years. For example, the assistance sent to the suffering believers in Judea may have continued over a multi-year span, since the famine occurred during the reign of Claudius (Acts 11:28), which ran from AD 41 to 54. Such examples demonstrate that long-term relief work, especially directed to or through churches, is a genuine part of apostolic and missionary service (Pocock 1996a, 164). Apart from famine relief, however, there are no examples of long-term dependence or of a group using financial inducements to control others.

Thus, it is appropriate to assume that churches, like individuals, were expected to trust God to supply all their needs (Phil. 4:19). This would imply a principle of self-support at the local level for the work of the church. Partnerships that developed into dependent relationships through long-term financial assistance would have been more difficult to sustain during New Testament times than they are today. Therefore, it is not surprising that this issue is not directly addressed.

The implications of the biblical evidence may be summarized as follows. First, God is the supplier of financial resources to accomplish the tasks he ordains. Second, God uses a variety of means to provide those resources, including business skills, hospitality, and generous giving.

Third, while "God blesses those who help the poor (Deut. 24:13, 19), since being kind to them is being kind to God (Prov. 19:17; see also Matt. 5:31–46)" (Moreau 2001c, 932), the abuse of power through financial control of people violates God's desire for relationships.

It is no wonder that generations of mission scholars have denounced paternalism, or the dominance of a sending culture over the mission process. Paternalism occurs when missionaries and their sending churches and agencies assume, sometimes unconsciously, that they possess superior knowledge, experience, and skills. As a result of these assumptions, they exert control over local Christians and their leaders. This control almost always involves financial arrangements and the implicit authority of money. Perpetuating this situation is the fact that young, local Christians are often reluctant to bite the hand of those helping them—even when that hand is manipulative.

With these principles in mind, we will now explore recent shifts in contemporary thinking about money in missions through the development of the ideas of indigeneity and partnership.

The Indigenous Perspective

For many decades, the indigenous philosophy informed missional understanding concerning the use of money in missions. In the mid-nineteenth century, Henry Venn of the Church Missionary Society in England and Rufus Anderson of the American Board of Commissioners for Foreign Missions developed the three-self formula (Terry 2000). They believed that young churches should be self-propagating, self-supporting, and self-governing from their inception. Venn and Anderson believed that spoon-feeding by missionaries created "rice Christians"—people who converted only for the benefits they received. They emphasized the need for true conversion, which was reflected by the willingness of local Christians to support the work of the church. The foreign mission, they said, is like scaffolding. When construction is finished, the scaffolding is removed. In many mission settings, however, what was built is unable to stand without the support of the scaffolding.

John Nevius, a Presbyterian missionary to China, applied the principles of Venn and Anderson in his classic book *The Planting and Development of Missionary Churches* (1958). Called the Nevius Plan, it was rejected by his contemporaries in China but became the guiding framework for Christian missionary work in Korea. These principles are:

(1) Christians should continue to live in their neighborhoods and pursue their occupations, being self-supporting and witnessing to their co-workers and neighbors. (2) Missions should only develop programs and institutions that the national church desired and could support. (3) The national

285

churches should call out and support their own pastors. (4) Churches should be built in the native style with money and materials given by the church members. (5) Intensive biblical and doctrinal instruction should be provided for church leaders every year. (Terry 2000, 484)

Of Nevius's five points, four deal with the wise use of finances in developing indigenous churches.

Melvin Hodges popularized indigenous perspectives in the 1950s with the publication of *On the Mission Field: The Indigenous Church.* He defined an indigenous church as "a native church . . . which shares the life of the country in which it is planted and finds itself ready to govern itself, support itself, and reproduce itself" (1957, 7). This formative definition expanded the three-self formula by saying that mission churches should be self-propagating, self-governing, and self-supporting while also reflecting God's will in culturally appropriate ways. The church, according to Hodges, must be like a banana plant in Central America—so indigenous to its environment that it requires no special attention to thrive. Banana plants grow in this climate wherever there is adequate water. A banana plant in Canada, however, cannot survive without special care. Before winter it must be dug up and transported indoors, and it seldom, if ever, is able to bear fruit (Hodges 1957, 7–8). The corresponding "fruit" of paternalism, according to Hodges, is anemic mission churches that are not allowed to grow naturally in the soils in which they are planted.

> *Some have chosen to find a solution to this dilemma [of sustaining long-term mission programs] by way of a simple equation: Western missionary dollars + African availability and zeal = missionary enterprise. . . . This model is simplistic. It attempts to address the problem, but in the process it has the potential of killing the very same African initiative that it purports to bring about. For us, it is of the utmost importance that this enterprise be truly indigenous. . . . The African church must be prepared to shoulder the bulk of the resource needs if indeed this African initiative is to be truly indigenous. If we have come of age as we say we have, then we must own every aspect of the vision.*
>
> Solomon Aryeetey (1997, 34–35)

Missionaries from other countries, not understanding that their roles are transitory, become indispensable in running the local church.

Glenn Schwartz advocates a strict indigenous approach. He believes that the use of Western money creates a dependency among mission-established churches (2000). Even though they live hand-to-mouth with little margin for the unexpected (illness, death, hunger, house or car

---

SIDEBAR 10.2
SEARCHING FOR MEANINGFUL WAYS TO HELP THE POOR

(Adapted from Schwartz 2001)

I (Glenn Schwartz) recently learned about a growing segment of the Christian movement in an Asian country where believers are a tiny minority. This unbelievable growth is not occurring because the leaders are making it easy to get into the Kingdom of God. The philosophy of the leaders is that if one wants to identify with the Christian faith in this part of the world, he or she will need to learn God's principles and live by them. This means doing at least four things. First, everyone must pay his or her debts. Christians are honorable people who pay what they owe. Second, Christians must pay their taxes. Christians are to show nonbelievers in government that they are law-abiding citizens. Third, believers are taught from day one that they should tithe. No excuses are tolerated, such as being too poor to give back to God. Salvation from day one means that everyone gives

something back to God from what he has provided. It is a recognition that everything we have comes from God. Fourth, believers are taught that they should put some of what they earn into savings. This helps them to be prepared for the time when the harvest is lean and also gives them a way to help those less fortunate when a crisis arises. In short, the fourth principle is designed to build a little margin into one's life as a believer.

REFLECTION AND DISCUSSION

1. What biblical principles are employed by the leaders of this movement?
2. How does Schwartz think accepting Christ changes patterns of economic life?
3. Is building a "little margin" in financial terms an idea taught in the Bible? Find examples from Scripture to support your answer.

---

repair), the poor must learn to build a margin. Schwartz writes, "The surest way for anyone to build margin into his or her life is to learn about and practice the principles which God has laid down for mankind" (2001). Christians must learn that "truly good news for the poor is discovering that God's way and his principles are the surest way to find margin" (Schwartz 2001).

This perspective, however, reflects the reality of Western individualistic cultures more than group-oriented cultures of the two-thirds world. David Maranz (2001) contrasts the survival pattern of microeconomics prevalent in Africa with the accumulation modes of macroeconomics typical in the West. The most fundamental economic consideration in Africa is "the distribution of economic resources so that all persons may have their minimum needs met, or at least that they may survive. This distribution is the African social security system" (Maranz 2001,

4). People act "to ensure the survival of family and kin" in a largely subsistence economy (Maranz 2001, 5). In the West, on the other hand, the most basic economic consideration is "the accumulation of capital and wealth. This is possible because natural resources are bountiful and rationally developed. Most citizens have had opportunity to achieve a comfortable life with ample material goods" (Maranz 2001, 5). Edward Stewart and Milton Bennett describe how individualism breeds American self-reliance:

> Of all the cultural norms associated with individualism, probably none is stronger than the idea of *self-reliance*. Americans talk fondly of "pulling themselves up by their bootstraps" to become "self-made men" (and women). Many of these ideas are based on myths of the Old West, when brave settlers carved out a new life without outside aid and lonely cowboys who shot straight imposed justice on equally lonely outlaws. (1991, 136)

Westerners tend to "emphasize personal possessions and personal rights above responsibility to others," while Africans, although they complain about the burden of the system, consider "people more important than possessions" (Maranz 2001, 13). Africans believe that "resources are to be used, not hoarded," and "being involved financially and materially with friends and relatives is a very important element of social interaction" (Maranz 2001, 16, 23). Westerners, on the other hand, "distrust friendships that regularly include financial or material exchanges" (Maranz 2001, 25). Paradoxically, "Africans readily share space and things but are possessive of knowledge," while "Westerners readily share their knowledge but are possessive of things and space" (Maranz 2001, 30). In the West, "the emotional component of friendship is emphasized," while in Africa, "friendship and mutual aid go together. . . . A friendship devoid of financial or other material considerations is a friendship devoid of a fundamental ingredient: mutual dependence. . . . It is only natural to expect material benefits from friendships " (Maranz 2001, 64–65).

> *[Westerners] are ignorant of the indigenous system that helps hold the whole . . . together.*
>
> Blaine Harden (Maranz 2001, viii)

Such contrasts are not limited to Africa. Western self-reliance is not particularly congenial to Africans, Latin Americans, Chinese, and Japanese, who consider mutual complementation more important than self-reliance (Stewart and Bennett 1991, 137–38). Missionaries from the West must, therefore, learn customs of gift giving and patterns of sharing

288

with people of the recipient culture while emphasizing and exemplifying the need for all Christians to give generously to God's work.

As noted in chapter 1, missional contexts are no longer separated from the rest of the world. They are interconnected socially, religiously, communicationally, and economically. New patterns of missions must acknowledge this reality. Christian religious groups holding to traditional indigeneity are seldom able to compete, for example, with Muslims in Africa south of the Sahara. Using Saudi money, Muslims build a mosque as soon as one family in a village is converted. They use these financial connections to draw people into their philosophical enclosure in a type of economic jihad. To Muslims, conversion does not deal simply with the soul but with the whole person and his or her relationship with the economic realities of culture.

The term *indigenous* literally means that which is "born from within"— what is local, innate, or native to a culture as contrasted with what is foreign, alien, or exotic (Kasdorf 1979, 72). These connotative meanings denote a limitation of the term. Because of their fallen nature, societies seldom uphold the values of God. Cultures, although created by God (when he instituted marriage, work, and covenants), rejected God at the fall. Although the indigenous perspective acknowledges that the church must speak the language of culture and be sensitive to people's understanding of reality, it can fail to call disciples of Christ for countercultural living in pagan settings. When Christianity becomes totally indigenous in this sense, it loses its divine distinctiveness.

A better phrase for the indigenous concept is "building *responsible* churches." The term *responsible* encompasses many of the intended meanings of *indigenous* with little of its baggage. *Responsible* implies that the church has grown to maturity in Christ and now walks side by side with its founder. An equality has been established, and mutual relationships that glorify God take place. The church is able to propagate itself, support itself, govern itself, and demonstrate the attributes of God in a non-Christian context.

Advocates of responsible church philosophy maintain that movements should ideally be self-supporting from their initiation. Money creates dependence and establishes paternalistic patterns. Though not always practiced well by missionaries, this perspective became a benchmark of mature Christian movements during much of the nineteenth and twentieth century.

The Partnership Perspective

As the world experienced significant changes in the twentieth century, a second perspective concerning the use of money in missions developed.

These changes moved mission leaders from the West toward greater cooperation with national leaders in other parts of the world. They realized that partnerships were essential to the mission of the church and especially vital in international, multicultural, urban contexts (for a more extended discussion, see chap. 9).

Luis Bush and Lorry Lutz identified four new realities of the world that create the need for partnering (1990). First, the world is shrinking. As the world is rapidly reduced to a global village by advances in communications and technology, greater dialogue and interdependency can be expected among different parts of the universal body of Christ. Second, majority world churches, which now comprise the majority of Christians, have grown to maturity. Third, the number of missionaries from the majority world has surpassed that of their Western colleagues. Fourth, Western and majority world mission organizations have much to learn from each other. Since they frequently target the same areas, they must learn to work collaboratively as brothers and sisters in Christ. Mission movements should no longer consider themselves separate communities of believers but part of a universal family of God that spans the globe.

During the 1990s, a significant transition occurred in the use of money in missions. In 1996, U.S. mission agencies reported that they employed 30,000 national missionaries of other countries and just under 40,000 American missionaries. By 1999, these same agencies were still supporting just under 40,000 U.S. missionaries, but the number of national missionaries they reportedly employed had grown to 71,000 (Moreau 2000f, 33–34). A. Scott Moreau, Gary Corwin, and Gary McGee comment, "This may or may not be good news for those countries [where U.S. missionaries serve]. It may only mean that the U.S. agencies are abandoning long-standing indigenous church-planting principles in favor of skimming off the leadership cream from indigenous churches" (2004, 285). Over 130 agencies in Canada and the United States "advocate and assist indigenous missions" (Linder 2002). The trend is obvious—a movement from indigenous self-support to international partnership.

At least two pragmatic factors have led to the need to consider international partnership. First, it is difficult for church movements to begin from scratch in highly specialized, time-limited, money-driven urban cultures without initial financial help. Urban churches that are initiated under the self-support principle seldom survive because they do not have the resources to influence a multicultural urban culture. They generally become isolated congregations on the periphery of the city. By way of contrast, newer charismatic churches from Brazil have recently arrived in Montevideo, Uruguay, and Buenos Aires, Argentina, with enough initial money to pay their missionaries, rent theaters, conduct crusades, and begin TV programs. A purely indigenous approach in a city the size of Montevideo or Buenos Aires would be seen as naive and shortsighted to these effective urban missionaries.

A second pragmatic reason for partnership is the need to enable mature movements within poorer areas of the world to develop the structures of continuity to nurture the local churches within their fellowship and to become mission-sending movements. Every mission agency can recount numerous stories of church-planting movements that disintegrated after foreign missionaries left. These missionaries failed to collaborate with local leaders to develop what Monte Cox calls "structures of governance, expansion, finance and theological education" (1999, 217).

These structures should be organized on both congregational and organizational levels. On the congregational level, the community of faith, guided by the Word of God, must determine how local churches are organized and how these local congregations relate to one another. On the organizational level, mature church leaders and missionaries must collaborate to develop teaching, equipping, and encouraging structures above the local church level. Vocational and full-time national evangelists must also form teams to complete the evangelization of their area and spread the gospel into adjoining and distant areas. Training schools on the association level almost always provide forums for creative reflection and for equipping leaders and youth for local churches (Van Rheenen 2000a, 43).

> *The church in Africa needs to work shoulder to shoulder with the church in North America, in Europe, in Asia, and in other parts of the world. No single one of us—regardless of how skilled, gifted, experienced, or rich we may be—can finish the task of world evangelization alone. It will take all the true Christian church. . . . The size of the task before us demands cooperation.*
>
> Tokunboh Adeyemo (2000, 268)

Luis Bush and Lorry Lutz define *partnership* as "an association of two or more Christian autonomous bodies who have formed a trusting relationship, and fulfill agreed-upon expectations by sharing complementary strengths and resources, to reach their mutual goal" (Bush and Lutz 1990, 46). These autonomous bodies may be mature churches, mission agencies, or a mixture of the two that partner with one another to evangelize an unreached people or accomplish some other agreed-upon Christian ministry. For example, the North Boulevard Church of Christ in Murfreesboro, Tennessee, is partnering with the eighteen-hundred-member Nsawam Road Church in Accra, Ghana, to support and oversee national preachers in Mali. OC International helped to initiate a mission society in Northeastern India, where the Christian movement is relatively strong, to send missionaries to Uttar Pradesh, an unreached area of India (Keyes 1994, 229–35).

Partnership, however, may be little more than a disguised form of paternalism. Money supplied by wealthy churches or mission agencies may unintentionally force national church leaders into unnatural patterns. Those providing the money may (even unconsciously) encourage local leaders to implement programs and communicate the gospel according to their foreign paradigms.

Such examples of paternalistic abuses, however, do not negate the need for wise partnership in international urban arenas and in contexts where churches have come to maturity. Samuel Chiang describes seven principles of effective partnership. He advocates that mission partners must (1) agree on doctrine and ethical behavior, (2) share common goals, (3) develop an attitude of equality, (4) avoid dominance of one over the other, (5) communicate openly, (6) demonstrate trust and accountability, and (7) pray together (1992, 288). These qualities imply that both partners must be mature in their Christian faith.

The definition of Bush and Lutz noted above also suggests that five significant qualities are imperative to effective partnership. These are (1) trust, (2) interpersonal relationships, (3) accountability, (4) mutual complementation, and (5) a well-defined goal (see Van Rheenen 1996, 191–95). Thus, partnership must not be naively constructed but governed by Christian principles. Many unauthentic partnerships are forged with young Christians who are spoiled by their newfound riches, work without local accountability, and seek to please the visitors from afar while not being responsive to the Christians who are near.

ENGAGING THE TREND: FOUR MODELS FOR THE USE OF MONEY IN MISSIONS

Frequently, church leaders operate without guidelines for determining how money is to be used within specific cultural contexts. This section offers four models of using money in missions that will help Christian leaders analyze how money should be used.

The Personal Support Model

Many of the abuses that McQuilkin cited are due to the frequent use of the personal support model. In this model, foreign churches and individual Christians, even mission agencies, send money directly to national preachers and evangelists without collaboration and oversight by mature church leaders on the field. This direct support may start when foreigners sponsor or participate in a short-term evangelistic campaign in a mission context and then begin supporting the minister of the local church that hosted them.

Abuses arise because foreign supporters are unable to discern the local situation. They are too far away, and the cultural barriers are too great. They are seldom able to perceive the real motives of those they support. Although they may be articulate and communicative, especially when visitors are present, those receiving support may not minister from a deep conviction of God's call. They may minister simply for an income that they would otherwise not have. For example, the executive director of a major Pentecostal group in Uganda said, "I would jump to another religious group if they paid me more. Currently I am not making enough to live on the level I desire. Many pastors under me feel the same" (Van Rheenen 1976, 101). Many supported leaders are guided by good motives, but financial pressures cause even them to cater to the theologies and methodologies of those who support them.

> *There is an element of mystery when the dynamism of mission does not come from above, from the expansive power of a superior civilization, but from below, from the little ones, those that do not have abundance of material, financial, or technical resources, but are open to the prompting of the Spirit.*
>
> Samuel Escobar (2000b, 28)

Dependency frequently becomes so great that local leaders believe they cannot initiate new churches without rich benefactors providing the funds. Jealousy between those who do and do not receive support erodes Christian community. Church leaders may undergo intense faith crises when their support is terminated and have even been known to join another religious group or turn their back on faith altogether.

This model is typically used to support pastoral rather than apostolic ministries. In other words, money from rich nations is employed to support local preaching ministers rather than church-planting missionaries. These churches, however, should be self-supporting. In rural areas of the world, where culture is informally organized and there is more time for ministry, vibrant churches should have a number of vocational ministers and pastors serving the flock. In urban contexts, where there is a cash economy, growing churches should support their own preaching ministers and pastors.

The personal support model is easy for Christians in rich lands to implement because they have only to write a check or, if they desire, to visit the national Christians they support. When they visit, supporters sometimes get a glamorized picture of the work with little understanding of what is actually occurring. The personal support model therefore tends to hinder rather than empower missions.

The Indigenous Model

In the indigenous model, missionaries seek to initiate churches that are self-supporting from their inception. For example, a church or agency supports its missionaries to plant new churches, nurture young Christians in these churches to grow to maturity, equip national leaders supported by their own people and resources, and then pass the baton of leadership to these developing Christian leaders.

The Partnership Model

The partnership model differs significantly from both the personal support and the indigenous model. The partnership perspective recognizes that there are certain contexts in this internationalizing world where foreign money, if appropriately used, can empower missions without creating dependency. This money, however, rather than going directly to the recipient goes through a local accountability structure of mature Christian leaders. As Bob Finley notes, "Providing financial support to indigenous ministries is effective *if* a clear distinction is made between directly supporting individual workers . . . and . . . supporting such workers indirectly through . . . boards that give oversight to the handling of funds" (1999, 73). Good partners cease to support stagnant, nongrowing works that through the guise of partnership have become dependent on outside support for the needs of the local church.

> *One of the most difficult problems facing the Christian movement at the beginning of the twenty-first century is the dependency on outside funding that has developed in many mission-established churches.*
>
> Glenn Schwartz (2000)

The Indigenous/Partnership Model

A mixing of the last two models—the indigenous approach and the partnership approach—forms the indigenous/partnership model. Missionaries work to establish initial beachheads of Christianity by leading people to a relationship with Christ, nurturing new Christians to maturity, establishing local churches, and training national leaders. Because the work is self-supporting during these formative years, early Christians come to Christ not because of financial inducements but because of faith commitments. When these churches reach maturity, they develop partnerships with agencies that nurture existing fellowships and train evangelists, enabling the churches to become mission-sending churches. In other words, national and missionary leaders as well as sending churches and agencies work together to develop structures that will enable a national church not merely to stand on its own but to become a redemptive, mission-sending movement.

Guidelines for the Use of Money in Missions

Mission leaders, both in local churches and in mission-sending organizations, need precise frameworks to guide them in the use of money in missions. The following suggestions provide such a framework.

First, churches, missionaries, and mission agencies must avoid the use of the personal support model. It is unwise to send money arbitrarily to people in other cultures without local oversight and coordination. The indigenous, partnership, and indigenous/partnership models can each be effectively employed in various world contexts.

SIDEBAR 10.3
QUESTIONS TO GUIDE FINANCIAL DECISION MAKING

Following is a list of specific questions that will aid in evaluating the use of money in missions. As you reflect on them, consider what types of policies you would develop if you were in the position of leading an agency wrestling with financial questions.

1. Are mission resources used to maintain local churches or to plant new ones?
2. Does support create unhealthy dependence or encourage national church initiative?
3. Are national church leaders ethically, morally, and spiritually responsible to other national church leaders who understand their culture?
4. Are missionaries ethically, morally, and spiritually responsible to teammates on the field, national church leaders, and church leaders of their sending congregation or agency?
5. Do supported national leaders expect to be supported by their own people in the near future?
6. Are national leaders supported on a level consistent with the local economy or on the economic level of members of the supporting church?
7. Does the support of one national leader create jealousy because other equally qualified people are not supported? Who determines who is qualified or not?
8. Does support unknowingly create hierarchies so that churches and institutions are controlled by the West rather than by local Christian leaders?
9. Do local Christians feel comfortable visiting and fellowshiping in the homes of missionaries?

295

CASE STUDY:
DILEMMAS ABOUT MONEY

Adapted from Van Rheenen (2002, 38–39)

Jim and Julie Beldon were excited. They had just returned from a short-term mission trip working among the Wachugi, a people group in which many were coming to Christ. During their brief stay at a local preacher's home, Jim and Julie sensed a strong conviction that God wanted them to commit their lives to missions and to serve him among the Wachugi. They reported this to the mission committee of Community Church, who in turn passed the information on to the pastor and the rest of the church. They were enthralled! They were especially excited that the Beldons would be Community Church missionaries, since both had grown up in the church.

Among other responsibilities, Jim and Julie would connect Community Church with the two existing Wachugi churches by helping with short-term mission trips taken by people from Community Church. They would also follow up with converts after the Community Church short-termers returned home as well as develop Wachugi Christian leaders.

Community Church was already supporting three Wachugi leaders to serve the church. One of the supported preachers, Simon, preached regularly at the larger of the two Wachugi churches. He had been a radio preacher for several years and considered himself the natural leader of the two churches. Another, Fanuel, was the preaching minister of the other Wachugi church. Having

Second, generally speaking, the indigenous and indigenous/partnership perspectives apply to rural cultures that do not have a high degree of specialization and do not relate extensively to the globalized world. In these contexts, the informal organization of the church should reflect that of the local culture. For example, these churches tend to be family focused. Visitors will likely be invited to preach. Decisions are almost always made by consensus or by the authority of older people. It would be superficial to impose a central bureaucracy, democratic decision making, and a full-time clergy on this informal setting. It is wise to allow God's mission to flow through the local patterns of interaction and to be planted in terms of the realities of the local economies rather than on the basis of Western economy. The indigenous/partnership model enables a mature, rural movement to develop what it needs to become a redemptive, mission-sending movement.

Third, in most urban settings, developing church movements have an extremely difficult time beginning without some type of partnership with churches and agencies from other countries. Building standards concluded that the best way to establish churches throughout the city was to train preachers, Community Church had also financed the building of a preacher's training school and had hired their third Wachugi, Daniel, as a teacher there.

Within six months of their move to take up long-term residence among the Wachugi, Jim and Julie became disillusioned. They had anticipated the stress of learning language and culture, but what had taken them by surprise were the stresses associated with finances.

All three of the preachers supported by Community Church were constantly asking for advances because of emergencies. They even started comparing their salaries to those of pastors from other churches! Further, most of the Wachugi assumed that Jim and Julie had control over the Community Church's mission budget. Even though Jim and Julie worked

hard to dissuade people of this belief, it persisted. Before they knew it, deciding money matters was consuming most of their time—and most of their energy.

At the same time, Wachugi lay leaders within the two congregations were also disillusioned. Some felt that those hired by Community Church were not the most qualified to lead them. Others demanded to know how much the hired preachers were making, since they lived at a higher economic level than their friends and neighbors. Yet another group began to grumble that it was Jim and Julie who were making church decisions for them, and they began to talk of starting a new church.

Tired and discouraged, Jim wrote home to the mission committee asking for advice. It took a series of emails and long phone calls, but in the end, after much deliberation and prayer, the committee and the Beldons decided they needed to …

are stringent, rent is high, and property is virtually inaccessible to those without significant financial means.

The sad reality is that many mission-sending churches and some agencies operate with no model for the use of money in missions. Their decisions about money and missions are, therefore, likely to be inconsistent, haphazard, and paternalistic. Mission history indicates that providing finances without a model for ministry and accountability often means that the mission endeavor will face corruption, controversy, and paternalism. It is imperative, therefore, that agencies and churches carefully consider the implications of their relative wealth if they truly want to support local churches that are healthy and vibrant.

11

The Impact
of New Technologies

Life in the Virtual World and Beyond

DOUGLAS MCCONNELL & J. TED ESLER

Assuming that the electricity is on and the phone lines are work-ing, a typical morning for the global missionary in this first decade of the twenty-first century begins with devotions, a cup of coffee, and an hour or more of email—assuming the cell phone does not interrupt this daily ritual. If frequent travel is a part of the mis-sionary's role, there is a good chance that the Bible and a commentary or study helps program is among the software on his or her laptop or handheld computer.

Technological tools are as normal for a missionary as they are for a business executive. As rapidly as new technology appears, it is incor-porated into the vocabulary and practice of missionaries around the world. Yet like everyone for whom connectivity is an important issue, a missionary also feels the pressure build with each new device that comes on the market. While going back to the days of snail mail offers no appeal for most of us, a certain lament is not uncommon even among those who communicate primarily through the virtual world provided by today's technology.

> **SIDEBAR 11.1**
> **IMPORTANT TERMS USED IN THIS CHAPTER**
>
> *connectivity:* The ability to communicate electronically. The more connected a person or organization is, the more it accesses communications technology (such as the Internet and cell phones) and the more accessible it is to others who are connected.
>
> *virtual:* An adjective used to describe electronic connections. The virtual world is distinguished from the real world in that it exists only in coded electronic form in a computer or network of computers. The Internet, for example, is a vast virtual world, though its real world components include computers, connective devices, and the people using them.

It is difficult to overestimate the impact of new technologies. For people living in the more developed world, technological tools are a part of life. From microwave ovens and coffeepots to electric shavers and hair dryers, it is difficult to leave the house without depending on some form of technology. But few of us realize the depth of the impact. Like it or not, many new technologies have the potential to change everything from the way we work to our worldview.

To see how quickly a new technology can affect a society, consider the introduction of television in Port Moresby, Papua New Guinea. The new National Broadcasting Network was launched one evening in mid-February 1987. After a rather painful hour of local news read by new broadcasters, the first program aired was *The A-Team*. The four soldiers of fortune blazed on to the screen with the well-known theme song and, best of all, a new hero for the Melanesian mind-set. Mr. T, a muscular African American man covered in gold chains, was the go-to guy when it came time to use brute force. As the most flamboyant of the foursome, he was the obvious candidate for a new-style guru.

Sure enough, the morning after this program aired, Doug McConnell was sitting in the front room of his apartment in Port Moresby when a group of school kids marched down the street locked arm in arm. Around their necks were strings of pop-tops reminiscent of Mr. T's chains. As they marched, they hummed the theme song from *The A-Team*. It was irreversible. A new hero had come to town.

The impact of new technologies spans the entire range of missionary activities from decision making to the methods employed in presenting the gospel. Increased connectivity has created virtual communities among missionaries and mission agencies around the globe. It is important, therefore, to explore the escalated pace of technology, which is changing the methods and culture of missions.

IDENTIFYING THE TREND: RAPID TECHNOLOGICAL CHANGES

Technological change has become the unchangeable axiom of our era. It is difficult to imagine a world in which continual technological advance did not exist. The pace of this change continues to accelerate and will dominate our lives for the foreseeable future. This trend changes not only how we go about missions but also what one's mission is. Technology is not a neutral tool that improves methodology. By applying technology to a problem, an entire issue can be reshaped (Postman 1992). In an effort to identify the trend, the following discussion focuses on (1) enhanced connectivity, (2) escalation of the pace of life, (3) high touch–high tech, (4) e-learning, (5) digital divide, (6) digital deflation, and (7) security issues.

Enhanced Connectivity

Cheap telephone rates, the Internet, cell phones, email, instant messaging, satellite television, low-cost radio transceivers, and DVDs are all a part of the global communication transformation of the world that has taken place during the past half century. While this trend affects almost everyone on the planet, the mission community already dispersed around the globe has been affected even more than the general population. Being connected is now an expected aspect of missionary practice for both missionaries and their supporters.

For example, in March of 1997, a missionary in Sarajevo sat down in front of his laptop. Perched precariously on the screen was a small web camera. After dialing into his local Internet service provider, he used an instant message service to connect with a coworker in Australia. On the other end of the connection was a web camera pointed out in the audience of a large Christian conference. Through this two-way video and audio connection, the missionary addressed the conference from halfway around the world using no more than a twenty-dollar computer camera. This event was among the earliest low-cost speaking engagements that connected two groups across the globe using only personal computers. It was also a harbinger of things to come.

Another example is the annual worship service that connects one of Egypt's largest Protestant churches located in Cairo with Northland Community Church in Orlando, Florida. The two congregations are connected via a live video feed and enjoy sharing reports and updates about their respective ministries. This new form of partnership has a significant effect on the worldviews of those attending. Mission fields can no longer be identified solely by geography.

Greater connectivity via the Internet also means that a mind-boggling amount of information is available at the fingertips of anyone who can access the Web. This has helped the mission community raise its standard of practice and strategic engagement. Missionary practices have been improved through greater levels of understanding made possible because of access to resources and greater interaction. Mission organizations have invested heavily in the development of websites with information ranging from opportunities for service to resources for the study of missions. Other websites that include forums, knowledge bases, organizational communication, and online chatting are also available. The many resources for accessing strategic missiological information on the Internet include the following:

- "Missions on the Web" (http://www.mislinks.org) is a regular feature of *Evangelical Missions Quarterly.*
- The Center for the Study of Global Christianity (Gordon-Conwell Theological Seminary) provides access to the world Christian database and "Status of Global Mission" online (http://www.world christiandatabase.org/wcd).
- The Gospel Communications website (http://www.gospelcom.net) provides access to English translations of the Bible and acts as a host to many valuable mission websites.
- The Network for Strategic Missions Knowledge Base offers an online collection of over thirteen thousand articles on missions (http://www.strategicnetwork.org/index.php?loc=kb&).

Another benefit of connectivity is the ease of transferring funds through the use of automated teller machines (ATMs) in centers around the world. International travelers have access to ATMs in airports and banks in order to withdraw funds in the local currency. Such immediate access has greatly improved the delivery of money to and the acquisition of local currency by the mission community. It allows mission agencies to deposit funds directly into the personal accounts of missionaries who can in turn access them when it is convenient. Missionaries who travel among various countries can carry ATM cards instead of large amounts of money or traveler's checks. This is a convenience and also minimizes currency exchange fees.

Individual missionaries also experience the benefits of enhanced connectivity. A first-term missionary no longer leaves behind her home culture. Instead, she heads to an Internet cafe (in Beijing, Budapest, or Brasilia) and finds out via email what Mom and Dad had for dinner that night. She sees that her friend back home is using an instant messaging website, and so they catch up on the latest news. Instant communication seems to be a great boon for the intercultural worker. It allows family members separated in distant lands to communicate regularly, reducing the pain of separation.

However, there are some costs associated with connectivity. Missionaries no longer step off a boat (or out of an airplane) and enter their new culture permanently. They now have a foot in each culture. They can easily switch back and forth, which requires greater discipline and fortitude to achieve the benefits of culture and language immersion. While missionaries of the 1800s packed their belongings in coffins with no thought of return, many of today's Western missionaries plan on spending Christmas at home with their families. During times of stress or crisis, it is easy to write emails while emotionally upset, communicating greater urgency and trauma than is often the case. Enhanced connectivity raises critical questions. Will these jet-setters truly imbibe the local culture to the point at which they can effectively communicate the gospel? What message does their link to the home culture send to the people they are trying to reach? Technological advances in communication and travel provide both challenges and opportunities.

Another problem associated with enhanced connectivity is the sharing of personal information. Not too long ago one could easily cross borders from country to country with some degree of privacy. That is no longer possible. Not only are information-sharing agreements common among nations, but a simple Web search of a person's name and affiliation can turn up significant personal information. An academic paper, posted by a university on a website, could become incriminating evidence against a person wishing to enter a country to serve. Automated teller machines allow government officials to monitor their citizenry. Similar methods are used to track missionary activity. It is important for intercultural workers to understand these dynamics so they can avoid unknowingly breaking the law or offending the local culture.

Escalation of the Pace of Life

James Gleick wrote the seminal book on the escalation of life's pace in technological societies (2000). Starting with the amount of time it takes for an elevator to open its doors, he demonstrates how impatient we have become. Technology is so focused on saving time that we have redefined quality to include the concept of speed. From a biblical perspective, this is a questionable value. Yet none of us wants to wait.

It is no wonder that intercultural missionaries struggle when they leave technologically advanced countries and enter cultures that are less time conscious. Clearly, there are advantages to the efficient use of time.

However, we betray our deeper values by our language. We have fast food, quickmarts, 24/7 access to our bank accounts, and rapid transit to almost any destination. Before indulging ourselves in immediate gratification, we need to pause and consider the implications. Certainly, the growth of character manifested by the fruit of the Spirit takes time to develop (Gal. 5:22–24). As we minister to others, we must recognize that time is one of our most precious resources and should be spent on those things that are most precious (Ps. 90).

Unfortunately, increased connectivity comes with a cost. Everyone knows the feeling of frustration when an important conversation is cut off because of a lack of reception on a cell phone. The pressures placed on us by expectations of an immediate reply to email drive many of us to the brink of communication despair. Ironically, even though we lament the pressures of immediate communication, we often find ways to check our email and voicemail even when we are on vacation. Speed and frequency of communication are addictive.

It is quite possible that technological advances affecting the pace of life are happening at the expense of relationships. For example, mass media may be an effective means to proclaim the gospel quickly to a large audience. Developing one-on-one relationships with leaders, however, while less efficient, provides more effective bridges for proclaiming the gospel in the long run.

High Touch–High Tech

"High touch–high tech" is a phrase that was coined to explain the tendency toward greater uses of technology while simultaneously requiring greater intimacy with other humans (Naisbitt 1984). Research demonstrated that technological solutions do not exist in isolation. They lead to an increased need for face-to-face relationships. For example, think back to the last time you called your church and instead of hearing a live person on the phone, you got an answering system. When we call a church, we expect a real person. When we do not hear a live person on the other end of the phone line, we may conclude that efficiency has taken precedence over human interaction. Thus, technology is interpreted as an affront to our humanity. The result is not an abandonment of the use of technology but the addition of more intimate human interaction. One way to demonstrate this is to observe the parallel growth in the number of computer engineers and licensed counselors.

Another way of looking at the phenomenon of high touch–high tech is to observe how computer systems make a higher level of human connection possible, even if it is virtual. For example, in the past it was nearly impossible for a missionary to have regular interaction with friends and family back home. Not so any more. Regular communication using email and cell phones keeps people in touch with the world they know. Therefore, the key is to see electronic systems as serving the development of relationships rather than controlling them.

E-learning

Technology has opened the door to new forms for delivering education, particularly through online courses. A major contributor to the success is Moodle, an educational website software package that is free for use by any educational institution (http://www.moodle.org). Originally a graduate project by Martin Dougimas, Moodle has been downloaded thousands of times and is currently running many educational courses at a wide array of schools and organizations. One school is using Moodle to deliver approximately thirty-seven hundred courses to over eighteen thousand students. Moodle, or a similar piece of software, allows just about anyone to manage an online course. This is an example of technology at its best.

E-learning in the missionary context has many applications. Over the past decade, seminaries and Bible colleges have increased the number of courses and even degree programs offered on the Web, allowing missionaries to take courses without leaving their field of service. The courses range from those that meet requirements for missionary service to more advanced subject specific courses designed to help missionaries deal with issues faced in various cultural or geographical contexts. New e-learning approaches are also beginning to supplement the theological and missiological education of local church and agency leaders.

Not only can e-learning overcome national boundaries and restrictive governments, but it is also a low-cost delivery method. Many e-learning environments are highly interactive. They incorporate video, chat rooms, bulletin boards, cohort groups (students studying together), and other more standard classroom techniques. Advantages include the ability to change or modify course material as the course is being taught, low-cost delivery, geographic dispersion, and the ability to study at one's own pace.

Of course, there are disadvantages as well. Certainly, face-to-face learning environments are more suited to imparting some forms of education, particularly in regard to character development. Another challenge is accessibility, which depends on location and infrastructure.

Digital Divide

The term *digital divide* refers to the widening gap between the information have-nots and the information savvy. Contrary to popular opinion in the West, the digital divide is a growing problem worldwide (Ujamaa 2005). Technological advances are growing by quantum leaps among wealthy nations, while poor nations, many of which are unable to feed their own populations, cannot afford to modernize and make use of increasingly complex, new technologies.

There are a number of reasons for the growing gap. The cost to set up a digital infrastructure is significant. While one can easily create a single-access point using a satellite dish or other small-scale technology, the large bandwidth trunk lines that a nation must possess to deliver broadband Internet access require significant government commitment. The growth of bandwidth availability in wealthy countries is also changing the use of the Internet. Graphics-intensive sites, video, and other data-rich media are creating a two-tiered Internet. Those with minimal bandwidth are not able to access these types of information.

How might this affect mission outreach? Let's assume a church in New York set up a web-based video system that allowed national ministries to address the congregation. This worked fine with the two or three ministries it supported. When the church considered new ministries, it discovered that one of the ministries was unable to tie into the system because of limitations in the availability of services in its country. The church decided that two-way dialogue was an important part of mobilizing the congregation's resources for missions and therefore decided to bypass the lower-tech ministry, effectively allowing digital resources to shape its decision.

Digital Deflation

A related concept is digital deflation (Tanaka 2003). This refers to the fact that products with greater value cost less because of increases in technology. Just a few years ago, two thousand dollars would purchase a reasonably fast personal computer. Today, you can still spend the same amount on a personal computer, but the machine you buy is far more advanced than the machine of a few years ago. The relative cost of a personal computer has deflated even though the price has remained the same.

Even though the term uses the word *digital*, this concept is not limited to digital technologies. It applies to all technologies. It also does not mean that new technologies are always cheaper. Sometimes a new technology is much more expensive but far more capable. The pharmaceutical industry is an example. The drugs that are being developed today are far more expensive than their counterparts just a few years ago. Their capabilities also far outpace those of just a few years ago. If you were suffering from a terminal illness, you would gladly pay the difference, assuming you had the money. In effect, the new drug is of greater value to you from an economic standpoint because of its greater attributes.

Digital deflation can feed the cycle associated with the digital divide. This is because it is increasingly easier for developed nations to take advantage of newer technologies because of their established infrastructures. The opposite is true of developing nations. The dramatic increase in the entry-level price for the infrastructure to support the new technologies makes them prohibitive.

Security Issues

Technological advances are creating a loss of anonymity and personal freedom. This may range from the obvious (border control on networked computers) to the subtle (computers that log speed on many new cars). When missionaries and mission leaders talk about security, they are typically referring to the confidentiality of their communication and the protection of those who work with them. Virtually all societies place limits on what can be communicated by its citizens. In those places where basic freedoms do not exist, where there is persecution of the local Christian population, or where missionaries are not welcome, privacy becomes very important.

Two technologies that are important when dealing with security are compression techniques and encryption algorithms. Compression techniques have changed the landscape of computing. While there is much talk about the advances in hardware that provide for greater and greater storage space, just as important is the software that makes large volumes of data fit into smaller and smaller spaces. Compression allows files to be sent through secure sites, which often have limited network capacity.

Just as important, encryption protects the security of the data sent. For missionaries living in areas of the world hostile to the gospel, encryption technologies have paved the way for the use of email. Yet it remains unclear just how secure this method of communication is. The most secure form provides point-to-point encryption, which means that data is encrypted when it is sent and is not decrypted until the intended recipient receives it. Most users, however, are not using this more sophisticated form of encryption. Secure Sockets Layer technology, commonly known as SSL, encrypts the connection only between the user's computer and the server, which is receiving the email. For many missionaries, this is acceptable because their goal is to keep their communications secure until they reach the server, which is usually located outside the country in which they are working. The problem with this arrangement is that from the server the email can proceed unencrypted to anywhere in the world.

In the wake of the September 11, 2001, terrorist attacks and the subsequent war on terrorism, there has been a heightened sense of concern regarding privacy and international travel. The world's governments are now tracking ATM transactions and are using facial recognition systems, fingerprinting, and a host of other means to offer security. While this has created a sense of security for U.S. citizens, it has had a chilling effect on those outside the United States. There is no doubt that the technology being developed to monitor people in the United States will find its way into countries that are less open to the spread of the gospel.

EVALUATING THE TREND: ASSESSING THE IMPACT OF NEW TECHNOLOGIES

Imagine a church in which nobody has ever actually met face-to-face. Is it possible? Many people think so. It is being advocated under the title "the Internet church" (Wilson 2000). These virtual fellowships are common among younger people. This approach to technology not only changes how we go about missions but also forces us to consider new categories of missions. It challenges an understanding of the church by raising the inevitable question, Isn't face-to-face fellowship a necessary element if the local church is to flourish? Responses to questions regarding the nature and impact of technological changes on the way we understand church are part of the growing literature on the church in a postmodern world (Careaga and Sweet 2001; Gibbs 2000; Jewell 2002; Slaughter 1998; Sweet 1999a, 1999b, 2002; Wilson 1999; Wilson 2000).

Changing methods of missions are not a new discovery for missiologists (Bosch 1991). What is new is the scale of the methods employed facilitated by the medium of technology. This section evaluates three ways in which technology has changed mission practice: (1) new horizons in church planting, (2) large-scale media efforts, and (3) virtual teams.

New Horizons in Church Planting

The virtual church has opened up a whole new avenue for ministry. In cultures where conversion means persecution, cyber-believers are able to fellowship in ways they have never known. Ali, a young engineer from the Middle East, recently affirmed his freedom to worship using a private message board: "I am able to tell others about my faith for the first time. I have learned, while using the Internet, that my country has many Christians. I have now found a few of them and we discuss our faith using email. It is dangerous, but I have a background in computers

SIDEBAR 11.2
DIGGING DEEPER ON THE WEB FOR SHORT-TERM MISSIONS

Read the questions below and then browse to http://www.mislinks.org/practical/shterm.htm (see also Moreau and O'Rear 2002) and several of the linked sites on short-term missions. Use a search engine such as Google (http://www.google.com) to find other sites and explore what is being said about short-term missions. Use what you find to discuss the issues raised below.

REFLECTION AND DISCUSSION

1. What agencies/groups seem to be the best organized for short-term missions? What made you choose the ones you chose?
2. What site(s) did you find the most helpful in understanding what short-term missions is all about? Why were they helpful?
3. Identify a short-term project that interests you in a country you would like to visit.

that allows me to protect my identity." Just a few years ago, a believer like Ali would have lived his entire Christian life in secret. Now he is able to fellowship with others from his own culture and grow deeper in his faith. Should we argue that this is not a valid form of the church?

As missionaries seek to plant churches, they must first ask, What are we seeking to plant? Technology has opened up new avenues that change the possible definitions of a church. This forces missionaries to look at the biblical model of the church in an entirely new way, to review definitions and approaches to find the best fit in the context of cyberspace. For example, how does the Internet church define its leadership? Does the webmaster, by virtue of his or her role, assume the leadership? What about the scriptural teaching on the role of elders, deacons, or other leaders?

New approaches to church planting, opened through the door of the Internet, are being stimulated by the dynamic use of new forms of media. Television, movies, and a host of web-based approaches are examples of the potential impact of new technologies on global movements of people toward faith in Christ.

Large-Scale Media Efforts

Media ministry has been a part of the missionary effort since Gutenberg published the first Bible using moveable type. Beginning in the 1930s, radio ministry was at the forefront of high-tech, mass-media outreach. Today, satellites and digital communications have taken over. The potential for these ministries is enormous.

SIDEBAR 11.3
CYBER-SALVATION?

It was a month before Christmas, and for George Ponsford, the prospects were not pleasing. Doctors had determined he had lymphoma and had only a few months to live. Matters of spirituality had not greatly concerned George during his adult life. Now, the closeness of eternity and concern for his standing with God brought fear and sadness.

Michael Pocock had come to know George and his family through one of his sons. Unknown to Pocock, George, using his extensive computer know-how, had begun to search the Internet for answers to his spiritual questions. One day, Pocock's son told him that George wanted to speak with him. He had been admitted to the hospital. Though in pain and discomfort, he was able to talk. He had been searching the Internet for answers, he said. When Pocock asked what he was looking for, he said, "Heaven, forgiveness, assurance."

"Did you find anything?" Pocock asked.

"Yes," he said and quoted several passages of Scripture and the Lord's Prayer. Pocock asked George if he believed the promises these passages contained. "Yes," he replied. As nurses worked on him, Pocock led him in a simple prayer of thanksgiving for God's salvation.

Two days later—with George feeling much better—they were able to talk alone and at length. It was a wonderful time of fellowship as they spoke about the Lord. Since George's health was still precarious, Pocock asked him about their conversation two days earlier. "George, if you were to stand in the presence of God today and he asked you why he should let you into heaven, what would you say?"

"No way," he replied. "I am a sinner."

"So that's it? You don't get to enter heaven?"

"Oh yes," he said, "because Jesus Christ died for my sin."

"George," Pocock said, "I believe on the basis of God's Word and your belief that you have been saved. Your answer was exactly what I hoped to hear."

Pocock then ventured to ask how he had used the Internet to find the answers he had been seeking. Using a search engine, he had done a key word search using "religion" and then "Bible." He had located the Dallas Theological Seminary website (http://www.dts.edu) and the Net Bible (http://www.bible.org) website. He had downloaded the applicable portions on heaven, sin, forgiveness, and assurance and had memorized several passages.

Cyber-salvation? Sounds a bit sensational, but there is no getting around it. God used his Word, the DTS website, the Net Bible, and the Internet to minister salvation to George Ponsford.

REFLECTION AND DISCUSSION

1. What are the strengths of using the Internet for evangelism, discipleship, and nurture?
2. Are there dangers associated with witnessing through an environment as open as the Internet?
3. Discuss some approaches to ensure that follow-up is given to such people.

One of the most visionary strategies is the SAT-7 project. Utilizing the Hotbird satellite, SAT-7 beams Christian programming into thousands of homes across the Arabic- and Farsi-speaking regions of the world. Launched in 1996, it has enjoyed continued growth and popularity. The major portion of programming on SAT-7 is aimed at Middle Eastern Christians, but the Muslim majorities watch many shows in the comfort of their own homes.

A second initiative, the *Jesus* film, has become a major evangelistic tool. From the outset, Bill Bright and Campus Crusade for Christ intended that the film be as close to the biblical text as possible. The film cost just over $6 million to produce, but since its release in 1979, it has become the single most viewed film in history. Since its debut, there have been more than 5.6 billion viewings. At the time of this writing, the Jesus Film Project had translated all or part of the film into 847 languages, with more planned. There is also an audio version of the film, a children's version, and over 5,500 people working on distribution teams.

A newer project similar in scope and potential is *The Hope*, produced by Mars Hill Productions, a nonprofit ministry that has produced videos and films used in over one hundred countries for over twenty-five years. Completed in 2002, it was designed from the outset to be both digital and a regular film; it can be viewed online along with additional supporting material (Mars Hill Publications 2002). *The Hope* introduces the story of salvation using the chronological approach so effectively used by agencies such as New Tribes Mission. The film begins with creation and ends with the church as we know it today. *The Hope* acts as a complement to the *Jesus* film and other tools and is easily accessed through the website.

The numbers that these large-scale media efforts have reached are impressive and reveal the potential that mass media has in reaching people with the gospel. While these statistics do not reveal much about the extent of spiritual transformation, they certainly attest to the power of mass media in proclaiming the gospel.

An important aspect of any large-scale outreach is designing and implementing an appropriate avenue for follow-up. SAT-7, for example, measures its success partly by the number of people who enroll in ongoing correspondence and discipleship courses. Any mass-media campaign without effective follow-up will not produce the intended long-term results and may use up valuable kingdom resources.

Virtual Mission Teams

Enhanced technology creates new possibilities for mission structures. Certainly, close proximity is a valuable asset to those who must work together. Inevitably, however, missionaries of the same agency are scattered in their service. This scattering creates problems of communication and participation. By using technology, mission teams can now be composed of individuals who live in different parts of the world. They are no longer bound by geography. These virtual teams may meet face-to-face only once or twice a year. In the meantime, conference calls, email, and instant messaging make a high level of communication possible.

Virtual teams provide obvious gains for the missionary endeavor. Not only can agency and church leaders more effectively engage with field personnel, but they can also directly participate in the accomplishment of team goals. More frequent communication, less frequent travel, and higher levels of accountability can be maintained. Because they are not bound by physical locations, organizations can also take on new forms that were previously impossible or at least impractical. With greater connectivity, distinctions between organizations may blur, particularly as leaders collaborate and seek ways to best use their staff capabilities.

Connectedness via technology has opened the way to virtual mission teams working on everything from administration to church planting. In countries where few if any of the workers are full-time, supporting team members located in other parts of the world can provide strategic input. The challenge for team leaders is to maintain a good working knowledge of the specific locations in which each team member lives and a good working relationship with each member. In most cases, the minimum amount of contact needed to maintain relationships and a commitment to the team purpose involves weekly emails, phone calls on a monthly basis, and at least three face-to-face meetings per year (McConnell 2002a).

Although virtual teams are increasingly a norm for agencies and other nonprofit organizations, the most common are teams that have a clear task orientation, such as administration, education, or communication. These teams are required to stay on task despite the challenges of separation and technological breakdowns. Four of the most common types of challenges involve the quality-quantity continuum of communication, team members' attitudes toward those with whom they communicate, high touch–high tech issues, and decision making (Esler and McConnell 2003).

In a world in which increasing numbers of people have access to email communication, the inevitable onslaught of emails to any one team member is a major problem. On a given day, it is not uncommon for one person to handle hundreds of pieces of communication. At the opposite end of the continuum is the quality of communication. Too often an email or a posting on a bulletin board is at best truncated and at worst undecipherable. A tendency to summarize and cut short responses means that members of a team must seek further clarification, leading to more messages. In addition, because of the natural tendency to validate communication if it is written, opinion becomes fact even when it is not.

A second problem for virtual teams is monitoring attitudes of team members. As weariness sets in, which is common when working away from teammates, people have a tendency to allow emotions to emerge that may or may not be warranted. This will inevitably surface in email communication. Messages can be read and reread to find all possible nuances, leading to growing suspicions fostered by isolation. Negative tendencies often emerge in the absence of regular meetings or when technical difficulties prevent regular correspondence from reaching all members (McConnell 2002b). A certain member may feel that he or she is being left out of the loop. Even worse, this may be purposefully done to marginalize certain team members. It is important that teams seek to honor God in all they do and make every effort to work in unity and to build trust.

A third type of challenge emerges from the high touch–high tech tendency. The list below summarizes the five most common issues faced by virtual teams:

1. Demands of working from home with inadequate office facilities and minimal interpersonal contact for long periods lead to questions of self-worth, influence, and a perception of loss of authority.
2. Logistical frustrations arise from differences in time and place. The reality is that someone somewhere is always working and, worse, expects you to be also.
3. High dependency on expensive technology systems that break down regularly leads to a desire to just chat with someone with a cup of tea and not a keyboard.
4. Virtual teams exacerbate the natural human tendency toward the formation of cliques (pressure groups), usually comprised of those who share a location and have the opportunity to hold face-to-face meetings.
5. Difficulties in collaboration cannot be assessed apart from reading emails. Such a process, however, is divorced from the senses of sight and sound, which are often key to interpreting interpersonal communication (Esler and McConnell 2003, 48).

The fourth type of challenge involves making decisions. Decision making is a natural part of leadership, and the traditional approaches require changes as new forms of technology emerge. For example, Pioneers adopted a consensus-based approach to decision making that was ideally

> *Virtual teaming should never be seen as a replacement for the richness of communication that comes only through face-to-face contact. This is particularly important when one considers the cultural differences, which already challenge mission leadership communication. Anecdotal evidence suggests that virtual team members will need to supplement their personal relationship needs with relationships outside their work life. While that is a completely acceptable approach to take in a secular work environment, it falls short of the ideal many missionaries seek among their co-workers. Unfortunately, those from more relationally oriented cultures will find this type of work style isolating.*
>
> Douglas McConnell (2002b, 6)

suited to a small organization with close and frequent contact of leaders and participants (McConnell 2002a). As the mission grew, however, there were inevitable changes facilitated by technology. Factors such as variations in both access to electronic communication and computer savvy affected the ability of the teams in the organization (over one hundred of them working in forty-five countries) to form a consensus.

Evaluating the impact of new technologies on missions is an ongoing task for leaders in every part of the missionary world. It is inevitable that issues that divide them along technological lines will change as rapidly as the technology. Leaders will be required to upgrade their diligence (Rom. 12:8) along with their computers if the mission force is to remain committed to the mission vision.

REFLECTING ON THE TREND: SERVANTHOOD AND STEWARDSHIP

Those involved in missions must reflect on the growing issues raised by new technologies—bioethics, justice for the poor, and a host of other vital concerns. To do so adequately requires that they have a deep commitment to be biblically and theologically informed. This section limits its focus to the biblical concepts of servanthood and stewardship as they relate to the trend of new technologies.

Servanthood

In clarifying his role for the disciples, Jesus often referred to servanthood. One of the clearest statements is found in the Gospel of Mark: "For even the Son of Man did not come to be served, but to serve, and to give his life as a ransom for many" (10:45). This statement was made in the context of clarifying not only his role but also the role of the disciples. In the most graphic demonstration of the meaning of servanthood,

---

SIDEBAR 11.4

A GROWING NEED FOR SOPHISTICATION IN VIRTUAL LEADERSHIP

During the first biannual evaluation of Pioneers' virtual leadership team approach, leaders determined that increased use of technology without a concurrent training program for leaders led to significant problems. The following excerpt addresses some of the issues faced by the team:

> As a by-product of the organizational systems developed to serve our [Pioneers] growing movement, we need to commit to greater levels of sophistication in our leaders. These systemic responses include an increasing dependence upon information technology, annual or biannual area conferences, procedures for member care, training opportunities, and performance standards for leadership roles. The logic behind the various systems is defensible from an administrative perspective; that is not the issue. The problems lie in the affects [*sic*] of these systems upon our members, from the team members who are working in more remote or difficult areas to the leaders for whom the organizational culture underlying the systems is foreign. Examples abound from the difficulty and costs to maintain efficient email contact with leaders, to the pressures on leaders to meet the expectations of mobilization bases in the care of their members. We are moving toward a degree of sophistication in administrative leadership that will require increasing amounts of financial support, which in turn will create new demands on our international funds. Beyond that, it requires that leaders of the international movement are truly international in their culture and skills plus an increased effort to socialize our members into our movement. (McConnell 2002b, 6).

REFLECTION AND DISCUSSION

1. Discuss the qualifications a person should have to join an international leadership team working in the virtual environment of technology.
2. Identify possible responses to the problems arising from the increased use of technology.
3. What are the primary strengths of a virtual team approach?

Jesus took the position of the lowest servant in the household. Jesus "got up from the meal, took off his outer clothing, and wrapped a towel around his waist . . . and began to wash the disciples' feet, drying them with the towel that was wrapped around him" (John 13:4–5). This action provoked concern and confusion (John 13:6, 8). It has always been difficult to understand that leading means serving. For Jesus, there was no mistaking the call. To lead is to serve.

Another statement is also helpful. "For you were called to freedom, brothers and sisters; only do not use your freedom as an opportunity for self-indulgence, but through love become slaves to one another"

(Gal. 5:13 NRSV). Building on the command to love one another, the invitation to "become slaves to one another" is also interpreted as "to serve one another in love" (NLT). Servanthood means being a servant of Christ and serving others in the community. Apart from the community, we cannot exercise servanthood. To serve is to engage in the world of those served. Those involved in missions must understand the world of others and adopt communication and patterns of behavior that are readily understood. How does this relate to the use of technology?

Because of the trend of new technologies, missionaries have access to an expanding number of technological tools, from palm pilots to cell phones, laptops, and digital cameras. As missionaries adopt new technologies, a critical question must be, Does this new solution help us serve others, and will they interpret it as service? Two critical issues to consider are the effect technology has on the task of building relationships and the divisions created by a disparity concerning possessions.

Central to missionary work is building relationships with local people. This involves a careful study of language and culture and time spent with people. The Internet has made it possible for missionaries to maintain relationships with people back home. While this is helpful in many ways, it also takes time away from the missionary task. Old friendships can fill the need for relationship, thereby reducing the need to form new friendships with local people. By spending time relating to local people, missionaries gain greater insights. But this takes time and a willingness to identify with the local community. Missionaries must remember the nature of Jesus' identification with us: "But he made himself nothing, taking the very nature of a servant, being made in human likeness" (Phil. 2:7).

Technology, though helpful to missionaries, can also create disparities between them and those they hope to serve. Such disparities may in fact become barriers that undermine the credibility of the gospel message. When disparities are eliminated, a closer bond is formed that assists missionaries as they share the gospel. As missionaries consider serving Christ within a community, they must assess the influence of both their attitudes and their possessions. Those things that facilitate greater service are assets to be developed. Those things that pull them away from serving Christ and the local community are liabilities to be eliminated.

Stewardship

Stewardship is to a large extent the call to be good stewards of the world and all that is in it. Yet it is often misunderstood or interpreted as being only a matter of looking after money. This is far short of the biblical view. Aspects of stewardship in the Bible include such things as responsibility for creation (Gen. 1:28), obedient use of God's gifts (1 Pet. 4:10), and a host of issues surrounding leaders and the church (1 Cor. 4:1–2; Eph. 3:2; Col. 1:25; Titus 1:7).

In most cases, people who read this book have a reasonable idea of the call to be stewards of the gospel. As those sent into the world to be servants and witnesses of the gospel of Jesus Christ, they are prepared to be obedient. As we focus on the nature of technology and its impact on the world, however, we are drawn more critically into other implications of stewardship.

By its very nature, technology is a product of human invention, thereby a direct extension of the minds used to create it. This means that both the lofty ideals of human minds created in the image of God and the despicable ideas that flow out of depraved human minds are intermingled. We do not have to go as far as nuclear technology to see this confusing juxtaposition. For example, consider the computers that most of us look at on a daily basis. While imbued

> *The modern emphasis on the stewardship of possessions, while true, may tend to obscure the fact that the Christian's primary stewardship is that of the gospel and includes the use of his [or her] whole life as well as his [or her] money.*
>
> Fred Lewis Fisher (1997, 1150)

with the capacity to act as a portal to new domains of knowledge on the Internet, they can also serve as windows into the evils of the sex industry or vehicles to websites proclaiming the virtues of racist ideals. Then, like most technology, computers inevitably become obsolete and must be either recycled or discarded. The hardware is full of toxic chemicals that find their way into the bodies of the poor who recycle them in Guiyu, China, or into the food and water supplies of populations close to dump sites. Thus, a staggering array of ethical issues surrounds new technology.

We must be good stewards of technology. We must resist the tendency to see technology as a neutral force for ever-increasing levels of efficiency and comfort. To be missional in the use of technology requires vigilance to protect those who will be affected by these new advances. We need wisdom in regard to the uses of technological solutions. Some of the issues raised previously must be in focus during the assessment phase. For example, what digital divide implications will result from this technology? How will we meet the human need for high-touch responses when we implement high-tech solutions? The final section of this chapter focuses on engaging the possibilities of this trend.

ENGAGING THE TREND: GUIDELINES FOR THE WISE USE OF TECHNOLOGY

A major challenge for anyone who tries to project how a given trend will affect missions is to avoid objectifying what is inevitably a subjective understanding. It would serve us all well to reflect on the comments of Samuel Escobar:

> Every characteristic of this [Western] missiology becomes understandable when perceived within the frame of that avowed quantifying intention. Concepts such as "people groups," "unreached peoples," "10/40 window," "adopt a people," and "territorial spirits" express both a strong sense of urgency and an effort to use every available instrument to make the task possible. . . . Missionary action is reduced to a linear task that is translated into logical steps to be followed in a process of management by objectives, in the same way in which the evangelistic task is reduced to a process that can be carried on following marketing principles. (2000a, 109)

Technological solutions often focus more on efficiency than on people. They are open to misinterpretation and misapplication. At this point, we do well to remember the creative tension that should exist between the needs of people and the stewardship of resources. As new technologies roll out of the labs and factories of the world, those involved in missions must evaluate each innovation for missiological implications (see sidebar 11.5).

There are many significant questions to be asked of any new technology. Without adequately considering potential impacts, it is doubtful that one can fully utilize the best new technologies. This is particularly true in the fields of health, nutrition, education, and lifestyle improvements. As the speed of technological developments escalates, so must our ability to discern what tools to use and how best to use them. The challenging world in which we live requires us to be vigilant, like the wise servants who used their master's resources to produce more than was left them initially (Matt. 25:14–30).

Because of the rapid development and influence of technology, the tough ethical questions are usually not asked before the fact. Missionaries must cope with them after Pandora's box has been opened. While some see technological advance as amoral, the implications can in fact be significant and positive (Postman 1992). If we are diligent in assessing the potential good, we may derive great benefit from new technologies.

The words of Jesus apply to this new world of the twenty-first century as readily as they did to the first century: "I am sending you out like sheep among wolves. Therefore be as shrewd as snakes and as innocent

SIDEBAR 11.5
CRUCIAL QUESTIONS FOR TECHNOLOGICAL SOLUTIONS

Below are several questions arranged in categories that help an organization think through issues of technology. Consider each question, reflecting on how your answers would affect an agency.

PURPOSE

1. How will this new technology assist us in achieving our purpose as a mission?
2. Specifically, will this tool facilitate new understandings of our purpose?
3. Will this technology assist missionaries in achieving our organizational purpose?
4. Will the investment in the technology take funding away from our purpose by creating new maintenance and replacement costs?

PEOPLE

1. What are the human costs in the adoption of this new technology?
2. Will members be required to learn additional operational skills or other applications to utilize its potential?
3. Is it worth the investment in personnel hours?
4. How much will the technology add to our capacity by reducing the workload of our members?
5. Will this new technology foster relationships or draw people away from them?

ETHICS

1. How was this new technology produced?

2. Were human or natural resources exploited in the process?
3. Can the applications of this technology be monitored sufficiently to guard against misuse by either our members or the ones we are called to serve?
4. Will environmental pollution be a direct result of the use or removal of this technology?
5. If so, can steps be taken to reduce these results?

CULTURE

1. What impact will the new technology have on the culture of our mission, church, or organization?
2. Can the change be seen as part of a healthy development of our organizational culture?
3. Does the technology undermine our cultural identification with the people we are called to serve?

IMPACT

1. How will the technology affect the population we are serving?
2. If it produces positive results, can we use this innovation widely to maximize the positive impact?
3. Is there a way to incorporate the production and/or distribution of the technology to provide needed jobs or development within the communities we serve?

CASE STUDY:
ARE WE A CHURCH?

Danielle had sensed a real call from the Lord to take on the task of cyber-evangelism. After many years of ministry in Southern Europe and North Africa, Danielle had been forced to reduce her travel to care for her aging mother. Her knowledge and skills in technology combined with fluency in Arabic, English, and her native French made her the ideal facilitator. After praying about ways to stay in touch with the people and places she knew so well, Danielle took up the challenge of creative-access approaches to missions. Within months of launching the website, she had shared the gospel with many enquirers. Before long, a regular group of people was responding to her comments and participating in a chat room. She then suggested that they begin to work through a discipleship program. Much to her delight, the group adopted a serious commitment to the discipleship materials and to the relational commitment it required.

After eighteen months of regular contact, Maria, one of the regular participants, asked about their relationship as a group to the church. Coming out of the Lutheran Church in Sweden, she wanted to understand the dynamic experiences they shared. Several members explained the negative connotation the word *church* had in their contexts. Words such as *division, competition, hegemony,* and *paternalism* seemed to characterize their concerns.

Building on Maria's question, Danielle facilitated a discussion that was part of their regular interaction for several weeks. The critical questions that surfaced included:

• Can a church exist without regular face-to-face fellowship and interaction?
• What are the basic requirements for a local church?
• What if any sacraments must be observed if a group is to be a church?
• How should they appoint leaders?
• Was Danielle the pastor?
• Should they make a commitment to a regular gathering in person?

Their enthusiasm grew as they realized the potential for their group. Danielle, feeling some responsibility for the group, decided to encapsulate their discussion in a statement of intent. Taking care with her words, she wrote ...

as doves" (Matt. 10:16). Those who are sent are required to be wise and discerning, and this applies to the use of technology. In the end, technology should be a tool for the advancement of the gospel, never a roadblock to its acceptance.

12

Contextualization

From an Adapted Message to an Adapted Life

A. Scott Moreau

Certainly, one of the geniuses of God's message of Christ as revealed in the Bible is that it is translatable into every culture in the world. It is in no small measure due to this reality that the church has exploded around the world (e.g., Sanneh 2003, 23–26; see also Walls 2002a). This fact of translatability is reflective of a reality: To make sense to a local people, the gospel—indeed, the Christian faith—must be enfleshed in their local culture. The faith is both universal *and* local, and therein lies a source of great tension.

The word *contextualization* was first used to express the tension between the two realities: (1) The Bible expresses universal truths, and (2) we live in a world of diverse and ever-changing cultures. These realities are deeply connected to a central concern every Christian faces: What is the relationship between the Christian faith and my culture? Contextualization is the process in which people wrestle with this and related questions. It is of crucial significance for all Christians—even those who never cross a cultural boundary—for every one of us lives in a cultural setting and has to incarnate the Word of God and the Christian faith appropriately in that setting.

IDENTIFYING THE TREND: FROM ACCOMMODATION TO TRANSFORMATION

As initially used in 1972, *contextualization* was intended to go beyond traditional terms such as *adaptation* and *indigenization* (Kinsler 1978). Its coinage was a natural result of the multiple shifts in mission thinking that had taken place during the twentieth century.

One of those shifts was the development and popularization of *missio Dei* (Latin for "the sending of God" [McIntosh 2000b]). *Missio Dei* "focuses on everything God does in his task of establishing his kingdom in all its fullness in all the world. While it includes what the Church does, it is not limited to that, for God works both in and out of the Church" (Moreau 2000d, 637). Since God is already at work in all cultures, it made sense for some missiologists, especially those on the more liberal end of the theological spectrum, to "let the world set the agenda" and "discern the signs of the times." They challenged the church to look to history and contemporary sociopolitical contexts to see how God was already working.

> *Contextualization may be one of the most important issues in mission today. Unlike the "Death of God" movement in theology, contextualization is no mere missiological fad that will fade when another "hot topic" catches our attention.*
>
> Darrell L. Whiteman (1997, 2)

Those who followed this orientation often advocated a particular method for discerning the signs of the times. They asserted that God's ultimate goal was justice through liberation from oppression wherever such oppression was found. No longer was Scripture to be exegeted and communicated to a new society through evangelism, discipleship, and church planting. Rather, local history and contemporary events were to be exegeted to expose where God was already at work bringing liberation and justice.

This was the milieu in which Shoki Coe first used contextualization. By it, he states:

> we try to convey all that is implied in the familiar term indigenization, yet seek to press beyond for a more dynamic concept which is open to change and which is also future-oriented. . . . Contextuality . . . is that critical assessment of what makes the context really significant in the light of the *Missio Dei*. It is the missiological discernment of the signs of the times, seeing where God is at work and calling us to participate in it. (1976, 21–22)

It is not surprising that the genesis and orientation of the term made some evangelicals reluctant to use it (see Fleming 1980). Even so, it was adopted by evangelicals by the time of the 1974 Lausanne Congress on World Evangelization (Buswell 1978; Kinsler 1978). However, they defined it using evangelical convictions. David Hesselgrave noted that the controversy was still not resolved by 1984, when he wrote, "Still in its infancy, that word has already been defined and redefined, used and abused, amplified and vilified, coronated and crucified" (693). Eventually, it was accepted and today is commonly used by both liberals and evangelicals. However, they use it in different ways, with the primary difference noted by D. A. Carson:

> The first [liberals] assigns control to the context; the operative term is praxis, which serves as a controlling grid to determine the meaning of Scripture. The second [evangelicals] assigns the control to Scripture, but cherishes the "contextualization" rubric because it reminds us the Bible must be thought about, translated into and preached in categories relevant to the particular cultural context. (1987, 220; see also Glasser 1979, 404)

The foundational idea of contextualization applies to more than just the Christian faith; it can be used of any religion transplanted by its adherents in a new setting. In this broadest sense, "contextualization is the process whereby representatives of a religious faith adapt the forms and content of that faith in such a way as to communicate and (usually) commend it to the minds and hearts of a new generation within their own changing culture or to people with other cultural backgrounds" (Hesselgrave 1984, 694; see also Nkéramihigo 1984, 22). Following this broad definition, then, Christian contextualization is the process whereby Christians adapt the forms, content, and praxis of the Christian faith so as to communicate it to the minds and hearts of people with other cultural backgrounds. The goal is to make the Christian faith *as a whole*—not only the message but also the means of living the faith out in the local setting—understandable.

> *Since the Gospel message is inspired but the mode of its expression is not, contextualization of the modes of expression is not only right but necessary.*
> Byang Kato (1975a, 1217)

Characteristics of Contextualization

What characterizes good contextualization? The following seven elements are not intended to be exhaustive but to stimulate further thinking about criteria to guide the work of bringing an eternal Word into ever-changing worlds (Conn 1984).

Good contextualization is grounded in Scripture. Through the history of the church, the standard for the Christian faith has been the canonical Scriptures. While church tradition plays a significant role in ensuring that we understand Scripture appropriately and how the church in the past dealt with issues faced today, ultimately, contextualizing efforts are judged based on fidelity to the teachings of the Bible. Contextualization that replaces the Bible with cultures themselves or the most recent analytic social science tools will eventually result in a relativism in which communities simply apply standards meaningful to them rather than God's standards (Glasser 1979).

Good contextualization is interdisciplinary in its approach to culture. While contextualization is anchored in the Bible, it brings to bear a number of disciplines, each of which has a distinct contribution to make. For example, history enables us to see how faithful Christian communities (and perhaps unfaithful ones as well) dealt with issues similar to those faced today. Theology helps us to think in biblical ways about a variety of issues. Anthropology offers insights into societies and cultural values, symbols, and artifacts that need to be brought into focus through the lens of Scripture. Sociology enables insight into social networks and associations that helps us understand church structures and polity. Linguistics gives insight into the word forms and language issues that are crucial to communication of the faith. Communication studies offer tools for analysis of methods of communication. Psychology helps us understand human dynamics—especially such things as motivations and decision making—as they are played out in faith settings. Economics helps us understand exchange processes (money, barter, social favors, etc.) that are essential to the survival of faith institutions and organizations. Politics helps us understand political and legal processes both in and out of the church. All can be invaluable in offering a comprehensive view of a local setting.

Good contextualization is dynamic. Contextualization, like local societies, should never be thought of as static. At the very least, each generation of Christians in a culture will need to contextualize the Christian faith in ways that are faithful to Scripture and indigenous to it. In times of radical cultural change (urbanization, acculturation, globalization), the process of contextualizing the faith will be a never-ending one, offering rich opportunities for the people of God to rethink their faith in light of the ways Scripture challenges them and their societies.

Good contextualization is concerned with the whole of the Christian faith. Contextualization is often applied only to theological formulation or expression. This is at best truncated contextualization. Unless we explore all elements of the Christian faith and how they may be indigenously expressed in a local context, we are in danger of simply reproducing our own forms and trying to fit them together with a local theology.

Good contextualization is aware of the impact of human sinfulness on the process. The realistic contextualizer does not overlook the impact of human sinfulness on the process or the product. Personal agendas can easily get in the way, and all too often they are driven by such things as a desire to exercise power, a fear of rejection, unresolved anger, revenge, and so on. While it is true that the church has the promised Holy Spirit to guide it in all truth, it is also true that unless we have a broken, humble attitude, sin may become the dominant factor in our contextualization rather than the Spirit's gentle promptings.

Good contextualization is both propositional and existential. Contextualization is concerned with both the ideas or truths that are expressed timelessly ("God is love") and the way those truths are to be lived out ("God wants us to obey him by _____") through the lives of those who follow Christ. It cannot be limited to propositional truths. It must be carried into the very warp and woof of church life and practice.

Good contextualization is a two-way process. Contextualization is not a one-way process in which people from one culture go to another to show those people how they should express their faith and live their lives. Rather, it should be a two-way process in which each side contributes. Contextualization should be done *with* those in the receptor culture rather than *for* them (Sprunger 1984, 6; for an example, see Gration 1983). Missionaries have much to learn from members of their target society about how to contextualize in the culture. Contextualization "is a form of mission in reverse, where we will learn from other cultures how to be more Christian in our own context" (Whiteman 1997, 4). Every society of the world has gifts of contextualized thinking to offer the universal church, and the church benefits from each contribution.

Terms Related to Contextualization

As noted above, contextualization is not understood by all missiologists in the same way. This section surveys some of the more significant terms related to contextualization, beginning with terms historically used to express the relationship between church and culture. These are the terms that set the stage for contextualization as we know it today.

HISTORICAL TERMS

Three terms in particular, though now rarely used, show how the church grew in its understanding of the relationship between faith and culture.

Accommodation, a term most typically used in Roman Catholic circles, referred to changing the rituals, practices, and forms of Christian practice in a missionary's culture to fit those of a local culture. The primary goal of accommodation as traditionally expressed was the planting of a local church as an extension of the church universal. Accommodation allowed local cultural practices that were seen as neutral or good to be incorporated into the local church's life (Luzbetak 1988, 67).

When used as a technical term, accommodation referred to the work of Matteo Ricci in China in the late 1500s and of Roberto de Nobili in India in the early 1600s. Each allowed what they considered biblically neutral local cultural practices to be brought into the Christian life (see Hunsberger 2000). Ricci allowed rites involving ancestors, and Nobili lived like a Brahmin holy man and affirmed the caste system. Both Jesuit pioneers maintained that these were simply social practices that were neutral in regard to the gospel (Neill 1971).

Dominican missionaries disagreed, however, and by the early 1700s, the so-called Chinese Rites Controversy had erupted. After a long dispute, in the mid-1700s, the pope sided with the Dominicans, condemning accommodation efforts in regard to all but the most trivial of social customs. That was not the last word, however. Vatican II reversed the Roman Catholic Church's orientation and opened the door to greater accommodation (Conn 2000).

Adaptation referred to finding ways to express the gospel in forms and ideas that were familiar to a culture so that they fit in it (Moreau 2000a). In practice, this ranged from incorporating new meaning into indigenous words (e.g., John invested the Greek term for "Word" [*logos*] with new meaning in his Gospel) to the adaptation of liturgy (e.g., baptism or the Lord's Supper) to changing church polity to fit local cultural ideals. This idea was jettisoned because those who practiced it did not take local culture seriously enough. Adaptation was a one-way effort in which the monolithic (global) faith was simply changed to fit a local setting, which was seen as having nothing to offer to the larger church in return (see Shorter 1988, 183; Schineller 1990, 16–17).

In 1960, Johann Bavinck, working from a Reformed perspective, coined the term *possessio* to refer to God's work in possessing a society for Christ by establishing beachheads for the gospel and gradually "conquering" the society by submitting all elements to God's control. This was done by investing every existing cultural value, symbol, and action with Christian significance (see McIntosh 2000a). As explained by Bavinck:

> The Christian life does not accommodate or adapt itself to heathen forms of life, but it takes the latter in possession and thereby makes them new.

Whoever is in Christ is a new creature. Within the framework of the non-Christian life, customs and practices serve idolatrous tendencies and drive a person away from God. The Christian life takes them in hand and turns them in an entirely different direction; they acquire an entirely different content. Even though in external form there is much that resembles past practices, in reality everything has become new, the old has in essence passed away and the new has come. . . . [Christ] fills each thing, each word, and each practice with a new meaning and gives it new direction. Such is neither "adaptation" nor accommodation; it is in essence the legitimate taking possession of something by him to whom all power is given in heaven and on earth. (1960, 178–79)

Peter Beyerhaus (1975, 120) describes three stages of *possessio*. First, God comes into the world and establishes beachheads of his sovereign rule, most specifically through the presentation and safeguarding of the gospel message. Second, these beachheads become the basis of outreach (leaven) in the culture and offer opportunities to invest the cultural values, practices, and symbols with Christian meaning. Third, and finally, Satan and his work are removed so that the transformation of human cultures into Christ-honoring ones can be completed. The ultimate conquest of any culture, in this sense, will not come until after this present age.

TERMS PARALLEL TO AND EXTENDING CONTEXTUALIZATION

Several other historical terms are still in use.

Indigenization was coined in the mid-1800s in Protestant mission circles to express the idea that a church must be local within its own context. In its broadest sense, "indigenization is a term describing the 'translatability' of the universal Christian faith into the forms and symbols of particular cultures of the world" (Conn 2000). Thus, while it preceded contextualization, it closely parallels contextualization's main focus. One important difference is that indigenization focuses on culture in a "foreign" setting, while contextualization takes place everywhere and incorporates social, political, and economic factors that indigenization does not include (see Tabor 1979; Haleblian 1983).

Indigenization was perhaps most clearly exemplified by the

> *The term "indigenous" comes from biology and indicates a plant or animal native to an area. Missiologists adopted the word and used it to refer to churches that reflect the cultural distinctives of their ethnolinguistic group. The missionary effort to establish indigenous churches is an effort to plant churches that fit naturally into their environment and to avoid planting churches that replicate Western patterns.*
>
> John Mark Terry (2000, 483)

327

three-self principle. The focus of this principle was on planting churches that were (1) self-propagating, (2) self-governing, and (3) self-financing. Developed independently by American Rufus Anderson and Briton Henry Venn, it is sometimes called the Anderson-Venn Formula.

Critics have noted that embedded within the indigenization focus are assumptions based on Western ideals. Alfred Krass points out that its claim of objectivity can no longer be accepted without severe qualifications and that the model of structural-functional anthropology on which it was based cannot handle cultural change adequately (1979). In addition, as Christians, we should rightly question what the idea of "self" means in each of the three "selfs." How much is the idea unconsciously framed by the perspective of Western individualism rather than by the more biblical perspective of Christ-centered interdependence (see Moreau 2001a)?

Since the 1970s, several missiologists have proposed adding more "selfs" to the formula (see Terry 2000). Alan Tippett (1987), for example, suggested that a church should have a "self-image" (see itself as independent of its founding mission). It should also be "self-functioning" (capable of carrying on its own functions) and "self-giving" (capable of knowing the needs of its local community and assisting in meeting those needs). The most widely accepted new "self," however, is "self-theologizing," which refers to the ability to develop biblically based theological expressions that meet the needs of the church's context (e.g., Hiebert 1985, 195–96, 216–19).

> *The New Testament has given us the pattern for cultural adaptation. The incarnation itself is a form of contextualization. The Son of God condescended to pitch his tent among us to make it possible for us to be redeemed (John 1:14).*
>
> Byang Kato (1975a, 1217)

As a term, *indigenization* continues to have wide and positive use among evangelical missiologists, though it is not as popular among ecumenicals and Roman Catholics.

Incarnational mission refers to the fact that Jesus' act of taking on humanity is a model for missionaries in their practice of adapting to local culture (see Neely 2001). Yet there is debate over the significance of the incarnation for Christian missions. Liberation theologians, for example, note Jesus' proclamation in Luke 4:18–19 that he came "to proclaim release to the captives." Therefore, we should do likewise, focusing on liberation as the primary concern of the incarnation (see Neely 2001 for other examples).

It is helpful to note that the extent of our ability to incarnate will always be limited. We cannot be born into another culture the way

Jesus was incarnated into Galilee. Still, *incarnation* is an important term when dealing with contextualization and points to the importance Jesus placed on being enfleshed in a particular context to communicate the gospel message.

Inculturation parallels contextualization, though it was coined in and continues to be used more widely in Roman Catholic circles than in Protestant ones (Moreau 2000c). It expresses the "dynamic relation between the Christian message and culture or cultures; an insertion of the Christian life into a culture; an ongoing process of reciprocal and critical interaction and assimilation between them" (Azevedo 1982, 11). It was originally defined by Pedro Arrupe as "the incarnation of Christian life and of the Christian message in a particular cultural context, in such a way that this experience not only finds expression through elements proper to the culture in question, but becomes a principle that animates, directs and unifies the culture, transforming it and remaking it so as to bring about a 'new creation'" (Schineller 1996, 109). Inculturation is not limited to theology or doctrines. As Peter Schineller notes, "In the final analysis, therefore, inculturation refers to the correct way of living and sharing one's Christian faith in a particular context or culture" (1990, 6).

> *Wherever one is, one tries to stir up the gospel values that are already present and to bring to bear the gospel values that are absent.*
>
> Peter Schineller (1990, 61)

Transformation focuses on the changing of a society into one that more adequately reflects the kingdom of God. It echos the idea of *possessio*, without the Reformed theological roots. Many evangelicals advocate that Christians transform society by leading individuals to Christ who will in turn work to transform their social networks and eventually will have a leavening effect on the entire society. Others strive for social change by mass persuasion or promoting and implementing legal changes that lead to the development of a transformed society. Current approaches to transformation can put too much weight on human capability and not enough focus on human sin (individual and corporate). Still, transformation is important, if for no other reason than to demonstrate God's kingdom values to a desperately needy world.

EVALUATING THE TREND: WHAT ARE THE DANGERS OF CONTEXTUALIZATION?

While contextualizing the Christian faith is not an option, this does not mean it is without peril. At least three potential dangers must be

329

noted: cultural imperialism, the fact that contextual realities can overwhelm biblical priorities, and syncretism.

Cultural Imperialism

There are many reasons cross-cultural workers inappropriately assume decision-making roles that stifle local church initiative and development. The workers may come from a culture that is technologically superior, or they may be more highly educated than those among whom they work. They may simply be wealthier or just more dogmatic and certain of themselves. In addition, indigenous people may be all too willing to assign the sojourners key decision-making roles.

Cross-cultural workers may too readily work to become indispensable to the local church in regard to decision making on deeply contextual issues, even when they do not know the local cultural values well enough to make wise, informed decisions. In cases in which they do have the wisdom, local leadership should still make the decisions (e.g., see Priest 1994), even when missionaries feel the decisions may be wrong. It is through the process of making such decisions that development happens. As long as the local people have the Bible as their sourcebook, they have a self-correcting resource that enables them to stay on track.

On the other hand, zealous missionaries may try to force contextual thinking on a church that has been in existence for generations, assuming that because of their training, background, or knowledge they know what is best for the local church. This too stifles local church development.

Contextual Realities Can Overwhelm Biblical Priorities

In some places in the world, people desperately need life's essentials—clean water, a nutritional diet, affordable shelter, employment, justice—causing the overwhelmed cross-cultural worker to put the deeper need of a living relationship with Christ on a shelf. It is necessary and good to be deeply engaged in people's search for the necessities of life but not at the expense of their eternal destiny. A more holistic approach to missionary engagement neglects neither. Certainly, there are times when temporal needs must be met and addressing eternal ones must be delayed. However, missionaries must never lose sight of the fact that when the eternal destiny of people is settled, they will have the resources (including the indwelling Spirit) to meet their more immediate needs in ways that reflect God's kingdom priorities.

The Danger of Syncretism

Perhaps the most often-noted danger associated with contextualizing is the possibility of crossing the line into syncretism. Contemporary scholarship has been gradually redefining syncretism as a neutral or even a good thing (see Schreiter 1993). If syncretism is defined only as one system adapting ideas or practices from another, then the church and everything related to contextualization is inherently syncretistic. However, such a definition does not do justice to the biblical concept of syncretism, which is "the replacement or dilution of the essential truths of the gospel through the incorporation of non-Christian elements." It is a violation of the first commandment to love God with all our hearts, souls, minds, and strength (Moreau 2000e).

Debate about syncretism has recently flared concerning contextualized approaches used among Muslims. For example, some people are actively building Jesus mosques, modeling them on messianic synagogues (see Parshall 1998; Travis 1998a; Gilliland 1998). In 1998, John Travis (pseudonym) listed a spectrum (C1 to C6) of contextualized efforts being practiced in ministry among Muslims (1998a). There is general agreement regarding the C1 to C4 efforts. The C5 and C6 practices raised questions among experienced missionaries such as Phil Parshall (1998) and Scott Woods (2003). The practices were defended by other notable scholar/practitioners such as Dean Gilliland (1998), John Travis (1998b), and Joshua Massey (2004). (Sidebar 12.1 presents the C4 through C6 part of the spectrum.)

Certainly, Christians must guard against syncretism. Paul Hiebert notes several safeguards (1994, 91). The most powerful one is a high view of the authority of Scripture. Another is the ongoing work of the Holy Spirit in the lives of Christians. To guard against a powerful individual leading a group astray, the church acts as a buffer (or "hermeneutical community") against possible extremes. Finally, the greater the variety of perspectives (gender, ethnic identity, nationality, socioeconomic class, etc.) among those who have a legitimate voice in a church, the less likely it is that a single voice or group can lead the church astray. The following guidelines can help guard against syncretism:

> Because of the convoluted nature of culture, the declaration of syncretism in a particular setting cannot be simply left in the hands of expatriate missionaries. The local community must be empowered to biblically evaluate their own practices and teachings. Missionaries must learn to trust that indigenous peoples are able to discern God's leading and trust God to develop and maintain biblically founded and culturally relevant faith and praxis in each local context. Finally, Christians of every culture must engage in genuine partnership with Christians of other cultures,

---

SIDEBAR 12.1
SELECTED ELEMENTS OF THE SPECTRUM
OF MUSLIM CONTEXTUALIZATION

(Adapted from Travis 1998a, 408)

The following chart shows the most radical part of the spectrum of practices in use today for contextualizing the Christian faith in Muslim settings.

C4: *contextualized Christ-centered communities using insider language and biblically permissible cultural and Islamic forms.* Biblically permissible Islamic forms and practices are utilized (e.g., praying with raised hands; keeping the fast; avoiding pork, alcohol, and dogs as pets; using Islamic terms and dress; etc.). Meetings are not held in church buildings. C4 communities are comprised almost entirely of Muslim-background believers. C4 believers, though highly contextualized, are usually not seen as Muslim by the

Muslim community. C4 believers identify themselves as followers of Isa the Messiah (or something similar).

C5: *Christ-centered communities of "messianic Muslims" who have accepted Jesus as Lord and Savior.* C5 believers remain legally and socially within the community of Islam, somewhat similar to the messianic Jewish movement. Aspects of Islamic theology that are incompatible with the Bible are rejected or reinterpreted if possible. Participation in corporate Islamic worship varies from person to person and group to group. C5 believers meet regularly with other C5 believers and share their faith with unsaved Muslims. Unsaved Muslims may see C5 believers as

since often the outsider's help is needed to enable local believers, blinded by culture and familiarity, to see that which contravenes scriptural adherence to the first commandment (Moreau 2000e, 924).

REFLECTING ON THE TREND: BIBLICAL AND THEOLOGICAL CONSIDERATIONS

Does Scripture contain examples of contextualization? This is an important question to ask and one that is easy to answer with a qualified yes (there are fewer examples in the Old Testament than in the New Testament).

Old Testament Reflections

It is difficult to find examples in the Old Testament of what we today call contextualization (see Hesselgrave and Rommen 1989, 3–7). In fact, one of the elements of God's call to the Israelites was that they remain separate from the cultures of the day so as not to be defiled by worship of other gods. Thus, it is not surprising that Old Testament theologically deviant and may eventually expel them from the community of Islam. Where entire villages accept Christ, C5 may result in messianic mosques. C5 believers are viewed as Muslims by the Muslim community and refer to themselves as Muslims who follow Isa the Messiah.

C6: *small Christ-centered communities of secret/underground believers.* C6 believers are similar to persecuted believers suffering under totalitarian regimes. Due to fear, isolation, or threat of extreme governmental/community legal action or retaliation (including capital punishment), C6 believers worship Christ secretly (individually or perhaps infrequently in small clusters). Many come to Christ through dreams, visions, miracles, radio broadcasts, tracts, Christian witness while abroad, or reading the Bible on their own initiative. C6 (as opposed to C5) believers are usually silent about their faith. This is not ideal, since God desires his people to witness and have regular fellowship (Heb. 10:25). Nonetheless, C6 believers are part of the family in Christ. Though God may call some to a life of suffering, imprisonment, or martyrdom, he may be pleased to have some worship him in secret, at least for a time. C6 believers are perceived as Muslims by the Muslim community and identify themselves as Muslims.

REFLECTION AND DISCUSSION

1. Where would you draw the line within this spectrum?
2. What approach would you take in teaching C6 people?
3. A friend of yours has decided to engage in Muslim evangelism using a C5 approach and asks for your advice. What would you say?

---

scholar Gleason Archer wrote, "It would be an error to look in the Old Testament for specific positive guidelines for contextualization" (1979, 200). Even so, Arthur Glasser discusses the "adaptive cultural response that characterized the ongoing history of the people of God" (1979, 405). By this he means that each period of history of the formation of God's people had as a major thrust ethical obligations and theologizing that arose out of their situation (Glasser 1979, 405–7). The prophets in Old Testament times also received God's messages and communicated them in contextually appropriate fashion to the people of God (Athyal 1997, 9).

Yet the particular nature of God's work in calling and setting aside a people who would follow him is not the whole story of the Bible. With the decimation of the nation of Israel and the domination of Rome, questions of culture and faith took on a far more prominent role.

New Testament Reflections

The New Testament itself is a contextualized document. On a basic level, Matthew was most likely composed for a Jewish audience, John

333

SIDEBAR 12.2
DIGGING DEEPER: SELECTED RESOURCES FOR CONTEXTUALIZATION IN THE NEW TESTAMENT

Abijole, Bayo. 1988. "St. Paul's Concept of Principalities and Powers in African Context." *Africa Theological Journal* 17 (April): 118–29.

Allen, Roland. 1927. *The Spontaneous Expansion of the Church.* London: World Dominion Press.

———. 1962. *Missionary Methods: St. Paul's or Ours?* London: R. Scott.

Bennett, Charles T. 1980. "Paul the Pragmatist: Another Look at His Missionary Methods." *Evangelical Missions Quarterly* 16 (July): 133–38.

Carson, Donald A. 1984. "Reflections on Contextualization: A Critical Appraisal of Daniel Von Allmen's 'Birth of Theology.'" *East Africa Journal of Evangelical Theology* 3, no. 1: 16–59.

Cope, Lamar. 1983. "Analogy, the Pauline Centre and Doing Theology Today." *Bangalore Theological Forum* 15, no. 2: 128–35.

Ericson, Norman R. 1978. "Implications from the New Testament for Contextualization." In *Theology and Mission: Papers Given at Trinity Consultation No. 1,* ed. David J. Hesselgrave, 71–85. Grand Rapids: Baker.

Gilliland, Dean S. 1989. "New Testament Contextualization: Continuity and Particularity in Paul's Theology." In *The Word among Us: Contextualizing Theology for Mission Today,* ed. Dean S. Gilliland, 52–73. Dallas: Word.

Peters, George W. 1973. "Pauline Patterns of Church-Mission Relationships." *Evangelical Missions Quarterly* 9 (Winter): 111–18.

Von Allmen, Daniel. 1975. "The Birth of Theology: Contextualization as the Dynamic Element in the Formation of New Testament Theology." *International Review of Mission* 64 (January): 37–52.

Wintle, Brian. 1992. "Doing Theology in Context: A Biblical Case Study." In *Doing Contextual Theology: A Festschrift in Honour of Bruce John Nicholls,* ed. Sunand Sumithra, 13–24. Bangalore, India: Theological Book Trust.

---

for an audience familiar with Greek categories of thought, and Luke/Acts for a Gentile named Theophilus. Each of Paul's epistles is an "occasional" letter—written for a specific purpose to a people located in a particular setting struggling to live out the faith.

We also see contextual issues lived out in the lives of New Testament characters. Certainly, the preeminent example is the previously noted incarnation of Jesus. The early church struggled over issues such as the extent to which Gentiles needed to follow Jewish law before they could be considered fully Christian (Acts 15). Contextual practice is seen in evangelism (Paul on Mars Hill; Acts 17:16–31), discipleship (Paul's decision to circumcise Timothy; Acts 16:1–3), church planting (Paul reasoning with the Thessalonians; Acts 17:1–4), and ongoing church growth (Paul's work in Ephesus; Acts 19). (For more information, see the sources listed in sidebar 12.2.)

Mapping Out Models of Contextualization

Numerous conceptual maps compare the multitude of contextualization models that have been proposed since the term was coined in 1972 (see, for example, Nicholls 1979; Fleming 1980; Schreiter 1985; Hesselgrave and Rommen 1989; Bevans 1992). All such maps take into account the fact that contextualization has two poles: Scripture and setting. Typically, the models are arranged by the way they prioritize the poles. This approach is followed in figure 12.1.

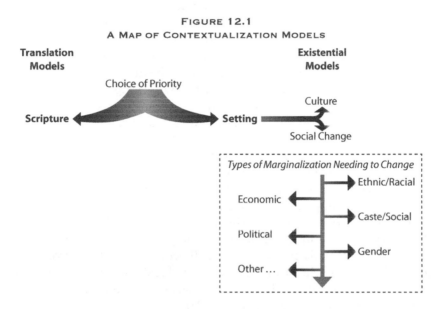

FIGURE 12.1
A MAP OF CONTEXTUALIZATION MODELS

Contextualization models that prioritize the pole of Scripture are typically called translation models. They take the Bible as normative, and the role of the contextualizer is to translate the message of the Bible so that it can fit indigenously in a new setting. The bulk of evangelical models are translation models, which is expected given that evangelicals see Scripture as the foundation of God's message for all humankind. Contemporary translation contextualizers pay careful attention to context but primarily so that the message is adequately conveyed. Examples of this type of approach are offered by Paul Hiebert (1984), William Larkin (1988), and David Hesselgrave and Edward Rommen (1989).

Contextualization models that prioritize the pole of setting are called by a variety of titles, but perhaps the most appropriate is existential

(Nicholls 1979). As figure 12.1 shows, such models can be divided into two orientations. The first focuses on the local culture and utilizes the tool kit of anthropology. Those who follow this model assume that God is already at work in the culture. Their task is not so much to *bring* a supra-cultural message as it is to *uncover* or *expose* the ways in which the message is already present. Vincent Donovan's (2003) work among the Maasai of Kenya is a typical example. The approach has been described as a treasure hunt that uses Scripture as a map or guide to discover the treasures to be found in the culture itself through anthropological analysis (see Bevans 1992, 49).

The second orientation within the existentialist camp focuses on social change on behalf of (or in cooperation with) marginalized populations. Proponents are driven by the conviction that God is deeply concerned with social justice and/or liberation of the oppressed. They look for marginalized populations and where those people are struggling for liberation. Marginalization may be seen in the areas of ethnicity (black or Hispanic theology), economics (Minjung theology; the "preferential option for the poor"), politics (liberation theology), caste or social class (Dalit theology), gender (feminist theology), and so on. The use of the Bible can range from a case book of how liberation was accomplished (e.g., the exodus) to a text that supports the theme of bringing justice to the nations of the world. By and large, this approach is driven by the process of discovering and joining in what is already happening (or what needs to happen) for justice in the local setting.

A third type of model is not shown in figure 12.1. This model, called the transcendental model, prioritizes the people rather than Scripture or setting. Essentially, it assumes that all people have a God-given ability to theologize, and the key is to enable the local church to tap into that process. Since few use it, it is not discussed here. (For an examination of this model, see Bevans [1992, 97–110].)

ENGAGING THE TREND: CONTEXTUALIZATION THAT IS CRITICAL AND COMPREHENSIVE

Certainly, Christians must be committed to the authority of God's Word for all cultures of the world. Therefore, a translation model is appropriate. This does not mean, however, that we can treat culture lightly or ignore the fact that through general revelation God has been speaking to all peoples on the planet. As a result, the model must incorporate valuable insights from the existential model, especially a deep respect for human cultures and God's clear desire for justice among the nations of the world.

Critical Contextualization

No translation model has been more widely accepted and used in evangelical circles than Paul Hiebert's four-step critical contextualization model (1984, 1987, 1994). The first step is exegesis of the culture. This is done by studying the local culture phenomenologically. A phenomenological approach is one in which missionaries temporarily suspend questions of what is right or true until they are sure they understand the phenomena being considered (Moreau 2001b). For example, when an issue or question arises that merits attention, the local church leaders (and, if necessary, the missionary) lead the congregation in *uncritically* gathering and analyzing the traditional beliefs and customs associated with the question at hand (see, for example, Gration 1983). The second step is exegesis of Scripture and employment of the hermeneutical bridge. Local leaders guide the community in a study of the Scripture passages related to the question at hand. They also have the responsibility to provide a larger framework that enables the community to translate the biblical message into all dimensions of their culture—bridging from the text of Scripture to their setting. The third step is the community's decision regarding how to respond to the situation. The community critically evaluates its beliefs and customs in light of its new biblical understanding and makes decisions based on the newfound truths. The community may choose to:

1. keep the old practice or belief because it is not unbiblical
2. reject the practice or belief as unbiblical
3. modify the practice or belief to give it a specific Christian meaning through appropriate rituals, actions, or symbols

Hiebert's fourth and final step is to develop a new contextualized practice. In this step, the leaders help the faith community arrange the practices and beliefs they have chosen into a ritual that expresses the Christian meaning of the event.

Obviously, this method can apply to almost every situation encountered. The focus, however, is not on developing a new theological system but on helping people deal theologically and practically with issues at hand.

Comprehensive Contextualization and the Religious Dimensions of Culture

While Hiebert's *method* is appropriate, an important second component of contextualization, if it is to be comprehensive, involves the areas of the Christian faith to which it must be applied.

To help us develop a comprehensive view of what is meant by contextualizing the whole of the faith, we will utilize the thinking of Ninian Smart, a religious studies scholar. Smart proposed a scheme of seven identifiable dimensions that apply to all religions (Smart 1996). These dimensions are widely used in introductory religious studies to help students develop a more comprehensive picture of a religion. Here they are used to reveal the comprehensive range of the Christian faith that must be contextualized. (For a searchable database of over two thousand bibliographic resources on contextualization covering the first six dimensions, browse to http://www.mislinks.org/biblio/query.php.)

Before we begin a discussion of the religious dimensions, we must remember the need to incorporate helpful insights from the existential model of contextualization. This can be done in two ways. First, for each dimension, we must look for biblical norms and models to bring to the culture, and we must also look in the culture to see the ways in which God has already revealed himself in it and prepared it for the reception of the Christian faith. Salvation cannot be found through general revelation—the specifics needed for salvation come through the special revelation Scripture alone provides. However, bridges for people to understand the gospel and its implications for church life are present in every culture, because God reveals himself to every culture long before missionaries arrive on the scene.

> *Contextualization can take place in the area of liturgy, dress, language, church service, and any other form of expression of the Gospel truth.*
>
> Byang Kato (1975a, 1217)

Second, the biblical message is clear that God is deeply concerned about justice in every human society. Therefore, we must pay attention

TABLE 12.1
QUESTIONS TO ASK OF SCRIPTURE AND SETTING

	Scripture	Setting	
		Cultural Bridges	Social Change
Questions	What has God revealed about the Christian faith that is essential to be incarnated or indigenized in the dimension?	How has God already been revealing himself in and through the dimension?	What areas within the dimension are in need of social change?
		What bridges for contextualization are present in the dimension?	Who and where are the oppressed and marginalized?
	What does the Bible affirm in the dimension, and what does it condemn?	How can they be used to make the whole of the faith indigenous in the setting?	How might the gospel enable them to live kingdom-centered lives in the midst of oppression?

338

to areas within cultures that are in need of kingdom-based social change or transformation. Further, we must consider the role local believers have in facilitating that change as a sign to the rest of the society that the kingdom of God is in its midst. Table 12.1 illustrates the types of questions to be asked for each dimension.

THE DOCTRINAL OR PHILOSOPHICAL DIMENSION

The doctrinal or philosophical dimension deals with important beliefs expressed in religious form (Smart 1996, 10). It could also be called the theological dimension. It answers questions such as, What is true about the world, people, the unseen powers, life, and death? Doctrines are religious beliefs about such things as the supernatural (e.g., demons exist), the created visible world and the universe (e.g., God made the world), and the relationship between people and God (e.g., all humanity has sinned). Religious beliefs may be organized in a doctrinal or philosophical fashion (such as systematic theology), or they may simply be embedded within the mythic, ethical, and ritual dimensions.

Among Christian contextualizers, this dimension—especially the contextualization of theology—is most typically discussed and debated. This dimension is expressed in liberation theology, African identity theology, feminist theology, black theology, Minjung theology, Dalit theology, ethno-theologies, and so on. In evangelical circles, Calvinistic, Arminian, Wesleyan, dispensationalist, and Pentecostal theologies are examples.

THE RITUAL DIMENSION

From simple greetings to formal state occasions, rituals are regularized ceremonies of life that provide "places" of security and are embedded in every culture. The ritual dimension includes such activities as worship, pilgrimage, meditation, and consecration (Smart 1996, 10). Finding ways to contextualize the ritual dimension of religious experience requires a general understanding of the concept of ritual as well as a more detailed understanding of the actions, symbolism, and myths of a particular ritual under consideration (see Zahniser 1997).

Rituals serve a variety of purposes in religion. They establish or affirm the social and historic identity of the participants, reminding them who they are and how they relate to others in the culture. They help people move from one social status to another. They serve as cultural drama libraries in which the history, values, and beliefs of the people are symbolized and stored. R. Daniel Shaw has identified three types of rituals (2000): (1) transition rituals, (2) crisis rituals, and (3) intensification rituals.

Transition rituals—such as baptism, confirmation, and membership ceremonies—usher people from one phase of life to another. Prior to such rituals, an individual is limited in participation and not considered a full member. Afterward, the individual enjoys the rights and privileges, as well as the expectations, of one who is on the inside. Many cultures of the world still have initiation rituals that bring a person from childhood to adulthood. Transition rituals typically contain three stages, as shown in figure 12.2: separation, transformation, and reincorporation (see also Zahniser 1997, 192).

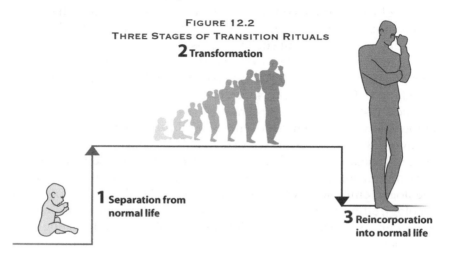

FIGURE 12.2
THREE STAGES OF TRANSITION RITUALS
2 Transformation
1 Separation from normal life
3 Reincorporation into normal life

The first phase is separation from normal life in preparation for the transformation that is about to take place. This may be accomplished through a symbolic act such as a staged kidnapping, taking off one's shoes, getting into a certain posture, putting on symbolic clothing, or going to a special location.

The second phase is transformation. During this stage, the applicants are in what is referred to as a liminal state (Hertig 2000). They have been removed from the normal course of life but have not yet undergone the transformation to the new form or stage of life. They are in limbo. This stage may involve symbolic acts expressing the liminalty, such as being cut off from communication with relatives. The transformation comes through various trials: physical, such as circumcision; cognitive, such as formal testing; or psychological, such as tests of courage. These trials enable participants to bond to a new role or status based on the meaning of the rituals (Zahniser 1997, 94–98). Successful completion of these trials results in a symbolic recognition of the new status, such as being given a new name or title or receiving a diploma.

The third and final phase of transition rituals is reincorporation or reintegration into normal life. Once the transformation is complete, the transformed person is reincorporated into the normal social fabric of life, although usually at a different level with different responsibilities. For example, in the United States, once a young woman passes her driving exam, she is given a driver's license and is legally free to drive anywhere on her own.

Crisis rituals, on the other hand, help people either prevent or deal with unexpected negative situations that arise in life. A prayer vigil for someone suddenly taken ill or an emergency board meeting to deal with a disciplinary issue are excellent examples, even though we may not think of them as rituals. Such rituals serve a deep need in people's lives by helping them feel that things are not as out of control as they may think they are. They give people hope that circumstances will change as God responds to their requests. In many cultures, crisis rituals involve such things as sacrifices to the spirit realm, visits to people of power such as shamans or diviners, and obtaining charms, potions, or fetishes to ward off attacks.

Intensification rituals help solidify a person's faith by reconnecting that person to religious values and beliefs. For Christians, the weekly worship service meets this need, helping people reconnect with God and with one another in a place where it is safe to express commonly shared beliefs and values. Other types of Christian intensification rituals include Christmas and Easter celebrations, personal devotional times, regular prayer meetings or Bible studies, and Sunday school. These are deeply cultural events, and the ways they are conducted are mediated by cultural values.

Many Western evangelical churches have distanced themselves from formal rituals, in some cases because of a fear of legalism and in others because of historical factors. However, God created us as ritualistic beings. This is clearly seen in John's visions of heavenly worship, such as the worship of the multitudes around the throne of God (e.g., Rev. 7:9–12).

Missionaries who grow up in churches that deny the importance of ritual can completely miss this as an important component of contextualization. While they may find local ways for communion, baptism, and membership, they may ignore or exclude other equally important indigenous rituals that may be adaptable to church life, such as those dealing with crises, initiation, and socialization. Wise missionaries will be observant of rituals in their new culture and will constantly think of ways such rituals can be used for evangelism, discipleship, or social transformation.

THE ETHICAL/LEGAL DIMENSION

The ethical/legal dimension focuses on how people are to behave as they interact with other people, the spiritual realm, and the physical world as well as how that behavior is regulated. Ethical systems apply from the individual to societal levels. They are deeply interwoven into the cultural values and doctrine and often enshrined in heroic (or evil) acts discussed in cultural myth. Doctrinal systems tell people what is right and wrong, but ethical systems tell people how they should live and act on the basis of what is right and wrong. The legal side maintains order.

The focus of the ethical/legal dimension in contextualization is to live out goodness through the practice of loving God and neighbor in a new cultural context. Few have wrestled with this as cogently as Bernard Adeney, and the following principles for guiding contextualizing ethics borrow heavily from his thinking (1995).

First, we must recognize the limitations of trying to identify a list of supra-cultural moral principles. Such a list of universally applicable moral principles will always be inadequate because the principles will focus on abstractions rather than on real contexts. For Christians, certainly one focus is to understand biblical prescriptions that are based on normative values for all humanity, but even these must be embedded in a particular context to be understood. For example, "Love your neighbor as yourself" (Matt. 19:19) applies to all people, but how that is expressed varies from culture to culture.

Second, Adeney notes that cultural values are more basic than principles, although they may be justified by principles. Usually we feel that our values are right because of experience or because we attribute them to a culturally recognized authority (God, other powers, leaders). We will even justify them by appealing to Scripture, and this is where great care must be taken. For example, many Americans read the command from Paul, "But everything should be done in a fitting and orderly way" (1 Cor. 14:40) and instinctively think that this refers to standard business practices such as establishing committees, having a well-defined authority structure, and taking votes to decide major issues. Certainly, Paul was not thinking along those lines when he wrote this command; his focus was on regulation of prophecy and tongue speaking during worship. Even so, our instinctive tendency is to take what he says and apply it in ways that make sense to us, which we determine by our cultural values and personal experience.

Developing a contextualized set of ethics and a legal system to maintain them, whether on the personal or the systemic level, requires a deep understanding of both Scripture and context to ensure that living wisely conforms to God's Word in ways that can be understood from within the setting. This certainly gives room for both commendation and condemnation of cultural values and practices. A missionary must be aware that it is easy to condemn those things that do not violate God's standards but do violate his or her cultural values (see Priest 1994). Things that need to be considered in contextualizing this dimension for church settings include formal and informal codes of conduct, standards for leadership, disciplinary measures for those who violate expected behavior, and so on.

THE EXPERIENTIAL DIMENSION

The experiential dimension consists of encounters with the transcendent (i.e., the supernatural). It includes how people experience the transcendent in their lives and interpret those experiences. Religious experience in this sense is particularly focused on experiencing God, the Holy Spirit, angels, or evil spirits. It is often in the intersection of needs and the daily issues of life that people encounter such experiences. They can range from quiet peace through meditative reflection to ecstatic worship, from Holy Spirit–filled charismata to demonic control.

This is the hardest area to contextualize because the supernatural realm is not at our beck and call. Further, many missionaries from North American conservative evangelical churches believe that such experiences are not to be talked about publicly (when was the last time you heard a sermon on dreams and visions?). When they are, they are explained through psychology. Missionaries with such backgrounds working in cultures that are more open to spiritual experiences feel ill equipped to handle them. As a result, they may stifle discussion of such things. The local church will learn to be silent on the topic or will talk about it only when the missionary is not around.

How do missionaries contextualize this dimension? First, they need to explore the biblical perspective of such phenomena with the local church. Second, together they need to develop rituals that will either enable such experiences (e.g., waiting on God) or stop them (e.g., demonic expulsion). Finally, they need to allow local believers to talk about their experiences and find indigenous ways that conform to Scripture to handle them.

THE MYTHIC OR NARRATIVE DIMENSION

The mythic dimension of religion refers to the stories of a culture that reflect its thinking about the world, itself, its laws, and its values. In academic discussion, myth is limited to the timeless stories of creation, redemption, and human/divine drama, examples of which are the Bible, the Koran, Hindu epics, and so on. In calling these "myth," scholars are not saying they are untrue. Rather, the focus is on the role they play in the culture.

Christians recognize *in this academic sense* that the Bible is myth. However, not only does it provide the God-inspired telling of the human/ divine drama, but it is the True Myth on which all other myths are based and judged. This belief was the inspiration for authors such as C. S. Lewis (The Chronicles of Narnia) and J. R. R. Tolkien (The Lord of the Rings). Both wrote their stories as reflections of the one True Myth, drawing from intimate knowledge of historical mythic themes and structures.

Ninian Smart broadened this category beyond the academic definition to include not only the classic myths but also stories of actual history in the culture that provide imagery of themes such as heroism, sacrifice, love, honor, power, and so on (1996, 130–31). In addition, folklore, fairy tales, and proverbs are part of the mythic structure of a culture that needs contextualized thinking and practice.

Myths concretize important values for a culture in story form and enable those values to be passed from generation to generation through constant retelling. As such, they have a vital impact on the development of theological systems in at least three ways. First, myths serve as a source of cognitive categories, especially for things people are unable to explain otherwise. Second, myths legitimize personal values and behavior as well as social institutional structures and operation. Finally, myths are the foundation for symbolic communication of the deep-seated aspirations, needs, and fears of a culture. They can provide a source for oppression on one hand and hope, motivation, and inspiration on the other (e.g., the "culture" and "myth" of poverty as it is manifested in various forms around the world) (adapted from Honko 1984, 46–48; Barbour 1974, 20–23).

The myth structure of a culture is important for contextualization because it grounds theological systems and cultural values. For example, if a culture's mythologies embody the idea of fatalism, then people of that culture may tend to develop theologies and values that emphasize God's sovereignty at the expense of human responsibility. On the other hand, if the society's mythologies focus on individualistic autonomy, then its theologies and values will more likely emphasize human freedom, possibly at the expense of God's sovereignty over all of life.

How then can missionaries contextualize in the mythic dimension? At the very least, they must recognize with C. S. Lewis that the Bible is the True Myth on which other myths are based and develop skill in using biblical stories in evangelism and discipleship (see Morton 2004). In addition, they can help local communities see whether their myths fit or do not fit with scriptural teaching. When a question arises about a local story or myth, it is an appropriate opportunity for a free-flowing discussion. The missionary should enable the local community of believers to talk openly about the myth, including the symbols or rituals that are part of it and the indigenous meanings associated with it. They should take the time to explore the possible range of meanings of the issues in question and always assume that there is more to be discovered. This provides an opportunity to explore Scripture together to see what it has to say about the values and ideas contained in the myth. While the missionary will serve as a resource, he or she must allow the community to provide leadership for the dialogue. The goal is for the local church to decide how it wants to deal with the myth at hand. If the people want to "Christianize" it and any associated practices, they must carefully think through the issues involved (both positive and negative).

THE SOCIAL OR ORGANIZATIONAL DIMENSION

The social or organizational dimension refers to the formal organization and leadership of a religion (Smart 1996, 215). Fellowships, associations, and denominations reflect the former; pastors, elders, priests, bishops, prophets, and so on reflect the latter. Organizational structures and leadership roles are built on the cultural values of how people are to relate socially in religious contexts.

This dimension includes several social institutions as well as the sense of belonging inculcated through socially experienced religious events. It focuses on issues such as leadership development and roles, gender relations and roles, and ethnic and religious affiliation. For the purposes of contextualization, four social institutions are found in every culture: association, kinship, education, and economics.

Association. The term *association* refers to the reality that a wide variety of groups and subgroups exists in every culture. They may be voluntary (clubs) or involuntary (caste). In Christian contexts, they include groups based on age (youth clubs), gender (women's guilds), education (alumni associations), ministry focus (mission agencies, churches), personal needs (Bible studies), institutionalization (committees), and so on. An understanding of the types of indigenous associations present and how they are organized is invaluable in ensuring that newly formed Christian associations are seen as indigenous rather than foreign.

Kinship. Kinship is a specialized form of association. All cultures recognize biological affiliations (including marriage) and the important role they play in continuing existence. Nearly everywhere the family (whether extended or nuclear) provides the basic context for socialization. Knowing kinship rules and expectations is essential for understanding such things as status, respect, and leadership roles and expectations (including nepotism) and dealing with ostracism (Muslim-background believers

345

CASE STUDY:
CAN A CHRISTIAN CELEBRATE DIWALI?

Simon P. David (Hiebert and Hiebert 1987, 84–85; used with permission)

It was Diwali time in India. As dusk began to settle over the village of Dipri in Uttar Pradesh, Victor Pakraj, a Christian missionary from Madras, trudged along the street to his home. His troubled mood was not lightened by the lights twinkling merrily from the little clay-pot lamps that decorated most of the homes he passed. In fact, they were part of his problem. He was trying to find an answer for the question Dhuwarak Prasad had asked him the night before.

Dhuwarak's voice had been respectful as always, but his eyes held almost a pleading look when he asked, "Why can't we light our house with beautiful little lamps and decorate our rooms at Diwali? Or, if we can't do it at our Hindu festival, could we do it at Christmas time?"

Two years had passed since Mr. and Mrs. Pakraj had come to Dipri from Tamilnadu. They had started their mission ministry by conducting Vacation Bible School. A handful of students participated, all of them from the Harijan community (untouchable caste that ranks at the bottom of the village society). During the summer, a number of them had accepted Christ as their Savior and Lord. Among these was twelve-year-old Dhuwarak Prasad. Dhuwarak's parents were happy for their son's conversion because they could see a real change in his life. In time, Mr. and Mrs. Prasad also wanted to become Christians, so they had come to the missionaries and were led to the Lord.

This had happened a few months before the annual Hindu festival of Diwali, which celebrates the victory of the god Siva over the powers of the evil god Narakhasura. The missionaries were encouraged by the Prasads' conversion and did their best to strengthen them in the faith. They visited the Prasads often and invited them to their own home as well. The Prasads had been socially ostracized by the other Harijans when they became Christians, so they

in need of a new family). All of these have a potential effect on church planting and development as well as social transformation.

Education. Education (formal, nonformal, and informal) is a facet of the socialization process. It refers to all activities that directly or indirectly contribute to providing new members, either by birth or by immigration, with the knowledge, values, and skills of a society. These are transmitted through educational processes to new members to prepare them to live and function within the society in a socially acceptable manner. Knowing indigenous educational systems and how they operate can be critical for developing relevant discipleship and ministerial training programs. For example, Sunday school and small group Bible studies may need to be radically different from those of a missionary's especially needed the fellowship of the missionaries and felt quite lonely when Victor Pakraj and his wife went to minister in other villages.

As Diwali approached, the villagers began to decorate their homes and prepare the many lamps they would place around them. They thatched their huts with new grass and bought new clothing to celebrate the festival, but this year, it was a depressing time for the Prasad family. Their own home was dark and undecorated. They were lonely and anxious for Mr. and Mrs. Pakraj to return from their ministry in a neighboring village. The missionaries finally returned on the evening of the day before the festival was to begin. The Prasad family had immediately gone to their house to welcome them home. It was while they were sitting together and Mrs. Pakraj was preparing the evening meal that Dhuwarak had asked the disturbing question. Mr. Pakraj had answered that he would think and pray about it. He invited the Prasad family to come again the following evening, and they would discuss it more.

As Mr. Pakraj neared his own home the next evening, he still was not sure exactly what he would say. He remembered that the first Christians in Europe had begun to celebrate the birth of Christ during the time of a pagan Festival of Winter because they were servants, and their masters gave them holidays at that time. After a while, the Christians had taken the pagan symbol of the evergreen tree decorated with lights and turned it into a symbol of their own evergreen hope for eternal life because of Jesus' coming into the world. Could the same kind of reinterpretation be applied to the Hindu festival of Diwali? Perhaps.

Victor Pakraj knew very well how important it was for new converts to make a clean break with Hinduism. If they did not really understand the difference, the Christian community might be absorbed back under the umbrella of Hinduism. Then its distinctiveness and its evangelical witness would be lost.

On the other hand, Mr. Pakraj also knew that he must help the Prasad family find a way to restore the joy of their salvation. He wondered just how he could do that.

home culture. At the very least, a missionary must understand the educational values and methods of the local setting so that those used for Christian education are indigenous rather than foreign.

Economics. Every culture must have a way of producing and distributing the goods and services that sustain the lives of its members. The institutions and roles organized around the performance of these activities constitute the economic system of the culture. Knowing the local economic system will be of great benefit, for example, in developing healthy churches that are not dependent on foreign economic assistance for survival. It also enables contextualization of a variety of exchanges that will reflect the Christian's biblical obligation to be generous. Further, models of communities that distributed wealth in the early church (e.g.,

Acts 4:32–5:10) can be used to help a local church find ways to engage in social transformation that reflects kingdom priorities.

THE MATERIAL DIMENSION

All religious systems of the world symbolically capture values and themes. Typically, they do so through artistic expression, whether architecture, art, ritualistic objects, or places. Smart includes as examples "buildings for worship and ritual, statuary and paintings, the dress and vestments of priests and so forth, books, amulets and the like, graves, burning-ghats [places in India where corpses are burned] and so on, sacrificial animals and the like" (1996, 277).

This is perhaps the area of greatest deficit for evangelical missionaries, especially the artistic expressions of faith. While missionaries certainly must be biblically faithful, they also should help churches in local settings express values, hopes, dreams, and aspirations in ways that make sense to them. This is an area that is being explored, but much more needs to be done. For help in thinking about areas from drama to visual arts to music, visit http://www.mislinks.org/practical/arts.htm.

Reference List

Aalen, S. 1971. *The New International Dictionary of New Testament Theology,* vol. 2, ed. Colin Brown, s.v. "Glory, Honor." Grand Rapids: Zondervan.

Adams, Eric, and Tim Lewis. 1990. "Making the Team! New Structures for Church Planting." *Mission Frontiers* 12 (December): 22–23.

Adeney, Bernard T. 1995. *Strange Virtues: Ethics in a Multicultural World.* Downers Grove, IL: InterVarsity.

Adeyemo, Tokunboh. 2000. "Profiling a Globalized and Evangelical Missiology." In *Global Missiology for the Twenty-first Century: The Iguassu Dialogue,* ed. William D. Taylor, 259–70. Grand Rapids: Baker.

Allen, C. Leonard. 1994. "Recovering the Economics of the Lamb: Affluence in Mission as an Eschatological Problem." *Journal of Applied Missiology* 5, no. 1 (April), http://bible.acu.edu/Missions/Page.Asp?ID=446 (accessed April 19, 2004).

Allen, Roland. 1962a. *Missionary Methods: St. Paul's or Ours?* Grand Rapids: Eerdmans.

———. 1962b. *The Spontaneous Expansion of the Church.* Grand Rapids: Eerdmans.

Anderson, Allan. 2001. *African Reformation: African Initiated Christianity in the Twentieth Century.* Trenton, NJ: Africa World Press.

Anderson, Gerald H., ed. 1998. *Biographical Dictionary of Christian Missions.* Grand Rapids: Eerdmans.

Anderson, Neil. 1990. *The Bondage Breaker.* Eugene, OR: Harvest House.

Anderson, Sarah, and John Cavanagh. 2000. "Top 200: The Rise of Global Corporate Power," http://www.ips-dc.org/reports/top200.htm (accessed June 28, 2004).

Anglican News Service. 2003. "A Statement by the Primates of the Anglican Communion Meeting in Lambeth Palace, 16 October 2003," http://www.anglicancommunion.org/acns/articles/36/25/acns3633.html (accessed April 20, 2004).

Ankeny, Jason. N.d. "Sinead O'Connor—Biography," http://launch.yahoo.com/ar-259638-bio--Sinead-OConnor (accessed February 22, 2005).

Araujo, Alex. 2000. "Globalization and World Evangelism." In *Global Missiology for the Twenty-first Century: The Iguassu Dialogue,* ed. William D. Taylor, 57–70. Grand Rapids: Baker.

Archer, Gleason L., Jr. 1979. "Contextualization: Some Implications from Life and Witness in the Old Testament." In *New Horizons in World Mission: Evangelicals and the Christian Mission in the 1980s: Papers Given at Trinity Consultation No. 2,* ed. David J. Hesselgrave, 199–216. Grand Rapids: Baker.

Arnold, Clinton. 1992. *Powers of Darkness.* Downers Grove, IL: InterVarsity.

———. 1997. *Three Crucial Questions about Spiritual Warfare.* Grand Rapids: Baker.

Aryeetey, Solomon. 1997. "The Road to Self-sufficiency in Africa's Missionary Development." *Evangelical Missions Quarterly* 33 (January): 34–38.

Athyal, Saphir. 1997. "The Old Testament Contextualisations." *World Evangelization Magazine* (September/October): 8–9.

Austin, James E. 2000. *The Collaboration Challenge: How Nonprofits and Businesses Succeed through Strategic Alliances.* San Francisco: Jossey-Bass.

Ayabe, Henry. 1992. *Step inside Japan: Language, Culture, Mission.* Tokyo: Japan Evangelical Mission, 1992.

Azevedo, Marcello de Carvalho. 1982. *Inculturation and the Challenges of Modernity.* Rome: Pontifical Gregorian University.

Baker, Dwight P. 2003. "William Carey and the Business Model for Mission." In *Between Past and Future: Evangelical Mission Entering the Twenty-first Century,* ed. Jonathan J. Bonk, 167–202. Evangelical Missiological Society Series, no. 10. Pasadena: William Carey Library.

Banks, Robert J. 1994. *Paul's Idea of Community: The Early Churches in Their Cultural Setting.* Rev. ed. Peabody, MA: Hendrickson.

———, and Julia Banks. 1998. *The Church Comes Home: Building Community and Mission through Home Churches.* Peabody, MA: Hendrickson.

Barber, Benjamin R. 1995. *Jihad vs. McWorld: Terrorism's Challenge to Democracy.* New York: Ballantine.

———. 1996. *Jihad vs. McWorld: How Globalization and Tribalism Are Reshaping the World.* New York: Ballantine.

Barbour, Ian G. 1974. *Myths, Models, and Paradigms: A Comparative Study in Science and Religion.* New York: Harper & Row.

Barnett, Mike. 2002. "Creative-Access Platforms: What Are They and Why Do We Need Them?" Paper Presented at EMS Regional Meeting, Dallas, March 9.

Barrett, David B. 1968. *Schism and Renewal in Africa.* Nairobi, Kenya: Oxford University Press.

———, ed. 1982. *World Christian Encyclopedia: A Comparative Survey of Churches and Religions in the Modern World, AD 1900–2000.* New York: Oxford University Press.

———, and Todd M. Johnson. 2004. "Annual Statistical Table on Global Mission: 2004." *International Bulletin of Missionary Research* 28 (January): 24–25.

———, and Todd M. Johnson, eds. 2001. *World Christian Trends, AD 30–AD 2200: Interpreting the Annual Christian Megacensus.* Pasadena: William Carey Library.

———, G. T. Kurian, and Todd M. Johnson, eds. 2001. *World Christian Encyclopedia: A Comparative Survey of Churches and Religions in the Modern World, AD 1900–2000.* 2nd ed. New York: Oxford University Press.

———, and James W. Reapsome. 1988. *Seven Hundred Plans to Evangelize the World: The Rise of a Global Evangelization Movement.* Birmingham, AL: New Hope.

Bavinck, Johann H. 1960. *An Introduction to the Science of Missions.* Trans. David H. Freeman. Phillipsburg, NJ: Presbyterian & Reformed.

Baylies, C. 2002. "The Impact of AIDS on Rural Households in Africa: A Shock Like Any Other?" *Development and Change* 33, no. 4: 611–32.

Bediako, Kwame. 1995. *Christianity in Africa: The Renewal of a Non-Western Religion.* Maryknoll, NY: Orbis.

Befus, David R. 2001. *Kingdom Business: The Ministry of Promoting Economic Activity.* Miami: Latin America Mission.

Berger, Peter L., ed. 1999. *The Desecularization of the World: Resurgent Religion and World Politics.* Grand Rapids: Eerdmans.

Bevans, Stephen B. 1992. *Models of Contextual Theology.* Maryknoll, NY: Orbis.

Beyerhaus, Peter. 1975. "Possessio and Syncretism in Biblical Perspective." In *Christopaganism or Indigenous Christianity?* ed. Tetsunao Yamamori and Charles Russell Taber, 119–42. Pasadena: William Carey Library.

Bonilla, Joshua. 2001. "Executive Summary: World Population Trends," http://www.prcdc.org/summaries/worldpopupdate02/worldpopupdate02.html (accessed April 20, 2004).

Bonk, Jonathan J. 1991. *Missions and Money: Affluence as a Western Missionary Problem.* Maryknoll, NY: Orbis.

———. 2000. "Thinking Small, Global Missions, and American Companies." *Missiology: An International Review* 28 (April): 149–61.

———, ed. 2003. *Between Past and Future: Evangelical Mission Entering the Twenty-first Century.* Evangelical Missiological Society Series, no. 10. Pasadena: William Carey Library.

Bosch, David J. 1991. *Transforming Mission: Paradigm Shifts in Theology of Mission.* Maryknoll, NY: Orbis.

Bretall, Robert, ed. 1946. *A Kierkegaard Anthology.* New York: Random House.

Brewster, D. 2003. "Children 'At Risk' Because They Have Not Heard the Good News: The 4/14 Window." In *Celebrating Children: Equipping People Working with Children and Young People Living in Difficult Circumstances around the World,* ed. G. Miles and J. J. Wright, 175–82. Cumbria, UK: Paternoster.

Brierley, Peter, ed. 1998–99. *UK Christian Handbook.* London: Christian Research.

Bromiley, Geoffrey W. 1985. *Theological Dictionary of the New Testament.* Grand Rapids: Eerdmans.

Brueggemann, Walter. 1993. *Notes under Negotiation: The Bible and Postmodern Imagination.* Minneapolis: Fortress.

Bubeck, Mark. 1991. *The Satanic Revival.* San Bernadino, CA: Here's Life Publishers.

Buhlman, W. 1986. *The Church of the Future: A Model for the Year 2000.* Maryknoll, NY: Orbis.

Burt, Ronald S., and Michael J. Minor, eds. 1983. *Applied Network Analysis.* Beverly Hills: Sage Publications.

Bush, Luis. 2000. "Where Are We Now?" *Mission Frontiers* 22 (June): 12–19.

———. 2002. "Catalysts of World Evangelization." Ph.D. diss., Fuller Theological Seminary, School of World Mission.

———. 2003. "The A.D. 2000 Movement." In *Between Past and Future: Evangelical Missions Entering the Twenty-first Century,* ed. Jonathan J. Bonk, 17–36. Pasadena: William Carey Library.

———, and Lorry Lutz. 1990. *Partnering in Ministry: The Direction of World Evangelism.* Downers Grove, IL: InterVarsity.

Buswell, James Oliver, III. 1978. "Contextualization: Theory, Tradition, and Method." In *Theology and Mission: Papers Given at Trinity Consultation No. 1,* ed. David J. Hesselgrave, 87–111. Grand Rapids: Baker.

Butler, Robby. 1995. "Edinburgh '80: The Roots of a Movement." *Mission Frontiers* (July–August), http://www.missionfrontiers.org/1995/0708/ja953.htm (accessed April 23, 2004).

351

Caldwell, Deborah Kovach. 1998. "A Spiritual Base: World Prayer Center Arms Itself with Technology in Evangelical Quest to Spread Its Message of Faith." *Dallas Morning News*, September 17, 26A.

Calver, Clive. 1999. "Postmodernism: An Evangelical Blind Spot?" *Evangelical Missions Quarterly* 35 (October): 430–31.

Campbell, Jonathan. 1999. "Postmodernism: Ripe for a Global Harvest—But Is the Church Ready?" *Evangelical Missions Quarterly* 35 (October): 432–37.

Campolo, Tony. 2004. *Speaking My Mind: The Radical Evangelical Prophet Tackles the Tough Issues Christians Are Afraid to Face.* Nashville: Thomas Nelson.

Careaga, Andrew, and Leonard Sweet. 2001. *eMinistry: Connecting with the Net Generation.* Grand Rapids: Kregel.

Carey, William. 1792. *An Enquiry into the Obligations of Christians to Use Means for the Conversion of the Heathens.* Leicester, UK: Ann Ireland.

Carson, D. A. 1987. "Church and Mission: Reflections on Contextualization and the Third Horizon." In *The Church in the Bible and the World: An International Study,* ed. D. A. Carson, 213–57. Grand Rapids: Baker.

———. 1996. *The Gagging of God: Christianity Confronts Pluralism.* Grand Rapids: Zondervan.

Chiang, Samuel E. 1992. "Partnership at the Crossroads: Red, Yellow, or Green Light?" *Evangelical Missions Quarterly* 28 (July): 284–89.

Cho, David. 2002. "Evangelicals Help Pace U.S. Growth in Church Attendance." *Washington Post*, September 17, A3.

Cho, Paul Yonggi. 1981. *Successful Home Cell Groups.* Plainfield, NJ: Logos International.

CNN.com. 2004a. "From Gang Leader to Strong Leader," http://www.CNN.com (accessed January 3, 2004).

———. 2004b. "Heather Mercer and Dayna Curry Profile," http://www.cnn.com/CNN/Programs/people/shows/curry.mercer/profile.html (accessed April 22, 2004).

Cockburn, Andrew. 2003. "Twenty-first Century Slaves." *National Geographic* 204, no. 3 (September): 2–25.

Coe, Shoki. 1976. "Contextualizing Theology." In *Mission Trends No 3: Third World Theologies,* ed. Gerald H. Anderson and Thomas F. Stransky, 19–24. New York: Paulist Press.

Conn, Harvie M. 1984. *Eternal Word and Changing Worlds: Theology, Anthropology, and Mission in Trialogue.* Phillipsburg, NJ: Presbyterian & Reformed.

———. 2000. *Evangelical Dictionary of World Missions,* gen. ed. A. Scott Moreau, s.v. "Indigenization." Grand Rapids: Baker.

Costas, Orlando E. 1974. *The Church and Its Mission: A Shattering Critique from the Third World.* Wheaton: Tyndale.

Cox, John. 1997. "The Tentmaking Movement in Historical Perspective." *International Journal of Frontier Missions* 14, no. 3 (July–September): 111–18.

Cox, Monte. 1999. "'Euthanasia of Mission' Or 'Partnership'? An Evaluative Study of the Disengagement Policies of Church of Christ Missionaries in Rural Kenya." Ph.D. diss., Trinity Evangelical Divinity School.

Crossroads International Church. 2004. "Our Story," http://www.xrds.nl/about.asp (accessed February 14, 2004).

Danker, William J. 1971. *Profit for the Lord: Economic Activities in Moravian Missions and the Basel Mission Trading Company.* Grand Rapids: Eerdmans.

DAWN Ministries. 2004. "Frequently Asked Questions," http://www.dawnministries.org/learn/faq.html (accessed February 7, 2004).

Dayton, Edward R., and David A. Fraser. 1990. *Planning Strategies for World Evangelization*. Rev. ed. Monrovia, CA: MARC.

DeLung, Jane S., and Becca Jones. 2003. "Executive Summary: International Migration," http://www.prcdc.org/summaries/intlmigration/intlmigration.html (accessed April 20, 2004).

Dickason, C. Fred. 1975. *Demon Possession and the Christian: A New Perspective*. Chicago: Moody.

Dixon, Larry. 1992. *The Other Side of the Good News: Confronting the Contemporary Challenges to Jesus' Teaching on Hell*. Grand Rapids: Baker.

Donovan, Vincent J. 2003. *Christianity Rediscovered*. Twenty-fifth anniversay ed. Maryknoll, NY: Orbis.

Douglas, J. D., ed. 1975. *Let the Earth Hear His Voice: The Proceedings of the Lausanne Committee on World Evangelism*. Minneapolis: World Wide Publications.

Dowsett, Rose. 2000. "Dry Bones in the West." In *Global Missiology for the Twenty-first Century: The Iguassu Dialogue*, ed. William D. Taylor, 447–62. Grand Rapids: Baker.

D'Souza, Joseph. 2000. "The Indian Church and Missions Face the Saffronization Challenge." In *Global Missiology for the Twenty-first Century: The Iguassu Dialogue*, ed. William D. Taylor, 391–406. Grand Rapids: Baker.

———. 2002. "A Report and Analysis after Three Months of the Dalit Revival." Dalit Update no. 2. Email (March).

Dyrness, William A. 1992. *Invitation to Cross-Cultural Theology*. Grand Rapids: Zondervan.

Edwards, Jonathan. 1741. "Sinners in the Hands of an Angry God," http://www.jonathan edwards.com/sermons/Warnings/sinners.htm (accessed February 14, 2005).

———. 1832. *A Narrative of Many Surprising Conversions in Northampton and Vicinity*. Worcester, MA: Moses W. Grout.

EFMA. 2004. "EFMA in Brief," http://community.gospelcom.net/Brix?pageID=7163 (accessed February 21, 2004).

Elder, Brett. 2003. "Dismantling the Ecclesiastical Welfare System." *Occasional Bulletin of the Evangelical Missiological Society* 15 (Fall): 1–2, 5.

Elkins, Phil. 1964. *Toward a More Effective Mission Work*. Dallas: Christian Publishing.

Elliot, Elisabeth. 1958. *Through Gates of Splendor*. New York: Harper & Row.

Endo, Shusako. 1976. *Silence*. New York: Taplinger Publishing.

———. 1982. *Samurai*. New York: Harper & Row.

Engelsviken, Tormod. 2001. *Spiritual Conflict in Today's Mission: A Report from the Consultation on "Deliver Us from Evil," Nairobi, Kenya, August 2000*. Lausanne Occasional Papers no. 29. Monrovia, CA: Lausanne Committee for World Evangelization.

Escobar, Samuel. 1994. "Missions and the New World Order." *Christianity Today*, July–December, 38, 48–52.

———. 2000a. "Evangelical Missiology: Peering into the Future at the Turn of the Century." In *Global Missiology for the Twenty-first Century: The Iguassu Dialogue*, ed. William D. Taylor, 101–22. Grand Rapids: Baker.

———. 2000b. "The Global Scenario at the Turn of the Century." In *Global Missiology for the Twenty-first Century: The Iguassu Dialogue*, ed. William D. Taylor, 25–46. Grand Rapids: Baker.

———. 2003. "Migration: Avenue and Challenge to Mission." *Missiology: An International Review* 31 (January): 17–28.

Esler, J. Ted, and C. Douglas McConnell. 2003. "Technological Solutions to Missionary Problems." *Evangelical Missions Quarterly* 39 (January): 40–48.

Evans, Tony. 1998. *The Battle Is the Lord's*. Chicago: Moody.

Fernando, Ajith. 2000. "Grounding Our Reflections in Scripture: Biblical Trinitarianism and Mission." In *Global Missiology for the Twenty-first Century: The Iguassu Dialogue*, ed. William D. Taylor, 189–256. Grand Rapids: Baker.

Field, David H. 1995. *New Dictionary of Christian Ethics and Pastoral Theology*, ed. David J. Atkinson and David H. Field, s.v. "Hospitality." Downers Grove, IL: InterVarsity.

Finley, Bob. 1999. "Send Dollars and Sense: Why Giving Is Often Better Than Going." *Christianity Today*, October 4, 73–75.

Fischer, Claude S. 1982. *To Dwell among Friends: Personal Networks in Town and City*. Chicago: University of Chicago Press.

———. 1984. *The Urban Experience*. 2nd ed. New York: Harcourt Brace Jovanovich.

Fisher, Fred Lewis. 2001. *Evangelical Dictionary of Theology*, 2nd ed., ed. Walter A. Elwell, s.v. "Stewardship." Grand Rapids: Baker.

Fleming, Bruce. 1980. *Contextualization of Theology: An Evangelical Assessment*. Pasadena: William Carey Library.

Ford, Leighton. 1990. Foreword to *Proclaim Christ Until He Comes: Calling the Whole Church to Take the Whole Gospel to the Whole World*, ed. J. D. Douglas, 10. Minneapolis: World Wide Publications.

Foster, Geoff, ed. 2003. "Study of the Response of Faith-Based Organizations to Orphans and Vulnerable Children: Preliminary Summary Report," http://sara.aed.org/ovc-tc/documents/day1/afternoon/6%20Cairns%20J--%20WCRP%20FBO%20Study.ppt (accessed April 20, 2004).

Fouch, Steven. 2003. "Globalization and Healthcare Mission." In *One World or Many? The Impact of Globalisation on Mission*, ed. Richard Tiplady, 123–42. Pasadena: William Carey Library.

Friedman, Thomas L. 1999. *The Lexus and the Olive Tree: Understanding Globalization*. New York: Farrar, Straus, Giroux.

———. 2000. "A Manifesto for the First World." In *Globalization*, ed. Katrin Sjursen, 7. New York: H. W. Wilson.

Friere, Paulo. 1986. *Pedagogy of the Oppressed*. Trans. Myra B. Ramos. New York: Continuum.

Frontiers. 2004. "About Frontiers," http://www.frontiers.org/about/index.htm (accessed February 14, 2004).

Fudge, Edward. 1994. *The Fire That Consumes: The Biblical Case for Conditional Immortality*. Cumbria, UK: Paternoster.

Garrison, David. 1990. *The Nonresidential Missionary*. Monrovia, CA: MARC.

———. 1999. *Church Planting Movements*. Richmond: International Mission Board of Southern Baptist Convention.

———. 2004. *Church Planting Movements: How God Is Redeeming a Lost World*. Midlothian, VA: WIGTake Resources.

GCOWE. 1997. "GCOWE '97 Business Executives Consultation Declaration," http://www.ad2000.org/gcowe97/Becdecl.htm (accessed March 8, 2004).

George, Sam. 2003a. "Emerging Youth Cultures in the Era of Globalization: TechnoCulture and TerrorCulture." In *One World or Many? The Impact of Globalisation on Mission,* ed. Richard Tiplady, 33–54. Pasadena: William Carey Library.

———. 2003b. "Missions in a Borderless World." *Connections* (June): 18–22.

George, Timothy. 1991. *Faithful Witness: The Life and Mission of William Carey.* Birmingham, AL: New Hope.

Gerstner, John H. 1990. *Repent or Perish: With a Special Reference to the Conservative Attack on Hell.* Morgan, PA: Soli Deo Gloria.

Gibbs, Eddie. 2000. *Church Next: Quantum Changes in How We Do Ministry.* Downers Grove, IL: InterVarsity.

Gifford, Kathie Lee. 2004. *Gentle Grace: Reflections and Scriptures on God's Gentle Grace.* Grand Rapids: Zondervan-Inspirio.

Gilliland, Dean. 1998. "Context Is Crucial in 'Islampur' Case." *Evangelical Missions Quarterly* 34 (October): 415–17.

Gillman, Ian, and Hans-Joachim Klimkeit. 1999. *Christians in Asia before 1500.* Ann Arbor: University of Michigan Press.

Glasser, Arthur F. 1979. "Help from an Unexpected Quarter or, the Old Testament and Contextualization." *Missiology: An International Review* 7 (October): 403–10.

Gleick, James. 2000. *Faster: The Acceleration of Just about Everything.* New York: Vintage Books.

Goudzwaard, Bob. 2001. *Globalization and the Kingdom of God.* Grand Rapids: Baker.

Gould, Melissa. 2001. "Executive Summary: The Status of Women around the World," http://www.prcdc.org/summaries/women/women.html (accessed April 20, 2004).

Granovetter, Mark. 1982. "The Strength of Weak Ties: A Network Theory Revisited." In *Social Structure and Network Analysis,* ed. P. V. Marsden and N. Lin, 105–30. Beverly Hills: Sage Publications.

Gration, John. 1983. "Willowbank to Zaire: The Doing of Theology." *Missiology: An International Review* 12 (January): 95–112.

Greenway, Roger S. 1992. "Eighteen Barrels and Two Big Crates." *Evangelical Missions Quarterly* 28 (April): 126–32.

Grogan, G. W. 1995. *New Dictionary of Christian Ethics and Pastoral Theology,* ed. David J. Atkinson and David H. Field, s.v. "Image of God." Downers Grove, IL: InterVarsity.

Guder, Darrell L., ed. 1998. *Missional Church: A Vision for the Sending of the Church in North America.* Grand Rapids: Eerdmans.

Gumbel, Nicky. 1999. *The Alpha Course Manual.* Brompton, UK: Holy Trinity Brompton.

Guthrie, Stan. 2000. *Missions in the Third Millennium: Twenty-one Key Trends for the Twenty-first Century.* Waynesboro, GA: Paternoster.

Gutiérrez, Gustavo. 1973. *A Theology of Liberation: History, Politics, and Salvation.* Maryknoll, NY: Orbis.

Haleblian, Krikor. 1983. "The Problem of Contextualization." *Missiology: An International Review* 11 (January): 95–111.

Hamilton, Don. 1987. *Tentmakers Speak: Practical Advice from Over Four Hundred Tentmakers.* Duarte, CA: TMQ Research.

Hamilton, Michael S., and Jennifer McKinney. 2003. "Turning the Mainline Around." *Christianity Today,* August, 34–40.

Hanciles, J. J. 2003. "Migration and Mission: Some Implications for the Twenty-first Century Church." *International Bulletin of Missionary Research* 27 (October): 146–53.

Harmon, Kendall. 1992. "The Case against Conditionalism: A Response to Edward William Fudge." In *Universalism and the Doctrine of Hell: Papers Presented at the Fourth Edinburgh Conference in Christian Dogmatics, 1991*, ed. Nigel M. De S. Cameroon, 193–224. Grand Rapids: Baker.

Haugen, Gary A. 1999. *Good News about Injustice: A Witness of Courage in a Hurting World.* Downers Grove, IL: InterVarsity.

Hertig, Young Lee. 2000. *Evangelical Dictionary of World Missions,* gen. ed. A. Scott Moreau, s.v. "Liminality." Grand Rapids: Baker.

Hesselgrave, David J. 1984. "Contextualization and Revelational Epistemology." In *Hermeneutics, Inerrancy, and the Bible,* ed. Earl D. Radmacher and Robert D. Preus, 693–738. Grand Rapids: Zondervan.

———. 1988. *Today's Choices for Tomorrow's Mission: An Evangelical Perspective on Trends and Issues in Missions.* Grand Rapids: Zondervan.

———. 2004. "Traditional Religions, New Religions, and the Communication of the Christian Faith." In *Encountering New Religious Movements: A Holistic Evangelical Approach,* ed. Irving Hexham, Stephen Rost, and John W. Moreland, 137–56. Grand Rapids: Kregel.

———, and Edward Rommen. 1989. *Contextualization: Meanings, Methods, and Models.* Grand Rapids: Baker.

Hexham, Irving, and Karla Poewe-Hexham. 2004. "New Religions as Global Cultures." In *Encountering New Religious Movements: A Holistic Evangelical Approach,* ed. Irving Hexham, Stephen Rost, and John W. Moreland, 91–111. Grand Rapids: Kregel.

Hiebert, Paul G. 1982. "The Flaw of the Excluded Middle." *Missiology: An International Review* 10 (January): 35–47.

———. 1984. "Critical Contextualization." *Missiology: An International Review* 12 (July): 287–96.

———. 1985. *Anthropological Insights for Missionaries.* Grand Rapids: Baker.

———. 1987. "Critical Contextualization." *International Bulletin of Missionary Research* 11 (July): 104–11.

———. 1994. *Anthropological Reflection on Missiological Issues.* Grand Rapids: Baker.

———. 1999. *Missiological Implications of Epistemological Shifts: Affirming Truth in a Modern/Postmodern World.* Harrisburg, PA: Trinity Press International.

———. 2000. "Missiological Issues in the Encounter with Emerging Hinduism." *Missiology: An International Review* 28 (January): 47–64.

———, and Francis Hiebert, eds. 1987. *Case Studies in Missions.* Grand Rapids: Baker.

———, Daniel Shaw, and Tite Tiénou. 1999. *Understanding Folk Religion: A Christian Response to Popular Beliefs and Practices.* Grand Rapids: Baker.

Hillerbrand, Hans J. 1964. *The Reformation.* New York: Harper & Row.

Himes, Judith, and Angelique Olmo. 2002. "Executive Summary: International Youth," http://www.prcdc.org/summaries/intlyouth/intlyouth.html (accessed April 20, 2004).

Hocking, William E. 1932. *Rethinking Missions.* New York: Harper & Brothers.

Hodges, Melvin L. 1957. *On the Mission Field: The Indigenous Church.* Chicago: Moody.

Hoefer, Herbert. 1991. *Churchless Christianity.* Pasadena: William Carey Library.

———. 2001. "Why Are Christians Persecuted in India? Root, Reasons, Responses." *International Journal of Frontier Missions* 18, no. 1 (Spring): 7–13.

Hofstadter, Richard. 1963. *Anti-intellectualism in American Life.* New York: Random House.

Honko, Lauri. 1984. "The Problem of Defining Myth." In *Sacred Narrative: Readings in the Theory of Myth*, ed. Alan Dundes, 41–52. Berkeley: University of California Press.

Howard, David M. 1979. *Student Power in World Evangelism*. Downers Grove, IL: InterVarsity.

———. 1999. "Student Power in World Missions." In *Perspectives on the World Christian Movement: A Reader*, 3rd ed., ed. Ralph D. Winter and Steven C. Hawthorne, 227–86. Pasadena: William Carey Library.

———. 2003. "An Army of One." *World Pulse* 38, no. 9 (May 30): 7.

Hughes, Philip E. 1962. *Paul's Second Epistle to the Corinthians*. New Commentary on the New Testament Series. Grand Rapids: Eerdmans.

———. 1989. *The True Image: The Origin and Destiny of Man in Christ*. Grand Rapids: Eerdmans.

Hunsberger, George. 2000. *Evangelical Dictionary of World Missions*, gen. ed. A. Scott Moreau, s.v. "Accommodation." Grand Rapids: Baker.

Huntington, Samuel P. 1993. "The Clash of Civilizations." *Foreign Affairs* 72, no. 3 (Summer): 22–49.

———. 1996. *The Clash of Civilizations and the Remaking of World Order*. New York: Touchstone Books.

Illich, Ivan. 1970. *De-Schooling Society*. Garden City, NY: Doubleday.

International Mission Board. 1995. *Roads Less Traveled: Journey into World A*. Videocassette.

International Teams. 2004. "General Facts," http://www.iteams.org/about/facts.html (accessed February 14, 2004).

Jaffarian, Michael. 2002. "The Statistical State of the Missionary Enterprise." *Missiology: An International Review* 30 (January): 16–31.

Jenkins, Philip. 2002. *The Next Christendom: The Coming of Global Christianity*. New York: Oxford University Press.

Jewell, John P., Jr. 2002. *New Tools for a New Century: First Steps for Equipping Your Church for the Digital Revolution*. Nashville: Abingdon.

Johnstone, Patrick. 1998. *The Church Is Bigger Than You Think*. Bulstrode Bucks, UK: WEC International.

———, and Jason Mandryk, eds. 2001. *Operation World: The Day-by-Day Guide to Praying for the Whole World*. Twenty-first century ed. Bulstrode Bucks, UK: WEC International.

Jones, Dale E., Sherri Doty, Clifford Grammich, James E. Horsch, Richard Houseal, Mac Lynn, John P. Marcum, Kenneth M. Sanchagrin, and Richard H. Taylor. 2000. *Religious Congregations and Membership in the United States*. Cincinnati: Glenmary Research Center.

Jongeneel, J. A. B. 2003. "The Mission of Migrant Churches in Europe." *Missiology: An International Review* 31 (January): 29–33.

Jordan, Ivan, and Frank Tucker. 2002. "Using Indigenous Art to Communicate the Christian Message." *Evangelical Missions Quarterly* 38 (July): 302–9.

Kaiser, Walter C. 1996. "The Great Commission in the Old Testament." *International Journal of Frontier Missions* 13 (January–March): 3–7.

———. 1999. "Israel's Missionary Call." In *Perspectives on the World Christian Movement: A Reader*, 3rd ed., ed. Ralph D. Winter and Steven C. Hawthorne, 10–16. Pasadena: William Carey Library.

———. 2000. *Mission in the Old Testament: Israel as a Light to the Nations.* Grand Rapids: Baker.

Kane, J. Herbert. 1976. *Understanding Christian Missions.* Rev. ed. Grand Rapids: Baker.

———. 1980. *Life and Work on the Mission Field.* Grand Rapids: Baker.

———. 1981. *The Christian World Mission: Today and Tomorrow.* Grand Rapids: Baker.

———. 1986. *Wanted: World Christians.* Grand Rapids: Baker.

Kasdorf, Hans. 1979. "Indigenous Church Principles: A Survey of Origin and Development." In *Readings in Dynamic Indigeneity,* ed. Charles Kraft, 71–86. Pasadena: William Carey Library.

Kato, Byang H. 1975a. "The Gospel, Cultural Context, and Religious Syncretism." In *Let the Earth Hear His Voice,* ed. J. D. Douglas, 1216–28. Minneapolis: World Wide Publications.

———. 1975b. *Theological Pitfalls in Africa.* Kisumu, Kenya: Evangel Publishing House.

Katzenbach, Jon R. 1998. *Teams at the Top: Unleashing the Potential of Both Teams and Individual Leaders.* Boston: Harvard Business School Press.

———. 2000. *Peak Performance: Aligning the Hearts and Minds of Your Employees.* Boston: Harvard Business School Press.

———, and Douglas K. Smith. 1993. *The Wisdom of Teams: Creating High-Performance Organization.* New York: HarperCollins.

———, and Douglas K. Smith. 2001. *The Discipline of Teams: A Mindbook-Workbook for Delivering Small Group Performance.* New York: John Wiley & Sons.

Keller, Tim. 1997. "Preaching Hell in a Tolerant Age: Brimstone for the Broad-minded," *Leadership* 18 (Fall), http://www.ctlibrary.com/le/1997/Fall/714042.html (accessed April 22, 2004).

Kennedy, James. 1983. *Evangelism Explosion.* 3rd ed. Wheaton: Tyndale.

Keyes, Larry. 1994. "OC International in an Indian Partnership." In *Kingdom Partnerships for Synergy in Missions,* ed. William D. Taylor, 229–35. Pasadena: William Carey Library.

Kinsler, F. Ross. 1978. "Mission and Context: The Current Debate about Contextualization." *Evangelical Missions Quarterly* 14 (January): 23–29.

Klaus, Byron D. 2000. *Evangelical Dictionary of World Missions,* gen. ed. A. Scott Moreau, s.v. "Marginal, Marginalized." Grand Rapids: Baker.

Klostermaier, Klaus K. 1989. *A Survey of Hinduism.* Albany: State University of New York Press.

Koyama, Kosuke. 1979. *Three Mile an Hour God.* Maryknoll, NY: Orbis.

Kraft, Charles H. 1989. *Christianity with Power: Your Worldview and Your Experience of the Supernatural.* Ann Arbor: Vine Books.

———. 1992. *Defeating Dark Angels: Breaking Demonic Oppression in the Believer's Life.* Ann Arbor: Vine Books.

———. 1995. "'Christian Animism' or God-Given Authority?" In *Spiritual Power and Missions: Raising the Issues,* ed. Edward Rommen, 88–136. Evangelical Missiological Society Series no. 3. Pasadena: William Carey Library.

———. 2002a. "Contemporary Trends in the Treatment of Spiritual Conflict." In *Deliver Us from Evil: An Uneasy Frontier in Christian Mission,* ed. A. Scott Moreau, Tokunboh Adeyemo, David Burnett, Bryant Myers, and Hwa Yung, 177–202. Monrovia, CA: MARC.

———. 2002b. "Contextualization and Spiritual Power." In *Deliver Us from Evil: An Uneasy Frontier in Christian Mission*, ed. A. Scott Moreau, Tokunboh Adeyemo, David Burnett, Bryant Myers, and Hwa Yung, 290–308. Monrovia, CA: MARC.

Krass, Alfred C. 1979. "Contextualization for Today." *Gospel in Context* 2, no. 3: 27–30.

Kristof, Nicholas D. 2003a. "Believe It, or Not." *New York Times*, August 15, A29.

———. 2003b. "God on Their Side." *New York Times*, http://query.nytimes.com/gst/abstract .html?res=F20B17FA38590C748EDDA00894DB404482 (accessed April 21, 2004).

Kuhn, Thomas S. 1970. *The Structure of Scientific Revolutions*. Chicago: University of Chicago Press.

Lane, William L. 1974. *The Gospel of Mark*. New International Commentary on the Bible. Grand Rapids: Eerdmans.

LaPierre, Dominique. 1990. *Beyond Love*. New York: Warner Books.

Larkin, William J. 1988. *Culture and Biblical Hermeneutics: Interpreting and Applying the Authoritative Word in a Relative Age*. Grand Rapids: Baker.

Larsen, Samuel H. 2002. "Early Asian Christianity and Buddhism." Paper presented at the Evangelical Missiological Society Regional Meeting, Dallas, March 15.

Latourette, Kenneth Scott. 1939. *A History of the Expansion of Christianity*. Vol. 3, *Three Centuries of Advance, A.D. 1500–A.D. 1800*. New York: Harper & Brothers.

Lausanne Committee for World Evangelization. 1974. The Lausanne Covenant, http://www .gospelcom.net/lcwe/statements/covenant.html (accessed April 24, 2004).

———. 1989. The Manila Manifesto, http://www.gospelcom.net/lcwe/statements/manila .html (accessed April 24, 2004).

Lencioni, Patrick M. 2002. *The Five Dysfunctions of a Team: A Leadership Fable*. San Francisco: Jossey-Bass.

Leonard, John S. 2004. "The Church between Cultures: Rethinking the Church in the Light of the Globalization of Immigration." *Evangelical Missions Quarterly* 40 (January): 62–70.

Lester, Toby. 2002. "Oh, God." *Atlantic Monthly* (February): 37–45.

Lewis, C. S. 1949. *The Weight of Glory and Other Addresses*. Grand Rapids: Eerdmans.

Linder, John. 2002. "Indigenous Missions for the Twenty-first Century." *Indigenous Mission* (Fall): 1, 3–4.

Lindsell, Harold. 1976. *The Battle for the Bible*. Grand Rapids: Zondervan.

Linn, David Bruce. 2000. "The Glory of God in Missions," http://www.breakfree.org/pages/ sermons/glorygod.htm (accessed April 22, 2004).

Lipman-Blumen, Jean, and Harold J. Leavitt. 1999. *Hot Groups: Seeding Them, Feeding Them, and Using Them to Ignite Your Organization*. New York: Oxford University Press.

Livingstone, Greg. 1993. *Planting Churches in Muslim Cities: A Team Approach*. Grand Rapids: Baker.

Love, Rick. 2000. *Muslims, Magic, and the Kingdom of God*. Pasadena: William Carey Library.

Lowe, Chuck. 1998. *Territorial Spirits and World Evangelisation?* Sevenoaks, UK: OMF.

Luther, Martin. N.d. *The Freedom of a Christian*, http://www.wsu.edu/~dee/reform/freedom .htm (accessed April 22, 2004).

Luzbetak, Louis J. 1988. *The Church and Cultures: New Perspectives in Missiological Anthropology*. Maryknoll, NY: Orbis.

Lyotard, François. 1984. *The Postmodern Condition: A Report on Knowledge*. Trans. Geoff Bennington and Brian Massouri. Minneapolis: University of Minnesota Press.

MAF. 2004. "What We Do," http://www.maf.org/about/index.html (accessed February 21, 2004).

Mangalwadi, Vishal. 2001. "An Indian Constantine?" *International Journal of Frontier Missiology* 18 (Spring): 19–22.

Mann, J. M., D. Taratola, and T. W. Netter, eds. 1992. *AIDS in the World*. Cambridge: Harvard University Press.

MAP International. 2004. "Journey to Hope," http://www.map.org/main.asp?menu=3&submenu=99&page=programs/features/AIDSjourney.inc (accessed April 20, 2004).

Maranz, David. 2001. *African Friends and Money Matters*. Dallas: SIL International and International Museum of Cultures.

Mars Hill Publications. 2002. "The Hope: God's Promise for All People," http://www.thehopevideo.com (accessed April 24, 2004).

Martin, Marie-Louise. 1978. "Kimbanguism: A Prophet and His Church." In *Dynamic Religious Movements: Case Studies of Rapidly Growing Religious Movements around the World*, ed. David Hesselgrave, 41–64. Grand Rapids: Baker.

Massey, Joshua. 2004. "Misunderstandings of C5." *Evangelical Missions Quarterly* 40 (July): 296–306.

Mbiti, John S. 1970. *African Religions and Philosophy*. New York: Doubleday.

———. 1976. "Theological Impotence and the Universality of the Church." In *Missions Trends Three: Third World Theologies*, ed. Gerald H. Anderson and Thomas Stransky, 6–18. New York: Paulist Press.

McClain, Alva J. 1968. *The Greatness of the Kingdom*. Chicago: Moody.

McConnell, C. Douglas. 1990. "Networks and Associations in Urban Mission: A Port Moresby Case Study." Ph.D. diss., Fuller Theological Seminary, School of World Mission.

———. 1997a. "Confronting Racism and Prejudice in Our Kind of People." *Missiology: An International Review* 25 (October): 388–404.

———, ed. 1997b. *The Holy Spirit and Mission Dynamics*. Pasadena: William Carey Library.

———. 2002a. "Issues of International Stewardship." Unpublished paper by the International Director, Pioneers, Orlando.

———, ed. 2002b. "The Internationalization of Pioneers: A Critical Review of the Issues." Unpublished paper by the International Coordinating Team, Pioneers, Orlando.

McDonald, Patrick. 2003. "Practical and Spiritual Lessons for the Church." In *Celebrating Children: Equipping People Working with Children and Young People Living in Difficult Circumstances around the World*, ed. G. Miles and J. J. Wright, 150–62. Cumbria, UK: Paternoster.

———, and E. Garrow. 2000. *Reaching Children in Need: What's Being Done—What You Can Do*. Eastbourne, UK: Kingsway.

McDowell, Josh. 1999. *More Evidence That Demands a Verdict: Historical Evidences for the Christian Scriptures*. San Bernadino, CA: Here's Life Publishers.

McGavran, Donald. 1975. "The Dimensions of World Evangelism." In *Let the Earth Hear His Voice: The Proceedings of the Lausanne Committee on World Evangelism*, ed. J. D. Douglas, 94–107. Minneapolis: Worldwide Publications.

———. 1979. *Understanding Church Growth*. 3rd ed. Grand Rapids: Eerdmans.

McIlwain, Trevor. 1987. *Building on Firm Foundations.* Vol. 1, *Guidelines for Evangelism and Teaching Believers.* Sanford, FL: New Tribes Mission.

———. 1991. *Firm Foundations: Creation to Christ.* Sanford, FL: New Tribes Mission.

McIntosh, John A. 2000a. *Evangelical Dictionary of World Missions,* gen. ed. A. Scott Moreau, s.v. "Christo-Paganism." Grand Rapids: Baker.

———. 2000b. *Evangelical Dictionary of World Missions,* gen. ed. A. Scott Moreau, s.v. *"Missio Dei."* Grand Rapids: Baker.

McLaren, Brian D. 2001. *A New Kind of Christian.* San Francisco: Jossey-Bass.

McLuhan, Marshall. 1964. *Understanding Media.* New York: McGraw-Hill.

McQuilkin, Robertson. 1999a. "Lost." In *Perspectives on the World Christian Movement: A Reader,* 3rd ed., ed. Ralph D. Winter and Steven C. Hawthorne, 156–61. Pasadena: William Carey Library.

———. 1999b. "Stop Sending Money: Breaking the Cycle of Missions Dependency." *Christianity Today,* March 1, 57–59.

McVey, Dan. 2003. Lectures on Islam. Seminar in Missions. Abilene Christian University, May 26–28.

Mellis, Charles J. 1983. *Committed Communities: Fresh Streams for World Missions.* Pasadena: William Carey Library.

Meyer, Ben. 1986. *The Early Christians: Their World Mission and Self-Discovery.* Wilmington, DE: Health Policy Advisory Center.

Miles, Glenn, and Josephine-Joy Wright. 2003. *Celebrating Children.* Cumbria, UK: Paternoster.

Mitchell, J. Clyde. 1974. "Social Networks." In *Annual Review of Anthropology,* ed. Bernard J. Siegel, 279–99. Palo Alto, CA: Annual Reviews.

Moffett, Samuel Hugh. 1998. *A History of Christianity in Asia.* Vol. 1, *Beginnings to 1500.* Maryknoll, NY: Orbis.

Moltmann, Jürgen. 1977. *The Church in the Power of the Spirit: A Contribution to Messianic Ecclesiology.* London: SCM.

———. 1984. *On Human Dignity: Political Theology and Ethics.* Trans. M. Douglas Meeks. Philadelphia: Fortress.

Molyneux, K. Gordon. 1993. *African Christian Theology: The Quest for Selfhood.* San Francisco: Mellen Research University Press.

Montgomery, Robert L. 2002. *The Lop-Sided Spread of Christianity.* Westport, CT: Praeger Publishing.

Moreau, A. Scott. 1995. "Religious Borrowing as a Two-Way Street: An Introduction to Animistic Tendencies in the Euro-North American Context." In *Christianity and the Religions: A Biblical Theology of World Religions,* ed. Edward Rommen and Harold Netland, 166–82. Pasadena: William Carey Library.

———. 1997. *Essentials of Spiritual Warfare.* Wheaton: Harold Shaw.

———. 2000a. *Evangelical Dictionary of World Missions,* gen. ed. A. Scott Moreau, s.v. "Adaptation." Grand Rapids: Baker.

———. 2000b. *Evangelical Dictionary of World Missions,* gen. ed. A. Scott Moreau, s.v. "Flaw of the Excluded Middle." Grand Rapids: Baker.

———. 2000c. *Evangelical Dictionary of World Missions,* gen. ed. A. Scott Moreau, s.v. "Inculturation." Grand Rapids: Baker.

———. 2000d. *Evangelical Dictionary of World Missions,* gen. ed. A. Scott Moreau, s.v. "Mission and Missions." Grand Rapids: Baker.

————. 2000e. *Evangelical Dictionary of World Missions,* gen. ed. A. Scott Moreau, s.v. "Syncretism." Grand Rapids: Baker.

————. 2000f. "Putting the Survey in Perspective." In *Mission Handbook: U.S. and Canadian Ministries Overseas,* ed. John A. Siewert and Dotsey Welliver, 33–80. Wheaton: Evangelism and Information Services.

————. 2001a. *Evangelical Dictionary of Theology,* 2nd ed., ed. Walter A. Elwell, s.v. "Church Growth Movement." Grand Rapids: Baker.

————. 2001b. *Evangelical Dictionary of Theology,* 2nd ed., ed. Walter A. Elwell, s.v. "Phenomenology of Religion." Grand Rapids: Baker.

————. 2001c. *Evangelical Dictionary of Theology,* 2nd ed., ed. Walter A. Elwell, s.v. "Poor, Poverty." Grand Rapids: Baker.

————. 2001d. *Evangelical Dictionary of Theology,* 2nd ed., ed. Walter A. Elwell, s.v. "Syncretism." Grand Rapids: Baker.

————. 2002a. "Deliver Us from Evil Consultation Statement," Lausanne Committee on World Evangelization Conference, Nairobi, Kenya, August 2000, http://www.gospelcom .net/lcwe/dufe/statement.htm (accessed February 21, 2005).

————. 2002b. "Gaining Perspective on Territorial Spirits." In *Deliver Us from Evil: An Uneasy Frontier in Christian Mission,* ed. A. Scott Moreau, Tokunboh Adeyemo, David Burnett, Bryant Myers, and Hwa Yung, 259–75. Monrovia, CA: MARC.

————. 2004. "Putting the Survey in Perspective." In *Handbook of North American Protestant Missions,* ed. Dotsey Welliver and Minnette Northcutt, 11–64. Wheaton: Evangelism and Missions Information Service.

————, Tokunboh Adeyemo, David Burnett, Bryant Myers, and Hwa Yung, eds. 2002. *Deliver Us from Evil: An Uneasy Frontier in Christian Mission.* Monrovia, CA: MARC.

————, Gary Corwin, and Gary McGee. 2004. *Introducing World Missions: A Biblical, Historical, and Practical Survey.* Grand Rapids: Baker.

————, and Mike O'Rear. 2002. "Missions on the Web: Missions and Arts on the Web." *Evangelical Missions Quarterly* 38 (July): 364–71.

Moreno, Pedro C. 1999. "Evangelical Churches." In *Religious Freedom and Evangelization in Latin America: The Challenge of Religious Pluralism,* ed. Paul E. Sigmund, 49–69. Maryknoll, NY: Orbis.

Morgan, T. C. 2003. "Mr. Jabez Goes to Africa." *Christianity Today,* November, 45–50.

Morris, Linus. 1993. *High Impact Churches.* Houston: Touch Publications.

Morton, Jeff. 2004. "Narratives and Questions: Exploring Scripture with Muslims." *Evangelical Missions Quarterly* 40 (April): 172–76.

Mullen, Peter. 2002. *The Magdalen Sisters,* a film by Miramax UK/Ireland.

Murray, John. 1965. *The Epistle to the Romans.* Grand Rapids: Eerdmans.

Myers, Bryant L. 2003. *Exploring World Mission: Context and Challenges.* Monrovia, CA: World Vision International.

Myers, Lewis, and Jim Slack. 1999. *To the Edge: A Planning Process for People Group Specific Strategy Development.* Richmond: International Mission Board.

Naisbitt, John. 1984. *Megatrends: Ten New Directions Transforming Our Lives.* New York: Warner Books.

Neely, Alan. 2001. *Evangelical Dictionary of Theology,* 2nd ed., ed. Walter A. Elwell, s.v. "Incarnational Mission." Grand Rapids: Baker.

Nehru, Jawaharial. 1946. *The Discovery of India.* New Delhi: Jawaharial Nehru Memorial Fund.

Neill, Stephen. 1964. *A History of Christian Missions*. London: Penguin.

———. 1971. *Concise Dictionary of Christian World Mission*, ed. Stephen Neill, Gerald H. Anderson, and John Goodwin, s.v. "Accommodation." Nashville: Abingdon.

Netland, Harold. 2001. *Encountering Religious Pluralism: The Challenge to Christian Faith and Reason*. Downers Grove, IL: InterVarsity.

Nevius, John L. 1958. *The Planting and Development of Missionary Churches*. Philadelphia: Presbyterian & Reformed.

———. 1968. *Demon Possession*. Grand Rapids: Kregel.

Newbigin, Lesslie. 1993. Preface to *Toward the Twenty-first Century in Christian Mission*, ed. James M. Phillips and Robert T. Coote, 1–6. Grand Rapids: Eerdmans.

Nicholls, Bruce J. 1979. "Towards a Theology of Gospel and Culture." In *Gospel and Culture: The Papers of a Consultation on the Gospel and Culture, Convened by the Lausanne Committee's Theology and Education Group*, ed. John R. W. Stott and Robert T. Coote, 69–82. Pasadena: William Carey Library.

Nkéramihigo, Théoneste. 1984. "Inculturation and the Specificity of Christian Faith." In *What Is So New about Inculturation?* Rome: Pontifical Gregorian University.

Nouwen, Henri. 1993. *In the Name of Jesus*. New York: Crossroad.

Nthamburi, Zablon. 1991. "Wealthy Missionaries: An African Viewpoint." Foreword to *Missions and Money: Affluence as a Western Missionary Problem*, by Jonathan Bonk, xiv–xvi. Maryknoll, NY: Orbis.

Núñez, Emilio A. 1985. *Liberation Theology*. Trans. Paul E. Sywulka. Chicago: Moody.

———, and William D. Taylor. 1989. *Crisis in Latin America: An Evangelical Perspective*. Chicago: Moody.

Nussbaum, Stan. 2003. "Goads on Globalization." *Connections* (June): 31–32.

Packer, J. I. 1990. "Evangelicals and the Way of Salvation: New Challenges to the Gospel— Universalism and Justification by Faith." In *Evangelical Affirmations*, ed. Kenneth S. Kantzer and Carl F. H. Henry, 107–36. Grand Rapids: Zondervan.

Pani, D. D. 2001. "Fatal Hindu Gospel Stumbling Blocks." *International Journal of Frontier Missions* (Spring): 23–32.

Parrish, Archie, and R. C. Sproul. 2000. *The Spirit of Revival: Discovering the Wisdom of Jonathan Edwards*. Wheaton: Crossway.

Parshall, Phil. 1998. "Danger! New Directions in Contextualization." *Evangelical Missions Quarterly* 34 (October): 404–6, 409–10.

Peacocke, Arthur. 1993. *Theology for a Scientific Age*. Minneapolis: Fortress.

Peck, Andy. 2004. "Emerging Churches: Insights and Concerns." *Christianity and Renewal* (January): 20–25.

Peters, George W. 1975. "Contemporary Practices of Evangelism." In *Let the Earth Hear His Voice: The Proceedings of the Lausanne Committee on World Evangelism*, ed. J. D. Douglas, 181–91. Minneapolis: Worldwide Publications.

Peterson, Robert A. 1995. *Hell on Trial: The Case for Eternal Punishment*. Philadelphia: Presbyterian & Reformed.

———. 2000. "Undying Worm Unquenchable Fire." *Christianity Today*, October 23, 30–37.

Pierson, Paul. 2000. *Evangelical Dictionary of World Missions*, gen. ed. A. Scott Moreau, s.v. "Moravian Missions." Grand Rapids: Baker.

Pierson, Steven. 2002. "We Sang Ourselves Free: Music Lessons from Estonia." *Evangelical Missions Quarterly* 30 (July): 314–22.

Pioneers. 2004. "Mission and Purpose," http://www.pioneers.org (accessed February 14, 2004).

Piper, John. 1993. *Let the Nations Be Glad!* Grand Rapids: Baker.

Pocock, Michael. 1996a. "Focus and Balance in Missionary Outreach." *Evangelical Missions Quarterly* 32 (April): 160–65.

———. 1996b. "Reasserting the Legitimacy of Spiritual Warfare." Paper delivered at the Fourth Biblical Conference on Spiritual Warfare, Sioux City, IA, February 29–March 2.

———. 1997. "Sources of the Conflict." *Moody Magazine,* July–August, 19–23.

———. 2001. "Speak of the Devil." *Moody Magazine,* April–May, 30–37.

———, and Joseph Henriques. 2002. *Cultural Change and Your Church.* Grand Rapids: Baker.

Pohl, C. D. 2003. "Biblical Issues in Mission and Migration." *Missiology: An International Review* 31 (January): 3–15.

Pond, Eugene. 2004. Director of Institutional Research, Dallas Theological Seminary, personal interview, February 10.

Population Issues. 1999. "Demographic Trends by Region," http://www.Unfpa.org/6billion/populationissues/dempgraphic.htm (accessed April 20, 2004).

Post Courier. 1998. "Papua New Guinea: Time to Change Gear?" *ACP-EU Courier* 171 (September–October): 13–17, http://europa.eu.int/comm/development/body/publications/courier/courier171/en/13_en.pdf (accessed April 20, 2004).

Postman, Neil. 1992. *Technopoly: The Surrender of Culture to Technology.* New York: Knopf.

Powell, John, and S. P. Udayakumar. 2000. "Race, Poverty, and Globalization." *Poverty and Race* (May–June), http://globalization.about.com/gi/dynamic/offsite.htm?site=http%3A%2F%2Fwww.globalexchange.org%2Feconomy%2Fecon101%2Fglobalization072000.html (accessed April 18, 2004).

Powlison, David. 1995. *Power Encounters: Reclaiming Spiritual Warfare.* Grand Rapids: Baker.

Priest, Robert J. 1994. "Missionary Elenctics: Conscience and Culture." *Missiology: An International Review* 22 (July): 291–315.

———, Thomas Campbell, and Brad Mullins. 1995. "Missiological Syncretism: The New Animistic Paradigm." In *Spiritual Power and Missions: Raising the Issues,* ed. Edward Rommen, 9–87. Evangelical Missiological Society Series no. 3. Pasadena: William Carey Library.

Rajendran, K. 2000. "Evangelical Missiology from India." In *Global Missiology for the Twenty-first Century: The Iguassu Dialogue,* ed. William D. Taylor, 307–32. Grand Rapids: Baker.

Reapsome, James. 2000. *Evangelical Dictionary of World Missions,* gen. ed. A. Scott Moreau, s.v. "Lausanne Movement." Grand Rapids: Baker.

———. 2002. "Middle East Christians Helping with Food Relief and Books." *World Pulse* 37 (December 6): 1–2.

Riddell, Peter G., and Peter Cotterell. 2003. *Islam in Context.* Grand Rapids: Baker.

Rivera, Luis N. 1992. *A Violent Evangelism: The Political and Religious Conquest of the Americas.* Louisville: Westminster John Knox.

Ro, Bong Rin, ed. 1989. *Christian Suffering in Asia.* Taichung, Taiwan: Evangelical Fellowship of Asia.

————, and Ruth Eshenauer, eds. 1984. *The Bible and Theology in Asian Contexts*. Taichung, Taiwan: Asian Theological Association.

Robertson, Roland. 2000. "Globalization and the Future of Traditional Religion." In *God and Globalization: Religion and the Powers of the Common Life*, vol. 1, ed. Max L. Stackhouse with Peter Paris, 53–68. Harrisburg, PA: Trinity Press International.

Rommen Edward, ed. 1995. *Spiritual Power and Missions: Raising the Issues*. Evangelical Missiological Society Series no. 3. Pasadena: William Carey Library.

Roof, Wade Clark. 1999. *Spiritual Marketplace: Baby Boomers and the Remaking of American Religion*. Princeton: Princeton University Press.

Rosen, Linda. 2001. "AIDS in Africa," http://www.prcdc.org/summaries/aidsinafrica/aid sinafrica.html (accessed April 20, 2004).

Ross, Allen P. 1988. *Creation and Blessing: A Guide to the Exposition of Genesis*. Grand Rapids: Baker.

Rothman, David H. 1997. "Will Bill Gates Buy *The Great Gatsby* for the Net—Or Just Fixate on Software and PCs?" http://www.teleread.org/update8.htm (accessed April 24, 2004).

Rouse, Ruth, and Stephen C. Neill. 1967. *A History of the Ecumenical Movement, 1517–1948*. Philadelphia: Westminster.

Rundle, Steve, and Tom Steffen. 2003. *Great Commission Companies: The Emerging Role of Business in Missions*. Downers Grove, IL: InterVarsity.

Sadowitz, Chris. 2004. "Recognizing World View and Its Relationship to Real Gospel Presentation and Understanding." *Occasional Bulletin of the Evangelical Missiological Society* 17 (Spring): 1–4.

Sanneh, Lamin. 2003. *Whose Religion Is Christianity? The Gospel beyond the West*. Grand Rapids: Eerdmans.

Saracco, Norberto. 2000. "Mission and Missiology from Latin America." In *Global Missiology for the Twenty-first Century: The Iguassu Dialogue*, ed. William D. Taylor, 357–66. Grand Rapids: Baker.

Schaeffer, Francis A. 1969. *The God Who Is There*. Downers Grove, IL: InterVarsity.

Schineller, Peter. 1990. *A Handbook on Inculturation*. Mahwah, NJ: Paulist Press.

————. 1996. "Inculturation: A Difficult and Delicate Task." *International Bulletin of Missionary Research* 20 (July): 109–10, 112.

Schreiter, Robert J. 1985. *Constructing Local Theologies*. London: SCM.

————. 1990. "Missions in the Third Millennium." *Missiology: An International Review* 18 (January): 3–12.

————. 1993. "Defining Syncretism: An Interim Report." *International Bulletin of Missionary Research* 17 (April): 50–53.

Schwartz, Glenn. 2000. "Is There a Cure for Dependency among Mission-Established Churches?" http://www.wmausa.org/art-cure.htm (accessed June 22, 2004).

————. 2001. "Searching for Meaningful Ways to Help the Poor," http://www.wmausa .org/art-helppoor.htm (accessed June 22, 2004).

Shank, David A. 1994. *Prophet Harris: The "Black Elijah" of West Africa*. Leiden: Brill.

Shaw, R. Daniel. 2000. *Evangelical Dictionary of World Missions*, gen. ed. A. Scott Moreau, s.v. "Rituals and Ceremony." Grand Rapids: Baker.

Shaw, Ryan. N.d. "This Generation for the Nations? Findings and Vision towards God's Global Announcement in this Generation," http://www.svm2.net/user_files/other/This GenerationFortheNations_RyansResearchPaper.pdf (accessed June 29, 2004).

Shenk, Wilbert R. 1980. "The Changing Role of the Missionary: From 'Civilization' to 'Contextualization.'" In *Missions, Evangelism, and Church Growth,* ed. C. Norman Kraus, 33–58. Scottdale, PA: Herald Press.

Shorter, Aylward. 1988. *Toward a Theology of Inculturation.* Maryknoll, NY: Orbis.

Shubin, Russell G. 1999. "The Synergy of Partnership." *Mission Frontiers* 21 (October): 28–29.

Siemens, Ruth E. 2004. "Ruth's Story—The Story behind GO," http://www.globalopps .org/ruths_story.htm (accessed March 6, 2004).

Sigmund, Paul E., ed. 1999. *Religious Freedom and Evangelization in Latin America: The Challenge of Religious Pluralism.* Maryknoll, NY: Orbis.

Simmons, Janet. 2003. News release of Interdev-US, November 4, 2003.

Sinclair, Matthew. 2003. "Giving Hits Record $240.9 Billion." *Nonprofit Times,* July 1, 2003, http://www.nptimes.com/Jul03/nptl.html (accessed April 24, 2004).

Sine, Tom. 1999. *Mustard Seed vs. McWorld: Reinventing Life and Faith for the Future.* Grand Rapids: Baker.

Slaughter, Michael, ed. 1998. *Out on the Edge: A Wake-Up Call for Church Leaders on the Edge of the Media Reformation.* Nashville: Abingdon.

Smart, Ninian. 1996. *Dimensions of the Sacred: An Anatomy of the World's Beliefs.* Berkeley: University of California Press.

Smart, R. 2000. *Children Living with HIV/AIDS in South Africa: A Rapid Appraisal.* Pretoria: Save the Children (UK).

Smith, Wilfred Cantwell. 1976. "The Christian in a Religiously Plural World." In *Religious Diversity: Essays by Wilfred Cantwell Smith,* ed. Willard G. Oxtoby, 3–21. New York: Harper & Row.

Snow, Donald B. 2001. *English Teaching as Christian Mission: An Applied Theology.* Scottdale, PA: Herald Press.

Solomon, Norman. 2004. "Kathie Lee, Disney, and the Sweatshop Uproar." *Albion Monitor,* http://www.monitor.net/monitor/sweatshop/ss-solomon.html (accessed May 15, 2004).

Spaugh, Herbert. 1999. "A Short Introduction to the History, Customs, and Practices of the Moravian Church," http://216.239.51.104/search?Q=Cache:opme-6v5plij:www .everydaycounselor.com/archives/Sh/Shistory.htm+&Hl=En&Ie=UTF-8 (accessed March 25, 2004).

Spitz, Lewis W. 1972. *World Book Encyclopedia,* s.v. "Reformation." Chicago: World Books.

Spong, John. 1998. *Why Christianity Must Change or Die.* San Francisco: Harper.

Sprunger, W. Frederic. 1984. "Six Lessons about Contextualization." *Mission Focus* 12, no. 1: 5–7.

Stackhouse, Max L., Don S. Browning, and Peter J. Paris. 2000. *God and Globalization: Religion and the Powers of the Common Life.* 4 vols. Harrisburg, PA: Trinity Press International.

Staples, B. L. 2000. *New York Times,* Book Review, November 26, 13.

Stearns, Bill. 1999. "Persecution Doesn't Scare Me." *World Christian Magazine* (September): 4.

Steuernagel, Valdir. 2000. "Learning from Escobar . . . and Beyond." In *Global Missiology for the Twenty-first Century: The Iguassu Dialogue,* ed. William D. Taylor, 123–32. Grand Rapids: Baker.

Stewart, Edward C., and Milton J. Bennett. 1991. *American Cultural Patterns: A Cross-Cultural Perspective*. Rev. ed. Yarmouth, ME: Intercultural Press.

Steyne, Phillip M. 1978. "The African Zionist Movement." In *Dynamic Religious Movements: Case Studies of Rapidly Growing Religious Movements around the World*, ed. David Hesselgrave, 19–40. Grand Rapids: Baker.

Stott, John R. W. 1975. *Christian Mission in the Modern World*. Downers Grove, IL: InterVarsity.

———. 1979. *The Message of Ephesians*. Downers Grove, IL: InterVarsity.

———. 1988. "The World's Challenge to the Church. Part 1. Griffeth Thomas Lectureship at Dallas Theological Seminary, 1988, on Christian Missiology in the Twenty-first Century." *Bibliotheca Sacra* 145, no. 578 (April–June): 123–32.

———. 1995. "Twenty Years after Lausanne: The Look Forward," http://www.gospelcom.net/lcwe/wemag/9506forward.html (accessed April 20, 2004).

Strachan, Kenneth. 1968. *The Inescapable Calling: The Missionary Task of the Church of Christ in the Light of the Contemporary Challenge and Opportunity*. Grand Rapids: Eerdmans.

Sweet, Leonard I. 1999a. *Aquachurch: Essential Leadership Arts for Piloting Your Church in Today's Fluid Culture*. Loveland, CO: Group Publishing.

———. 1999b. *Soul Tsunami*. Grand Rapids: Zondervan.

———. 2002. *SoulSalsa: Seventeen Surprising Steps for Godly Living in the Twenty-first Century*. Grand Rapids: Zondervan.

Taber, Charles R. 1979. "The Limits of Indigenization in Theology." In *Readings in Dynamic Indigeneity*, ed. Charles H. Kraft and Tom N. Wisley, 372–99. Pasadena: William Carey Library.

Tanaka, Graham. 2003. *Digital Deflation: The Productivity Revolution and How It Will Ignite the Economy*. New York: McGraw-Hill.

Taylor, Harold. 2004. "Contextualized Mission in Church History." In *Encountering New Religious Movements: A Holistic Evangelical Approach*, ed. Irving Hexham, Stephen Rost, and John W. Moreland, 43–60. Grand Rapids: Kregel.

Taylor, William D. 1994. *Kingdom Partnerships for Synergy in Missions*. Pasadena: William Carey Library.

———. 2000a. *Evangelical Dictionary of World Missions*, gen. ed. A. Scott Moreau, s.v. "Latin America." Grand Rapids: Baker.

———, ed. 2000b. *Global Missiology for the Twenty-first Century: The Iguassu Dialogue*. Grand Rapids: Baker.

Tebbe, Elizabeth. 1999. "Postmodernism, the Western Church, and Missions." *Evangelical Missions Quarterly* 35 (October): 426–29.

Tentmaker Track, Lausanne II Congress. 1989. "Tentmaker Declarative Appeal," http://www.csonline.net/Tie/Whatis.htm (accessed March 8, 2004).

Terry, John Mark. 2000. *Evangelical Dictionary of World Missions*, gen. ed. A. Scott Moreau, s.v. "Indigenous Churches." Grand Rapids: Baker.

Tiplady, Richard. 2000. "Let X = X: Generation X and World Mission." In *Global Missiology for the Twenty-first Century: The Iguassu Dialogue*, ed. William D. Taylor, 463–76. Grand Rapids: Baker.

———. 2003a. "One World or Many?" *Connections* (June): 10–17.

———, ed. 2003b. *One World or Many? The Impact of Globalisation on Mission*. Pasadena: William Carey Library.

Tippett, Alan Richard. 1973. *Verdict Theology in Missionary Theory.* Pasadena: William Carey Library.

———. 1987. *Introduction to Missiology.* Pasadena: William Carey Library.

Toulmin, Stephen. 1990. *Cosmopolis: The Hidden Agenda of Modernity.* New York: Free Press.

Travis, John. 1998a. "The C1 to C6 Spectrum." *Evangelical Missions Quarterly* 34 (October): 407–8.

———. 1998b. "Must All Muslims Leave 'Islam' to Follow Jesus?" *Evangelical Missions Quarterly* 34 (October): 410–15.

Tuck, Jim. 2005. "Bartolomé de las Casas: Father of Liberation Theology, 1474–1566," http://www.mexconnect.com/mex_/history/jtuck/jtbartolome.html (accessed February 14, 2005).

Tucker, Ruth A. 1983. *From Jerusalem to Irian Jaya: A Biographical History of Christian Missions.* Grand Rapids: Zondervan.

Ujamaa, Nia. 2005. "Robert Fairlie on the Economics of the Digital Divide," http://www.digitaldivide.net/articles/view.php?ArticleID=61 (accessed February 13, 2005).

Unger, Merrill. 1957. *Biblical Demonology.* Wheaton: Scripture Press.

———. 1977. *What Demons Can Do to Saints.* Chicago: Moody.

UNICEF. 2002. "UNICEF Calls Global Response to Children Orphaned by AIDS Grossly Inadequate," http://www.unicef.org/newsline/02pr64windhoek.htm (accessed April 20, 2004).

———. 2003. "Countries in Crisis: Child Soldiers," http://www.unicef.org/emerg/index_childsoldiers.html (accessed April 20, 2004).

United Nations Population Division. 2002. "International Migration Report 2002," http://www.un.org/esa/population/publications/ittmig2002/2002ITTMIGTEXT22-11.pdf (accessed June 4, 2004).

———. 2003. "The Impact of AIDS," http://www.un.org/esa/population/publications/AIDSimpact/AIDSWebAnnounce.htm (accessed April 30, 2004).

USAID. 2003. "Building Community-Based Partnerships to Support AIDS Orphans and Vulnerable Children. Bureau for Global Health, Success Stories HIV/AIDS," http://www.usaid.gov/our_work/global_health/aids/News/successpdfs/zambiastory3.pdf (accessed June 4, 2004).

Valerio, Ruth. 2003. "Globalisation and Economics: A World Gone Bananas." In *One World or Many? The Impact of Globalisation on Mission,* ed. Richard Tiplady, 13–31. Pasadena: William Carey Library.

Van Engen, Charles. 1991. *God's Missionary People: Rethinking the Purpose of the Local Church.* Grand Rapids: Baker.

Van Gelder, Craig. 1996. "Mission in the Emerging Postmodern Condition." In *The Church between Gospel and Culture,* ed. George R. Hunsberger and Craig Van Gelder, 113–38. Grand Rapids: Eerdmans.

Van Rheenen, Gailyn. 1976. *Church Planting in Uganda: A Comparative Approach.* Pasadena: William Carey Library.

———. 1991. *Communicating Christ in Animistic Contexts.* Grand Rapids: Baker.

———. 1996. *Missions: Biblical Foundations and Contemporary Strategies.* Grand Rapids: Zondervan.

———. 2000a. "Learning . . . Growing . . . Collaborating . . . Phasing Out." *Evangelical Missions Quarterly* 36 (January): 36–47.

———. 2000b. "Monthly Missiological Reflections #2: Money and Mi$$ion$," http://www.missiology.org/mmr/mmr2htm (accessed April 22, 2004).

———. 2001a. "Monthly Missiological Reflections #15: Using Money and Missions: Four Perspectives," http://www.missiology.org/mmr/mmr15.htm (accessed April 22, 2004).

———. 2001b. "Monthly Missiological Reflection #22: The Changing Cultural Ethos of Latin America," http://www.missiology.org/mmr/mmr22.htm (accessed July 9, 2004).

———. 2002. "Using Money in Missions: The Good, the Bad, and the Ugly." *Evangelical Missions Quarterly* 38 (January): 38–45.

———. 2004a. "Monthly Missiological Reflection #30: Encountering Religious Pluralism," http://www.missiology.org/mmr/mmr30.htm (accessed April 20, 2004).

———. 2004b. "Monthly Missiological Reflection #32: Modernity Sweeps Africa," http://www.missiology.org/mmr/mmr32.htm (accessed April 20, 2004).

———. 2005. "A Theology of Power." *Evangelical Missions Quarterly* (forthcoming).

Viva Network. 2003. "Sexual Exploitation," http://www.viva.org/tellme/aboutcar/risks.php?icode=RJE (accessed April 20, 2004).

———. 2004a. "About Children at Risk," http://www.viva.org/tellme/car (accessed April 20, 2004).

———. 2004b. "Child Soldiers," http://www.viva.org/tellme/aboutcar/risks.php?icode=RJES (accessed April 20, 2004).

Wagner, Peter C. 1973. *Look Out! The Pentecostals Are Coming.* Carol Stream, IL: Creation House.

———. 1988. *The Third Wave of the Holy Spirit: Encountering the Power of Signs and Wonders Today.* Ann Arbor: Servant Publications.

———. 1996. *Confronting the Powers.* Ventura, CA: Regal.

———. 1997. "Contemporary Dynamics of the Holy Spirit in Missions." In *The Holy Spirit and Mission Dynamics,* ed. Doug McConnell, 107–22. Evangelical Missiological Society Series no. 5. Pasadena: William Carey Library.

Walls, Andrew F. 1996. *The Missionary Movement in Christian History: Studies in the Transmission and Appropriation of the Faith.* Maryknoll, NY: Orbis.

———. 2002a. *The Cross-Cultural Process in Christian History: Studies in the Transmission and Appropriation of the Faith.* Maryknoll, NY: Orbis.

———. 2002b. "Eusebius Tries Again." In *Enlarging the Story: Perspectives on Writing World Christian History,* ed. Wilbert Shenk, 1–21. Maryknoll, NY: Orbis.

———. 2003. "Landmarks in African Christian History." Missions and Evangelism Lectureship at Dallas Theological Seminary, November 4–7.

Wang, Thomas. 1989. "The Year 2000: Is God Trying to Tell Us Something?" In *Countdown to the Year 2000,* ed. Thomas Wang, xiv–xx. Pasadena: A.D. 2000 Movement.

Warner, Timothy. 1991. *Spiritual Warfare: Victory over the Powers of This Dark World.* Wheaton: Crossway.

Waters, Malcolm. 2001. *Globalization.* 2nd ed. New York: Routledge, 2001.

Webber, Robert E. 2002. *The Younger Evangelicals.* Grand Rapids: Baker.

Wellman, Barry, S. D. Berkowitz, and Mark Granovetter, eds. 1997. *Social Structures: A Network Approach. Contemporary Studies in Sociology.* Greenwich, CT: JAI Press.

Wenham, John W. 1992. "The Case for Conditional Immortality." In *Universalism and the Doctrine of Hell: Papers Presented at the Fourth Edinburgh Conference in Christian Dogmatics, 1991,* ed. Nigel M. De S. Cameroon, 161–91. Grand Rapids: Baker.

369

West, Martin. 1975. *Bishops and Prophets in a Black City: African Independent Churches in Soweto Johannesburg.* Cape Town: David Phillip.

White, Karen L. 1998. "Overcoming Resistance through Martyrdom." In *Reaching the Resistant,* ed. J. Dudley Woodberry, 155–79. Evangelical Missiological Society Series no. 6. Pasadena: William Carey Library.

Whiteman, Darrell L. 1997. "Contextualization: The Theory, the Gap, the Challenge." *International Bulletin of Missionary Research* 21 (January): 2–7.

Wilkinson, Bruce. 2004. Walk through the Bible, a seminar, http://www.walkthru.org (accessed May 20, 2004).

Williamson, J. 2000. *Finding a Way Forward.* Washington, DC: USAID.

Willow Creek Association. 2004. "The Purpose of Willow Creek Association," http://www.willowcreek.com/wca_info (accessed February 7, 2004).

Wilson, J. Christy, Jr. 1979. *Today's Tentmakers: Self-Support—An Alternative Model for Worldwide Witness.* Wheaton: Tyndale.

Wilson, Len. 1999. *The Wired Church: Making Media Ministry.* Nashville: Abingdon.

Wilson, Samuel. 2000. *Evangelical Dictionary of World Missions,* gen. ed. A. Scott Moreau, s.v. "Peoples, People Groups." Grand Rapids: Baker.

Wilson, Walter P. 2000. *The Internet Church: New Rules for Ministry in the Age of . . . the Local Church Just Can't Be Just Local Anymore.* Nashville: Word.

Wimber, John 1986. *Power Evangelism.* San Francisco: Harper & Row.

Wink, Walter. 1992. *Engaging the Powers: Discernment and Resistance in a World of Domination.* Minneapolis: Fortress.

Winter, Ralph D. 1975. "The Highest Priority: Cross-Cultural Evangelism." In *Let the Earth Hear His Voice: The Proceedings of the Lausanne Committee on World Evangelism,* ed. J. D. Douglas, 213–41. Minneapolis: Worldwide Publications.

———. 1993. "Can You Sense the Spirit Blowin' and the Momentum Building?" *Mission Frontiers* (January–February), http://www.missionfrontiers.org/archive.htm (accessed April 23, 2004).

———. 1996. "Do We Need Heresies on the Mission Field? Can Heresies Be Clouds with a Silver Lining?" *Mission Frontiers* 18 (September–October): 6.

———, and Steven C. Hawthorne, eds. 1999. *Perspectives on the World Christian Movement: A Reader.* 3rd ed. Pasadena: William Carey Library.

Woodberry, J. Dudley, ed. 1998. *Reaching the Resistant: Barriers and Bridges for Missions.* Evangelical Missiological Society Series no. 6. Pasadena: William Carey Library.

Woods, Scott. 2003. "A Biblical Look at C5 Muslim Evangelism." *Evangelical Missions Quarterly* 39 (April): 188–95.

World Vision. 2002. "HIV/AIDS Hope Initiative," http://www.wvi.org/wvi/aids/global_aids.htm (accessed April 20, 2004).

———. N.d. "What Is Love INC?" http://www.worldvision.org/worldvision/wvususfo.nsf/stable/loveinc (accessed April 24, 2004).

Wuthnow, Robert. 1998. *After Heaven: Spirituality in America since the 1950s.* Los Angeles: University of California Press.

Yamamori, Tetsunao. 1987. *God's New Envoys: A Bold Strategy for Penetrating "Closed Countries."* Portland, OR: Multnomah.

———. 1993. *Penetrating Missions' Final Frontier: A New Strategy for Unreached Peoples.* Downers Grove, IL: InterVarsity.

————, and Kenneth A. Eldred, eds. 2003. *On Kingdom Business: Transforming Missions through Entrepreneurial Strategies*. Wheaton: Crossway.

Yung, Hwa. 2002. "A Systematic Theology That Recognizes the Demonic." In *Deliver Us from Evil: An Uneasy Frontier in Christian Mission*, ed. A. Scott Moreau, Tokunboh Adeyemo, David Burnett, Bryant Myers, and Hwa Yung, 3–27. Monrovia, CA: MARC.

Yungen, Ray. 2002. *A Time of Departing: How a Universal Spirituality Is Changing the Face of Christianity*. Silverton, OR: Lighthouse Trails.

Zacharias, Ravi. 2000. *Jesus among Other Gods*. Nashville: Word.

Zahniser, A. H. Mathias. 1997. *Symbol and Ceremony*. Monrovia, CA: MARC.

Zwingle, Erla. 2000. "A World Together." In *Globalization*, ed. Katie Sjursen, 153–64. New York: H. W. Wilson.

Subject Index

Scripture Index

Contributing Authors

J. Ted Esler was a church planter for several years in the Balkans and is now executive vice president of Pioneers USA.

Mike Barnett (Ph.D., Southwestern Theological Seminary) is the Elmer V. Thompson Chair of Missionary Church Planting at Columbia Biblical Seminary. He served for twelve years with the International Mission Board of the Southern Baptist Convention, working in the 10/40 Window. He has a business background and continues to work in international business development.

A. Scott Moreau is professor of missions and intercultural studies at Wheaton College Graduate School and the general editor of the *Evangelical Dictionary of World Missions*.